PRAGMATISM, REASON, & NORMS

American Philosophy Series

1. *Peirce and Contemporary Thought: Philosophical Inquiries*, edited by Kenneth Laine Ketner

2. *Classic American Philosophers*, edited by Max H. Fisch; introduction by Nathan Houser

3. John E. Smith, *Experience and God*

4. Vincent G. Potter, *Peirce's Philosophical Perspectives*, edited by Vincent Colapietro

5. *Philosophy in Experience: American Philosophy in Transition*, edited by Richard E. Hart and Douglas R. Anderson

6. Vincent G. Potter, *Charles S. Peirce: On Norms and Ideals*, introduction by Stanley M. Harrison

7. *Reason, Experience, and God: John E. Smith in Dialogue*, edited by Vincent M. Colapietro

8. Robert J. O'Connell, S.J., *William James on the Courage to Believe*

9. Elizabeth Kraus, *The Metaphysics of Experience: A Companion to Whitehead's PROCESS AND REALITY*

PRAGMATISM, REASON, & NORMS

A REALISTIC ASSESSMENT

Edited by

Kenneth R. Westphal

Fordham University Press
New York
1998

Copyright © 1998 by Fordham University Press
LC 97-38942
ISBN 0-8232-1818-x (hardcover)
ISBN 0-8232-1819-8 (paperback)
ISSN 1073-2764
American Philosophy Series, No. 10
Vincent M. Colapietro, Editor
Vincent G. Potter (1929-1994), Founding Editor

Library of Congress Cataloging-in-Publication Data

Pragmatism, reason & norms : a realistic assessment / edited by
Kenneth R. Westphal.
    p. cm. -- (American philosophy series ; no. 10)
Includes bibliographical references and index.
ISBN 0-8232-1818-X (hardcover : alk. paper). --
ISBN 0-8232-1819-8 (pbk. : alk. paper)
  1. Will, Frederick L. 2. Pragmatism. 3. Realism. I. Westphal,
Kenneth R. II. Series.
B945.W494P73 1998
191--dc21   97-38942
                                           CIP

Printed in the United States of America

Contents

Editor's Introduction   vii

1 Perspectives on Pragmatism   1
  Nicholas Rescher

2 Transcendental Reflections on Pragmatic Realism   17
  Kenneth R. Westphal

3 Perception and Conception   59
  William P. Alston

4 How to Teach a Wise Man   89
  Michael Root

5 Presuppositions of Inference   111
  Marcus G. Singer

6 Education as Norm Acquisition   145
  Thomas F. Green

7 Some Comments on the Later Philosophy of Frederick
  L. Will   185
  Marcus G. Singer

8 Frederick L. Will on Morality   193
  William H. Hay

9 Moral Intuitions and Philosophical Method   203
    Martin Perlmutter

10 Two Problems in Hans Kelsen's Legal Philosophy   219
    Stanley L. Paulson

11 The Spirit of the Enterprise   243
    James D. Wallace

12 Rationality Beyond Deduction: A Guide for the Perplexed
    and the Disappointed   265
    James E. Tiles

13 Reasons in a World of Practices: A Reconstruction of Fred-
    erick L. Will's Theory of Normative Governance   293
    Matthias Kettner

Contributors   341

Biographical Notice on Frederick L. Will   345

Index   347

Editor's Introduction

The essays published here are presented in critical appreciation of Frederick L. Will's penetrating philosophical work. In his foreword to Will's *Pragmatism and Realism*, Alasdair MacIntyre contends that Will's work is "one of the more remarkable achievements of twentieth-century North American philosophy" and that philosophy can prosper only by taking Will's "splendid" work with "great seriousness."[1] Each contributor to this collection spontaneously realized that the only proper honor to Will is to contribute to the on-going discussion of central philosophical issues. These essays may be read independently of Will's views. Yet each of them also casts light on the character and significance of his philosophy. In introducing the essays I shall, naturally enough, highlight the bearing they have on his views. I begin with a sketch of Will's work and development and then turn to the essays presented here.

Frederick L. Will (b. 1909) trained at Cornell and began his philosophical career a devoted follower of Hume, convinced that in both style and in substance Hume's *Enquiry Concerning Human Understanding* was the epitome of philosophy. He devoted several decades to dissolving the problem of induction through ordinary language analysis. Some of his essays from that period are widely anthologized. In the mid-1960s Will's thought took a profound and highly illuminating pragmatic turn. He criticized the presuppositions of the problem of induction and, by drawing on resources in history and philosophy of science, in ethics, and in law, and on the work

---

[1] Will 1997, ix, xii.

of Hegel, Peirce, Dewey, and the later Wittgenstein, he developed a penetrating pragmatic analysis of reason, justification, and knowledge. The basis of Will's pragmatic turn sets the stage for the issues investigated in the essays presented here.

In 1964 Will completed a book-length manuscript that proposed a definitive solution to the problem of induction. His solution relied on what he called "principles of factual reasoning." Like Peirce's "leading principles of inference" or Ryle's "inference tickets," such principles formulate supposed factual relations among events or objects, such that the occurrence or observation of one would reliably warrant inferring the occurrence or observation of the other. In the manuscript Will contended that such principles are constantly generated, assessed, and revised in the course of our ordinary and specialized (technical or scientific) affairs, always in conjunction with other such principles.

During final revisions he realized that his solution was inadequate on two main counts. First, the inductive skeptic could grant those contentions while denying that they had anything to do with genuine, philosophically legitimate justification. Given the essentially Cartesian terms in which the problem of induction is formulated, admissible premises cannot be justified on the basis of other "principles of factual reasoning," and they must be "analytic" or necessary truths, because the justification of synthetic principles is precisely what Hume's problem challenges.[2] Second, treating inferential reasoning in terms of "principles of factual reasoning" inherits the basic foundationalist model of knowledge as charting our inferential way from one basic experience to another.

Hume's problem of induction and its foundationalist presuppositions required instead radical critique and replacement. This involved going far beyond Will's earlier argument, that Hume's problem of induction is incoherent. It is incoherent because eliminating all unjustified synthetic principles from the solution to the problem also eliminates all "the considerations necessary for under-

---

[2] Will discusses Goodman's "riddle" of induction in Will 1988, 117–18.

standing what the inference is about, and thus for grasping not only the scope and significance but, therewith, the very meaning of the inductive conclusion that is supposed to be in question."[3] To take only one example, to strip Newton's famous inductive generalization which ascribed mass and gravity to all planets of every "synthetic" proposition,[4] would leave one bereft of any principles for understanding Newton's problem as part of an astronomical investigation of planetary motions relying on data collected with a variety of observational instruments.

Will's critique of foundationalism and the problems of induction it generates began with his 1969 presidential address to the Western (now Central) Division of the American Philosophical Association, "Thoughts and Things."[5] His full critique was delivered in *Induction and Justification*.[6] Part One of that book placed the problem of induction in the context of foundationalist models of knowledge. Part Two examined the main root of foundationalist models of justification, the regress argument, and argued that neither the alleged sensory foundations of human knowledge nor the various analytic, postulational, or inductive principles for justifying nonfoundational beliefs met the requirements of the skeptical model of knowledge underlying the regress argument. Part Three sketched an alternative, social and pragmatic account of knowledge and justification, which he developed in a series of articles.

In a second book, Will extended his critique of foundationalism by criticizing the deductivist model of justification on which it rests; hence his title, *Beyond Deduction*. On the deductivist model of justification, norms are treated as kinds of templates (mental, physical, or otherwise) of performance, resident in agents, which determine unilaterally what kinds of thought or action accords with them. This view has led to multiple perplexities; the most important concern evaluating, justifying, and rectifying such unilaterally

---

[3] Will 1959, 371.
[4] Newton 1934, Rule 3.
[5] Will 1997, ch. 1.
[6] Will 1974.

determining entities. Sometimes one can appeal to other, supervening norms; but the need to terminate the regressive procedure typically leads to appeals to dubious "foundations," to conventions, or to sheer prejudice. In addition to this negative case against deductivism, Will showed both that it is possible, and how one can, while reasoning about some specific problem (whether moral, legal, scientific, or technical), revise one's original principles and concepts—one's understanding of the nature of both the problem and its solution—in the course of solving it. On this basis, Will showed that a pragmatic, social account of knowledge can be reconciled with realism, the idea that things have characteristics regardless of what we say or think about them.

Will has investigated very broad, fundamental issues about human reason and its objects. His views about rationality, justification, and knowledge are very distinctive and have both direct and indirect implications for many areas of current philosophical debate. Many of these implications are developed or at least touched upon in his own writings.[7] Several more are developed in the following essays.

A central theme in pragmatism is that thought is rooted in action, theoretical reason is based in practical reason. The essays below divide roughly into two parts following this theme. The first six essays concern epistemology; the last seven essays concern moral and social philosophy. The first essay in each group is brief and highlights some key issues in pragmatic accounts of knowledge and morality, respectively. These first essays are then followed by extended essays on specific issues concerning knowledge and the guidance of action.

A perennial issue about pragmatism is its relation to realism. In "Perspectives on Pragmatism," Nicholas Rescher initiates the first group of essays by stressing a point too often overlooked in current discussions, namely, that some versions of pragmatism—primarily those which offer a pragmatic theory of *justification*—are consistent with realism. Rescher joins Peirce and C. I. Lewis in the realist

---

[7] A detailed summary of Will's views is given in my introduction to Will 1997.

camp of pragmatists, and queries whether Will sides with them or with the "postmodern" antirealist camp of neo-pragmatists.

Two key points in Will's defense of a realist pragmatism about knowledge are the dependence of human thought on the things and events around us and the exposure of a widespread non sequitur which rejects pragmatism if "knowledge by acquaintance" is possible, or rejects realism if it is impossible. In "Transcendental Reflections on Pragmatic Realism," Kenneth R. Westphal shows that, in very similar ways, both Kant's and Carnap's rejections of realism shatter on Will's anti-Cartesian point that our thoughts depend for their very possibility on the things and events around us, and that the non sequitur Will identifies is still pervasive and influential.

A pragmatic realism about knowledge requires a middle ground between concept-free perceptual knowledge by acquaintance and "conceptualism," which reduces perception or perceptual knowledge to its conceptual components or propositional content. This middle ground is developed by William P. Alston in "Perception and Conception." Alston's criticism of conceptualism is especially vigorous, and it avoids the pitfall of propositional knowledge by acquaintance.

Pragmatism provides a social account of knowledge. One important element in a social account of knowledge concerns the role of testimony in human knowledge and the principles governing our assessment of the testimony of others. In "How to Teach a Wise Man," Michael Root develops a modified Humean account of principles of testimony.

One of the central themes in Will's pragmatism is that there is more, far more, to a norm than any explicit formulation we may give it. This view runs contrary to one prominent trend of analytic philosophy that tries to account for rational principles in terms of precise and explicit formulae. In "Presuppositions of Inference," Marcus G. Singer explores several kinds of presuppositions involved even in explicit logical deduction—presuppositions that cannot be explicated and set among the explicit formulae comprised in formal deductions.

Another central theme in pragmatism, highlighted and developed by Will, is that the norms of thought and action do not descend to us from a Platonic heaven by rational insight. Norms are culturally and historically developed, and they are embodied by and in agents who are educated in particular traditions. On pragmatic principles, education is a central aspect of our collective cognitive and practical abilities and resources. In "Education as Norm Acquisition," Thomas F. Green presents a compelling analysis of the moral character—broadly construed—of education and its philosophical centrality to the analysis of reason and action.

A longstanding concern about pragmatic accounts of moral or political norms is that pragmatism appears to subordinate the right to the useful, the effective, or the expedient. In "On the Later Philosophy of Frederick L. Will," Marcus Singer raises this concern in connection with Will's views. Singer's begins the second group of essays, each of which responds to this concern, either directly or indirectly.

Will's pragmatic account of reason and justification is based on considerations in common sense, science, mathematics, morality, and law. Although Will has not written on ethics, in "Frederick L. Will on Morality' William H. Hay argues that Will's nondeductive account of reason provides rich resources for both describing and assessing moralities, both in theory and in practice.

One of Will's clues to the nondeductive character of much legitimate and legitimating reason is the frequent and often somewhat embarrassed recourse to intuitionism in ethics, even among philosophers of an otherwise rationalist persuasion. In "Moral Intuitions and Philosophical Method," Martin Perlmutter amplifies Will's critique by arguing that our moral intuitions do not behave in the well-ordered ways by which alone they could perform the role assigned to them recently by much prominent moral theory and argument.

Will criticizes the strictly deductive view of justification in part because it generates a regress to ultimate master norms, the status and justification of which are highly problematic. One example of these problems is provided by "legal realism," which rests the authority of legal norms on the decisions actually rendered by courts of law. In "Two Problems in Hans Kelsen's Legal Philosophy," Stanley L. Paulson complements Will's critique of legal realism by showing how Kelsen's theory of "legal fictions" also fails to resolve the problem of justifying ultimate legal norms.

One of the most original features of Will's account of norms is his distinction—and integration—of the explicit and implicit aspects of norms. He contends that any norm has an explicit or "manifest" aspect in terms of which we conceive of and can formulate that norm. However, the manifest aspect of a norm is only an aspect; any norm also has implicit or "latent" aspects. These latent aspects are crucial to the guiding function of norms, both in terms of how they relate to specific contexts of action and how they relate to and function with other norms in those contexts and in related contexts. The manifest and latent aspects of norms are explored by James Wallace in "The Spirit of the Enterprise." Wallace makes a case for the existence and importance of the latent aspects of norms by examining a range of examples, both ordinary and technical, and scientific as well as political.

The deductive model of rationality and justification is so pervasive that it can be difficult to understand an expressly nondeductive model like Will's, and it can be especially difficult to appreciate the kind of guidance and basis for assessing norms and practices it provides. This difficulty is addressed by James E. Tiles in "Rationality Beyond Deduction: A Guide for the Perplexed and the Disappointed." Tiles contends that Will's nondeductive model of rationality can indeed provide genuine guidance and grounds for assessing norms and practices. In this regard Tiles also emphasizes very important respects in which Will's philosophy extends classical American pragmatism.

Pragmatic accounts of norms and justification are contextualist and may appear to undermine traditional claims about the universality of our most basic norms. In "Reasons in a World of Practices: A Reconstruction of Frederick L. Will's Theory of Normative

Governance," Matthias Kettner argues that Will's emphasis on the concreteness of norms is correct and salutary, but that his opposition to abstractness leads him needlessly to downplay reflective modes of governing norms and to reject important aspects of the universality of reasons. Drawing on semiotics, pragmatic speech-act theory, and discursive theory of democracy, Kettner argues that Will's pragmatic stress on the contextual nature of norms is consistent with the methodological centrality of reflective governance and with significant generalizability of justifying reasons.

I would like very much to thank each of the contributors for their enthusiasm for this project, and for the high caliber of their contributions. I wish also to thank Mark Singer for advice on various matters. The Center for the Humanities at the University of New Hampshire kindly defrayed some of the initial costs incurred by this project. On behalf of all the contributors I wish most of all to thank Fred Will for the tremendous philosophical stimulation and guidance he has provided each of us over the many years of his illustrious and productive philosophical life.

Kenneth R. Westphal

References

Newton, Isaac. 1934. *The Mathematical Principles of Natural Philosophy.* A. Motte, tr., revised F. Cajori. Berkeley: University of California Press.

Will, Frederick L. 1959. "Justification and Induction." *Philosophical Review* 68 No. 3: 359–72.

Will, Frederick L. 1974. *Induction and Justification.* Ithaca: Cornell University Press.

Will, Frederick L. 1988. *Beyond Deduction.* New York and London: Routledge.

Will, Frederick L. 1997. *Pragmatism and Realism.* K. R. Westphal, ed. Lanham, Md.: Rowman & Littlefield.

1

Perspectives on Pragmatism

Nicholas Rescher

An interesting—and rather curious—aspect of contemporary American philosophy relates to the fate of "pragmatism." The founding father of this quintessentially American tendency of thought, C. S. Peirce, emphatically insisted on the central point that there is a cogent *standard* for assessing the merit of cognitive products (ideas, theories, methods)—a standard whose basis of validity reaches outside the realm of pure theory into the area of practical application and implementation. For him the ultimate test of our intellectual artifacts lay in seeing them as instrumentalities of effective praxis—in their ability to serve the communal purpose for whose sake and publicity available resources are instituted. But in recent years various philosophers who have laid claim to the label of "pragmatism" have subjected the doctrine to a drastic sea change. Whereas Peircean pragmatism sought in applicative efficacy a test of objective adequacy—an individual-transcending reality principle to offset the vagaries of personal reactions—later pseudopragmatists have inclined to follow William James in turning their backs on the pursuit of objectivity and impersonality. For classical pragmatism's impersonal concern with "what works out *for anyone* (for humans in general)" they have perversely substituted an egocentrism of "what works out *for me* or for the 'us' who constitute some limited group." In their hands the defining object of the pragmatic tradition——the search for objective and impersonal standards—has shattered into a fragmentation of communities in the parochial setting of a limited cultural context. We have a total dissolution—that is, destruction—of the classical pragmatic approach that saw the rational validity of intellectual artifacts to reside in the capacity to provide effective guidance in the successful conduct of our extratheoretical affairs—in matters of prediction, planning, successful intervention in the course of nature, and other similar aspects of the successful conduct of our practical activities. Various aspects of this phenomenon deserve closer consideration.

Ever since Arthur Lovejoy's provocative 1908 paper on "The Thirteen Pragmatisms" it has been recognized that pragmatism has a serious identity crisis.[1] For there seem to be as many pragmatisms as pragmatists—and perhaps more if Lovejoy was right regarding the equivocation at work among pragmatist thinkers. One particularly striking aspect of the situation involves the split between a pragmatism of the Left that sees this position as a doorway to flexibility, to cognitive relativity and pluralism, and a pragmatism of the Right, that sees the position as a source of stability, a pathway to cognitive security and substance. The latter is the pragmatism of C. S. Peirce, C. I. Lewis, and, among contemporaries, the present writer; the former is the pragmatism of William James, F. S. C. Schiller, and Richard Rorty. The two approaches involve diametrically opposed positions.

The pragmatists of the Left take roughly the following line:

> The core of pragmatism is utilization of the standard of "what works." But this splinters apart when we add the question: For whom? Different people have different purposes—different needs, preferences, and goals. They have a different personality-structure (as per William James's tough-minded and tender-minded). Accordingly, pragmatism countenances a live-and-let-live multiplicity of views that is as broad and flexible as the range of human idiosyncrasy and cultural variation.

A good example of this stance is the position of the early John Dewey. In his three 1911 Harrison lectures at the University of Pennsylvania on "The Problem of Truth," Dewey extended and

---

[1] Lovejoy 1908.

reaffirmed William James's lines of thought. Hard-and-fast, capital-T Truth as idealistic philosophers conceive of it is simply an illusion. Ideas and beliefs are nothing but artificial thought-instruments, mere conveyers of man-made meanings, shaped by social processes and procedures. Truth is that which gets endorsed and accepted in the community. Its sole validation is the sanction of social approbation and custom, and when those "truths" no longer satisfy social needs others are found to replace them. Truth resides in agreement: social consensus does not merely *evidentiate* truth, but is its *creator*. It is a social constraint that is at issue.[2]

To this general line of approach, Richard Rorty adds certain characteristic emphases:

> Let me sum up by offering a . . . characterization of pragmatism: it is the doctrine that there are no constraints on inquiry save conversational ones—no wholesale constraints derived from the nature of the objects, or of the mind, or of language, but only those retail constraints provided by the remarks of our fellow inquirers . . .. The pragmatist tells us that it is useless to hope that objects will constrain us to believe the truth about them, if only they are approached with an unclouded mental eye, or a rigorous method, or a perspicuous language. . . .. The only sense in which we are constrained to truth is that . . . we can make no sense of the notion that the view which can survive all objections might be false. But objections—conversational constraints—cannot be anticipated. There is no method for knowing *when* one has reached the truth, or when one is closer to it than before.[3]

---

[2] Dewey 1911. The later Dewey seems to have hardened his line, however. Thus in his reply to Arthur Murphy (Dewey 1951, 556–68), Dewey endorses the stronger classical doctrine. Discussing his earlier theories that "[s]cientific conceptions are not a revelation of prior and independent reality" (Dewey 1929, 165), Dewey now indicates that the negative emphasis belongs on "revelation" and *not* on "prior and independent reality" (1951, 560–61, 563, 565). Frederick Will cites this discussion in "The Concern about Truth" (1997, 45 note), and ends §3 of that essay with the declaration: "We shall be poorer in our understanding of human knowledge if we permit our proper scepticism of these [problematic] entities [such as "facts" or "states of affairs"] to obscure and cause us to neglect the concern [for the truth/falsity distinction] from which they arose" (1997, 47).

[3] Rorty 1982, 165–66.

Such a pragmatism of the Left looks to the doctrine as a means of loosening up our thinking—of asserting its idiosyncratic and parochial diversity. It abolishes constraints in the interests of achieving an outcome that is subjectivistic, personalistic, and relativistic. The crux of such a freewheeling ("postmodernist") pragmatism lies in its abandonment of the ideal of objectivity—its dismissal of the traditional theory of knowledge's insistence on judging issues by impersonal or at any rate person-indifferent standards. Truth is viewed as a matter of social convention—of the mores of the tribe.

The pragmatism of the Right is diametrically opposed to these disintegrative tendencies. It sees pragmatism's concern for efficacy as a means of substantiation, solidification, and objectification. The pragmatists of the Right take roughly the following line:

> Pragmatism is concerned with what works—with the effective and efficient achievement of purpose. And the purposes at issue are not idiosyncrasies of individuals, but rather those collective human enterprises whose rationale roots in the nature of the human condition at large. Our empirical knowledge, in particular, is concerned with the achievement of active (interactionistic) and passive (predictive) *control* over nature. Those ways of proceeding which prove themselves effective and efficient here are *ipso facto* substantiated, so that people engaged in the project are rationally impelled to adopt them. Pragmatism is a road that leads not to subjectivity but to objectivity; it speaks not for relativistic preferences but for objective constraints.[4]

Such an approach looks to pragmatism as a "reality principle" that imposes rather than abolishes constraints and limitations. Whether the key opens the lock or jams it or whether the mushroom nourishes or kills us is not dependent on the predilections of people but on the *modus operandi* of impersonal nature. What actually works for the realization of human needs is, after all, something independent of our idiosyncratic wants and preferences.

The pragmatism of the Left holds a Jamesean view, "what works for the satisfaction of personal wishes and desires" is justified. The

---

[4] The author's fullest defense of this version of pragmatism is in Rescher 1977.

pragmatism of the Right holds that "what is efficient/effective for the satisfaction of needs (general human desiderata)" is justified. The one is concerned with peoples desires, the other with recalcitrant realities (people's actual needs included). These are two very different sorts of "pragmatism"; the one is consensual and relativistic, the other objectivistic and universalistic. The one is a postmodern pragmatism of people's desires and inclinations, the other a rationalistic pragmatism of generic needs and impersonal standards.

The fact is that pragmatists of the Right tend to follow Peirce into an adherence to metaphysical realism. In metaphysics they hold that reality is what it is independently of what we think about it. In epistemology they incline to the view that conscientiously contacted inquiry leads to at least roughly correct views about the matter. And in any case, existence precedes knowledge: inquiry does not engender reality but rather models it. It is our view of reality that is a human social constraint, and not reality itself (as with the soft pragmatists of the Left).

With this basic dichotomy clearly in view, we can now pose the focal question of the present essay: Where does Frederick L. Will stand with regard to this chasm that splits pragmatism into two distinct and very different doctrines? Does he favor the soft social pragmatism of the relativistic Left? Or does he side with the more tough-minded pragmatism of the objectivistic Right?

As far as I can see, this is an issue on which Will is somewhat of two minds.[5] On the one hand he recognizes pragmatism's pull to solidity and objectivity: He acknowledges its "great service in stressing something that now especially needs to be stressed, namely, that in external and internal nature there are, as well as opportunities for the development of practices, limitations upon the kinds of practices which may be developed, and that these limitations we ignore at the risk of the health and well-being of the system of

---

[5] All references here are to F.L. Will, "The Rational Governance of Practice" (Will 1997, ch. 9).

practices and the quality of the life that is lived through them."[6]
And moreover:

> All these limitations upon the variability of practices and governance,
> not least of which is that independent character of the objects of
> investigation with which in scientific and other cognitive practices we
> are directly concerned, represent sources of stability greatly counter-
> balancing any tendency there may be in governance and practices
> toward general, unmanageable instability.[7]

All of this sounds very much like a pragmatism of the Right.
But occasionally Will begins to manifest second thoughts:

> The function of [inquiring] reason is much more homely, modest,
> mundane and, to change the myth, less Promethean than this. Draw-
> ing upon the most pertinent features of practices and governance we
> are able to say that, with these as with other things, new revised
> versions are not necessarily better; new manifestations of reason itself,
> are not necessarily improved ones; though they sometimes are. And
> who, or what, is to say? Who, but us?[8]

Now this is still on reasonably firm ground provided the "us" at
issue is construed normatively as the idealized community of strictly
rational inquirers and not empirically as the historical scattering of
schools of thought (let alone of idiosyncratic individuals). But
occasionally the bottom line, the fashionable relativism of the
present day seems to gain the upper hand with Will:

> Nothing that has been said so far about the processes of rational
> governance provides any guarantee that what these processes yield at
> one time . . . may not at other times and from other points of view
> be rightly judged to have been deficient in rationality. There are some
> who readily concede the possibility of reversal in steps taken by
> individuals in the governance of habits in their own lives, but would
> demur in some degree concerning governance viewed on the broad
> stage of world history, where individuals, as agents of governance,

---

[6] Will 1997, 79.
[7] Will 1997, 79.
[8] Will 1997, 82.

are to a considerable extent replaced by social groups or institutions. Yet the hard facts of social life and proximate history count heavily against placing unqualified trust in any social agent of governance, however grand and impressive . . ..[9]

But if we follow Will into this rejection on making what is large-scale, long-run, and to some extent idealized, then we are left in the end with the views of atomic individuals and contingently constituted groupings. We are shunted into the shifting sands of individual vagaries.

As I see it, the basic problem with Will's position lies in his preoccupation with the issue of failproof assurances.[10] Of course there are no guarantees in this imperfect epistemic disposition. But just why should this be such a big deal? Surely it is old hat—being among other things the lesson of the Genesis story of the expulsion from Eden.

As I see it, Will leaves us stranded somewhat betwixt and between. The great strength of his position is his naturalism. This comes to the fore in "Thoughts, and Things"[11] and to prominence in part 3 of *Induction and Justification*. And it remains on deck in his later essays and in *Beyond Deduction*. But when it comes to the question of how firm a ground this naturalism leaves under our feet—of just where and just how it provides for objective, wish-and-thought–independent modes of quality control that go deeper than the shifting sands of social consensus—the position in which Will leaves us is not altogether satisfactory.

To give to this issue of guarantees the pride of place is to do serious pragmatism a serious injustice. All we need ask for is the reasonable assurance of a balance of plausibilities—to require full-fledged *guarantees* is surely to go too far. The basic issue is that of regulative ideals. In the end, the pivotal issue for rationality remains what people *ought* to think, and not what they do happen to think.

---

[9] Will 1997, 81.

[10] Will's elaborate—and surely right-minded—critique of the pursuit of epistemic guarantees is especially developed in Will 1988.

[11] 1997, ch. 1.

And here the question arises as to the justificatory rationale behind that *ought*.

Still, if we abandon the subjective wishes of atomic individuals (individual wants) for the collective purposes of people-in-general (human needs), then how are we to judge those issues of normative adequacy?

Obviously this will have to be done at the collective level. ("Who but us?" Will rightly asks.) The extent to which "our" purposes are effectively served by particular arrangements and mechanisms will indeed have to be appraised by *us*. But the focus of the question has changed. It is now not a matter of what we want but of what we need. The point (to reemphasize) is something that is not for us to *decide* but for us to *discover*.

Kant was indeed right: All of our pretensions to the truth are shadowed by an inseparable *I think*. But that is not the end of it. For it does not impede us from dealing with the communal issue of what *we think* nor yet with the normative issue of what *sensible people think*. The question of the way things are never simply collapses into that of the way people think them to be, unless and until those "people" at issue are construed normatively as "ideally rational individuals working under epistemically ideal conditions."

But where do we ground that normativity if we are reluctant to jump into the epistemic pool at the deep end of idealization? And just what is to say that we will judge the matter rightly? *Securus judicat orbis terrarum* is surely an eminently problematic contention, even though St. Augustine was its author. All this is true enough, but it does not get to the heart of the matter. The long and short it is that reliance on the general position of the group is our best bet only insofar as we have reason for confidence that "general group" consists largely or substantiality of rational individuals. Here, as elsewhere, we can do no better than the best we can manage in the circumstances. But the project is and remains that of endeavoring to implement impersonal standards of objective cogency.

Of course, reasonable assurance and promising plausibilities afford no categorical guarantees of adequacy. But this really doesn't matter. For the point is *not* that the community will judge rightly by some sort of cosmic necessity. In concentrating on this unavailability of guarantees Will is to some extent flogging a dead horse. What matters is that the collective wisdom of the group is likely to avert some of the biases and eccentricities to which many or most of its individual member are subject. For the very reason that certainties are not available in this domain we have to be satisfied with probabilities and rest satisfied with the best *estimates* of the real truth that we can make in the circumstances. And just here lie the advantages of a pragmatic approach with its enhanced impetus to objectivity.

A sensible pragmatism of the Right accordingly has four key features: (1) It adopts an objectivistic stance that averts the subjectivistic relativism. (2) It is communally geared, but with *normatively* constituted groupings and not just *contingently* constituted ones.[12] Accordingly, (3) it places an emphasis on impersonally normative rationality that enables it to implement the pursuit of objectivity. Finally, (4) it locates the quality control of our cognitive proceeding, not in the sphere of human activity itself, but in the impersonal dealings of nature in their (often unwelcome) impact upon us. Overall, the salient fact is that the quality controls we require at this stage are best obtained from the realm of pragmatic considerations. They pivot on the question of functional efficacy in the achievement of our objectives. And this is not something that we make up as we go along—it lies in the objective nature of things.

The key lies in mediating between extremes. On the one hand we have those philosophers wedded to evident certainties and a deductivist instance of proliferation. On the other hand we have those who think that the cognitive domain is one of opinions all the way down and envision nothing save "conversational constraints." Here Will is on the side of the angels. He sees the demand for certainty as unrealistic. He holds that conceptual frameworks can be rational. He rejects relativism and absolution in all their forms. But there yet remains what is (in my view) a weakness in his armor. For the

---

[12] [Compare Durkheim's distinction between "mechanical" and "organic" solidarity, discussed by Thomas Green below in Essay 7, §5.1—Ed.]

tenor of his social pragmatism is such that Will is prepared to settle for the convenience of a contingently constituted community rather than for the harder version of a normatively constituted one.

Such a tough-minded pragmatism can certainly grant both the frailties of individuals and groups and the diversity and not infrequent perversity of human aims and purposes. But it can and will go on to insist both that rational comportment is an open option for us, and that it is an option which, given the realities of the human condition, yields palpable benefits. And above all, such a pragmatism does not allow the matter to rest with the idiosyncratic wishes of scattered individuals or with the parochial predilections of contingent groups. Whether those ideas and beliefs actually work or not—whether the engine starts or the bulb lights—is not a matter of social custom but of the world's impersonal ways. Pragmatism of the Right pivots on a self-subsistent and person-indifferent reality principle—its cutting edge lies not with people's connections but with the world's ways assessed in a normative perspective.

The classic pragmatists of the Left (James, Dewey) and their epigones saw the idealistic tradition (and Royce in particular) as the enemy. And at first thought this seems plausible enough. For in cognitive matters at the level of generality and precision at issue in theories of natural science, conceptions such as "knowledge," "truth," "law," "completeness," "system," and the like are all geared to the ideal level. They are not realizable results whose attainment we can (if realistic) see as achievable projects. All of them involve an element of normative idealization that renders their full actualization unrealistic.

Acknowledging the impracticability of a full concretization of a normative goal—with its concomitant foregoing of guarantees—is thus no insuperable obstacle to the validation of an ideal. This issue of its actualization is simply beside the point, because what counts with an ideal is not the question of its attainment but that of the benefits that accrue from its pursuit. What matters in the final analysis is not the achievement of perfection but an improvement on alternatives. All in all, it seems to one that Will is so focused upon the *theoretical* governance of cognitive norms that he fails to do justice to the centrality of their *practical* governance.

But credit should be given where credit is due. Will is concerned *both* to insist on the unavailability of epistemic guarantees and to avert succumbing to skeptical relativism. My only caveat is that he does not seem to me to acknowledge sufficiently the extent to which a traditionalistic pragmatism of the Right is able—and indeed was in Peirce's thought *designed*—to accomplish this job. Here Peirce's only shortcoming was (as I see it) to look to the long-range future rather than to a time-transcending idealization. Some may see this as an advantage—but this is something I would emphatically question.[13]

As Max Weber observed with characteristic perspicacity, even in the domain of politics—that "art of the possible"—"the possible has frequently been attained only through striving for something impossible that lies beyond one's reach."[14] To attain the limits of the possibilities inherent in our powers and potentialities, we must aim beyond them. And just here lies the great importance of the ideal realm. Ideals are visionary, unrealistic, and utopian. But by viewing the world in the light of their powerful illumination, we see it all the more vividly—and critically. We understand the true nature of the real better by considering it in the light reflected from ideals, and we use this light to find our way about more satisfactorily in the real world.

To be sure, our ideals ask too much of us—cognitive ideals included. We cannot attain perfection in the life of this world—not in the moral life, or in the life of inquiry, or in our economic, social, or religious life. Authentic faith, comprehensive knowledge, genuine morality, or perfect markets are all idealizations, or destinations that we cannot actually reach. They are hyperboles that

---

[13] See especially Will 1988, part 3.

[14] "Nicht minder richtig aber ist, daß das Mögliche sehr oft nur dadurch erreicht wurde, daß man nach dem jenseits seiner Kraft liegenden Unmöglichen griff" (Weber 1922, 476).

beckon us ever onward, whose value lies in their practical utility as a motivating impetus in positive directions.

But what can possibly justify our adhesion to such unconcretizable ideals? The answer is that they represent not bare goals but actual *values*. They orient and guide our action in certain particular directions. And it is in this action-guiding role that their legitimation lies. For their validation is ultimately pragmatic: Their justification lies in their utility, their efficiency in promoting the furtherance of the enterprise as issue. On this telling, ideals, despite their superior and splendid appearance, are actually of a subordinate status in point of justification. They are not ultimate ends but instrumental means, subservient to the controlling aims and goals whose realization they facilitate. They are indeed important and valuable, but their worth and validity ultimately reside, not in their intrinsic desirability ("wouldn't it be nice if . . ."), but in their eminent utility—in their capacity to guide and to facilitate the cultivation of the objectives of the enterprises to which they are affiliated. Dedicating ourselves to those unrealizable ideals and staging our contact in their light enhances our performance through enabling the realization of results at the level of actual attainment superior to what we would otherwise be able to achieve. Their validation may reside, not in providing an achievable declaration, but rather in benefits we realize in the course of the pursuit itself. The striving after an ideal science that affords us "the ultimate truth" about the workings of nature seems to be a telos of just this sort. (We arrive at the perhaps strange-sounding posture of an invocation of practical utility for the validation of an ideal.) Paradoxical though it may seem, the validation of such ideals ultimately lies in the pragmatic domain.

The validation of an ideal is thus something derivative. It does not lie simply in the nature of the (unrealizable) state of affairs that it contemplates—in the inherently unachievable perfection that it envisions. Rather, it lies in the influence it exerts on the actions of its human exponents through the mediation of thought. The justification and power of an ideal inhere in its capacity to energize and motivate human effort toward positive results—in its practical efficacy, in short. Ideals may involve unrealism, but this in no way annihilates their impetus or value, thanks to the positive consequences that ensue upon our adoption of them.

Such an approach to the issue of legitimating ideals has a curious aspect of seeing our commitment to an ideal as lying in its practical utility for our dealings with the real through its capacity to encourage and facilitate our productive efforts. Such an approach does not adopt a Platonic view of ideals that sees them as valuable strictly in their own right as abstract embodiments of worth. Rather, their value comes to be seen as instrumental or pragmatic: ideals are of value not for their own sake, but for ours, because of the good effects to be achieved by using them as a compass for orienting our thought and action amid the shoals and narrows of a difficult world. And so a sensible idealism is one which, in the final analysis, takes its stand on a pragmatic basis geared to a praxis that roots in the actualities of our human situation.

To be sure, an objective pragmatism need not deny the harsh fact of a human fallibility that makes the pursuit of rationality a chancy and uncertain proposition. Of course it cannot provide absolute guarantees—here Will is entirely right. But what it can and does offer us are certain not insubstantial *advantages*. An objective pragmatism need not argue that purposive rationality is a failproof option. All it needs to do is to establish its superiority to the alternatives. In this context as in so many others we can achieve no guarantees. The best we can do is to play the odds intelligently.

In the end, then, there remains the critical advantage of an objectivistic and traditionalistic over a relativistic and postmodern pragmatism. A tough-minded pragmatism of impersonal standards coheres with a commitment to the life of reason. It enables us to make sense of the classical epistemic project of caring for evidence, argumentation, and the pursuit of truth. Of course we have to recognize that in this project as in all other human endeavors the attainment of perfection will be beyond our grasp. But this, surely, is no reason to abandon the venture. For since when is the inability to secure perfection an appropriate excuse for not doing the best we can?

At this point, the issue of values comes to the fore.[15] For if we join in with objective pragmatism and take purposive efficacy addressed to need satisfaction as our normative guide, then the question of what justifies this normative decision arises. And the answer here lies ultimately in the place that we assign to rationality in the evaluative scheme of things. Here the crucial point is—or should be—that if we want a justification at all, it is surely a *rational* justification that we want. And rationality more or less by definition consists in the intelligent pursuit of appropriate objectives.[16] Now the effective and efficient satisfaction of our needs (that is our *real* as opposed to our merely *felt* needs, which is to say mere wants) serves as the pivot-point of this justifactory venture. It is therefore rationality itself that speaks on behalf of a sensibly realistic pragmatism that need not apologize for its commitment to objectivity.[17]

University of Pittsburgh

References

Dewey, John. 1911. *Brief Studies in Realism*. Chicago: University of Chicago Press.

Dewey, John. 1929. *The Quest for Certainty*. New York: Minton Back.

Dewey, John. 1951. "Experience, Knowledge and Value: A Rejoinder." In *The Philosophy of John Dewey*. P. Schilpp, ed. 2nd ed., La Salle Ill.: Open Court, 515–608.

Lovejoy, A. O. 1908. "The Thirteen Pragmatisms." *The Journal of Philosophy, Psychology, and Scientific Methods* 5: 5–12, 29–39.

Rescher, Nicholas. 1977. *Methodological Pragmatism*. Oxford: Blackwell.

Rescher, Nicholas. 1988. *Rationality*. Oxford: Clarendon Press.

Rorty, Richard. 1982. *Consequences of Pragmatism*. Minneapolis: University of Minnesota Press.

---

[15] On this issue see Will's instructive 1993 paper, "Philosophical Governance of Norms," (in Will 1997, ch. 9).

[16] For a development of this point see Rescher 1988.

[17] I am grateful to Ken Westphal for constructive comments in a draft of this essay.

Weber, Max. 1922. "Der Sinn der 'Wertfreiheit' in den soziologischen und ökonomischen Wissenschaften." *Logos* 7, 1917–18: 40–88. Rpt. in *Soziologie, Universalgeschichtliche Analysen, Politik.* J. Winckelmann, ed. Stuttgart: Kröner, 1973, 263–310.

Will, Frederick L. 1974. *Induction and Justification.* Ithaca, N.Y.: Cornell University Press.

Will, Frederick L. 1988. *Beyond Deduction.* New York and London: Routledge.

Will, Frederick L. 1997. *Pragmatism and Realism.* K. R. Westphal, ed. Lanham: Md., Rowman & Littlefield.

2

Transcendental Reflections on Pragmatic Realism

Kenneth R. Westphal

> Not empiricism and yet realism in philosophy,
> that is the hardest thing. (Against Ramsey.)[1]

1 INTRODUCTION

At the end of his introduction to *Essays in Quasi-Realism*, a set of essays in which he probes whether there is a significant debate between realism and antirealism, Simon Blackburn tentatively offers as his meta-philosophical creed the observation that "there are too many ideologies and too few works wondering about the foundations underlying their differences."[2] Blackburn's creed is both salutary unto itself, suggesting as it does the need for far more careful and self-critical reflection on our own philosophical orientations and specific views, and also suggestive of the merit of Frederick Will's work, for Will has been steadily probing the foundations underlying skepticism and various epistemological currents and problems for well over thirty years. Some of Will's results are so finely distilled that their significance, regrettably, has gone unnoticed. Here I shall explicate two of Will's basic insights, into the dependence of thoughts on the ordinary things they are about, and

---

[1] Wittgenstein 1978, §VI–23 (p. 325).
[2] Blackburn 1993, 11.

into a primary reason that this relation has been widely overlooked, first by setting those insights into a broader philosophical and historical context, and subsequently by showing a few of the myriad ways in which his insights remain pertinent to current discussions. The significance of Will's insight into the dependency of thoughts on things develops directly out of a common problem afflicting both Kant's and Carnap's rejections of realism—ordinary realism of the sort according to which there is a way things are that is not generated by our thought or language, and that we can know something about those things. The reason this dependency has been overlooked, and the reason this kind of commonsense realism has seemed so problematic, stems directly from a very prevalent and still influential non sequitur undergirding the debate between foundationalism and coherentism in epistemology. In §§2 and 3 I develop parallel internal criticisms of Kant's and Carnap's rejections of commonsense realism. In §4 I discuss Will's parallel insight, which he developed out of ordinary language analysis, and the non sequitur he identifies in the dispute between foundationalism and coherentism. In §5 I show that his insights have important bearing on the views of Michael Williams, John Haldane, and Crispin Wright.

2 KANT

2.1   *The Affinity of the Manifold of Intuition Is a Transcendental Condition of Possible Human Experience*[3]

A primary characteristic of Kant's "formal" idealism is that the matter of experience is given to us *ab extra*. This is a transcendental condition of experience.[4] Precisely how this matter is given to us remains controversial, but this condition itself is unproblematic.[5] The

---

[3] The following summary is drawn from my much more detailed treatment in Westphal 1997a.

[4] See Allison 1983, 250.

[5] Paton 1936, 1:139–40, recognizes that the matter of sensation must result from affection by things in themselves. I defend this thesis in Westphal 1997b.

only other transcendental material condition of human experience recognized by Kant is, however, quite controversial, namely, the transcendental affinity of the manifold of empirical intuition. This condition is perplexing because it is both transcendental and formal, but neither conceptual nor intuitive. This is to say, the transcendental affinity of the manifold of intuition is transcendental, because it is a necessary *a priori* condition of possible human experience. It is a formal condition because it concerns the orderliness, indeed the regularity of the matter of empirical intuition. However, this condition is not fulfilled by the *a priori* conditions of intuition necessary for human experience (analyzed in Kant's "Transcendental Aesthetic"), nor by the *a priori* conceptual conditions necessary for human experience (analyzed in the first part of Kant's "Transcendental Logic," the "Transcendental Analytic"). As Kant twice affirms, this condition is fulfilled by the "content" or the "object" of experience.[6]

According to Kant, appearances must be associable if we are to be able to make cognitive judgments. If (self-conscious) experience is possible at all, Kant holds, then this associability of appearances must have an objective ground. Kant calls this ground the "affinity" of the manifold of intuition.[7] Kant stresses that a complete sensibili-

---

[6] *KdrV* A112–13, 4:85.3–10; A653–54=B681–82, 3:433.14–29. I cite Kant's works (1902–) by volume, page, and line numbers; I cite the two editions of the first *Critique* by the usual designations, "A" and "B."

[7] The following is the most important passage on this topic: "Now if this unity of association did not also have an objective ground, so that it would be impossible for appearances to be apprehended by the imagination otherwise than under the condition of a possible synthetic unity of this apprehension, it would be entirely accidental that appearances should fit into a connection in human knowledge. For even though we should have the capacity to associate perceptions, it would remain entirely undetermined and accidental *whether they themselves were associable*; and in case they were not associable, then a multitude of perceptions, and indeed an entire sensibility would be possible, in which much empirical consciousness would be found in my mind, but separated, and without belonging to *one* consciousness of myself, which, however, is impossible. For only because I ascribe all perceptions to one consciousness (original apperception) can I say of all perceptions that I am conscious of them. There must, therefore, be an objective ground (that is, one that can be comprehended *a priori*, antecedent to all empirical laws of the imagination) upon which rests the possibility, indeed, the necessity, of a law that extends to all appearances—a ground, namely, for regarding all appearances as data of the senses that must be associable in themselves and subject to universal rules of a

ty and understanding, capable of associating perceptions, does not of itself determine whether any appearances or perceptions it has are in fact associable. If they weren't, there may be fleeting episodes of empirical consciousness (*i.e.*, random sensations), but there could be no unified, and hence no self-conscious, experience. In part this would be because those irregular perceptions would not admit of any reproductive synthesis; they wouldn't admit of any psychological association, and so couldn't afford a basis for developing empirical concepts or for applying categorical concepts to objects.

Kant makes this point especially clear in a passage found in both editions of the first *Critique* in which he specifies an empirical and a transcendental principle of "genera":

> If among the appearances which present themselves to us, there were so great a variety—I do not say in form, for in that respect appearances might resemble one another; but in *content*, that is, in the diversity of existing entities—that even the acutest human understanding could never by comparison of them detect the slightest similarity (a possibility which is quite conceivable), the logical law of genera would absolutely not obtain, and there would not even be the concept of a genus, or any other universal concept, or indeed any understanding at all, since it has to do solely with such concepts. If, therefore, the logical principle of genera is to be applied to nature (by which I here understand only those objects which are given to us), it presupposes a transcendental principle [of genera]. In accordance with this latter principle, homogeneity is necessarily presupposed in the manifold of possible experience (although we cannot determine *a*

---

thoroughgoing connection in their reproduction. *This objective ground of all association of appearances I entitle their affinity.* It is to be found nowhere else than in the principle of the unity of apperception, in respect of all cognitions which should belong to me. According to this principle all appearances, without exception, must so enter the mind or be apprehended, that they conform to the unity of apperception. Without synthetic unity in their connection, which is thus objectively necessary, this would be impossible.

"The objective unity of all (empirical) consciousness in one consciousness, that of original apperception, is thus the necessary condition of all possible perception; and the *affinity* of all appearances, near or remote, is a necessary consequence of a synthesis in imagination which is grounded *a priori* on rules." (*KdrV* A121–23, 4:90.6–91.2; tr. Kemp Smith 1929, 144–45; translation emended, some emphases added.)

priori its degree); for without homogeneity, no empirical concepts, and hence no experience, would be possible.[8]

It is significant that Kant identifies the relevant kind of similarity as a matter of the content (*"dem Inhalte"*), rather than the form, of appearances. This is Kant's own indication that the issue of the regularity of the objects of (or in) experience is a material condition. The fact that it concerns *relations* among the characteristics of the contents of experience indicates that this is also a "formal" condition, in Kant's sense; it concerns something's being orderable. The oddity for Kant is that this is a formal condition, although it is not an intuitive or a conceptual condition. The consequences of the lack of such similarities are of transcendental import: failing such recognizable regularities, we would have no empirical concepts, indeed no (functioning) *understanding*, and hence no conscious experience. Kant does not speak here of the "principle of affinity."[9] Instead he speaks of a "logical [*i.e.*, cognitive] principle of genera," which he claims presupposes a "transcendental principle of genera." Although such a principle is presupposed by the reflective use of rational principles in organizing our experience (the topic of much of the Dialectic of the first *Critique* and most of the third *Critique*), this transcendental principle concerns the application of the logical law of genera to nature in the broad sense of "objects given to us," and it also concerns the very possibility of experience itself. Consequently, this principle is also a constitutive principle of experience directly relevant to the transcendental analysis of the necessary conditions of possible experience. Below some minimum degree of regularity among appearances, the matter of sensation, or the objects of experience, there can be no recognition of objects or regularities; hence there could be neither empirical concepts nor *any* employment of the understanding; hence there could be no experience.

---

[8] *KdrV* A653–54=B681–82, 3:433.14–29; tr. Kemp Smith 1929, 539–40; translation emended, emphasis added. Notice that the last sentence rightly emphasizes that this law of genera concerns a constitutive, and not only a regulative, issue.

[9] *KdrV* A766–67=B794–95, 3:500.2–25.

(Above that minimum, there is then a reflective or regulative issue concerning how much those recognized regularities can be systematized.)

It is important to note that, in both cases, the necessity of the associability of the manifold of intuition is a *conditional* necessity, holding between that manifold and any self-conscious (human) subject. Necessarily, if a human subject is aware of any object or event through a manifold of intuition, then the content of that manifold is associable. The associability of this content *is* its "affinity." The fact that affinity is necessary for the possibility of experience entails that this affinity is transcendental. The question now is, What is the status of the principle of affinity in Kant's transcendental analysis, and is his idealist account of that status adequate?

2.2   Kant's Idealist Explanation of the Affinity of the Manifold of Intuition

Kant's transcendental idealism explains the "necessity" of transcendental conditions of possible human experience in terms of the structure and functioning of our cognitive capacities, because these unavoidably and inevitably structure our experience of objects.[10] Kant tries repeatedly to explain the affinity of the manifold of intuition in the same way. His most detailed argument for this is the following:

> I therefore ask, how do you make comprehensible to yourselves the thoroughgoing affinity of appearances, whereby they stand under constant laws, and *must* belong under such laws?
>
> On my principles it is easily comprehensible. All possible appearances, as representations, belong to the totality of a possible self-consciousness. But as self-consciousness is a transcendental representation, numerical identity is inseparable from it, and is *a priori* certain, because nothing can come to cognition except through this original apperception. Now, since this identity must necessarily enter into the synthesis of all the manifold of appearances, so far as this

---

[10] *KdrV* B41, A23=B37–38, A26–28=B42–44, A195–96=B240–41, 3:54.21–27, 52.8–14, 55.1–56.19, 171.25–172.9; A101–02, A113–14, A121–123, A125–26, 4:78.20–33, 85.10–28, 90.6–91.2, 92.14–24; *Prolegomena* §36, 4:319.11–30.

synthesis is to become empirical knowledge, the appearances are subject to *a priori* conditions, with which the synthesis of their apprehension must be in complete accord. Now the representation of a universal condition according to which a certain manifold can be uniformly posited is called a *rule*, and, when it *must* be so posited, a *law*. Thus all appearances stand in thoroughgoing connection according to necessary laws, and therefore in a *transcendental affinity*, of which the *empirical* is a mere consequence.[11]

In this passage Kant states the principle of the affinity of appearances as a principle which, *prima facie*, is open to alternative explanations, he challenges non-Kantians to explain it, and he claims that it is easy to explain on his own transcendental idealist principles. However, his argument is unsound; in fact transcendental idealism cannot explain the satisfaction of the transcendental principle of affinity at all.

2.3   Criticism of Kant's Idealist Explanation of the Affinity of the Manifold of Intuition

I contend that Kant is quite right, for reasons given above, that the affinity of the manifold of intuition constitutes a transcendental condition of possible human experience. Apperceptive (*i.e.*, self-conscious) experience requires that we are able to identify objects, and identifying objects requires that they display recognizable regularities (both similarities and differences). Otherwise, our discursive understanding could neither develop empirical concepts nor apply general concepts (both empirical and categorial) to intuited objects, yet such application of concepts is necessary to distinguish and identify objects, and to contradistinguish oneself from the objects one perceives. (Kant cannot give up this doctrine without giving up the entirety of his rationalist critique of empiricism or his "Refutation of Idealism."[12]) Such a thesis is inherent in any non-

---

[11] *KdrV* A113–14, 4:85.10–28, tr. Kemp Smith 1929, 139–40; translation emended.

[12] Kant's opposition to empiricism is indicated, *e.g.*, in his contention that there may be sensory consciousness without thought. That is precisely the prospect encountered whenever there is no affinity. See, *e.g.*, A90–91=B123 (quoted above, note 6).

skeptical epistemology which, like Kant's, rejects both knowledge
by acquaintance and innate ideas.

The problem is that Kant cannot explain how or why this condition is satisfied. In brief, the problem is that Kant's attempted
explanations of the transcendental affinity of the manifold of intuition conflate its *ratio cognoscendi* (which follow from Kant's
transcendental analysis of the conditions of possible experience)
with its *ratio essendi* (which Kant's idealism cannot explain at all).

Kant's first contention on this head is that the "empirical affinity"
of a manifold of intuition (or a set of appearances) is the mere
consequence of its "transcendental affinity."[13] This cannot be correct. That an empirical manifold has affinity—in order for us to be
self-consciously aware of it—is indeed entailed by the requirements
for unitary self-consciousness, but this entailment expresses a *conditional* necessity: Whenever unitary self-conscious (human) experience occurs, that subject is presented with a manifold of associable
appearances. However, the associability of that manifold of appearances is an independent fact, a *sine qua non*, of self-conscious
experience; *empirical* affinity is an independent factor, needed to
satisfy the transcendental principle of affinity.

Kant's related claim, second, that the affinity of appearances is a
necessary consequence ("*notwendige Folge*") of the (transcendental)
synthesis of imagination, is equivocal.[14] Like the English "consequence," the German "*Folge*" can denote either logical or causal
consequence. The affinity of a manifold is a logical consequence of
the occurrence of the transcendental synthesis of imagination requisite for unitary apperception. Neither synthesis nor apperception
could occur if the manifold of intuition lacked affinity. However,
this affinity cannot be a *functional product* (causal consequence) of
that synthesis, unless Kant were to give up his carefully qualified
transcendental idealism and adopt full-blown subjective idealism.[15]

---

[13] *KdrV* A114, 4:85.27–28; quoted above, p. 23.

[14] *KdrV* A123, 4:90.37–91.2.

[15] *Cf.* Paton: "I believe that the empirical differences in the shapes and sizes of
objects, like their empirical qualitative differences, must be ascribed to the 'influ-

Unified self-conscious experience is the *ratio cognoscendi* of the occurrence of transcendental affinity of the manifold of intuition; but the occurrence of such transcendental affinity is the *ratio essendi* of unified self-conscious experience. In fact, transcendental idealism cannot *explain* the occurrence of transcendental affinity at all.[16]

Third, transcendental idealism is not at all the only possible explanation of affinity.[17] The satisfaction of the principle of affinity is a distinct factor from its transcendental status as a necessary condition of unified self-conscious experience. This is because the "necessity" that this principle be satisfied is conditional. Once this is recognized, then it is possible to recognize that the satisfaction of the principle of affinity is a function of the *de facto* orderliness of nature, just as Hume (in effect) argued.[18]

Finally, it also cannot be the case that we are solely responsible for introducing order and regularity into the appearances we call nature, as Kant also claims.[19] The basic reason is the same in each case: if the matter of sensation is given us *a posteriori*, then *ex hypothesi* we cannot generate its content. Consequently, we also can neither generate nor otherwise insure the regularities, the recognizable similarities and differences, within that content or among any set of given intuitions. The satisfaction of the transcendental principle of affinity by any manifold of intuitions or appearances cannot be generated, injected, or imposed by that subject; in Kant's terms, it cannot be a "transcendentally ideal" condition of possible experience. The satisfaction of the principle of affinity can be *required* by the cognitive nature of a subject, and thus it can be a *transcenden-*

---

ence' of things-in-themselves . . .. Only what is strictly universal is imposed by the mind upon objects. Empirical differences are particular determinations of the universal, but their particularity is not due to the mind and must be due to things. If this view be given up, I do not see how the Critical Philosophy can be made intelligible" (1936, 1:139–40). Affinity consists in the regularities among the specific contents of empirical intuitions.

[16] *Contra KdrV* A101–2, A113–14, A122; 4:78.20–33, 85.10–28, 90.26–30.
[17] *Contra KdrV* A101–2, A113–14, A122; 4:78.20–33, 85.10–28, 90.26–30.
[18] Hume 1975, §§IV Part 1, VIII; 44, 82.
[19] *KdrV* A125, 4:92.14–24.

tal condition for the possibility of that subject's unified self-conscious experience. This is a *conditional* necessity. The satisfaction of the transcendental principle of affinity is a contingent function of the specific characteristics of *a posteriori* matter of sensation, namely the (recognizable) similarities among those characteristics. Kant was quite right to say that the principle of affinity concerns the content of experience, and that its ground lies in the object of experience.[20] Consequently, the principle of affinity is no more explicable on Kant's transcendental idealist account than on any naturalist account of the objects of knowledge.[21]

2.4   Interim Conclusion

From these considerations I conclude that a transcendental analysis of the conditions of possible human experience, along the lines set out by Kant, can in fact be turned against Kant's idealism and put in service of common sense realism. Kant is right that "inner experience in general is only possible through outer experience in general."[22] However, this insight *cannot* be defended by Kant's transcendental idealism. Indeed, it can only be defended by naturalism, because we humans are only capable of self-conscious thought if we in fact experience a world naturally structured by events and objects with identifiable similarities and differences.[23] In the next section I shall argue for a similar conclusion through criticism of Carnap's rejection of realism.

---

[20] *KdrV* A112–13, 4:85.3–10; A653–54=B681–82, 3:433.14–29.
[21] *Contra KdrV* A113–14, 4:85.10–28.
[22] *KdrV* B276–77, B278–79; 3:192.10–13, 193.20–21.
[23] This conclusion is broader than what I have argued here. The broader conclusion turns on the fact that the criticism of Kant sketched here ultimately affords a derivation of the standard objection to Kant's arguments for transcendental idealism, the so-called "problem of the neglected alternative," from principles internal to Kant's own analysis. This is because the objection sketched here shows that objective, natural features of the world can fulfill the *a priori* requirements of a certain kind of cognitive subject. See Westphal 1997a.

3 CARNAP

3.1   Carnap's Attempt to Dissolve the Issue of Realism

According to Carnap's syntactic program for analyzing scientific knowledge, sentences (including observation sentences) are compared with other sentences, not with "facts" or "reality."[24] Traditional philosophical "theses" about concepts or knowledge are confused expressions in the material mode of speech of syntactical propositions, propositions that ought, for clarity's sake, to be formulated in the formal mode of speech as relations said to hold between statements, predicates, and other elements of a specified language.[25] Syntactical propositions do not express facts but rather are either rules or proposals for a language of science we are to (re)construct (depending upon whether the language is extant or yet to be built), and so are matters of practical decision rather than of knowledge.[26] Carnap takes empiricism for granted,[27] but since any principle of empiricism is a principle formulated in the metalanguage that specifies the syntax of a specific (re)constructed language, it is not a matter requiring theoretical justification.[28] Accepting a principle of empiricism is part of accepting one or another linguistic framework, and such acceptance is a practical rather than a cognitive matter.[29]

Carnap's rejection of epistemological realism comes to a head in "Empiricism, Semantics, and Ontology" in the distinction between internal and external questions—a distinction whose cognitive import Carnap himself traces back to the early Vienna Circle and his own essay on Scheinprobleme (pseudoproblems).[30] Carnap claims

---

[24] Neurath 1931–32, 396–96, 403, 404 (1959, 285, 291, 292); 1932–33, 208–09 (1959b, 203); 1934, 352; Hempel 1935a, 54; 1935b, 94. This summary is drawn from my much more detailed treatment in Westphal 1989, ch. 4.

[25] Carnap 1931, 23; cf. Hempel 1935a, 54.

[26] Carnap 1932–33, 216; 1936–37, 430, 19-20, 26; 1956a, 207, 214, 215 note 5; 1956b, 44-45; Hempel; 1935b, 95.

[27] 1936–37, 2.

[28] 1956a, 214, 218.

[29] 1956a, 207–8, 214, 215 note 5.

[30] 1956a, 215; cf. 1928.

that the question, 'Are there any *x*s?', is ambiguous and divides into three questions: a question internal to a linguistic framework, a question about adopting a linguistic framework, and a question about the utility of adopting a linguistic framework.[31] He holds that the internal question is answered by formal analysis and observation. Within a framework, there are *x*s if the framework contains variables ranging over a specified domain of objects. If there are such variables, then there are such things. The answer to the second question of whether to adopt a framework is a practical rather than a theoretical question and thus a matter for decision rather than an assertion.[32] Thus it is not a matter for proof, for proofs conclude in assertions. The supposed framework-independent question about the supposed "reality" of an entity or its kind is senseless because any kind of entity can only be specified through the use of a particular framework, and because there are no framework-independent "facts" on the basis of which such a question could be answered.[33] (The third practical question about the advisability of accepting a framework is discussed below.) These are the main points of Carnap's dissolution of the traditional philosophical questions about the reality of various kinds of entity.

3.2   Carnap's Subjectivism

Carnap's formal semantics renders truth as truth in a specified formally (re)constructed language.[34] This is not just a matter of what one can say about the world being a function of what language one uses to speak. The problem is that his semantics makes the way the world is a function of the language applied to it. He states this implication explicitly in "Truth and Confirmation" in the course of criticizing talk of the comparison of statements with reality and recommending talk of "confrontation" instead:

---

[31] 1956a, 213.
[32] See notes 23–25 above.
[33] 1956a, 207-8, 213, 215 note 5, 221; *cf.* 1934, §17.
[34] 1963, 901.

Furthermore, the formulation in terms of "comparison," in speaking of "facts" or "realities," easily tempts one into the absolutistic view according to which we are said to search for an absolute reality whose nature is assumed as fixed independently of the language chosen for its description. The answer to a question concerning reality however depends not only upon that "reality," or upon the facts but also upon the structure (and the set of concepts) of the language used for the description.[35]

However ontologically benign the last of these sentences might be interpreted, Carnap here quite explicitly eschews the notion of a reality the nature of which is what it is ("fixed") independently of the language chosen for its description, and thus "absolute." And should anyone hope for the contrary, Carnap goes on to talk about the impossibility of complete translatability between different theoretical languages in a way that prefigures Kuhn.[36] Consider Carnap's 1958 statement about the logical structure produced by his constructive procedures:

> [T]he structure can be uniquely specified but the elements of the structure cannot. Not because we are ignorant of their nature; rather, there is no question of their nature.[37]

By this reasoning, any purported answer to a supposedly external question about the characteristics or reality of any kind of entity is groundless, precisely because there is no such thing or because there are no such characteristics independent of one or another linguistic framework.

---

[35] Carnap 1949, 126; *cf.* Hempel: "We may say that searching for a criterion of absolute truth represents one of the pseudo-problems due to the material mode of speech: indeed the phrase that testing a statement is comparing it with facts, will very easily evoke the imagination of one definite world with certain definite properties, and so one will easily be seduced to ask for the one system of statements which gives a complete and true description of this world, and which would have to be designated absolutely true. By employing the formal mode of speech, the misunderstanding which admits no correct formulation disappears, and with it the motive for searching for a criterion of absolute truth" (1935a, 55).

[36] 1949, 126; *cf.* 1956b, 51, regarding scientific "revolutions."

[37] 1956b, 46.

3.3   *Criticism of Carnap's Program*

Both Warner Wick and Wilfrid Sellars noticed the weakness of Carnap's program, which lies in the fact that he never developed explicit views about the posing or answering of practical questions about the adoption of any particular linguistic framework.[38] In fact, the problem is much worse than they suggest. Carnap's rejection of the "external" reality of things or their characteristics in fact subverts any possible basis for answering such practical questions.

According to Carnap, the question of whether or not the decision to adopt a framework is justified is a matter of the fruitfulness, convenience, efficiency—in short, the utility of adopting that framework. However, Carnap's position makes it impossible even to investigate such questions, to say nothing of answering them, because according to his position there are no facts about entities or their characteristics, which are relevant to the utility of a framework (and thus also to its assessment), independent of the very framework whose acceptance stands in question. That conclusion follows from the fact that there simply are no facts or entities regarding which the acceptance of a framework could be efficient, at least not independent of that very framework. The "entities" within a framework ultimately are supposed to be the objects or events investigated by a natural science. However, if there is strictly *no* question about their characteristics or reality independent of a framework, then there are also no kinds or frequencies of objects or events (or data). And if there are no framework-independent kinds or frequencies of objects or events, then there is no basis for one framework providing, *e.g.*, better predictions than another or in any other way being more utile than another. This is the same problem that undermined Kant's rejection of (commonsense) realism: The world must have unto itself at least some characteristics consisting in kinds and frequencies of events or objects that we can recognize and distinguish if we are at all able to engage in the kinds of activities these philosophies ascribe to us. In Kant's case those activities consist in

---

[38] Wick 1951, 50; Sellars 1963, 433.

bringing empirical intuitions under *a priori* concepts in order to experience objects. In Carnap's case those activities consist in developing and assessing the utility of various alternative linguistic frameworks in order to decide which among them to accept.

3.4 *Carnap's Non Sequitur*

Carnap had of course anticipated roughly this line of criticism and tried to deflect it. However, in discussing these practical questions about accepting or rejecting frameworks he draws the following inference: The answer to the practical question is a matter of degree, hence the answer does not have a determinate (note: not determin*able*) truth-value, hence the answer does not allow a correspondence notion of truth. It is worth quoting Carnap's two most explicit statements on the matter at length:

> The decision of accepting the thing language, although itself not of a cognitive nature, will nevertheless usually be influenced by theoretical knowledge, just like any other deliberate decision concerning the acceptance of linguistic or other rules. The purposes for which the language is intended to be used, for instance, the purpose of communicating factual knowledge, will determine which factors are relevant for the decision. The efficiency, fruitfulness, and simplicity of the use of the thing language may be among the decisive factors. And the questions concerning these qualities are indeed of a theoretical nature. But these questions cannot be identified with the question of realism. They are not yes-no questions but questions of degree. The thing language in the customary form works indeed with a high degree of efficiency for most purposes of everyday life. This is a matter of fact, based upon the content of our experiences. However, it would be wrong to describe this situation by saying: "the fact of the efficiency of the thing language is confirming evidence for the reality of the thing world;" we should rather say instead: "This fact makes it advisable to accept the thing language."[39]

> [The question] may be meant in the following sense: "Are our experiences such that the use of the linguistic forms in question will be expedient and fruitful?" This is a theoretical question of a factual,

---

[39] 1956a, 208.

empirical nature. But it concerns a matter of degree; therefore [*sic!*] a formulation in the form "real or not" would be inadequate.[40]

The inference Carnap draws in these statements is quite curious. He denies bivalence (and hence a truth-value) for the question of whether or not any statements of the framework are true because the question of efficiency of the use of a linguistic framework is a matter of degree.[41] The theoretical question of whether a linguistic framework would be effective may well be answerable only by indicating degrees. But this does not meet the realist's contention. The realist may ask about two possible correspondences here. One of these concerns the efficiency of the framework. The question asked of any statement concerning the efficiency of the framework (whether this be a matter of stating degrees to, or aspects in, which the framework would or would not be efficient) is, Is the statement true or false? Does it accurately represent the degree or the aspects of the framework's efficiency or inefficiency? It is important to note that the last sentence quoted above misstates the issue. The question of the "reality" of the objects denoted by a variable in a linguistic framework is the question that is supposed to be a yes-or -no matter; the efficiency of adopting a linguistic framework containing this variable is a question of degree. The range of latitude allowable in the latter in no way entails a lack of bivalence of the former. Unfortunately, this is the principal argument Carnap offers for rejecting bivalence for the question of the reality of objects denoted by the variables of a linguistic framework or for rejecting the question of the nature of these objects.[42] As his inference is a *non sequitur*, he has failed to undermine the issue of epistemological realism.

Moreover, Carnap cannot undo the question of realism and of a determinate, "externally" characterized, truth-value for the answers

---

[40] 1956a, 213.

[41] Carnap 1956a, 208 (quoted above); *cf.* 1956b, 46; Hempel 1935b, 94-95.

[42] 1956b, 46; *cf.* 1936–37, 19, 20, 44-45; 1956a, 207-8; Hempel 1935a, 55; 1935b, 95.

to these questions by reinvoking the distinction between internal and external questions. Invoking this distinction would require formally reconstructing the language in which the questions of the utility of a proposed framework are posed and answered. However, this reconstruction would generate in turn the same kinds of questions about the fruitfulness, utility, *etc.*, of adopting this second framework. These questions would be "external" to the newly reconstructed framework and so would want (for reasons given in the preceding paragraph) a straightforwardly realist answer. Carnap could in turn reconstruct this language, but an infinite regress is in the offing. The regress, however, is damaging to Carnap's position, for any such reconstructed language poses the same unreconstructed external questions about the utility of its adoption, and Carnap has no good argument to show that the answers to these questions do not have a determinate truth value. We have no grounds for accepting a framework without assessing its utility, and (on this kind of reiterated construction of frameworks for assessing the utility of previous frameworks) we never have grounds for accepting the last framework of the series, and so cannot use that framework for assessing the utility of its predecessor, and so on right back to the framework originally at issue. Carnap thinks it is odd in advance of accepting a framework to try to determine whether there is a certain kind of entity, in order on that basis to decide to accept the framework that designates or describes that entity.[43] He didn't notice, however, that his dissolution of framework-independent (including commonsense) realism removes any basis for deciding whether to adopt a framework—and indeed, any basis for the kind of "theoretical knowledge" which he admits must guide such decisions. Without a minimal kind of realism, according to which there are determinate (if only broad) kinds of things or events that recur in determinate and (broadly) determinable frequencies, we couldn't possibly select an appropriate framework. But once this kind of realism is accepted, one must reject Carnap's own "framework" (set out in

---

[43] 1956a, 213–14.

"Empiricism, Semantics, and Ontology") concerning linguistic frameworks and its intended dissolution of framework-independent (including commonsense) realism.

4 ORDINARY LANGUAGE ANALYSIS AND TRANSCENDENTAL PRAGMATISM

Having derived essentially the same conclusion through parallel internal criticisms of two prominent rejections of realism, I now turn to the positive case Will makes for accepting realism. In his 1968 Presidential Address to the Western (now Central) Division of the American Philosophical Association, "Thoughts and Things," Will takes issue with the basically Cartesian notion that human thought and experience can or might be radically divorced from their putative objects. Will blocks the skeptical generalization, from occasional perceptual error to universal ignorance, with resources found in ordinary language analysis. Drawing on the notion of the "open texture" of concepts and such "bizarre fictions" as Austin's exploding goldfinch, Will shows how without the general and recognizable stability of the things around us, we would not be able to think or speak at all. Will's basic pragmatic point about human thought is that it is based in and depends on the structure and regularity of the environment, of the world itself in which we live.

This dependence of thought on things was touched on by Wittgenstein, Waismann, Austin, and before them by Leibniz. Wittgenstein touched on this dependence in connection with our not having complete rules for the use of empirical terms, Waismann in connection with the "open texture" of empirical concepts. All four of them consider it in connection with what Leibniz called "bizarre fictions": Wittgenstein's chair that disappears and reappears (or at least seems to);[44] Waismann's friend who does the same, and his cat which grows gigantic or revives in circumstances where cats surely die;[45]

---

[44] Wittgenstein 1958, §80.
[45] Waismann 1965, 125.

Austin's goldfinch which explodes, or quotes Virginia Woolf, or "does something outrageous";[46] Leibniz's angels or inhabitants of the moon who display rational thought, speech, and action like humans, but who have extraordinary powers or machines.[47] The most important point of these bizarre fictions is not simply that there are always borderline cases for applying empirical terms, or that we don't have fully explicit or explicable rules for using empirical terms. The fundamental point is touched on by Austin's negative remark that in such cases "we don't know what to say" because "words literally fail us,"[48] by Leibniz's positive remark that "we are spared these perplexities by the nature of things,"[49] and by Austin's conclusion that "what the future can always do, is to make us revise our ideas about goldfinches or real goldfinches or anything else."[50] Although these philosophers noticed these puzzling kinds of cases, and concluded that they show something important about human understanding, they did not develop their analyses beyond a criticism of verificationist or rule-following theories of meaning.[51]

Will uses these examples to reconsider thought and its objects and to criticize both the broad Cartesian tradition and the conventionalism found in many recent theories of meaning or of knowledge inspired, if not directly espoused, by logical empiricism, by the later Wittgenstein, or by Derrida. One main reason that the foundationalist-*cum*-skeptical project of establishing the link between thoughts and things is gratuitous is that, if there were no such link, as the examples of "bizarre fictions" show, we would simply be

---

[46] Austin 1965, 354.
[47] Leibniz 1960, Bk. 3 ch. 6 §22; 5:292–94.
[48] Austin 1965, 354.
[49] Leibniz 1960, Bk. 3 ch. 6 §22.
[50] Austin 1965, 354.
[51] This is not simply a summary of their points; I have reported the entirety of their oft repeated, but always quite brief considerations on this topic. Wittgenstein's comment about alternative general laws of nature (1958, Pt. xii) suggests there is more to this issue, perhaps along Will's lines. In Leibniz's view, such examples require distinguishing between nominal and real definitions.

incapable of thinking. Skeptics and traditional epistemologists (closet Cartesians all) may retort that Will begs the question by insisting that thought depends upon things, the stability and identifiability of which transcend our experience; they may retort that such alleged stability and identifiability cannot be assumed or demonstrated precisely because they transcend our experience.

This retort rests upon the very supposition Will, in keeping with the pragmatic tradition, challenges, namely, that thought can be identified with those supposedly mental episodes to which we (supposedly) have incorrigible access and can fully explicate descriptively. The point of the examples of "bizarre fictions" is to show that this identification is unwarranted. These examples concern not simply the extent of our evidence, but the fact that what "content" of thought we can explicitly formulate and identify by means of descriptions, classifications, and demonstratives is only part of the content of our thought, and this explicit aspect of our thought is neither *sui generis* nor self-sufficient. The portion of our thought that we can explicitly articulate is always outstripped by the specificity, and sometimes by the unexpected characteristics or capacities, of the things we engage with by thinking about them and doing things with them. The most important point about "open texture" is that our thought occurs and proceeds only on the basis of and in conjunction with the relatively stable and identifiable things with which we interact and about which we think and speak.[52] Will puts his point this way:

> Thinking is an activity which we engage in not only in the world of things, but by means of things in this world, supported and sustained by them. And when these things fail us in certain ways, as they sometimes do, then, to extend Austin's pronouncement, words do literally fail us, because our thoughts fail us.[53]

---

[52] G. P. Baker and P. M. S. Hacker (1980, 1:433) seriously underestimate the philosophical significance of the "open texture" of the meanings of ordinary descriptive terms.

[53] Will 1997, 14.

Our cognitive predicament is not one of establishing a link between our thoughts and their supposed objects, it is instead one of exploiting the links our thinking does and must have with things in order to discriminate the genuine characteristics of things. This may sound like a minor reformulation of the problem, but it is not. It blocks the skeptic's generalization from occasional perceptual error to universal empirical ignorance and it provides a major philosophical reorientation, away from both Cartesian skepticism and conventionalism toward recognizing the natural conditions of the possibility of human thought and experience. In this regard, Will emphasizes, with Dewey and Peirce, the natural bases of thought and belief (something notably absent from current versions of "pragmatism"), and advocates a version of what was later designated (by David Armstrong) as an "externalist" account of the content of thoughts and beliefs.[54]

Accepting this insight into the dependency of many of our most common thoughts on the ordinary objects and events in our surroundings may seem to involve a relapse into a long-discredited "knowledge by acquaintance." This is not the case. Another important insight of Will's is that the appearance of such a relapse rests on a still very pervasive *non-sequitur*. In "The Concern about Truth,"[55] Will shows that Kantian tradition discredited the Cartesian model of knowledge as revelation by developing a complex philosophy of mind and philosophy of language, the very complexity of which seemed to undermine the possibility of making, much less making truly, such statements as "the cat is on the mat." Once such statements appeared problematic, so did the correspondence notion

---

[54] See Armstrong 1973, 157–59. At this point, Will's analysis also links up with the views of Dretske and Nozick, who restrict the "relevant" alternatives regarding justifying conditions of knowledge to those conditions that are causally possible, rather than all those that are logically possible (see Will 1997, ch. 7, §12).

[55] Will 1997, ch. 3. Will's pragmatic realism requires a theory of perception that recognizes the complex conceptual mediations involved in perception and the interdependence of perceptual beliefs, and yet does not reduce the object or the content of a perceptual belief to its conceptual component. The prospects for such a theory of perception are explored by William Alston in "Perception and Conception," Essay 3 in the present volume.

of truth. A wide variety of considerations suggest that human knowledge is active and that knowledge of individual objects, events, facts or states of affairs is interdependent with our knowledge of other facts (*etc.*)—knowledge is at least to some extent holistic. Examples of considerations of this sort are that our "forms of intuition" transform what we perceive; that statements can only be compared with other statements, not with "things"; that there can be no conclusive verification of individual statements; that the meaning of individual protocol sentences is in part a function of their syntax, which is a function of the linguistic framework within which they are formulated; or that the formation of a perceptual belief about one thing or event involves other beliefs about the physical conditions under which one perceives or about other things or events in its environs.

Philosophers convinced by such considerations in philosophy of mind and language that facts are not knowable singly by direct acquaintance have tended to argue that individual facts, things, or states of affairs must be expunged from philosophy. By contrrast, philosophers who retain confidence in their abilities to know facts, things, or states of affairs singly have tended to argue on that basis against such philosophies of mind and language. The pervasive, influential underlying assumption has been that, if there is no knowledge by acquaintance, then there are no individual facts (*etc.*) to be known. As Will notes, those influenced by Kantian philosophy tended to affirm the antecedent, their opponents to deny the consequent.[56] Both sides found this inference compelling. It can be found explicitly, arguing *modus tollens* against complex activist accounts of cognition, in Russell, Schlick, Ayer, and C. I. Lewis. It is found, arguing *modus ponens* against the tenability of individual objective facts or states of affairs, in Neurath, Hempel, Reichenbach, Waismann, and Blandshard. This inference also forms the crucial entheme undergirding Richard Rorty's dismissal of realism in *Philosophy and the Mirror of Nature*. (Carnap, uncharacteristical-

---

[56] Will 1997, 42.

ly, waffled on this issue.)[57] Each of these philosophers saw the fate of the correspondence conception of truth hanging in the balance. However, despite how pervasive and persuasive this inference has been, it is a *non-sequitur*; the consequent does not follow from the antecedent. Its being a *non sequitur* does, however, cut the ground out from under the debate between the two sides, especially when a clear distinction between a criterion of truth and the nature of truth is not only noted but maintained. Criteria of truth must be indicative of truth, but their capacity to indicate truth must rest on our capacities as cognitive subjects and the suitability of those capacities for gaining knowledge of the objects and events around us. Identifying the nature of truth with its criteria, or defining truth in terms of satisfying its criteria gives priority to epistemology over ontology in a way that necessarily leads to subjectivism—to the view that the existence or the characteristics of the objects of knowledge depend on our thought, beliefs, or ways of talking about them.[58] Will's point about the dependence of thought on things shows that subjectivism of this sort is unwarranted. Consequently, his point also gives important grounds for distinguishing the nature of truth from the criteria of truth, and linking them contingently, rather than identifying or interdefining them. Once knowledge by acquaintance is rejected, these reflections lead to a correspondence analysis of truth combined with coherence criteria of truth; a correspondence analysis of truth does not require using 'correspondence' as a criterion, nor does it require 'knowledge by acquaintance.'

---

[57] I document the acceptance of this *non-sequitur* by these philosophers in Westphal 1989, 62–64, 245, and in my Introduction to Will 1997, xxvii–xxxi. In §5 below I extend this list to some current discussions.

[58] I have made this case in detail against Descartes, Kant, and Carnap in Westphal 1989, Introduction and chs. 2–4. This case is developd in detail against an array of recent views by William Alston (1995) in his critique of "epistemic" conceptions of truth. Williams (1993, 195) reiterates Brand Blanchard's concern that distinguishing the nature of truth from its criteria ultimately leads to their disintegration. He claims this objection has "considerable intuitive force," but he completely overlooks its subjectivist *cum* skeptical implications. I must insist that, contrary to widespread misunderstanding, Peirce did *not* "define" truth in terms of the ultimate scientific consensus. His "hypothesis of science" (1877) plainly shows that he regards that consensus as itself resting on the dilligence and insight of scientists and on the generally cognizible nature of the world. (Peirce's more well known essay of 1878 *must* be read together with its 1877 predecessor.) Ironically, Nagel, who recognizes the pitfalls of subjectivism, espouses precisely the view Peirce holds, but denies its true authorship (1986, 83)!

Plainly much more needs to be said about each of these points, and about related points, in order to develop a philosophical position, and not simply an orientation. Will has developed these points and their associates throughout his later writings. Their explication and further development cannot be undertaken here. However, some of their significance can be indicated and further articulated by seeing how just these two points have significant bearing on the views of Michael Williams, John Haldane, and Crispin Wright.

5 CURRENT RELEVANCE OF WILL'S PRAGMATISM

5.1   Contextualism and Traditional Epistemology

In *Unnatural Doubts*, Michael Williams contends that skepticism about the external world withstands ordinary language and verificationist critique.[59] However, skepticism is committed to knowledge of the external world as a whole being a suitable object of philosophical investigation and to the priority of our knowledge of appearances over our knowledge of the world.[60] Williams agrees that at least the neutrality of experience with regard to its supposed objects is supported by examples such as Descartes's Evil Deceiver and Putnam's Brain in a Vat.[61] The priority of "experiential" knowledge (*i.e.*, knowledge of the apparent content of our experiences) over knowledge of the world stems from the epistemological-*cum*-skeptical aim of assessing our knowledge of the world wholesale.[62] Because of the intuitive force of the Evil Deceiver and the Brain in the Vat, skepticism does not (Williams claims) admit of definitive refutation; skepticism is intuitively far more plausible than any theoretical response to or refutation of it.[63] However, Williams denies that our beliefs about the world form any natural kind of whole suited to wholesale investigation by philosophical reflection.[64] The assumption that they do is a major, contentious theoretical commitment on the part of skepticism and traditional epistemology.[65] In opposition to this assumption, Williams espouses a contex-

---

[59] Williams 1996, 59, 92–93, 139–44, 158, 160, 166–71, 176.
[60] Williams 1996, xii, 23, 43.
[61] Williams 1996, 53, 73–74, 77.
[62] Williams 1996, 90–92, 101, 124–25, 210; *cf.* 138, 171, 218, 246.
[63] Williams 1996, xvii, xix, 44, 59, 153, 201.
[64] Williams 1996, 45, 64, 102.
[65] Williams 1996, 103, 219, 318; *cf.* 201.

tualism according to which the epistemic status of any belief, statement, or proposition is solely a function of the interests and methodological constraints that guide any particular line of disciplinary or informal inquiry.[66] Consequently, though philosophical doubts may be raised about our knowledge of the world as a whole,[67] those doubts depend on the methodological constraints of philosophical inquiry and do not generalize from the context of philosophical reflection to the contexts in which our various beliefs (*etc.*) about the world are generated, investigated, or otherwise assessed.[68] According to Williams, only contextualism affords an adequate response to skepticism, because only contextualism challenges the skeptical presumption that beliefs (*etc.*) possess an intrinsic epistemic status.[69]

Will and I agree with Williams that "it is a large assumption [made by Descartes and traditional epistemology] that, independently of our place in the world, we have *any* epistemic position at all."[70] However, there are problems with how Williams develops his critique of this assumption. Williams attacks, not the attempt to reflect on empirical knowledge as a whole, but the alleged *object* of such reflection.[71] The key to that object, according to Williams, is that beliefs, propositions, or statements have an intrinsic epistemic status.[72] One problem with Williams's thesis is that he states different constraints on the relevant kind of intrinsic epistemic status. At first he states this claim quite generally.[73] However, later the intrinsic status of beliefs (*etc.*) is supposed to be a function of their content,[74] and ultimately it is supposed to be a function of whatever of their content is accessible to the kind of solipsistic, skeptical philosophical reflection carried out, *e.g.*, in Hume's study.[75] Conse-

---

[66] Williams 1996, 102, 106, 109–10, 113, 118–19, 123–24, 166–67, 222–23, 349; *cf.* 321, 328, 338–39.

[67] Williams 1996, 189, 223.

[68] Williams 1996, 130, 158, 164–67, 199–200, 358–59; *cf.* 148, 170, 194–95, 213–14, 222–23, 250, 259, 282.

[69] Williams 1996, xx, 118–19, 130, 133, 158, 168, 199–200, 221.

[70] Williams 1996, 168.

[71] Williams 1996, 194.

[72] *Cf.* Williams 1996, 118–19, 158.

[73] Williams 1996, xx.

[74] Williams 1996, 118–19, 329.

[75] Williams 1996, 119, 329, 358–59. At one point Williams states, "[t]o reject epistemological realism is to hold that a proposition's epistemic status is a func-

quently, Williams's critique is directed primarily at internalist accounts of "intrinsic" epistemic status, and does not address the
broader issue of epistemic status *per se*. Consequently, his criticism
of naturalistic externalist theories of knowledge misfires.[76]

More importantly, Will's reflections on bizarre fictions show that
there is much more to develop in Austin's views than the hints of
contextualism Williams stresses.[77] Will's reflections on bizarre
fictions shows that the alleged priority of knowledge of the content
of our experiences over knowledge of the world is false. Indeed,
Will's reflections show that even the alleged neutrality of sensory
experience with regard to the world is false. This is a substantive,
though faulty, assumption of wholesale Cartesian inquiry and of
skepticism, an assumption Williams shares. Moreover: Will's reflections show it to be false at the same "intuitive" level at which
skeptical possibilities supposedly have their great appeal. That is,
Will's critique succeeds without appeal to epistemological theory,
which Williams thinks must inevitably be less "intuitive" and hence
less convincing than the original skeptical problem. Will's pragmatic
realism thus shows the falsehood of the skeptical hypotheses while
preserving the commonsense platitudes about truth and realism.[78]
Not detachment from everyday certainties,[79] but detachment from
any and all worldly roots of thought is impossible. This is a presupposition of ordinary thought and action that remains invisible in
ordinary affairs, and in much philosophical reflection—but not in
Will's pragmatic reflections. Will's reflections on bizarre fictions
block the crucial skeptical move from the universal possibility of
illusion to the possibility of universal illusion.[80]

---

tional matter, not an intrinsic characteristic" (158). To contrast "functional" and
"intrinsic" in this way sits ill with the externalism with which Williams often
expresses sympathy, and the only "functions" he considers are contextual functions
of elective methods and interests, not the kinds of reliable belief-forming functions
analyzed by reliabilists or by Dretske.

[76] I think his treatment of externalism is seriously flawed, but I cannot go into
detail here. For one thing, Williams does not adequately understand Dretske's
information theoretic epistemology, or how it preserves and develops the sound
core of a relevant alternatives analysis of knowledge. See Williams 1996, 330–6;
cf. Westphal, Introduction to Will 1997, xliii–xlvi.

[77] Williams 1996, 113, 166–67.

[78] *Contra* Williams 1996, 40.

[79] Williams 1996, 178.

[80] *Cf.* Williams 1996, 215, citing Bernard Williams 1978, 54.

Now Williams would likely respond that Descartes's Evil Deceiver or Putnam's supercomputer stimulating a brain in a vat are designed to preserve the apparent coherence of our sensory experience and thus avoid confronting us with bizarre fictions just as well as nature does. Indeed they are; that is why they supposedly show the neutrality of experience with regard to the world. However, the fundamental question in epistemology is, What *are* our cognitive abilities and how do we know objects or events (if we do know any)? The skeptical possibilities rest on counter-factual hypotheses about what our cognitive abilities and circumstances *might* be. These possibilities are relevant only if the only suitable principles for analyzing human knowledge are necessary truths. One can cavil about whether this quest concerns "certainty,"[81] but even Williams cannot avoid locutions about "guarantees," where the only relevant kind of guarantee is a deductively sound one.[82]

One problem with this deductivist aspiration is that contingent truths do not follow logically from necessary ones. To avoid this problem, philosophers have taken recourse to sensory "appearances" whose occurrence is logically contingent, but whose contents necessarily are exactly and only what they seem to be. The problem is that appearances of this kind are a philosophical invention, conjured into existence to fulfill the requirements of a particular kind of Cartesian quest for logically irrefutable guarantees. The sleight-of-hand by which these sorts of "appearances" are conjured into existence can be found in Williams. Williams states:

> What [the skeptic] calls our attention to, someone might say, is the more-than-purely logical point that I could *know* all about how things appear without knowing anything about how they are, whereas I could not know anything about how they are without knowing about how they appear . . . .. The point is that I could not know *anything* about how the world is without knowing *something* about how it appears; whereas I could know all about how it appears and yet know nothing about how it is. So there is a fundamental asymmetry here after all.[83]

---

[81] Williams 1996, 218–20.

[82] Williams 1996, 56, 73–74. For criticism of the assumption that legitimate, sufficient justification must be deductive, see Will 1988.

[83] Williams 1996, 77.

Williams recognizes that, at most, this line of argument establishes that it is possible to know the contents of our experiences without knowing anything about the world, but not *vice versa*; this does not prove the priority of knowledge of the contents of our experiences over knowledge of the world.[84] The problem, however, lies in the notion of knowing the supposed "contents" of our experiences without knowing anything about the world. Williams calls this "experiential knowledge." This phrase is fatally ambiguous and misleading. One would think, ordinarily, that "experiential knowledge" is knowledge of some object or event that one gains (at least in part) by experience of that object or event. Williams uses this phrase, not in this objectual sense, but in an introspective, phenomenal sense concerning knowledge of the manifest or apparent content, that is, the qualitative or sensory character, of one's experiences. To accept Williams's terminology is already to start sliding down the slippery slope into solipsism. Notice that the passage just quoted requires very particular stresses in order to have any skeptical import:

> I could *know* all about how things **appear** without knowing anything about how they **are**, whereas I could not know anything about how they **are** without knowing about how they **appear** . . .. I could not know *anything* about how the world **is** without knowing *something* about how it **appears**; whereas I could know all about how it **appears** and yet know nothing about how it **is**.

These emphases stress the supposed contrast between appearances and reality, and do so in a way that reifies appearances into something distinct from things or events that happen to appear to us. Compare the following alternative stressing:

> I could *know* all about how **things** appear without knowing anything about how **they** are, whereas I could not know anything about how **they** are without knowing about how **they** appear . . .. I could not know *anything* about how **the world** is without knowing *something* about how **it** appears; whereas I could know all about how **it** appears and yet know nothing about how **it** is.

These emphases stress the commonsense idea that the world, or things and events that are parts of the world, appear to us in our

---

[84] Williams 1996, 77, 79.

experience. With these emphases, however, these statements are patently false: It is not possible to know "all" about how *things* appear without knowing at least something about how *they* are, and it is impossible to know "all" about how *the world* appears "and yet know nothing about how *it* is." If in fact things or events in the world appear to us in experience, then "experience" is not neutral in the way required by wholesale skeptical doubt. Will's reflections on bizarre fictions graphically highlight (*inter alia*) the fact that experiences are not neutral in the way Williams and others suppose. And it suffices for knowledge of the world that it *is* the case that things and events in the world appear to us in our experiences. This need not be a necessary or otherwise irrefutable truth.[85] Now the skeptical hypotheses of Evil Deceivers or Brains in Vats are germane only if "appearances" have already been abstracted from things and events that appear in our experience and reified as a surrogate for them. And the introduction of such abstract surrogates is motivated by the quest for deductive guarantees of knowledge claims. This is precisely how Cartesians (broadly speaking) manufacture for themselves an epistemic veil which then cannot be breached—precisely because it is designed to be unbreachable.[86] All possible experience is equally compatible with the existence or with the nonexistence of the world *only* if "experiences" are abstracted from the world and interposed between us and it.[87] But there is no good reason to erect this veil to begin with, and, as Will shows, excellent reason not to.[88]

Williams comments:

> Perhaps the most striking illustration of the tendency to underestimate the theoretical commitments of skeptical arguments is what seems to be an almost irresistible temptation to think that, to raise the specter of skepticism, it is sufficient to point to the "logical gap" between

---

[85] [This kind of approach to perceptual appearances is developed by William Alston in the next chapter.—Ed.]

[86] *Cf.* Williams 1996, 56; *cf.* Will 1997, ch. 3 §4.

[87] *Contra* Williams 1996, 73–74; and Stroud 1984, 179.

[88] This shows that Williams's analysis of the problems of foundationalism is far closer to traditional diagnoses than he realizes (Williams 1996, xviii). Also, to the extent that wholesale skeptical doubt requires equivocations of the kind just highlighted, it reinforces Williams's point that skepticism is a theoretically loaded view, but it undermines the significance of the supposed "intuitive" character of skepticism. Our intuitions are too often confused or ambiguous to deserve the kind of emphasis Williams gives them.

statements about appearances and statements about reality. But this cannot be right. It is not the logical gap alone that threatens us with skepticism but the thought that, pending heroic efforts, we are stuck on one side of it.[89]

Williams is right that it is a substantive assumption that we are stuck on one side of a logical gap. However, it is also a substantive assumption of skepticism that this logical gap between kinds of statements is relevant to human knowledge, and relevant in a way that supports skepticism. Williams's observation sounds plausible, but on investigation it reveals a closely related tendency to erect a cognitively opaque veil between ourselves and the world. The logical gap between *statements* of these kinds is, strictly speaking, irrelevant. What matters is the cognitive—not the logical—link between our *experiences* and the *world*. Recording our experiences in the form of statements, and then subjecting our *statements* (or propositions) to logical analysis can and too often has led epistemologists away from the evidential character and merit of experiences themselves. Substituting statements or propositions for appearances or experiences greatly assists abstracting experiences from things that appear. Fixation on the logical gap Williams highlights leads philosophers to divorce appearances from things or events that appear to us and thus to distinguish them numerically. And this sets us almost irresistibly on the road to "coherence" theories of truth and to relativism. Epistemologists have, unfortunately, not learned as quickly as modal logicians that we must very carefully distinguish which features of a logical model represent features of the situation modeled, and which features of the model are mere artifacts of the modeling.[90] The logical gap between statements about appearances and statements about reality does not, of itself, show anything about any alleged gap between how things appear to us in our experiences and how things are. Cognitive "appearances" to us are a joint product of objects or events that appear, our senses, and our conceptions and beliefs by which we form and hold explicit, articulate beliefs about those objects or events. If in Cartesian reflection it is easy to lose track of the fact that worldly objects and events are what appear to us, Will's pragmatic reflections bring it graphically home to us again. Consequently, Will's pragmatic

---

[89] Williams 1996, 73.
[90] Kaplan 1975, 722. *Cf.* Will 1997, chs. 1 (§§4, 7.2), 3 (§§2, 6), 5 (§6), 7–9.

realism offers a powerful alternative to traditional epistemology *and* to Williams's contextualism.

5.2 *Aquinas's Empiricism Rehabilitated?*

In opposition to Putnam's internal realism, John Haldane advocates a return to Aquinas's empiricism, according to which we are able, with luck and careful sifting of experience, to grasp through our concepts the essential natures of things.[91] Haldane is right that Putnam caricatured pre-Cartesian rationalism. However, Haldane's recourse to Aquinas is triply anachronistic. It is anachronistic because classical skeptics were able to distinguish between appearances and reality without relying on the Stoic and Cartesian view that our sensory presentations or ideas intervene between us and the alleged objects of knowledge.[92] It is also anachronistic because it disregards (rather than responds to) the now widespread recognition that human thought is intimately dependent upon language, and that human languages vary historically and culturally. However much "intrinsic intentionality" the human mind must possess such that infants survive and learn a language, beyond a very elementary level, no human being can think about, recognize, or know any of the myriad aspects of reality we engage with without linguistic training and linguistically conditioned representations.[93] Haldane's recourse is furthermore anachronistic because his position involves opting for one side (in his case, the currently unpopular side) of a false dichotomy, the very one identified by Will in the *non sequitur* discussed above. Haldane indeed comes quite close to formulating the dichotomy Will identifies, namely, that an active model of cognition appears to be incompatible with realism about the objects of knowledge,[94] but he doesn't recognize that this dichotomy itself deserves critical rejection. He does recognize that there appears to be a tension between the (realist) thesis that "the world is ontologically independent of thought" and the thesis that "concepts and what they represent are intrinsically related."[95] However, because he does not address the dependence of concepts on language, and the

---

[91] Haldane 1993, 19–24, 29–32.

[92] Haldane 1993, 21. For a summary of Sextus Empiricus's skepticism, see Westphal 1989, 11–16.

[93] Haldane overlooks this point also in his 1994.

[94] Haldane 1993, 16.

[95] Haldane 1993, 24–25.

significant dependance of language on culture and history, he doesn't recognize why realists cannot simply "avail" themselves "of the general view of concepts suggested by Aquinas, and claim that they are mental counterparts of extra-mental features acquired by the subject through his encounter with the world."[96] Aquinas's view of concepts suffers the same problem as Modern empiricism's and indeed some early logical positivist views of concepts, namely, the idea that concepts are more or less direct copies of the objects that give rise to them. Will recognizes that there is a point to this kind of empiricism, namely, that many of our most basic concepts do depend on the structure of the worldly things and events with which we interact, but Will's linguistic analysis shows both that this dependency is far more indirect than Aquinas, Modern empiricists, some positivists, and now John Haldane recognize, and also that this dependency is nevertheless present and essential to our cognitive functioning. Like Sellars, Will notes that the epistemological "given" faded in the wake of recognizing the genuine complexities of philosophical psychology.[97] The interdependence of linguistic or conceptual bearers of meaning and the interdependence of cognitive judgments or evidential states (including, *e.g.*, beliefs about one's perceptual circumstances) bring in tow some kinds of coherentism, though not necessarily the unqualified kind of holism often rejected as "the coherence theory." Will is right to insist that the content of our beliefs about things in our environment are doubly dependent on our language and the things with which we interact.

5.3   *Quasi-Realism*
The point made above (§4) about the roles of worldly circumstances and of a correspondence conception of the nature of truth applies directly to Blackburn's "quasi-realism." In his original presentation Blackburn described the "quasi-realist" as someone who, "starting from a recognizably anti-realist position, finds himself progressively able to mimic the intellectual practices supposedly definitive of realism."[98] So far as the basis of human thought lies in identifying ordinary objects and events around us, Will's point shows that anti-realism in this domain is a nonstarter. Blackburn's quasi-realist isn't

---

[96] Haldane 1993, 25.
[97] Will 1997, 40–44.
[98] Blackburn 1993a, 15.

entitled to his Ramseyian point of departure.[99] Moreover, Black-burn's quasi-realist explanations themselves require realism, at least within one crucial domain. Quasi-realist explanations of a domain of judgment or discourse purport to account for their content and nature on the basis of a "thin, Humean view of the world" according to which the world presents us with patterns of stimulation to which we respond by projecting various supposed properties.[100] To mount such quasi-realist, projectivist explanations of a domain of discourse thus requires identifying both the occasioning causes of the psychological states that stimulate our alleged projections, and the psychological needs and capacities that allegedly generate the character of those projections.[101] According to Blackburn, "[p]roperties are abstractions from predicates; predicates come from judgments; judgments from discriminations."[102] Discriminations, however, are differential reactions to distinct characteristics of various things or events we confront. That is true even if we express our discriminations in terms of "response-dependent" concepts. This is shown by my criticisms of Kant and Carnap and by Will's argument, discussed above.[103] How much we may transfigure or "project" the

---

[99] Blackburn simply assumes that a redundancy theory of truth is tenable. See Will 1997, ch. 3 *contra*. For brief, incisive criticism of the redundacy theory (with further references) see Horwich 1990, 37–41, and Alston 1995, 41–51.

[100] *Cf.* Blackburn 1993a, 5, 9, 80, 93.

[101] *Cf.* Blackburn 1993a, 153.

[102] Blackburn 1993b, 375, *cf.* Blackburn 1993a, 8.

[103] In this connection it is worth noting that Blackburn consistently misrepresents his two main sources of inspiration in order to trim them to his theoretical aims. He makes much of Hume's essay, "Of the Standard of Taste," in setting up his quasi-realist programme. He fails to notice, however, that Hume treats judgments of taste as reports based on the pleasurable feeling of beauty, which he analyzes as a tertiary quality, that is, as a regular response to objective features of works of art. (He insists on this point five times in his essay. Most directly he states: "Though it be certain, that beauty and deformity, more than sweet and bitter, are not qualities in objects, but belong entirely to the sentiment, it must be allowed, that there are certain qualities in objects, which are fitted by nature to produce those particular feelings" (1964, 3:272, *cf.* 271–2). Hume has a much stronger basis for characterizing the possibility of improved or mistaken judgments than Blackburn recognizes (1993a, 20, *cf.* 104). In his interpretation of Wittgenstein (most elaborately presented in Blackburn 1990) Blackburn disregards those passages, such as *Philosophical Investigations* 1:§230, in which Wittgenstein contends that our sense of logical or mathematical necessity and our ability to formulate and follow logical or mathematical rules depends on extremely general characteristics of our natural environment. Such passages are crucial to Wittgenstein's views on rules; their significance is elaborated by Will 1988, and 1997, chs. 7 and 9.

character of what we take ourselves to discriminate, and how much
that projection may be a function of our physiology (colors) or our
socialization (etiquette) may be an open question.[104] But if we
project in the Humean way Blackburn's quasi-realist supposes, then
our discriminations have an objective basis, and his claims about
that basis require a realistic, correspondence account of truth.
Denying either of these points would scuttle the quasi-realist's
whole programme. It is thus little surprise that Blackburn moves
quickly from his (inconclusive) discussion of common sense and
scientific realism to the issues in ethics and modality that really
interest him.[105] However, the basic kind of realism required by
quasi-realist explanations of our use of predicates shows that the
quasi-realist cannot *begin* with an anti-realist Ramseyan redundancy
theory of truth. Instead, it is incumbent on quasi-realists to show
where and why a realist correspondence account of truth must give
way to an anti-realist notion of truth because we (supposedly)
project rather than comprehend the characteristics of things or
events in some specified domain.

Blackburn contrasts his quasi-realist approach with standard forms
of realism in the following way:

> [W]hen our project is to place ethical or modal or probabilistic
> discourse, that is, to understand why we go in for it and what its role
> is in our activities and lives, a simple explanation of our judgements
> as responses to the facts is markedly inferior to the longer story
> explaining their functional role, the reason why we have them and
> give them the importance we do.[106]

Blackburn supposes that the functional explanation of a kind or
aspect of discourse is an *alternative* to explaining that fragment of

---

[104] *Cf.* Blackburn 1993b, 378. Also William Hay 1975.

[105] He does this both in Blackburn 1984, chs. 5–7, and 1993a. Blackburn's first
quasi-realist essay, "Truth, Realism, and the Regulation of Theory" (1993a, 15–34),
requires more discussion than I can give it here. Blackburn grants that the quasi-
realist either must deny that there is convergence in scientific consensus or seek an
explanation of it which does not refer to the supposed facts about which scientific
consensus is reached (*ibid.*, 30). That is an extremely tall order, and so it is little
surprise that Blackburn's discussion of this topic peters out inconclusively. I cannot
discuss the success of Blackburn's efforts to grapple with morals and modals here.
See Hale 1993a, 1993b, and Blackburn 1993b. I tend to believe (with Crispin
Wright [1992, 11 & note]), that Hale's criticisms are sound.

[106] Blackburn 1993a, 8.

our discourse in terms of its elucidation of facts. Why should such a functional account be a complete account? Why, more important-ly, should those be exclusive options (as Blackburn here supposes)? Will's pragmatism points out that Blackburn's dichotomy is alto-gether dubious. Our abilities to discriminate facts are socially and historically developed. But that fact alone does not require rejecting realism about the objects of our commonsense or scientific inquir-ies. That is the moral of Will's exposure of the *non-sequitur* dis-cussed above. Blackburn is quite right that our use of concepts and theses needs to be earned, but he is quite wrong to suppose that only the quasi-realist can be or is engaged in doing this.[107]

5.4   Beyond—or Rather, Before—Cognitive Command and Best Explanation

In his recent writings Crispin Wright has distinguished minimalism or deflationism about truth (in the form of the "correspondence platitude") from realist accounts of truth.[108] He contends that the burden of proof lies with the realist to go beyond the minimal notion of truth. The minimal notion of truth, which is neutral between realism and antirealism, he claims,

> regulates any statement-making practice which displays the interlock-ing set of characteristics [. . . such that it] is disciplined by acknow-ledged standards of justification and justified criticism, which has the syntax to be subjected to ordinary sentential logic, which sustains embeddings within propositional attitudes, and where ignorance and error are possible categories of explanation of aberrant performances by its practitioners.[109]

Wright describes here some characteristics of a statement-making practice. There may be domains in which the requisite stability and structure of practice Wright describes may not require (and so would not justify) going beyond the minimal notion of truth to a realist correspondence notion of truth. Wright contends that the proper initial attitude to take about truth is the parsimonious mini-mal (anti- or nonrealist) view; minimalism suffices until proven

---

[107] *E.g.* 1993a, 8, 34.

[108] A preliminary version of his account appears in Wright 1993; a much fuller discussion appears in Wright 1992.

[109] Wright 1993, 69. This is his most sucinct statement of his "minimal" view of truth. *Cf.* Wright 1992, 74–76, 140.

otherwise.[110] Wright considers two features of a discourse that would require transcending minimalism and adopting realism: "Cognitive Command" and "Best Explanation." "Cognitive Command," roughly, is the *a priori* requirement that, waiving certain understandable and remediable causes of disagreement, differences of opinion within some domain must be explained in terms of some sort of cognitive deficiency of at least one of the parties to the dispute.[111] "Best Explanation" of the relevant sort comes in two varieties. At the least, if the best explanation of true beliefs registered in a discourse must cite "truth-conferring states of affairs," then realism is required in that domain of discourse. Better yet, if the "cosmological role" of those states of affairs is "wide" because they enter into explanations, not only of our true beliefs about them, but also into explanations of a lot of other phenomena, then once again realism is required in that domain of discourse.[112] Wright recognizes that this condition is indeed met in the case of perceptible objects and events in our environment.[113]

Wright's discussion shows that the kinds of "explanations" he considers are scientific, or at least empirical explanations.[114] The requirement of "Best Explanation" is not an *a priori* requirement.[115] Notice, however, that even the *a priori* constraint involved in "Cognitive Command" concerns a putative necessary constraint on the explanation of divergent *outcomes* of inquiry. Both of Wright's constraints are *ex post facto* with respect to formulating and undertaking an investigation. In this regard, Will's discussion of "bizarre fictions" reveals a lingering Cartesianism in Wright's minimalism about truth. Will's reflections on the dependence of thought on the recognizable characteristics of things around us shows that our statement-making practices about them do require realism, including correspondence, about such objects. Without the general stability and identifiability of things and events in our environment, our

---

[110] 1992, 149–50; 1993b, 69.

[111] 1992, 144–46.

[112] 1992, 182, 189, 196–98; 1993b, 73.

[113] 1993, 76–77, 82; *cf.* 1992, 199. This line of argument is developed in detail by Ian McFetridge (1993), who presents a splendid critique of Dummett. It is also endorsed by Johnston (1993, 95). At first glance this kind of argument may appear viciously circular, but if it is properly constructed it need not be. See Alston 1986, and 1993.

[114] 1992, 192.

[115] 1992, 186.

commonsense practices of describing, referring to, and engaging with objects (in part through our language) would not be possible as stable practices in the way described by Wright's minimalism about truth (quoted above). Obtaining this result does not require determining the best philosophical interpretation of the outcomes of various lines of inquiry. Will's treatment of "bizarre fictions" shows that we—as the human beings we are—could not be in a position to wonder about the sources of our sensory experience, or about our grasp of common facts, or the truth (or other suitability) of our utterances, if we were not generally able to identify objects and events in our environment. To suppose that we could have the sophisticated intellectual practices indicated in Wright's minimalist conception of truth, and that we still could have an open question about commonsense realism, is to suppose that human thought is radically independent of objects in our natural environment. Will's discussion of "bizarre fictions" shows that this supposition is radically mistaken.[116] The pervasiveness of this kind of supposition in contemporary philosophical discussion, also found above in Michael Williams, shows how Cartesian much of contemporary semantics and epistemology has remained, official disavowals not withstanding. If we are *able* to use the truth-predicate in Wright's "minimal" sense, we are *entitled* to use it in his "realist" sense. This is because, as Kant saw, "inner experience in general is only possible through outer experience in general." And this is true, as Fred Will demonstrated, because we human beings are only capable of thinking if we experience a common-sense world of real objects and events which are naturally structured by identifiable similarities and differences.[117]

---

[116] Cartesians and Putnamians (*ca.* 1981) may retort that we might, *e.g.*, be deceived by an evil spirit or be brains in vats. The presumption to argue against any and all logical possibilities in order to justify claims to knowledge is a mainstay of traditional foundationalism which Will, along with the classical pragmatists, rejects as an abject failure. As mentioned above, at this point Will's views converge with the naturalism represented, *e.g.*, by Dretske and Nozick, who contend that the relevant alternatives to consider are determined by the causal possibilities that naturally structure one's actual cognitive circumstances (see Will 1997, ch. 7, esp. §12). I have argued elsewhere (1987–88) that the classic foundationalist attempt made by Descartes inherently suffers five vicious circularities.

[117] As this is going to press I note the appearance of Melnick 1997, which develops a very sophisticated naturalized semantics, including a correspondence theory of truth, compatible with Will's pragmatic naturalism. Melnick's book is pioneering, insightful, and compact; it both requires and deserves careful attention.

6 CONCLUSION

The point of Will's pragmatic reflections in his later writings on cognitive and practical norms and their natural bases in our physiology and in our environment is to show that we need both an historical and social account of the development and justification of norms, coupled with a realist account of the natural world (including our physiology) that make those developments possible, and that provide the basis for any further creative constructions we may make in our social practices, whether moral, legal, or procedural. This kind of naturalism, so prominent in Peirce's and Dewey's pragmatism, regrettably has been not only lost but positively undermined by recent versions of neopragmatism. One of the virtues of Will's pragmatism is to call our attention to it again. I hope these remarks may indicate how important such a re-engagement could be. My own success in this endeavor aside, Will's work repays careful study because of the persistent ways in which he probes the fundamental points underlying many ongoing philosophical debates.[118]

University of New Hampshire

References

Allison, Henry. 1983. *Kant's Transcendental Idealism*. New Haven: Yale University Press.

Alston, William. 1986. "Epistemic Circularity." *Philosophy and Phenomenological Research* 47 No. 1: 1-30.

Alston, William. 1993. *The Reliability of Sense Perception*. Ithaca: Cornell University Press.

Alston, William. 1995. *A Realist Conception of Truth*. Ithaca: Cornell University Press.

Armstrong, David M. 1973. *Belief, Truth and Knowledge*. Cambridge: Cambridge University Press.

Austin, John L. 1965. "Other Minds." Rpt. in *Logic and Language: First and Second Series*. A. Flew, ed.. Garden City, N. J.: Double Day, 342-80.

Ayer, Alfred J. ed. 1959. *Logical Positivism*. New York: Free Press

Baker, G. P. and P. M. S. Hacker. 1980. *Wittgenstein: Understanding and Meaning*. Chicago: University of Chicago Press.

Blackburn, Simon. 1984. *Spreading the Word*. Oxford: Clarendon Press.

Blackburn, Simon. 1990. "Wittgenstein's Irrealism." In *Wittgenstein: Eine Neubewertung/Towards a Re-evaluation*. R. Haller & J. Brandl, eds. Vienna: Hölder-Pichler-Tempsky, vol. 2, 13–26.

Blackburn, Simon. 1993a. *Essays in Quasi-Realism*. New York: Oxford University Press.

Blackburn, Simon. 1993b. "Realism, Quasi, or Queasy?" In Haldane & Wright, 1993, 365–83.

Carnap, Rudolf. 1928. "Scheinprobleme in der Philosophie." Appendix to *Der logische Aufbau der Welt*. Hamburg: Meiner; "Pseudoproblems in Philosophy." Appendix to *The Logical Structure of the World*. R. A. George, tr. Berkeley: University of California Press, 1969.

Carnap, Rudolf. 1931. *The Unity of Science*. London: Routledge & Kegan Paul.

Carnap, Rudolf. 1932-33. "Über Protokolsätze." *Erkenntnis* 3: 215–28.

Carnap, Rudolf. 1934. *Die logische Syntax der Sprache*. Wien: Springer. *The Logical Syntax of Language*. A. Smeaton, tr. Paterson, N.J.: Littlefield, Adams, and Co., 1959.

Carnap, Rudolf. 1936–37. "Testability and Meaning." *Philosophy of Science* 3: 419-71, and 4, 1937: 2-40F.

Carnap, Rudolf. 1949. "Truth and Confirmation." *Readings in Philosophical Analysis*. H. Feigl & W. Sellars, eds. New York: Appelton-Century--Crofts, 119-27.

Carnap, Rudolf. 1956a. "Empiricism, Semantics, and Ontology." In *Meaning and Necessity*. Chicago: University of Chicago Press, 205-21.

Carnap, Rudolf. 1956b. "The Methodological Character of Theoretical Concepts." *Minnesota Studies in Philosophy of Science* 1: 38-76.

Carnap, Rudolf. 1963. "Replies and Systematic Expositions." In Schilpp, 1963, 859-1013.

Carrier, Martin. 1991. "What is Wrong with the Miracle Argument?." *Studies in the History and Philosophy of Science* 22 Nr. 1: 23–36.

Carrier, Martin. 1993. "What is Right with the Miracle Argument: Establishing a Taxonomy of Natural Kinds." *Studies in the History and Philosophy of Science* 24 Nr. 3: 391–409.

Haldane, John and Crispin Wright, eds. 1993. *Reality, Representation, and Projection*. New York: Oxford University Press.

Haldane, John. 1993b. "Mind-World Identity Theory and the Anti-Realist Challenge." In Haldane & Wright, 1993, 15–37.

Haldane, John. 1994. "The Life of Signs." *Review of Metaphysics* 47 No. 3: 451–70.

Hale, Bob. 1993a. "Can There Be a Logic of Attitudes?" In Haldane & Wright, 1993, 337–63.

Hale, Bob. 1993b. "Postscript." In Haldane & Wright, 1993, 385–88.

Hay, William. 1975. "Under the Blue Dome of Heaven." *Proceedings and Addresses of the American Philosophical Association* 48: 54–67.

Hempel, Carl. 1935a. "On the Logical Positivists' Theory of Truth." *Analysis* 2 Nr. 4: 49-59.

Hempel, Carl. 1935b. "Some Remarks on "Facts" and Propositions." *Analysis* 2 Nr. 6: 93-96.

Horwich, Paul. 1990. *Truth.* Oxford: Blackwell.

Hume, David. 1964. *David Hume: The Philosophical Works.* T. H. Green & T. H. Grose, eds. Rpt. Aalen: Scientia.

Hume, David. 1975. *An Enquiry Concerning Human Understanding.* In P. H. Nidditch, ed. *Enquiries Concerning Human Understanding and Concerning the Principles of Morals*, 3^d ed. New York: Oxford University Press.

Johnston, Mark. 1993. "Objectivity Refigured: Pragmatism Without Verificationism." in Haldane & Wright, 1993, 85–130.

Kant, Immanuel. 1902–. *Kants Gesammelte Schriften.* Königlich Preußische (now Deutsche) Akademie der Wissenschaften. Berlin: G. Reimer (now De Gruyter), usually referred to as "Akademie Ausgabe."

Kant, Immanuel. 1929. *Immanuel Kant's Critique of Pure Reason.* N. K. Smith, tr. New York: St. Martin's.

Kaplan, David. 1975. "How to Russell a Frege-Church." *Journal of Philosophy* 72: 716–29.

Leibniz, Wilhelm. 1960. *Nouveaux Esssais.* In *Philosophische Schriften.* Gerhardt, ed.. Hildesheim: Olms, vol. V; *New Essays Concerning Human Understanding.* P. Remnant & J. Bennett, trs. Cambridge: Cambridge University Press, 1981.

McFetridge, Ian. 1993. "Realism and Anti-Realism in a Historical Context." In Haldane & Wright, 1993, 39–61.

Melnick, Arthur. 1997. *Representation of the World: A Naturalized Semantics.* New York: Peter Lang.

Nagel, Thomas. 1986. *The View from Nowhere.* New York: Oxford University Press.

Neurath, Otto. 1931–32. "Soziologie im Physikalismus." *Erkenntnis* 2: 393–431.

Neurath, Otto. 1932–33. "Protokolsätze." *Erkenntnis* 3: 204–14.

Neurath, Otto. 1934. "Radikaler Physikalismus und Wirkliche Welt." *Erkenntnis* 4: 346-62.

Neurath, Otto. 1959a. "Sociology and Physicalism." In Ayer, 1959, 282—317.

Neurath, Otto. 1959b. "Protocol Sentences." In Ayer, 1959, 199–208.

Paton, Herbert J. 1936. *Kant's Metaphysic of Experience*, 2 vols. London: George Allen & Unwin.

Peirce, Charles S. 1877. "The Fixation of Belief." In *The Collected Papers of Charles Saunders Peirce*. C. Hartshorne and P. Weiss, eds. Cambridge, Mass.: Harvard University Press, 1932–1934, vol. 5, 358–87.

Peirce, Charles S. 1878. "How to Make Our Ideas Clear." In *The Collected Papers of Charles Saunders Peirce*. C. Hartshorne and P. Weiss, eds. Cambridge: Mass., Harvard University Press, 1932–1934, vol. 5, 388–410.

Sellars, Wilfrid. 1963. "Empiricism and Abstract Entities." In Schilpp, 1963, 431-468.

Schilpp, Paul A., ed. 1963. *The Philosophy of Rudolf Carnap*. The Library of Living Philosophers.

Stroud, Barry. 1984. *The Significance of Philosophical Scepticism*. Oxford: Clarendon Press.

Waismann, Friedrich. 1965. "Verifiability." Rpt. in *Logic and Language: First and Second Series*. A. Flew, ed. New York: Anchor, 123–51.

Walsh, W. H. 1952. "A Note on Truth." *Mind* 61: 72–74.

Westphal, Kenneth R. 1987–88. "Sextus Empiricus *Contra* René Descartes." *Philosophy Research Archives* 13: 91–128.

Westphal, Kenneth R. 1989. *Hegel's Epistemological Realism*. Dordrecht and Boston: Kluwer.

Westphal, Kenneth R. 1997a. "Affinity, Idealism, and Naturalism: The Stability of Cinnabar and the Possibility of Experience." *Kant-Studien* 88: 139–89.

Westphal, Kenneth R. 1997b. "Noumenal Causality Reconsidered." *Canadian Journal of Philosophy* 27 No. 2: 209–46.

Wettstein, Howard. 1991. *Has Semantics Rested on a Mistake?* Stanford: Stanford University Press.

Wick, Warner. 1951. "The "Political" Philosophy of Logical Empiricism." *Philosophical Studies* 2 Nr. 4: 49-57.

Will, Frederick L. 1988. *Beyond Deduction*. New York and London: Routledge.

Will, Frederick L. 1997. *Pragmatism and Realism*. K. R. Westphal, ed. Lanham, Md.: Rowman & Littlefield.

Williams, Bernard. 1978. *Descartes: The Project of Pure Inquiry*. Harmondsworth and New York: Penguin.

Williams, Michael. 1993. "Realism and Skepticism." In Haldane & Wright, 1993, 193–214.

Williams, Michael. 1996. *Unnatural Doubts*. Princeton: Princeton University Press (originally published, Oxford: Blackwell, 1992).

Wittgenstein, Ludwig. 1958. *Philosophical Investigations/Philosophische Untersuchungen*. London: Macmillan, 3d ed.

Wittgenstein, Ludwig. 1978. *Remarks on the Foundations of Mathematics.*
G. H. von Wright, R. Rhees, G. E. M. Anscombe, eds. G. E. M.
Anscombe, tr. Cambridge, Mass.: M. I. T. Press, revised edition.
Wright, Crispin. 1992. *Truth and Objectivity.* Cambridge, Mass.: Harvard
University Press.
Wright, Crispin. 1993. "Realism: The Contemporary Debate—W(h)ither
Now?" In Haldane & Wright, 1993, 63–84.

3

Perception and Conception

William P. Alston

1 In this paper I will turn a critical eye on what I will call *conceptualist* accounts of perception, accounts that take all *perceptual cognition* of (external) objects to be mediated by concepts, and hence deny any non- or subconceptual mode of perceptual cognition of objects. More specifically, I will be constrasting such views with a particular rival, the theory of appearing, and arguing for the superiority of the latter. I will approach this task by first giving a brief characterization of the theory of appearing, and then turning my attention to conceptualist theories, their varieties, and their vicissitudes.

2 I look out my study window and observe a variegated scene. There are maple, birch, and spruce trees in my front yard. Squirrels scurry across the lawn and up and down the trees. Birds fly in and out of the scene, hopping on the lawn in search of worms. Cars and vans occasionally drive by. My neighbor across the street is transplanting some geraniums. A truck pulls up in his driveway.

What is a natural and philosophically illuminating way of describing what is happening in these episodes? It will help to prompt an answer of that sort if I arrange for this seeing to follow a period of visual deprivation. First my eyes are shut. In that condition I think about the scene before me. I remember the trees in my yard. I wonder whether there are squirrels and robins out there at the moment. I hypothesize that my neighbor across the street is working in his garden. That is, I form various propositional attitudes con-

cerning what is or might be in front of me. Then I open my eyes
and take a look. My cognitive condition is radically transformed.
Whereas before I was just thinking about, wondering about, remembering the trees, the squirrels, the houses, and so on, these items (or
some of them) are now *directly presented* to me, to my awareness.
They are, to use a currently contentious phrase, *given* to my consciousness. They are *present* to me, whereas before I was merely
dealing with propositions *about* them. This, I submit, is an intuitively plausible way of describing the difference, and hence a plausible
way of bringing out what is distinctive of perception as a mode of
conscious cognition. This would seem to be what differentiates
conscious perceptual cognition of the world from judging, believing,
remembering, wondering, hypothesizing, reasoning about the world.
These reflections contain the germ of the account of perception that
is (was) called the *Theory of Appearing*.[1] According to that theory
what it is to consciously perceive an object is for that object to
appear to one in a certain way—to *look* so-and-so, or to *sound* so-
and-so, or to *feel* so-and-so . . .. That may not be all that is involved in perceptual experience, and shortly I shall be acknowledging that it is not, but it is the heart of the matter. It is this that
distinguishes perception from other modes of cognition, and it is
this on which all the other components of perceptual consciousness
are based. As the language just used indicates, when in this essay
I speak of a theory or an account of *perception*, I will be thinking
of perception as a mode of *conscious cognition of something*,
usually of something in the immediate environment, rather than, for
example, a physical-physiological process that eventuates in such a
conscious cognition.

---

[1]   The theory is espoused in Prichard 1909; Hicks 1938; and Barnes 1945. A
clear statement, without a whole hearted endorsement, is found in Moore 1922,
220, 252). It is criticized in Broad 1925, ch. 4; Price 1932, ch. 3; and Chisholm
1950. Since these attacks the theory has all but dropped from sight, though there
is a recent critical discussion by Jackson (1977). Although Dretske does not use
this term, I would classify his account of "non-epistemic seeing" in Dretske 1969,
ch. 2, as a form of the theory.

To go into this just a bit more, the theory of appearing takes the relation of *X's appearing so-and-so to a subject, S,* to be basic and irreducible. Everyone who recognizes perceptual experience at all will agree that there is such a thing as *X*'s looking red or round or like a tree or like a house. But other theories proffer analyses of this in other terms. The sense datum theory holds that *X*'s looking red to *S* is a matter of a relation between *X* and *S*'s being aware of a red sense datum. This relation is specified differently by different forms of the theory. The adverbial theory will give a similar analysis with 'being aware of a red sense datum' replaced by 'sensing redly.' Propositional content theories, with which I will be much concerned here, may analyze *X*'s looking red to *S* as something like *S's being in a certain kind of attitude to the proposition that X is red.* And so on. But the theory of appearing rejects all such attempts and takes the appearing relation to be a basic unanalyzable relation that is obviously exemplified in experience but not subject to conceptual unpacking.

Just another word about the relation. It does not bear the usual marks of an intentional relation. *X appears* ϕ *to S entails X exists.* No 'intentional inexistence' here. And it is refreshingly transparent. If *X appears* ϕ *to S* and *X=Y*, it follows that *Y appears* ϕ *to S.* So though *S*'s being *directly aware* of *X* (to switch to the converse of the relation of appearing) is obviously a mode of cognition, a way of being aware of *X* (and so satisfies one intuitive root of intentionality, *viz.,* being *of* something), it is not a mode of intentionality on the currently most popular criteria for this.[2]

At this point it looks as if I am launching a full-dress defense of the theory of appearing, but it is time to pull back my horns and remove that from the agenda of this paper. Such a defense would have to deal with various difficulties, the most serious of which concerns how to handle hallucinations. According to the theory, perceptual consciousness is, at bottom, a matter of something's appearing to one as so-and-so. In normal perception that something

---

[2] Smith (1989) treats *acquaintance,* the term he uses for this relationship as intentional in the traditional sense of being *of* or *about* something.

is an object in S's environment. But what about hallucinations? If the theory were limited to veridical perception (*i.e.*, veridical in having a physically existent object in the 'right place,' not necessarily in giving rise to true beliefs about that object), there would be no need to worry about this. But since, like other accounts of perceptual consciousness, the theory aspires to give a unified account of all experience that is phenomenologically of a perceptual sort, it has to locate something that is doing the appearing in hallucination. But that is a task for another occasion. My aim in this paper, as far as the theory of appearing is concerned, is to defend it against a certain rival, *conceptualism*, which takes all perceptual cognition to be mediated by concepts. Clearly the relation of appearing/direct awareness is non-conceptual. Otherwise, it would bear the standard marks of intentionality I have just pointed out that it lacks. So what I will do in this paper is take a look at conceptualist theories of perception, consider what has been or can be said in their favor, and bring out difficulties in them that tell in favor of the theory of appearing. This will constitute a partial disposal of rivals, as a prelude to a complete defense of the theory.[3]

3 Now for an account of conceptualism and a survey of its varieties. I won't attempt an account of the nature of concepts. Suffice it to say that to apply a concept to X is either to think of X as belonging to a certain kind or as possessing a certain property. The basic claim of conceptualism is that all perceptual cognition of objects involves something(s) like this. To avoid easy refutation the view must allow that the application of the concept can be more or less implicit; it need not be something the subject is doing with full deliberateness and full consciousness. Nothing in my discussion will

---

[3] Elsewhere, in Alston 1990, I have done another ground-clearing job by criticizing all theories that take object perception to be a matter of a causal or other relation between the object and sensory experience, where the latter is construed as wholly a state within the subject. Such theories are, or can be, opposed to conceptualism as well. They typically hold that one perceives an object, X, when one is in a sensory state with respect to which X stands in a certain kind of causal relation. It is natural to suppose that no concept deployment is necessarily involved in any of that.

hang on the degree of conscious accessibility of the conceptualization that, on this view, is always involved in perceptual cognition. But I do take it as definitive of conceptualism, in the sense in which I use the term, that it maintains that perceptual cognition of an object involves conceptualization of the object that is conscious to some degree. Thus, in opposing conceptualism I do *not* thereby oppose psychological theories of perception that posit unconscious conceptual or propositional processes that generate or underlie perceptual consciousness.[4]

Many conceptualists make the further claim that the conceptualization involved in perceptual cognition always takes a propositional form. I will call this variety *propositionalism*. It is not always distinguished from mere conceptualism, but it is a special form thereof. One could be employing a concept in seeing a tree, thinking it of it as a tree, using that concept to 'locate' it in one's total cognitive state, without entertaining any proposition that involves that concept, not even the proposition *that's a tree*. If this seems mistaken to you, simply dismiss it. All my criticisms will apply equally to a propositional and a non-propositional form of conceptualism.

There are conceptualists who go beyond propositionalism and maintain that all perception involves *belief* (judgment), or something in the neighborhood thereof, such as a tendency to belief. Thus David Armstrong[5] and George Pitcher[6] hold that perception is *nothing but* the acquisition of beliefs about the environment or tendencies to such beliefs. Brand Blanshard,[7] following the Anglo-American absolute idealist tradition, holds that perceiving an object is a matter of making a judgment about it, and Michael Pendlebury[8] holds a similar view. John Heil[9] oscillates between the two

---

[4] For a good presentation of such a theory see Rock 1983. Unlike many psychologists, Rock makes a clear distinction between perceptual experience and the unconscious processes that generate it.

[5] Armstrong 1961; Armstrong 1968.

[6] Pitcher 1971.

[7] Blanshard 1939.

[8] Pendlebury 1987, 91–106.

views. These are forms of conceptualism, because I can't believe or judge that X is ϕ without using the concept of ϕ, but they are particularly strong and vulnerable forms. I can employ the concept of *house* in seeing an object, and even entertain the proposition that it is a house, without believing it to be a house or even, I would say, acquiring a tendency to believe that it is a house. I might realize that it is part of a movie set and is only a fake house facade. Though these belief-judgment views seem obviously false to me, I will not be discussing them in this essay but will, rather, confine myself to criticisms that apply to any form of conceptualism.

There is another important distinction in this territory. Moderate conceptualists do not deny that perceptual experience involves more than concept deployment, though they deny that this 'more' constitutes any cognition of objects. The more extreme conceptualism does deny the former, taking perception to be nothing but a kind of conceptual cognition. Moderate conceptualists differ as to what that this extra nonconceptual component is. Thus Blanshard, while construing the perception of X as a judgment that X is before one, recognizes that such a judgment is based on *sensation*, which itself is nonconceptual in character, though it never appears in perception as a distinct element. John Searle,[10] while holding that "the content of the visual experience . . . is always equivalent to a whole proposition" (40), also acknowledges at one point that there can be distinguishable visual experiences with the same propositional content (*there being a tree over there*), thus implying that there is more to visual experience than propositional content. He seems to take this to be an awareness of sensory qualia. Christopher Peacocke[11] asserts that "the representational content of a perceptual experience has to be given by a proposition, or set of propositions, which specifies the way the experience represents the world to be"

---

[9] Heil 1983, chs. 4, 5.
[10] Searle 1983.
[11] Peacocke 1983.

(5).[12] But he takes pains to distinguish this from *sensation*, which he also takes to be an essential element of perception. Heil also recognizes the presence of nonconceptual sensation, though he takes it to be inessential for perception (63).[13] One nonconceptual aspect that doesn't figure in this list is a direct awareness of external objects, since countenancing that would exclude them from conceptualism.

Before proceeding further I need to say something about the fact that we have seen Searle and Peacocke formulate their position in terms of what constitutes the *content* of perceptual experience, rather than, as I have been doing, in terms of what is required for *perceptual cognition of an object*.[14] In these writers 'content' is often tied to *representation*, as in the above quotation from Peacocke. Sensory experience *represents* the world as being a certain way. My present visual experience, for example, represents it as being the case that such-and-such sentences are currently showing on the screen of my computer. Furthermore, Peacocke makes it explicit that he is thinking of perceptual experience as *intrinsically* representational; its having a certain representative function is at least an essential part of what makes it the experience that it is. It is not just that the experience *could* be used to represent something. Searle has a similar idea, which he more often expresses in terms of 'intentionality' and 'conditions of satisfaction.' A visual experience, like a belief, has built into it certain conditions of satisfaction, conditions under which it will be 'successful,' *i.e.*, represent some bit of the world as it actually is.

The notion of *content* is often explicitly (and, no doubt, often implicitly) *limited* to the representational aspect of perceptual experience, and in this way distinguished from the nonpropositional aspects like sensation, where these are recognized.

---

[12] In later writings Peacocke also recognizes a "non-conceptual" mode of perceptual representation. See, *e.g.* Peacocke 1992. This latter Peacocke is not a pure conceptualist in my sense.

[13] We should not assume that all these thinkers understand *sensation* in the same way.

[14] This is typical of contemporary conceptualists.

I will use the phrase 'content of experience' only for the representational content of an experience, and never for a type of sensation. (Peacocke 1983, 5)

We need not be committed to a representative theory of perception to think that perception in some sense represents the world. We can express this by saying that perceptions have content. (Crane 1992, 136)

And contemporary opponents of conceptualism often accept this ground on which to fight the battle. They too put their position in terms of 'representational content,' and deny that it is always conceptual or propositional. (See, *e.g.*, Crane 1992.)

When conceptualism is put in terms of what constitutes the representational content of perception, this complicates the task of comparing it with the theory of appearing, for the latter does not share the assumptions in terms of which the conceptualist claim is made. It is not that whereas the conceptualist says that *content*, in her sense, is wholly conceptual, the appearing theorist denies this. It is rather that the latter rejects this whole way of thinking of content because she does not take perceptual experience to be inherently representational. The reason for this incommensurability of the views is that conceptualists take perceptual experience to be in itself objectless and wholly within the subject's mind-brain, while the appearing theorist takes it to be, at bottom, a relation of the subject to an object, which is, in veridical perception, an external physical object, not part of the mind. It is natural for one who accepts the former construal to think of perceptual experience as *representing* states of affairs in the environment. But according to the theory of appearing, in normal perception the external world is already, so to say, 'in' the experience. The experience wouldn't be what it is without being a relation between subject and external object. Hence the experience doesn't *represent* the external object; it rather, so to say, *makes the object present to the subject*.[15] Thus

---

[15] Searle, strangely enough, feels constrained to point out that perceptual experience differs from, *e.g.*, belief in that it doesn't just 'represent' its objects but

the difference between the views goes deeper than a disagreement over the nature of content. It is rather a disagreement over how to think of what makes an experience the experience that it is.

This is why I formulated the basic issue in terms of whether there is a nonconceptual *cognition* of external objects in perception. Though there is an impasse over 'content,' both sides will, presumably, share at least a pretheoretical notion of cognition. Even if the conceptualist considers the concept of *immediate awareness* to be radically defective, she would at least be prepared to recognize that if there were such a thing, it would be a mode of cognition, or awareness, of something.[16] And the appearing theorist will, like everyone else, freely grant that there is such a thing as conceptual cognition. Hence, it would seem the better part of valor to bypass content and fight it out over cognition. What is needed to complete the translation is the point that conceptualists assume that all perceptual cognition of objects is effected by way of perceptual *representations*. I don't find them saying this, but, as I take it, they regard this as too fundamental to need explicit notice.

I now turn to the more extreme form of conceptualism. It is not easy to find an unambiguous advocate, but Joseph Runzo, of whom more below, seems fairly definite, when he says "I will be arguing that there is no identifiable 'pure perceptual' element in perception, which is independent of the mind's conceptual ordering" (1982, 205). And the view of Armstrong and Pitcher, referred to above, that perception is nothing but the acquiring of beliefs (or tendencies to belief) about the environment, would seem to imply that there is nothing to be said about the character of perception or perceptual

---

'presents' them. It gives 'direct access' to them. "The experience has a kind of directness, immediacy, and involuntariness which is not shared by a belief I might have about the object in its absence" (Searle 1983, 45–46). Searle does not, in my opinion, succeed in harmonizing this admission with his basic thesis that the content of perceptual experience is wholly propositional.

[16] It is true that conceptualists tend to assume that cognition is essentially of the nature of belief or at least is propositionally structured. See, *e.g.*, Heil 1983, 33, 74, 120, and Bonjour 1985, ch. 4. But this may be a terminological matter. In any event, what I am primarily concerned to insist on is a nonconceptual *awareness* of objects in perception. I am less interested in whether this is properly called 'cognition.'

experience except for the propositional content of the beliefs in question.

I will not be directing my arguments against the extreme view as such. It is too easy a target. One need only reflect on the distinctiveness of perception in contrast to abstract thought, as illustrated in my opening scenario, to realize that there must be more to perception than conceptualization or propositional attitudes. In that episode I had plenty of the latter before I saw anything at all. My arguments will be directed against any form of conceptualism.

There are various claims typically associated with conceptualism, and that might well be confused with it, to the denial of which I am not committed. Here are the most important ones.

1. Perception is typically conceptually (or propositionally) structured.
2. There is (can be) no perception without conceptual structuring.
3. Conceptual-propositional thought influences the character of sensory experience.

Indeed, I accept both (1) and (3) Let me take a moment to enlarge on this. First, as to (1), I am far from being the most radical possible deconceptualist. I am not so pre-Kantian as to suppose that concepts play no role in perception. On the contrary, I take adult human perception to be heavily concept laden. When I look out my study window my visual experience bears marks, obvious on reflection, of being structured by my concepts of *house*, *tree*, *grass*, *pavement*, *etc.*, *etc.* I see various parts of the visual field *as* houses, trees, *etc.*, employing the appropriate concepts in doing so. Perception is, typically, a certain kind of use of concepts, even if, as I am contending, the cognition involved is not only that. My thesis is that there is a cognitive element, aspect, or component of perception that is nonconceptual. Moreover, it is this element that gives perception its distinctive character vis-á-vis other modes of cognition. It is this element that distinguishes perception from memory, (mere) judgment, reasoning, wondering, hypothesizing, and all forms of abstract thought.

As for (3), it is almost equally obvious that one's concepts, beliefs, assumptions, expectations, and the like affect the way things look. There is much experimental evidence for this, but it is also apparent from common experience. My house looks very different to me after long familiarity than it did the first time I saw it. And complex musical compositions sound quite different after we have learned to recognize themes and follow their development. As for (2), although I reject it and hold that it is very likely that infants, and adults in conditions of reduced cognitive activity, perceive things without any conceptualization, I will not argue for that in this paper.

These disavowals are important because much of the argumentation of conceptualists is designed to support (1), (2), or (3). Such arguments have no bearing on my contentions in this paper.

There are other familiar arguments of conceptualists that, for one reason or another, do not make contact with my position. First, it is standard practice for conceptualists to contrast their position with sense-datum theory and to support their view by pointing out defects in the latter. But since the view I oppose to theirs is radically different from a sense-datum theory, this is of no concern to me. Second, the same is to be said for epistemological attacks on 'the given,' arguments to the effect that nothing is presented to us in perception in a foolproof, infallible way that renders mistake about the character of the given impossible. Though my view is that sensory experience essentially involves a *givenness* or *presentation* of something, it is definitely not committed to the epistemological views in question. Hence these arguments, too, pass me by.

The importance of the distinctions I have just been making is apparent from the frequency with which they are ignored. Consider the beginning of Runzo 1982, 205:

> Perceptual experience does not consist in a mere passive reception of sensations which come ready-marked with their identities and inter-relationships. A child sees an animal, where we see a camel, and a biologist might see a dromedary. I see a Picasso, you see the work

of someone obsessed with blue; I hear noise, you hear a composition by John Cage. Thus, the content of our perceptual experience is, surely to some extent, structured by the *conceptual* resources which we possess. But to what extent? In this paper I will defend the view, which I will call the "conceptualist" view, that the possession of concepts is a *necessary* condition of all perceptual experience.

Centrally, I will be arguing that there is no identifiable "pure perceptual" element in perception, which is independent of the mind's conceptual ordering.

In this passage we can discern the following importantly different theses:

1. The things we are aware of in perception do not bring their identities with them. We have to use concepts to identify them.
2. *What* one perceives depends on how it is conceptualized.
3. The content of perceptual experience is conceptually structured.
4. One cannot have perceptual experience without possessing concepts.
5. There is no element in perception the nature of which is independent of concepts.

I do not suggest that Runzo makes no distinction at all between these. For example, he says, in effect, that (4) makes explicit the extent to which (3) holds. But he is obviously identifying some of them with others. Thus he takes (2) to spell out the import of (1). And yet they are radically different. I take (2) to be obviously false. It belongs to the 'grammar' of perception verbs like 'see' and 'hear' that where they take a direct object, that object place is transparent. That is, if I see X and $X=Y$, then it follows that I see Y, whether or not I realize that $X=Y$, or whether I even have the concept of Y. Thus if a child sees an animal which is in fact a camel, then the child sees a camel, whether or not she has an concept of a camel, or can recognize camels when she encounters them. Similarly, even if you can't make anything of a certain composition except noise, if that composition was in fact written by

Cage you heard a composition by Cage. Thesis (1), in contrast, is obviously true. It is a conceptual achievement to *recognize* what you see as a camel. Thus (2), so far from spelling out what (1) says is sharply differentiated from it, as sharply as error differs from truth. Nor does (2) follow from (3); much less are they equivalent. Runzo is equally misguided in supposing (4) to be a further specification of (3). Concept possession might be necessary for perceptual experience but not by way of structuring it. It might be necessary, for example, because until one had reached the level of cognitive development at which one has concepts, no experience one has could be called 'perceptual.' (I am not affirming the latter, only putting it forward as conceivable.) Finally, (5), what I am concerned to deny in this essay, is not equivalent to (3), nor does it follow from (3). Even if all perceptual experience is conceptually structured, there could still be an *element* in that experience that is independent of conceptualization.

4 I now turn to what each of our contenders has to say by way of recommending its perspective on perceptual experience over that of its rival. And first are the arguments of the conceptualists.

In reading these theorists one cannot avoid being struck by the paucity of support they adduce for their position. It is the rule rather than the exception that they present their view as something too obvious to require argument, proceeding as if they think their only task is to determine the best way to formulate the position. A good example of this is Searle. In the chapter on perception in Searle 1983, ch. 2, he announces his intention as follows.

> My aim in this chapter is not, except incidentally, to discuss the traditional problem of perception, but rather to place an account of perceptual experiences within the context of the theory of Intentionality that was outlined in the last chapter. (37)

This announcement leads the reader to expect little argumentative support, and these expectations are not disappointed. The closest we come to an argument is this.

> I want to argue for a point that has often been ignored in discussions
> of the philosophy of perception, namely that visual (and other sorts
> of perceptual) experiences have Intentionality. The visual experience
> is as much *directed at* or *of* objects and states of affairs in the world
> as any of the paradigm Intentional states that we discussed in the last
> chapter, such as belief, fear, or desire. And the argument for this
> conclusion is simply that the visual experience has conditions of
> satisfaction in exactly the same sense that beliefs and desires have
> conditions of satisfaction. (39)

Some argument! It does have this virtue: the premise strongly
supports the conclusion. But it is hard to imagine anyone who was
not antecedently disposed to accept the conclusion accepting the
premise. Nor is Searle an isolated case. Peacocke 1983, ch. 1
simply lays it down that the content of experience is propositional
and proceeds to develop the view. Sometimes a conceptualist refers
to Kant as having established that percepts without concepts are
blind. Never mind the fact that most of those who invoke the
authority of the sage of Königsberg would never dream of using his
arguments for the conceptual structuring of perception.

I suspect that this situation is due largely to a failure to realize
what is needed for a successful defense. For one thing, since conceptualists typically do not distinguish their position from the
weaker view that perception always involves conceptualization, they
fail to realize that this latter thesis is compatible with the claim that
there is also a nonconceptual cognition of objects in perception.
Hence they spend a lot of time pointing out the pervasiveness of
conceptualization in ordinary perception, mistakenly supposing that
this suffices to establish their stronger position.[17] Again, they regularly inveigh against sense-datum theory, supposing that eliminating it leaves conceptualism in possession of the field.[18] Analogous

---

[17] See, *e.g.*, Runzo 1982, 206–7, 210–11; Runzo 1977, 214; Heil 1983, ch. 4.
Much of the criticism of Dretske on "non-epistemic seeing" (1969, ch. 2) is
directed at Dretske's claim that such seeing can occur in the absence of any
conceptualization.

[18] See Runzo 1977, 216; Searle 1983, 58–59; Pendlebury 1987, 94.

remarks can be made about the other misguided arguments I listed above.

This situation makes it difficult to assess the position in the standard way, by assessing the strength of the arguments for it. But I will do the best I can with what I have to work with.

Pendlebury (1987) is unusual in proferring arguments that are not based on mistakes about the dialectical situation. First, he contends that taking perceptual experience to be propositional enables us to accommodate the fact that perceptions are said to be veridical or nonveridical. For a proposition is just the sort of thing that is assessable in that way (93).[19] But this doesn't amount to much. We can easily explain this kind of talk by taking it to be directed to beliefs or judgments based on perceptual experience rather than directed to the experience itself. Or, alternatively, it could be directed to the tendency of the experience to give rise to true or false judgments, rather than to the possession of truth or falsity by the experience itself.

Second, he points out that "the view enables us to accommodate so-called contradictory sense experiences in a quite straightforward way" (94). An example would be having simultaneously an experience of A and B being the same color, an experience of B and C being the same color, and an experience of A and C being different in color. Pendlebury points out that it is quite possible for all three propositions to be entertained at the same time, whereas the phenomenon cannot be accounted for on the sense-datum view. (If A, B, and C, are sense-data, they can't actually be related in this fashion.) But he ignores the point that the theory of appearing can easily handle the data. A can look the same color as B, B can look the same color as C, while A looks different in color from C, all at the same time.

Runzo also attempts to support the position. Some of his arguments are based on conflations I exposed above in commenting on the beginning of his 1982 article. Others will be discussed below.

---

[19] Blanshard 1939, 94 presents essentially the same argument, concentrating on *judgment* rather than on *proposition*.

Two that can be dispatched as quickly as the Pendlebury arguments, and in the same way, consist of two alleged advantages of the propositional content view over a 'pure presentation' view.[20] (1) The former is simpler since we have to recognize propositionally structured awareness in perception anyway. True enough, and this would be sufficient for the conclusion, provided there were not strong enough reasons for preferring the more complex account, as I will be arguing there are. (2) The propositional view "can account both for the differences in the way things are and the variant ways they appear, and for the subsequent phenomena of mistake and illusion in perception . . ." (215). But the theory of appearing has no difficulty with these data either. It can easily recognize that things can appear perceptually to be other than they are. The appearance relation need not be construed as foolproof.

I now turn to reasons that I am prepared to take somewhat more seriously. (A) It is widely held that the (alleged) concept of *immediate awareness* or *direct presentation* that is at the heart of the theory of appearing is unintelligible, incoherent, or otherwise radically defective. My impression is that the dissatisfaction with the notion stems largely from the fact that it cannot be analyzed in any way. It can explained only by pointing to examples in our experience, which are, of course, legion. This is the classic device for conveying the concept.[21] And ostensively definable concepts, especially mental ones, are out of fashion today.[22] Another bar to recognizing the concept comes from a confusion between direct awareness of objects and direct awareness of facts. It is arguable that the latter essentially involves conceptual-propositional deployment; and if it is not distinguished from the former, the same will be said of

---

[20] See Runzo 1977, 215.

[21] See, *e.g.*, Moore 1953, 46; Moore 1910, 36–62; Broad 1925, 145.

[22] People who are worried by this and who also want to preserve such talk often give 'direct awareness' an epistemological construal. To be directly aware of X is to be aware of it in such a way that what one believes about it on the basis of that awareness could not be mistaken. (See, *e.g.*, Malcolm 1963, 73–95.) But that is no help to the theory of appearing. The concept of appearing employed there is not an epistemic concept. It is not defined in terms of the infallibility or incorrigibility of beliefs that stem from it, or in any other way.

it.[23] In any event, each person must decide whether she or he can understand a concept of direct presentation that has the features I spelled out in §2.

An argument that was more popular in the heyday of absolute idealism than at present is that all perceptual cognition of objects essentially involves inference. And if the perception of an object is generated by inference, it must be judgmental, or at least propositional. A good presentation is in Blanshard 1939, ch. 2. Blanshard was thinking of the inference as going from "sensation" to a judgment about an external object. This idea immediately runs into the objection that sensation, which is itself not propositional, cannot function as a premise of an inference. More recently those who emphasize inference in perception have appealed to work in the psychology of perception that hypothesizes unconscious inference that underlies conscious perceptual experience.[24] But even if some of these theories are correct, they tell us only what is causally responsible for perceptual experience, not what the character or structure of the latter is. This conflation, which we earlier saw Runzo making, is also very common among psychologists, though Rock (1983) is careful to avoid it. Once all this is cleared up, the fact, if it is a fact, that perceptual experience is influenced by unconscious inference can be seen to pose no difficulty for the thesis that there is a basic nonconceptual awareness of external objects involved in perception.

Now I come to the most serious argument of the conceptualist for his position vis-à-vis the theory of appearing. According to the latter, to perceive X is for X to appear to one in some way. Restricting ourselves to vision for the sake of concreteness, it is for X to *look so-and-so* to one. But, says the conceptualist, that itself essentially involves concepts. X's looking so-and-so to me (looking round, red, like a house or a tree) *is* just for me to see X *as* round, as red, as a house, or as a tree. That is, it is to *take S* to be a

---

[23] For a good example of the failure to make this distinction see Bonjour 1985, ch. 4. The distinction is discussed in Alston 1989, 302.

[24] A good source for this is Rock 1983.

house, or at least to have a tendency to do so. It is to apply the concept of a house to it. Hence, the supposed nonconceptual awareness of X's looking some way to S turns out to involve the use of concepts after all.[25]

Though this argument can sound impressive, and though it has been convincing to many, it will not survive careful scrutiny. The move from 'X looks ϕ to S' to 'S sees X as ϕ' looks plausible. But just how are we to understand the latter? It is natural to understand 'seeing X as a house' as '(perceptually) *taking, believing,* or *judging* X to be a house.' But on that construal the position is hopeless. It is perfectly clear that X can look ϕ to me without my believing it to be ϕ. If I know that X is a white object in red light it can look red to me without my taking (believing, judging) it to be red. And if I know that X is a house façade on a movie set, it can look like a house to me without my taking it to be a house. Hence, the conceptualist adds the disjunct 'tends to take it to be ϕ.' He then equates the disjunction with 'applies the concept of ϕ to X.' But in order to evaluate the movement to and from the disjunction, we would have to look at the concept of *tendency* involved, and I want to avoid (here) that rather tedious task if possible. Fortunately it is possible, since it is 'apply the concept of ϕ to X' in which the conceptualist is really interested. So let's move directly to examining the relation of that to 'X looks ϕ to S.'

It is clear, from reasons just given, that the application of the concept of ϕ to X will have to be possible in the absence of belief that X is ϕ if it is to have any chance of being equivalent to X's looking ϕ to S. And the prospects for this may seem dim. Doesn't perceptually applying the concept of tree to X just mean *judging that X is a tree*? What else could it be? Well, perhaps 'apply' is not quite the right term here. If a look amounts to *some* use of a concept, that will give the conceptualist all she wants. And it does seem clear that, in general, I can use a concept vis-á-vis X without judging that the concept is true of X. When I wonder whether X is a house or test the hypothesis that X is a house or hope that X is

---

[25] Runzo 1977, 214–15; Searle 1983, 40–42.

a house, I have made use of the concept of a house in thinking about X, without committing myself to X's being a house. But the question is whether anything like this is possible in *perceptual* cognition. It seems so. Perhaps the best entering wedge here is the phenomenon of ambiguous pictures. Take the one that can be seen either as a pair of faces or as a vase, depending on what is taken as figure and what as ground. I can be employing the concept of a vase in looking at it in that way without taking anything to be a vase.[26] To this it may be replied that I at least take something to be a picture of a vase (or a picture that can be seen as a picture of a vase). But even if that is so, it remains that I can be using the concept of vase perceptually (even if it is only as a component of the concept of a picture of a vase) without taking anything to be a vase.

To be sure, it doesn't follow from this that when X looks red without my believing it to be red, I *must* be using the concept of red. But the ambiguous figure example at least opens up this possibility. Let's say that it is possible in perception to be conceptualizing something as red or as a house without believing it to be red or a house. I can be seeing X as a house, in one sense of that phrase, if I use the concept of a house to, so to say, 'mark out' that part of the visual field, without believing it to be a house. And if so, it is at least a coherent supposition that X looks ϕ to me *iff* I am using the concept of ϕ in visually perceiving X.

But even if coherent, this account is not true. The most obvious and the most decisive reason for this is that X can look ϕ to S even if S lacks the concept of ϕ. Where that happens there is the look without the corresponding concept application. Something may look like a mango to me (present the kind of appearance that mangoes typically present to normal perceivers in this kind of situation) even though I lack the concept of a mango. Hence, X's looking ϕ to S cannot *be* S's using the concept of ϕ in perceiving X.

---

[26] I am not claiming that one has to be employing the concept in order to see the picture in that way, only that one may be doing so.

This negative judgment may be resisted in more than one way. Some of these embody simple confusions. For example, it may be said that I couldn't report or believe that X looks like a mango without using the concept of a mango. But that is neither here nor there with respect to what it is for X to look like a mango to me. The supposition that it does is based on a confusion between the fact that p and the belief, report, or thought that p. Without the concept of a mango I can't realize that X looked like a mango to me. But in the same way if I lack the concept of a muscular spasm I cannot realize or report that I am having a muscular spasm. That doesn't show that *having* a muscular spasm involves using the concept of a muscular spasm.

But it may be replied that even if looking red does not necessarily involve using the concept of red, when it comes to kind terms the concept of looking like a K essentially involves the concept of a K.[27] We can't explain what it is to look like a mango without using the concept of a mango. And so how could X look that way to S without S's being able to recognize what it is that X looks like, in which case S would be wielding the concept in question after all.

To get to the bottom of this we must distinguish different kinds of *look* concepts, and relate them to looks themselves. Chisholm and others have distinguished what I will call *phenomenal* look-concepts and *comparative* look-concepts. The basic distinction is this. A phenomenal concept is simply the concept of the distinctive phenomenal qualitative character of a look. It is something one cannot understand without having experienced that kind of look. S cannot understand the phenomenal concept of *looking red* without having experienced things looking red.[28] Whereas a comparative *looks*-concept is a concept of the way in which a perceivable object of a certain sort typically or normally looks, or looks under certain

---

[27] See Runzo 1982, 206.

[28] That is not to say that nothing other than the experience is required to grasp the concept. Experiences of the character in question constitute a *necessary* condition for concept possession, not a sufficient condition.

circumstances. This kind of concept involves the concept of the sort of object in question, and it does not involve a specification of the phenomenal distinctiveness of the look in question.

Thus a *comparative* concept of looking ϕ involves the concept of ϕ, whereas a *phenomenal* concept of looking ϕ does not. It is of the first importance to realize that this is a distinction between kinds of look-concepts, not a distinction between kinds of looks. One and the same look can, in principle, be conceptualized in both ways. With simple sensory qualities this is a live possibility. In saying 'X looks red' I can mean either (a) X presents an appearance with a certain distinctive but unanalyzable phenomenal quality (phenomenal concept) or (b) X looks the way red objects typically look, or something of the sort. Where more complex looks, like *look like a maple tree*, are concerned we always, or almost always, use comparative concepts, for the very good reason that we are unable to analyze the look into its sensory quality components and their interrelations. Nevertheless, there is in principle a phenomenal *look like a maple tree* concept that would, if we could get our hands on it, make the phenomenal distinctiveness of that look explicit. Of course with respect to kind terms, the 'typical look' is an enormous disjunction of looks rather than a single uniform look. Not all houses, or all maple trees, or even all mangoes, look exactly alike, not by a long shot. But with respect to any look in the disjunction, a phenomenal concept that captures it is possible in principle, though typically not in practice. For there must be some organization of sensory qualities such that by being visually aware of an example of that, we are capable of recognizing the object as a maple tree or as a mango.

The point of all this is that the supposed contrast between 'looks red' and 'looks like a mango,' according to which even if the former can be nonconceptual the latter cannot, is an illusion. In both cases, the concept of the object property (or kind) comes into one alternative way of *conceptualizing* the look, rather than into the look itself. To report or think of the look in comparative terms (to use a comparative *concept* to conceptualize the look) we have to be using the concept of the property (red) or the kind (mango). But for

X to look that way to us, no concept deployment is required. The possibility still stands for X to look that way to the person innocent of any such concept.[29]

There are other considerations that might mislead one into rejecting my conclusion. There is the point, already mentioned more than once, that one's conceptual repertoire, readinesses, activity, and so on, can influence how things look. To one with a firmly internalized bacteriological conceptual scheme things look very different under the microscope than they do to the neophyte. Thus my denial that X's looking ϕ to S *is* S's employing the concept of ϕ in perceiving X should not be taken as a denial that conceptual possession and/or utilization can *affect* the way X looks. But even where this happens it is not the case that concept utilization is what looking a certain way amounts to. The mere fact that the influence in question is not invariable is sufficient to make that point.

One more caveat. It may be alleged, with some show of reason, that whenever X looks ϕ to S, if S has the concept of ϕ, then S has some tendency to apply that concept to X. But, again, even if this is true, it by no means shows that looking ϕ to S amounts to such concept application. It doesn't even show that whenever X looks ϕ to S and S has the concept of ϕ, S does apply that concept to X.

A final reason for rejecting the conceptualist understanding of 'looks' has to do with the richness of perceptual appearances, particularly visual appearances. When I look at my front lawn it presents much more content to my awareness than I can possibly capture in concepts. There are indefinitely complex shadings of color and texture among the leaves and branches of each of the trees. That is perceptually *presented* to me in all its detail, but I can make only the faintest stab at encoding it in concepts. My repertoire of visual property and visual relation concepts is much too limited and much too crude to capture more than a tiny propor-

---

[29] For that matter, even if the contrast does hold so that X could look red to S without S's deploying the concept of red, though X couldn't look like a mango to S without S's deploying the concept of a mango, it still would not be the case generally that looking ϕ is a matter of using the concept of ϕ, though the possibility would be left open that this is true for some looks.

tion of this detail. This is the situation sometimes expressed by saying that while perceptual experience has an 'analog' character, concepts are 'digital.'[30] Since looks are enormously more complex than any conceptualization available to us, the former cannot consist of the latter.

5 In discussing the question whether 'X looks ϕ to S' can be construed as 'S applies the concept of ϕ to X' we have reached the boundary separating arguments for conceptualism (vis-à-vis the theory of appearing) and arguments for the theory of appearing (vis-à-vis conceptualism). For in disposing of the case for an affirmative answer to the above question I have both refuted a major argument for conceptualism and validated a major argument for the theory of appearing. Since X's looking ϕ to S does not amount to S's wielding the concept of ϕ, this constitutes the central form of nonconceptual cognition of external objects that is affirmed by the theory of appearing. And so the above discussion amounts to a defense of that affirmation. I now proceed to some other reasons for preferring the theory of appearing to conceptualism.[31]

1. The theory of appearing makes much more of a contribution to the solution of problems of reference than conceptualism does. Perceptual experience provides us with a basis for beliefs about particular perceived objects. Even if background beliefs also enter into the basis for perceptual beliefs about the environment, as they often do, they are not enough by themselves to ground perceptual beliefs. The antecedent beliefs I bring with me to the situation do not suffice by themselves to tell me whether the leaves have turned on a tree I see. The visual presentation plays an essential role in both engendering and justifying the belief I form about that. But how do I succeed in referring to one particular tree, T, when I believe, or assert, that the leaves on T have begun to turn? Presum-

---

[30] See Dretske 1981, ch. 6; Peacocke 1992.

[31] Actually, the point just made suggests that in more than one case there is a certain artificiality in distinguishing the arguments of §4 from those of §5 in the way I do. But the important thing in any event is the substance of the discussion, not how one or another part of it is pigeon-holed.

ably my perceptual 'contact' with a particular tree is what enables me to pick it out. And what is there about that contact that brings this off? What else could it be than my perceptual awareness of the tree? But, according to conceptualism, that perceptual awareness (the tree's looking a certain way to me) is just a matter of my applying certain concepts *to that tree*. And, as the italicized phrase makes explicit, the look, as the conceptualist construes it, already presupposes the reference. I can apply concepts *to that tree* only if I am already capable of referring to that tree. Application of concepts to *X presupposes* reference to *X*. And so, on conceptualism, we are still left with the question of what directs our belief, speech, or thought to *that tree*, rather than to something else in the world.[32] The theory of appearing has an answer. It is by virtue of being directly aware of *that tree* looking a certain way that I am enabled to refer to *it* rather than to anything else. The nonconceptual awareness of the object gives me something to conceptualize, form beliefs about, and, more generally, think about in various ways.[33]

2. A conceptualist is faced with the question of why we apply concepts in perception as we do, what basis we have for this. When I look out my window, the conceptualist thinks of my perceptual cognition of the scene as essentially involving the use of the concepts of *tree*, *driveway*, *house*, *bird*, and so on. But why those concepts and not others? Why don't I conceptually structure the scene by the use of the concepts of *microscope*, *airplane*, and *mountain*? The theory of appearing has an obvious answer to this. It is because what I see *looks like* trees, houses, birds, a driveway,

---

[32] It is noteworthy that conceptualists typically couch the alleged propositional content of perceptual experience in existential, rather than in singular referential, terms. See, *e.g.*, Searle 1983, ch. 2, where for most of the chapter Searle uses as his chief example a visual perception with the content *There is a yellow station wagon in front of me*. Near the end of the chapter in §*vi* he attempts to show how reference to a unique particular can be brought into his account, but I cannot see that he is successful in doing so.

[33] For a complete defense of the claim that the theory of appearing is necessary to bring out the way in which perception provides a basis for reference I would also have to consider the popular idea that I can refer to the tree I am currently seeing by virtue of its causal relation to my non-object-directed visual experience. That lies beyond the scope of this essay.

etc. Since these looks do not themselves consist of concept applications, they can provide a basis for using certain concepts rather than others. This prevents my 'choice' of concepts from being arbitrary, and contributes to the justification of the beliefs I use those concepts to form. But conceptualism itself can have nothing to say in answer to the question. How could it, since it 'starts' with the concept application and is silent as to what, if anything, underlies that.

For the extreme conceptualist this is the last word. Since he recognizes nothing in perception except what involves concepts, he is left with no resources at all for providing a justifying explanation for a particular choice of concepts. But the moderate conceptualist has more cards in his deck. He can claim that the nonconceptual (though also noncognitive) element in perception provides a basis for the conceptualization. It is because one has a sensory experience of a certain qualitative sort that one draws the concept of *tree* rather than some other from one's stock of concepts, and it is the fact that it was a sensation of that qualitative sort (plus, perhaps, background knowledge) that justifies one in applying the concept of *tree* in this instance. But that leaves us with the question of how the fact that one is undergoing a sensory experience with a certain qualitative character justifies us in supposing that there is a tree in front of one rather than something else. On the theory of appearing it seems clear that *X*'s looking like a tree provides at least prima facie justification for thinking that it is a tree. But where is the comparable bridge from intrinsic qualities of sensation to that judgment?

3. My last point is one that I cannot claim to be as conclusive as the preceding ones, but I will throw it out for the reader's consideration. If all perceptual cognition of objects is by way of concepts, how does the perceiver come by those concepts? Obviously some concepts can be derived from others. If I have the concepts of an *institution* and *learning* I can put them together to form the concept of a *school*. But what about the earliest concepts? It is a fundamental principle of empiricism that the most basic concepts are acquired by abstraction from experience. On repeatedly experiencing round

things, I form the general concept of *round* as what they have in common. But if things can't look round to me without my using the concept *round*, how do I get started on this project? Even if I am born with certain innate concepts, or conceptual proclivities, they presumably don't include such specific items as the various sensory qualities, much less concepts of the kinds of objects we find in the world.

I believe that this argument is decisive against extreme conceptualism. But before it can amount to a conclusive refutation of moderate conceptualism, we will have to dispose of the possibility that the concepts in question could be acquired by abstraction from non-object-directed, nonconceptual experience, such as sensations are often thought to be. And that would require going into the matter more deeply than I am able to do here. Hence, I will leave the question dangling as to whether moderate conceptualism can generate a viable theory of the origin of empirical concepts.

6 Let me remind the reader as to what I have and have not purported to do in this essay. My central aim was to discredit what I call "conceptualism." I have sought to do this both by undermining the arguments in its favor and by supporting a rival view, the theory of appearing. I distinguished more extreme and more moderate forms of conceptualism. The former takes perception to be nothing but a certain employment of concepts. The latter recognizes a nonconceptual component of perception but maintains that all perceptual cognition of objects is by way of concepts; there is no nonconceptual cognition of objects. The theory of appearing contradicts both forms of conceptualism, but in this essay I have been mostly concerned with the moderate form.

I take the considerations of this essay to be decisive against conceptualism in both of its forms. But I do not claim to have provided conclusive support for the theory of appearing. If it is true, as I believe, that the theory of appearing is the only serious alternative to moderate conceptualism, then disposing of the latter will leave the former in possession of the field. But I have not attempted to justify that belief here, and until that is done, the refutation of moderate conceptualism will not suffice to establish the theory of appearing. Moreover, there are difficulties with the theory that I have not attempted to address in this essay. Hence, I must content myself with claiming to have refuted conceptualism and to have suggested where this leaves us in our thinking about perception generally.

Finally, it may help to flesh out that suggestion if I am more explicit about just how the theory of appearing can be connected with what I have unreservedly conceded to be the role of concepts in normal adult human perception. We can think of it this way. Still sticking to visual perception, at the foundation of a case thereof there are one or more objects looking certain ways to the subject, where looking is the visual form of *appearing* as characterized earlier. Typically (some will say, invariably) one does not simply receive these nonconceptual lookings but applies concepts to the presented objects. It is quite compatible with the theory of appearing to suppose that this concept application is an intimate part of the total experience, not distinguished from the rest except by painstaking reflection. Furthermore, the conceptualization can, and often does, affect the way the object looks. And typically all this will issue in a number of beliefs, which may be short-lived but can guide one's responses to the environment so long as they are active. Under certain conditions these beliefs can take the form of attentive judgment that some perceived object(s) is (are) so-and-so. Thus, all the aspects of perception emphasized by the conceptualist can find a place in the total phenomenon along with the nonconceptual mode of awareness of objects that is stressed by the theory of appearing. The claims to exclusivity made by even moderate conceptualism constitute an unfortunate exaggeration of insights that are eminently valid when kept within bounds and assigned their proper place in a comprehensive view of our perception of the environment.

Syracuse University

References

Alston, William P. 1989. *Epistemic Justification*. Ithaca, N. Y.: Cornell University Press.

Alston, William P. 1990. "Externalist Theories of Perception." *Philosophy and Phenomenological Research* 50, Supplement: 73–97.

Armstrong, D. M. 1961. *Perception and the Physical World*. London: Routledge & Kegan Paul.

Armstrong, D. M. 1968. *A Materialist Theory of the Mind*. London: Routledge & Kegan Paul.

Barnes, W. F. H. 1945. "The Myth of Sense-Data." *Proceedings of the Aristotelian Society* 45: 89–118.

Blanshard, Brand. 1939. *The Nature of Thought*. London: George Allen & Unwin.

Bonjour, Laurence. 1985. *The Structure of Empirical Knowledge*. Cambridge, Mass.: Harvard University Press.

Broad, C. D.. 1925. *The Mind and Its Place in Nature*. London: Routledge & Kegan Paul.

Chisholm, Roderick M.. 1950. "The Theory of Appearing." In *Philosophical Analysis*. M. Black, ed. Ithaca, N. Y.: Cornell University Press, 102–18.

Crane, Tim. 1992. "The Nonconceptual Content of Experience." In *The Contents of Experience*. T. Crane, ed. Cambridge: Cambridge University Press, 136–57.

Dretske, Frederick. 1969. *Seeing and Knowing*. London: Routledge & Kegan Paul.

Dretske, Frederick. 1981. *Knowledge and the Flow of Information*. Cambridge, Mass.: MIT Press.

Heil, John. 1983. *Perception and Cognition*. Berkeley, Cal.: University of California Press.

Hicks, G. Dawes. 1938. *Critical Realism*. London: Macmillan.

Jackson, Frank. 1977. *Perception*. Cambridge: Cambridge University Press.

Malcolm, Norman. 1963. *Knowledge and Certainty*. Englewood Cliffs, N.J.: Prentice-Hall.

Moore, G. E. 1910, "The Subject Matter of Psychology." *Proceedings of the Aristotelian Society* 10: 36–62.

Moore, G. E. 1922, *Philosophical Studies*. London: Routledge & Kegan Paul.

Moore, G. E. 1953. *Some Main Problems of Philosophy*. London: George Allen & Unwin.

Peacocke, Christopher. 1983. *Sense and Content*. Oxford: Clarendon Press.

Peacocke, Christopher. 1992. "Scenarios, Concepts, and Perception." In *The Contents of Experience*. T. Crane, ed. Cambridge: Cambridge University Press, 105–35.

Pendlebury, Michael. 1987. "Perceptual Representation." *Proceedings of the Aristotelian Society* 87: 91–106.

Pitcher, George. 1971. *A Theory of Perception.* Princeton, N.J.: Princeton University Press.

Price, H. H. 1932. *Perception.* London: Methuen.

Prichard, H. A. 1909. *Kant's Theory of Knowledge.* Oxford: Clarendon Press.

Rock, Irvin. 1983. *The Logic of Perception.* Cambridge, Mass.: MIT Press.

Runzo, Joseph. 1977. "The Propositional Structure of Perception." *American Philosophical Quarterly* 14 No. 3: 211–20.

Runzo, Joseph. 1982. "The Radical Conceptualization of Perceptual Experience." *American Philosophical Quarterly*, 19 No. 3: 205–17.

Searle, John. 1983. *Intentionality.* Cambridge: Cambridge University Press.

Smith, David Woodruff. 1989. *The Circle of Acquaintance.* Dordrecht: Kluwer.

4

How to Teach a Wise Man

Michael Root

1 In *An Inquiry Concerning the Human Understanding*, David Hume advanced four principles for a wise man to live by.[1]

   (1) A wise man proportions his beliefs to the evidence.

   (2) Testimony is good evidence for a wise man only if he has good evidence that the witness is credible.

   (3) A wise man has good evidence that a witness is credible only if he observes a constant conjunction between his reports and the truth.

   (4) A witness A's testimony that p to a wise man B is good evidence for B only if B believes that A is more credible than p is unlikely.

Though each principle is plausible, together they are not, for a man who is defined by (1)–(4) is unwise. In particular, he learns little from the testimony of others and seldom believes the word of a teacher or the teachings of a text.[2]

---

[1] This essay is written in honor of my teacher Frederick Will.

[2] Hume uses the phrase 'wise man.' I don't know whether he meant 'man' to include women. When I use 'wise man,' I intend the phrase to cover both men and women, since I believe that wisdom knows no gender. But a growing number of philosophers think gender matters here as everywhere. They might want to read

Truths in science and history pass in his one ear and out his other, for the wise man proportions his beliefs to the evidence, and few of his teachers or texts offer testimony which, given principles (2) and (3), count for him as good evidence.[3] Since he seldom has other evidence of these truths, he believes little of science or history.

In science he is taught that magnesium is a chemical element, that Neptune has an equatorial diameter of 27,000 miles, that women have two X chromosomes, that water is H_2O, and much more. But he accepts little, for he has too little evidence that his teachers or texts are credible, since he has little chance to hold their teachings up to the truth.

In history he is taught that the Magna Carta was signed in 1215, that Napoleon commanded the French troops in the battle of Water-loo, that the Chicago Cubs last won the World Series in 1908, and

---

the term 'man' in this paper to mean man.

[3] Hume discusses belief based on testimony in 1955, §10, the section on miracles. Hume advances (1) when he writes: "A wise man, therefore, proportions his belief to the evidence." (118); he advances (2) when he writes: "The reason why we place any credit in witnesses and historians is not derived from any connection which we perceive *a priori* between testimony and reality, but because we are accustomed to find a conformity between them." (120–21) and "Were not the memory tenacious to a certain degree, had not men commonly an inclination to truth and a principle of probity, were they not sensible to shame when detected in a falsehood—were not these, I say, discovered by experience to be qualities inherent in human nature, we should never repose the least confidence in human testimony. A man delirious or noted for falsehood and villainy has no manner of authority with us." Hume advances (3) when he writes: "It will be sufficient to observe that our assurance in any argument of this kind is derived from no other principle than our observation of the veracity of human testimony and the usual conforming of facts to the reports of witnesses" (119); finally, he advances (4) when he writes: "The plain consequence is (and it is a general maxim worthy of our attention) that no testimony is sufficient to establish a miracle unless the testimony be of such a kind that its falsehood would be more miraculous than the fact which it endeavors to establish" (123). The occasion for Hume's discussion of testimony is evidence for the truth of the Christian religion. Our evidence for the resurrection of Christ and other tenets of such a religion, according to Hume, is the testimony of the witnesses, *viz.* the Apostles. However, his discussion applies equally to evidence for the truth of modern science. Our evidence for the theories of physics and chemistry is the testimony of witnesses, *viz.* those who conducted the experiments that confirm the theories. Without belief in their testimony there would be little science to believe in. That is, testimony is the basis for a system of science as much as religion.

much more. But again he accepts little, for he has too little evidence that his teachers or texts are credible, since he has had little chance in the past to compare their words with the world. The wise man is more skeptic than scholar; on most matters, whether questions of science or religion, he sits on the fence. Show me, he says, but showing him is limited to what he has already seen.

By Hume's standards, few in science or history are wise, since most are trusting when they should be dubious and, in particular, believe when they have too little evidence. In other words, Hume's principles do not fit how people in science or history really think; his principles do not match their considered judgments of when it is wise to base their beliefs on testimony.

Hume's principles don't portray the world of science or history as they are. Is Hume's art bad or the science sloppy? Do we change the portrait or the way scientists respond to testimony— revise Hume's theory or alter scientific practice? A theory about X—whether in philosophy or in science—should be in reflective equilibrium with our considered judgments about X. In science, we adjust theory and observations to get a better fit. In philosophy, we adjust definitions and intuitions. As Nelson's Goodman argues in *Fact, Fiction and Forecast*, there should be dual adjustment between definition and usage. "A rule is amended," he wrote, "if it yields an inference we are unwilling to accept; an inference is rejected if it violates a rule we are unwilling to amend."[4] The process of justifying our reasoning is one of making mutual adjustment between our canons and our accepted practices.

We revise our canons and prune our principles until we reason as we should and require what we do. In other words, there isn't one but two directions of fit. An error can be in us or in the normative theory about us. According to Goodman, our aim should be to change both ourselves and our theories until each comes into line with the other.

Hume's canons do not pass Goodman's test. They match too few of our considered judgments. They require too much doubt; were

---

[4] Goodman 1965, 64.

we to follow them, we would disbelieve too many of the witnesses (teachers or texts) in whom we place our greatest trust. Some adjustment needs to be made in the canons. Which ones?

2 Some philosophers would question (1), the principle that a wise man proportions his beliefs to the evidence. Blaise Pascal and William James adjusted this principle. Always requiring evidence, they thought, divides—implausibly—theoretical and practical wisdom. On their view, the wise man sometimes proportions his belief beyond the evidence; at times he believes because it pays him to. Believing is wiser than not believing that God exists, according to Pascal, because belief maximizes the best and minimizes the worst outcome. In particular, in the absence of all evidence—under conditions of uncertainty—belief is wiser than disbelief when preferred by both the maximax and minimax rules of rational choice theory. Pascal adjusts (1) to the canons of practical wisdom and, in particular, revises (1) to incorporate his principles of rational choice under conditions of uncertainty.[5]

James also applies the standards of practical reason and, in particular, rational choice theory, to our epistemic attitudes, and he offers the following practical or pragmatic alternative to (1):

(1*)   If *p* concerns a matter that B cares about and B does not have good evidence for either *p* or not-*p*. Then B is wise to believe that *p* if and only if the expected benefits to him of doing so exceed the expected costs.[6]

---

[5] The argument is referred to as Pascal's wager. Pascal offers it in his *Pensees* (1904, 2:§233; 1966, §418, 149–153). Recent commentators have shown that his reasoning can be represented as a case of decision making under uncertainty and, in particular, as a game against nature in which no estimate of the likelihood of each of the possible outcomes is available. According to this way of looking at the argument, given what Pascal takes to be the payoff matrix, one's preferences over the outcomes, the rational decision whatever one's outlook—whether pessimistic or optimistic—is to believe that God exists. [Editions of Pascal's *Pensées* vary significantly; the two editions cited here are good standards.—Ed.]

[6] James 1979 offers this account of reasonable belief. Like so much of the historical discussion of reasonable belief, the account was occasioned by an interest in religious belief.

Like Pascal, he revises (1), because it deprives the wise men of much he cares about, *e.g.*, religion, and, like Pascal, he has trouble seeing the wisdom in such self-denial.

But the adjustment James and Pascal propose is extreme. Where (1) makes wisdom scarce and costly, (1*) makes it common and cheap. Witnesses needn't be credible, as long as their testimony tells us what we want to hear. We buy their words as long as the words buy us happiness. If we are too easily pleased, our body of belief becomes fat, since we often believe or disbelieve under conditions of uncertainty. In short, given (1*), it can be wise for B to believe that *p* based on A's testimony even though B has no evidence that A is honest or knows what he is talking about.

Pascal defended the practical or pragmatic approach, *i.e.*, principle (1*) over (1), by arguing that it could purchase salvation, while James argued that it could purchase truth. His argument was this. Let S be a set of propositions and their denials, and let B be completely uncertain about which of the propositions is true. If B follows Hume's advice, principle (1), he remains agnostic about all the propositions in S. If he follows James's principle (1*), he believes one whenever it pays him to. If that proposition is true, he acquires a truth. Thus, if B follows (1*), he has a chance of acquiring the truths in S but no chance if he follows (1). Moreover, where the propositions are really momentous, as in the case of religion, acquiring the extra truths could be very rewarding.

Though James is the father of American pragmatism, he argues here as if he were a realist. He assumes that the truth of a proposition is independent of any reasons for believing it or, in other words, that propositions are determinate in truth value even though no one knows or would ever have the means to find out what truth value the propositions have. His argument is empty if truth is equated—as pragmatists seem to do—with reasonable belief. But let's take a realist perspective and consider whether the argument for (1*) over (1) is a good one?

The argument is poor for at least two reasons. First, the wise man has no evidence that the proposition it pays for him to believe is true, and so no evidence that (1*) will lead him to more truths than (1);[7] second, the argument ignores an important cost: the revision of other parts of his body of belief. Belief in a proposition p in S requires an adjustment in attitude toward propositions he already believes. For example, if the proposition in S is that God performs miracles, then, the wise man has to adjust his prior belief, q, that nature is uniform, and all of his other beliefs that rely on q. If many of these were true, then, in willing to believe that p, the wise man loses these other truths.[8]

Replacing (1) with (1*) is too great an adjustment. Whatever it wins for religious belief, it loses for belief in science or history. There our practice is not to credit a man with wisdom when he allows his beliefs to overreach his evidence and, in particular, when he believes—in the absence of evidence—what it pays him to. In science, a wise man's conjectures can precede the evidence but his beliefs must await it.

We would do better to revise another of Hume's principles and stick with (1). Perhaps we should adjust (2) or (3), *i.e.*, grant the relation between wisdom and evidence but revise the one between evidence and testimony. Evidence that p is true is the only reason for believing that p (a chance at salvation doesn't count). A wise man, we might allow, proportions his belief to the evidence, but he doesn't need evidence that a witness is credible; here we adjust (2). Alternatively we could adjust (3) and say that a wise man can have all kinds of evidence, including testimonial, that a witness is credible. Principle (3) is clearly the most vulnerable.

---

[7] James might have believed in the principle of indifference (named and rejected by Keynes), that if there is no known reason for believing any one of two opposing hypotheses, then relative to our knowledge they have equal probability. Left unrestricted this principle leads to contradiction but if suitably restricted, it can't be used to support James's argument.

[8] James does not come to his canons, as Goodman recommends, by mutual adjustment and pruning. His argument is not that (1*) fits more considered judgments than (1) but that the end of inquiry is truth and (1*) is a better means to that end than (1). However, in assessing the claim that one canon is a better means to truth, we rely on our considered judgments, *viz.*, what we believe with confidence the truth to be. So, James's method of arguing is not very different from Goodman's after all.

3 Hume is committed to (3) because he believes that testimony is good evidence—A's testimony that p makes it reasonable for B to believe that p—only if there is good nontestimonial evidence that the witness is credible and, in particular, only if B remembers that when, in the past, A testified that q, he himself observed that q. That is, Hume is committed to the view that the credibility of testimony is founded on the evidence of memory and observation and, thus to a familiar form of foundationalism.[9] The beliefs of the wise man must have foundations, and the foundations are the evidence of observation, memory and introspection; any other evidence, *e.g.*, the evidence of witnesses of teachers or texts—rests on these. Thus, any reasons for believing that testimony is evidence of truth must be nontestimonial. A man who cites testimony in making the case for testimonial evidence is, on Hume's view, begging the question.

But why assume foundations? The process of justifying our reasoning from one body of evidence to another is, as Goodman says, one of mutual adjustment between how we do reason between them and the canons of how we ought to. The canon that our beliefs be founded on certain or indisputable truths or that we only reason to the credibility of testimony from the evidence of memory and observation would have us amend too many of our most respected epistemic practices. The canon must be adjusted to allow that testimonial and nontestimonial evidence can be mutually supporting. The coherence of bodies of evidence rather than certainty or self-evidence is the better basis or standard of reasonable belief, for that standard fits better with our most respected examples of actual epistemic inquiry.

Once we adjust (3), to cite testimony as evidence for testimony begs no questions. Now to believe that a witness is credible on the basis of testimonial evidence can be wise. The wise man proportions his belief to both testimonial and nontestimonial evidence. Moreover, nontestimonial evidence—what is remembered or ob-

---

[9] See Coady (1992) for a discussion of Hume's view that testimony rests on a foundation of non-testimonial, and, in particular, observational evidence.

served—is no more basic than testimony; each plays an equal role in supporting his wisdom.

Following the method of reflective equilibrium, we adjust Hume's third principle, (3), to read like this.

(3*)   A wise man has good evidence that a witness is credible only if he has good testimonial or nontestimonial evidence that the witness is a reporter of truths.

A wise man who lives by (1), (2) and (3*) is more teachable; he can learn a great deal from what teachers and texts would tell him. Science and history don't pass in his one ear and out his other. His epistemic practices resemble those of actual communities of science and history. Still he is epistemically self-reliant; he is committed to principle (2); he doesn't believe that p simply because a witness tells him that p. He considers whether to believe what witnesses tell him and only believes when he has evidence that the witnesses are credible. In short, the wise man does not accept their word on trust.

But should a wise man keep so much to his own counsel? Would he be more wise were he more accepting and believe what others —teachers or texts—tell him simply because they tell him? There is a growing consensus that he would be and that (2) should be adjusted to allow him to be more credulous.[10] He should believe what others would teach him, not because he has evidence that they are credible, but because he and they are part of the same community. Epistemology, according to this view, should become more socialized and be less a matter of what each individual can learn on his own and more a matter of what we can know or learn together.

The source for a more social epistemology or a more communally wise man seems to be Thomas Reid.[11] Reid would adjust all of Hume's principles. According to Reid, a wise man does not disbelieve until he has proof or evidence. Often he believes unless he

---

[10] See, for example, Foley 1994, 53-73; Coady 1992; Hardwig 1985; Welbourne 1986; Will 1997, chs. 4, 5, and 8.
[11] Reid 1969, 1975.

has good evidence to the contrary. The burden is not on him to prove to a skeptic that his beliefs are true, but the burden is on a skeptic to prove that they are likely not to be. A wise man, according to Reid, does not proportion his trust in a witness to the evidence that the witness is credible but rather his distrust to the evidence that he is not.

The attitude of believing until defeated seems especially appropriate in dealing with testimony. Reid writes:

> The wise and beneficent Author of nature, who intended that we should be social creatures, and that we should receive the greatest and most important part of our knowledge by the information of others, hath, for these purposes, implanted in our natures two principles that tally with each other.[12]

> The first of these principles is, a propensity to speak truth, and to use the signs of language so as to convey our real sentiment . . ... Another original principle implanted in us by the Supreme Being, is a disposition to confide in the veracity of others, and to believe what they tell us. This is the counterpart of the former; and, as that may be called the principle of *veracity*, we shall, for want of a more proper name, call this *the principle of credulity*.[13]

Reid would have us adjust the canons of wisdom not only at (3) but at (2) as well. Principle (2), he seems to suggest, should be replaced with (2*).

(2*)   Testimony is good evidence for a wise man unless he has good evidence that the witness is not credible.

This corresponds to credulity. Reid would also have us add another principle to the canons, *viz.* (5).

(5) A wise man does not dissemble when being a witness and giving testimony to others.

---

[12] Reid 1975, 93.
[13] Reid 1975, 94–95.

This corresponds to veracity. Reid's principle of veracity and credulity are connected, for the fact that each wise man conforms his testimony to (5) gives every wise man a reason to be credulous and believe what a wise-man witness tells him, *i.e.*, to conform to (2*).

Though Reid presents his principles as if they describe how people actually think and speak—he says that we have the propensity for veracity and the disposition for credulity—he also treats them as norms by which to regulate thought and talk.

> It is evident that, in the maker of testimony, the balance of human judgment is by nature inclined to the side of belief; and turns to that side of itself, when there is nothing put into the opposite scale. If it were not so, no proposition that is uttered in discourse would be believed, until it was examined and tried by reason; and most men would be unable to find reasons for believing the thousand part of what is told them. Such distrust and incredulity would deprive us of the greatest benefits of society, and place us in a worse condition than that of savages.[14]

Reid says that we are inclined to believe a witness and that we ought to (given that we don't desire to be deprived of the greatest benefits of society). He thinks that (2*) is superior to (2), because (2*) better fits our actual epistemic practice and our practice is better for following (2*), for by following (2*) rather than (2) we are led to the greatest benefits of society: a broader grasp of the truth.

According to (2), a wise scientist must obtain evidence that colleagues in another lab whose experimental observations bear on his own research are credible before he believes their reports. This greatly limits the reports he is able to believe and limits the data against which he can formulate and test his theories. Even his own data come into doubt, since the methods of science require that his data be replicated, but if he fails to believe the reports of colleagues, he has little evidence that they are, *i.e.*, too few other

---

[14] Reid 1975, 94–95.

reports to compare them with. Thus, the distrust and incredulity sanctioned by (2) deprive the scientist of data and limit his ability to apply the methods of science to the study of nature.

4 Both Reid and Hume are internalists. Both offer canons for the wise man to live by. They are intended to direct his epistemic decisions—to help him decide whom to believe and when. Thus, all the factors needed for a belief to be epistemically justified—in order for the wise man to make it his own—must be internal to his cognitive perspective, *i.e.*, cognitively accessible to him. The evidence they require must be evidence in his eyes—that he is aware of and able to reason with. The fact that there is evidence that a witness is credible has no bearing on whether a man is wise to believe it, on Hume's view, unless the man believes that the witness is credible on the basis of that evidence.

An externalist looks at the matter differently. The canons of wisdom, on his view, are for the epistemic assessors rather than the epistemically assessed to live by. A third person, C, employs the canons in deciding whether to credit B with wisdom, when B believes that *p* on the basis of A's testimony that *p*. In this case, the factors needed for a belief to be justified—for a man to be wise—need not be ones that the man is aware of or able to reason with. C could credit B with wisdom in believing that p based on A's testimony when there is evidence that A is credible, even though B does not possess it.

Externalism eliminates the debate over the wisdom of incredulity —over whether wisdom is an individual or social achievement. Where A conforms to (5), there is evidence that A is credible even if B does not have it. In such a case, (2) and (2*) match the same considered judgments of whether B is wise in believing that *p*. That is, the issue over whether trust or doubt is a mark of wisdom assumes internalism. The contrast between sociality and individualism is lost unless we assume that the canons of wise testimony are designed to serve the first person, A or B, rather than the third person C.

However, even if we assume internalism, the contrast between sociality and individualism is not so sharp as it appears to be. On Reid's view, if there is good evidence that a witness is not credible, then it is not wise to believe him. That is, when doubt over a witness's integrity or authority is raised, Reid's wise man and Hume's proceed the same way. The crux of the difference between them is in the burden of proof. Reid's wise man believes unless there is good reason to doubt the witness's credibility, unless the assumption that he is credible is defeated. So, according to Reid, often a man is wise to believe that a witness is credible even though he has no good evidence that he is. Hume disagrees.

But if Reid's wise man is bound by (4), then he will have to assess the degree of credibility of a witness whenever he receives his testimony, contrary to what he is told to do by (2*). Canon (4) tells him to compare the prior probability that p with the credibility of the witness who is testifying that p. But this requires him to assess the witness's credibility. As Hume writes:

> [When] the fact which testimony endeavors to establish partakes of the extraordinary and the marvelous—in that case the evidence resulting from the testimony admits of a diminution, greater or less in proportion as the fact is more less unusual.[15]

He goes on to illustrate the point by reminding us of the Roman proverb "I should not believe such a story were it told to me by Cato." The incredibility of the fact would invalidate an authority as great as Cato. Hume's point is simple: the more implausible the proposition, the more credible the witness must be before we are wise to believe him. Most of us accept the proverb. Thomas Jefferson did. He thought it very unlikely that extraterrestrial matter, a meteorite, could survive passage through the atmosphere and land on the surface of the Earth. So unlikely that he remarked of a report of a meteor landing by two professors at Yale: "It is easier to believe that Yankee professors would lie than that stones would

---

[15] Hume 1955, 120.

fall from the heaven."[16] Jefferson apparently had more confidence in the Earth's atmosphere than in the reliability of Yankee scientists.

So, the force of (2*) is lost if the canons of wisdom include (4). Both Hume and Reid agree that a wise man believes the testimony of others only if he does not doubt their authority or honesty, but Reid says that the wise man will not doubt it unless he has particular reasons to. But (4) requires him always to assess his confidence in the witnesses, and such an assessment requires him to assess his evidence of the witnesses' credibility. In short, the individualist requires the wise man to apply his own reason as best he can in developing his own understanding of the world. A more social approach is supposed to allow him to rely on the reason of others. But if the social approach includes (4), the wise man must again apply his own reason as best he can, and the contrast between the two approaches is lost.

Should the canons of wisdom include (4)? Does a wise man update his beliefs on the basis of the weight of new evidence and prior probabilities? He does if he conforms to the mathematical principles of probability theory and, in particular, to Bayes' theorem.[17] That is, it is possible to read (4) as a version of Bayes-Laplace theorem (for incompatible hypotheses).[18] On this reading, the wise man considers a witness's propensity to error and veracity in relation to his prior confidence in the truth of what the witness tells him. The less his prior confidence the more confidence he must have that the witness is not prone to error or dishonesty.

Principles (2*) and (4) are opposed; while (2*) tells him ignore priors, (4) tells the wise man to weigh them in. One of them has to

---

[16] Brown and Mussett 1981, 58.

[17] Owen (1987) believes that Hume had something like Bayes' theorem in mind when he endorsed (4). See Sobel 1987, for an opposing view.

[18] The theorem says that $P(h/e) = P(h) \times P(e/h)$ divided by $[P(h) \times P(e/h)] + [P(\sim h) \times P(e/\sim h)]$, where '$e$' is the evidence, '$h$' the hypothesis and '$P(h/e)$' is the probability of h on the evidence e. The theorem can be applied to A's testifying that p to B by replacing 'h' with 'p' and 'e' with 'A says p.' In this case, '$P(A$ says $p/p)$' can be interpreted as the reliability of A with respect to p, where the reliability of A with respect to p is a function of both A's veracity and his propensity to error.

be adjusted or abandoned. The social epistemologist might abandon (4). When a wise man updates his (degrees of) beliefs on the basis of testimony, he might argue, the man ignores prior probabilities, *i.e.*, the degree of implausibility that *p*, and relies on A's testimony that *p* alone (unless he has good evidence that A is not credible).[19]

But, according to many considered judgments, to ignore the prior probabilities is unwise. In updating one's beliefs or initial confidence in a proposition *p* on the basis of new evidence, whether the evidence of testimony, memory, or observation, a person is not wise to ignore the prior probability that *p*, for to ignore it is to ignore relevant evidence, *viz*. the evidence on which one's initial confidence in *p* is based. Though, according to some psychological experiments, people do sometimes ignore the initial probabilities when updating, this does not mean that even these subjects consider such a practice wise.[20] According to most considered judgments, it is unwise to ignore base rates in updating one's belief or degree of belief, even if some seemingly wise men sometimes do it.[21]

The social epistemologist, in the face of such considered judgments, might revise rather than abandon (4). He might argue that simple Bayesian assessments are not always wise (as against maintaining that they are never wise), and, in particular, they are not wise when the new evidence is testimony and there is no evidence that the witness is prone to error or dishonesty. The question then is whether (4) so adjusted fits the considered judgments of the men of science or history.

When witnesses in Utah testified that cold fusion occurred during experiments in their laboratory, did other scientists consider their initial confidence that cold fusion occurred in judging whether to believe them? I suspect they did and that it was the considered

---

[19] Cohen (1981) advances the view that a wise man ignores priors and does not conform to Bayes' theorem.

[20] See Tversky and Kahneman 1974.

[21] According to Laplace, employing base rates is a matter of common sense. He wrote: "[t]he probability of . . . the falsehood of the witness becomes as much greater as the fact attested is more extraordinary. Some authors have advanced the contrary . . .. Simple common sense rejects [their] strange assertion" (1951, 114).

judgment of most of them that it was wise to do so. That is, the reason why they were so reluctant to believe what Pons was telling them was that cold fusion, on the world view of physics, is very implausible. The credibility of Pons was less than the prior probability that fusion was occurring at such low temperatures, and so Pon's testimony was doubted.

I defer to careful social studies of science here, but I doubt that a revision in (4) is needed to reflect the way scientists actually think or practice. I suspect that when revising their scientific beliefs in light of new testimonial evidence, scientists do not, as a rule, ignore base rates, and, as a result, that they do judge how credible a witness is before they decide to accept his testimony.

5 Do the practices of science favor a less over a more self-reliant wise man? Do Hume's principles (1) and (2) fit our convictions that to be wise in science is to be trusting? Hume, according to the social epistemologist, portrays teaching and learning as an adversarial practice. His wise man always considers whether others have an interest in misleading him. To proceed this way, the critic allows, is wise when others are adversaries, as in a court of law, but not wise in science when others are prone to be cooperative. Here Reid's canons are better reflections of wise practice.

The social epistemologist has a point. The courtroom is not a wise man's natural habitat. Much of the evidence possessed by juries is testimonial, but the witnesses who appear before them are unusual; they come as partisans. They aren't simply there to tell the truth but to speak for one side or another. The burden of proof is on the lawyers to convince a jury that their witnesses are credible, and it is reasonable for a juror to suspect that a witness is prone to error or dishonesty. Moreover, while the practices of cross-examination and redirection are part of reaching a verdict in the law, they are not part of reaching truth in science or history.

Plato knew that the aim of a trial is not to make the jury wise and the intention of lawyers is not to seek the truth. In the *Theaetetus*, Socrates explains why we should not look to the courts to understand how wisdom is best acquired:

If you compare people who have been knocking about in lawcourts and such places since they were young with people who have been brought up in philosophy and other such pursuits, it's as if you were comparing the upbringing of slaves with that of free men . . .. [The philosophers] carry on their discussion in peace with time to spare . . .. [The lawyers] aren't allowed to make speeches about anything they please but the opposing counsel stands over them, equipped with compulsion in the shape of a document specifying the points outside which they may not speak . . .. And their contests are never for some indifferent prize, but always for one that concerns themselves . . .. Because of all that they become tense and sharp, knowing how to flatter their master with words and fawn him with deeds, but small and crooked in their mind.[22]

People knocking about in the law are not wise men. The lawyers do not know how to acquire wisdom.

Hume's wise man seems to be knocking about in the law and to believe that every room is a courtroom or worry that every witness is a hostile witness. But appearances mislead. The wise man knows the difference between a laboratory and a law court. He relies on himself, but this does not prevent him from placing a great deal of trust on others if he has reason to believe that he is living in a trustworthy world.

In the laboratory, in contrast to the courtroom, a wise man is likely to have evidence that others are worthy of trust. In labs, people acquire the ability to find the truth and the propensity to speak it. There they observe Reid's principle of veracity and, so, in listening to their speech, a man is wise to observe Reid's principle of credulity. He does not need evidence that each individual witness is credible if he has evidence that being in the lab is enough to make a witness credible. He trusts each witness, because he has evidence that the lab keeps them all trustworthy.

The wise man simply takes each witness at his word—on trust. His practice seems to fit nicely a social account of wisdom: what anyone knows others learn simply by querying him. Wisdom is transmitted by his testimony; his testimony is not evidence that

---

[22] Plato 1973, 173ab (49).

what he is saying is true but rather serves to carry the truth. His testimony is the medium, his truth the message. No one is looking for or thinking about evidence here.

But again appearances mislead. There is evidence behind the scenes. The wise man trusts the witness because he has evidence that the lab holds members to the principle of veracity. B does not have evidence that A is credible when A testifies that p to B, but B does have evidence that A is a member of a community that expects its members to observe norms whose observance assures that the members are credible witnesses. In believing that A is a credible witness, B relies on the lab to see that the norms are observed, but in requiring evidence that the lab is equipped and disposed to enforce the norms, he is being epistemically self-reliant. He assures himself that each witness is credible, but he does so with little epistemic labor not because he, B, is such a social animal but because A is. B acts trustingly, not because he is naturally trusting, but because he has discovered that the community he resides in is the Leviathan rather than the State of Nature.

Here we have Hobbes's account of trust. Hobbes thought that in the absence of regulation, a man was not wise to trust that others would act cooperatively. In a world in which one man's gain is another's loss, trust can be injurious to your health. But regulations and dependable enforcement can change the world; they can change the games men play from a Prisoner's Dilemma to an Assurance Game.[23] In a properly regulated world, each man can trust that others won't do him wrong without knowing much about them. With the sword of an enforcer of honesty over everyone's head, B does not need to know much about A to know that A will not act dishonestly. Hobbes showed how men who were committed to self-

---

[23] If x_1 is the situation in which a player X does not cooperate, and x_0 one in which she does, then the preference schedule of player A in the Assurance Game is $a_0b_0 > a_1b_0 > a_1b_1 > a_0b_1$ and the schedule of player B is $a_0b_0 > a_0b_1 > a_1b_1 > a_1b_0$. With the preference schedule of the Prisoner's Dilemma, cooperation requires enforcement, but with the preference schedule of the Assurance Game, cooperation does not. Each player in the Assurance Game has a reason to cooperate, as long as she believes that the other will.

reliance could still win for themselves the benefits of sociality. Science, on my view, learned the lesson that Hobbes had to teach us.

6 Riddle: How does a wise man know that members of a community are committed to giving true testimony, except by having evidence that each member is a credible witness? Answer: He knows that a condition of membership is that members conform to principles—like Reid's principle of veracity—that require them to be credible witnesses. Such a community resembles the kind of cooperative communities Paul Grice describes in his papers on the logic of talk exchanges.[24]

According to Grice, members of speech communities are committed to the cooperative principle: make your conversational contributions such as is required by the purpose of the talk exchange in which you are engaged. Given the purpose and direction of many exchanges, *e.g.*, to spread the truth, to follow the cooperative principle, a participant must follow what Grice calls the maxims of 'Quality', 'Quantity', 'Relation', and 'Manner'. The maxim of quantity tells the participant to make his contributions as but not more informative than necessary (given the aims of the exchange); the maxim of quality tells him to make his contributions true and base them on evidence. The maxim of relation requires that his contributions be relevant, and the maxim of manner, that they be perspicuous. Participants in such exchanges can be expected to conform to these maxims and can expect other participants to as well (expect others to because they expect that others expect them to). In virtue of these expectations, a participant is able to infer what a speaker is conversationally implying (Grice uses the term 'implicating') by what he says (in contrast to saying or entailing).

Grice's maxims are like Reid's principles. They lead men to be cooperative witnesses and to be honest and credulous when giving and accepting testimony. Grice does better than Reid. His maxim of quality, for example, goes further than Reid's principle of veracity

---

[24] See Grice 1989.

because the latter only requires the participant to be honest, while the former requires that he base his testimony on evidence (which lessens his proneness to error) as well. A participant has more reason to conform to Reid's principle of credulity if he believes that other participants conform to Grice's maxim of quality than merely conform to Reid's principle of veracity.

Not every exchange has purposes that are advanced by Grice's maxims. The kinds of exchanges that are characteristic of the courtroom and other adversarial proceedings are not, for example. The purpose of winning a verdict for a plaintiff or a defendant is not advanced, as a rule, by conforming to the maxim of quality or manner. Here participants are wise to conform to other and perhaps opposing norms. In an adversarial proceeding, Grice's cooperative principle might require maxims that direct participants to be "unco-operative," *e.g.*, to be obscure, ambiguous or irrelevant or to give unsubstantiated testimony.

The purpose of the exchanges within science, in contrast, are more likely served by Grice's maxims. As a result, when members of a scientific community give testimony, they follow and expect others to follow his maxims. The purposes of science are better served if testimony is governed by these maxims than by those that govern testimony in the courtroom, but there is nothing in my idea of epistemic self-reliance that opposes such norms or that prevents a wise man from relying on them.

According to Grice, observance of the cooperative principle and (given certain aims) the four maxims is reasonable (wise), given that the goals of conversation, *e.g.*, giving and receiving information or influencing and being influenced by others, are best attained when everyone observes them. However, in scientific communities there are additional reasons to observe the maxims, *viz.* official sanction. Flouting them carries a steep price; witnesses who testify dishonestly about their own experimental observations risk their reputations and membership in the community. The costs of nonob-servance are known by participants in scientific talk exchanges to far exceed the benefits.

Thus, each participant is wise to observe the maxims and to believe that every other participant is wise to observe them as well. In such a case, a participant does not need to have evidence that a particular witness is credible in order to be wise to believe that he is. Because the participant knows that observance is wise, he is wise to believe that the testimony is offered in accordance with the maxims, and, in particular, that the witness is fitting his words to the maxims of quality and manner. The participant is wise to trust a witness even though he has not observed the witness in the past or has evidence of his record of speaking the truth, for he knows that the witness has good practical reasons to be credible. Society is important here. An individual's trust in a witness—his belief that the witness is credible—is based on the belief that the witness is a member of a society whose members observe a certain set of norms. But such a trust is consistent with the canon, (2), that a wise man has good evidence that witnesses are credible before he believes their testimony, and, if (2) makes the portrait individualistic, then trust (given the appropriate beliefs about a witness's community) is consistent with an individualistic approach to wisdom.

7 Hume is accused of being out of touch with scientific practice. His portrait of wisdom is said to leave too little room for trust. But these accusations are mistaken. His canons, once we adjust (3), do fit our considered judgments and the importance of testimony to science. I have argued that (2) does not overlook the importance of trust and that trust does not oppose self-reliance. The wise man must have his own evidence, but his evidence can show him that he is wise to accept the word of others on trust. The wise man—no longer looking for foundations—is able to learn much from the testimony of others and benefit often from the words of a teacher or the teachings of a text. In short, with one adjustment, Hume's portrait fits our actual epistemic practice very well.[25]

---

[25] There are other and perhaps more interesting ways to understand the claim that wisdom or testimony is socially grounded than the one I adopt here. In a series of

University of Minnesota

References

Brown G. C. and A. E. Mussett. 1981. *The Inaccessible Earth*. London: George Allen & Unwin.

Coady, C. A. J. 1992. *Testimony: A Philosophical Study*. Oxford: Oxford University Press.

Cohen, L. Jonathan. 1981. "Can Human Irrationality be Experimentally Demonstrated?" *The Behavioral and Brain Sciences*, 4: 317-70.

Foley, Richard. 1994. "Egoism in Epistemology." In *Socializing Epistemology*. F. F. Schmitt, ed. Lanham, Md.: Rowman and Littlefield, 53-73.

Goodman, Nelson. 1965. *Fact, Fiction, and Forecast*. New York: Bobbs-Merrill.

Grice, G. P. 1989. "Logic and Conversation." In *Studies in the Way of Words*. Cambridge, Mass.: Harvard University Press, 20-40.

Hardwig, John. 1985. "Epistemic Dependence." *Journal of Philosophy*, 82, No. 7: 335-49.

Hume, David. 1955. *An Inquiry Concerning Human Understanding*. C. W. Hendel, ed. New York: Bobbs-Merrill.

James, William. 1979. "The Will to Believe." In *The Will to Believe and Other Essays in Popular Philosophy*. Cambridge, Mass.: Harvard University Press, 13-33.

Laplace, Pierre. 1951. *Philosophical Essay on Probabilities*, 2nd ed. F. W. Truscott and F. L. Emory, trs. New York: Dover.

Owen, David. 1987. "Hume Versus Price on Miracles and Prior Probabilities: Testimony and the Bayesian Calculation." *Philosophical Quarterly*, 37: 187-202.

Pascal, Blaise. 1904. *Pensées de Blaise Pascal*. In *Oeuvres complètes* (14 vols.) XI-XIII. L. Brunschvicg, ed. Paris: Hachette.

Pascal, Blaise. 1966. *Pensees*. A. J. Krailsheimer, tr. Baltimore: Penguin.

Plato. 1973. *Theaetetus*. J. McDowell, tr. Oxford: Clarendon Press.

---

papers, Fred Will argues that knowledge is a human institution and as such is constituted by social practices (*e.g.*, 1997, chs. 5, 6, and 8). His idea is not that Reid's canons better portray wisdom than Hume's but that a wise man is able to understand or apply any canon or principle only because he engages with others in a process that is fundamentally social. Will might be correct, but whether he is does not resolve my question, *viz.*, whether epistemically self-reliant men, *i.e.*, ones committed to (2), can carry out the practice of history or science as well as epistemically social men, *i.e.*, ones committed to (2*).

I thank my colleague Naomi Scheman for helpful comments on previous drafts of this paper.

Reid, Thomas. 1969. *Essays on the Intellectual Powers of Man*. B. Brody, ed. Cambridge, Mass.: MIT. Press.

Reid, Thomas. 1975. *An Inquiry into the Human Mind on the Principles of Common Sense*. In *Thomas Reid's Inquiry and Essays*. R. Beanblossom and K. Lehrer, eds. New York: Bobbs-Merrill.

Sobel, Jordan Howard. 1987. "On the Evidence of Testimony for Miracles: A Bayesian Interpretation of David Hume's Analysis." *Philosophical Quarterly*, 37: 166-86.

Tversky, A. and D. Kahneman. 1974. "Judgment under Uncertainty: Heuristics and Biases." *Science* 185: 1124-31.

Welbourne, Michael. 1986. *The Community of Knowledge*. Aberdeen: University of Aberdeen Press.

Will, Frederick. 1997. *Pragmatism and Realism*. K. R. Westphal, ed. Lanham, Md.: Rowman & Littlefield.

5

Presuppositions of Inference

Marcus G. Singer

1 INTRODUCTION

To suppose is to assume or take for granted. To presuppose is to assume, or take for granted, in advance, prior to the activity or enterprise in which one is engaging. It is to take for granted implicitly, unconsciously, unwittingly. If we say, "Let us suppose" or "Let us assume," our supposition is deliberate, conscious, explicit. "Let us presuppose," though the usage is admissible, borders on self-contradiction, is akin to saying "Let us suppose in advance, unwittingly, unconsciously, implicitly." To presuppose is also to assume or suppose silently—though we can break the silence—as we can also succeed to some extent in making our presuppositions explicit, in becoming aware of them, and subjecting them to the light of intelligence. Every art and every inquiry has its presuppositions, and to examine these presuppositions, in various areas of activity and inquiry, is a central aim of philosophy.

The term 'presupposition' is one of a family of terms beginning with 'pre-,' where this prefix signifies something prior to or in advance of, either logically or temporally, or superior in rank or quality or force. Some other members of this family, arranged in no predetermined order, are 'preoccupied,' 'prerequisite,' 'prearranged,' 'preview,' 'presentence,' 'pre-eminent,' 'predisposed,' 'predominant,' 'prenatal,' 'prejudge,' 'prepackaged,' 'prerecorded,' 'prehistoric,' and 'precondition.' In this set, the prefix in 'preoccupied,' 'predominant,' 'precondition,' and 'presupposition' clearly signifies a logical rather than a temporal priority, as a premise is logically though not temporally prior to a conclusion. This precondition on 'presupposition' has not always been adequately attended to. To be preoccupied is to be occupied or absorbed by something in an overwhelming or dominant way; something that predominates dominates over and above and beyond anything else, no matter how dominant something else is. A precondition is a condition in advance, prior to any other conditions that can be laid down or come upon. Similarly, a presupposition is something supposed or assumed prior to and in a way that is necessary for whatever activity or belief presupposes it. Without the presupposition it could not be the activity or belief that it is.

When do presuppositions become preconceptions? Do they? The question presupposes that they do. And they do not. Notice that the question does not preconceive that they do—such an assertion is nonsense. Notice also that "to presuppose" functions as a verb; "to preconceive" does not. "Let us preconceive" is nonsense *per se*. Preconceptions are ideas formed in advance before one can possibly know or form a reliable opinion, encrusted remains of previously living ideas, the stuff of ideology, not of inquiry. Presuppositions may become preconceptions, prejudices, hardened attitudes. That is a danger to be guarded against. We can do without preconceptions, we cannot do without presuppositions. They govern us in all we do, in all we say, in all we think, whether we do, say, or think well or badly.

Presuppositions are like habits and, like habits, can be examined and criticized and modified. In the process of examining them, making them explicit, we are still engaging certain habits, still presupposing. We can break a habit only by acquiring a contrary habit; arguably, we can dispense with a presupposition only by presupposing its contrary. We are not limited merely to presupposing it, we can establish or prove its contrary, but there are presuppositions in this process as well. A necessary presupposition is a presupposition that cannot be dispensed with.

Presuppositions are typically though not always social, acquired in and through one's culture, and tend to be common in a culture.

The presuppositions of a culture provide that culture's implicit philosophy and outlook on life and morals. Whitehead has nicely epitomized this:

> When you are criticising the philosophy of an epoch, do not chiefly direct your attention to those intellectual positions which its exponents feel it necessary explicitly to defend. There will be some fundamental assumptions which adherents of all the variant systems within the epoch unconsciously presuppose. Such assumptions appear so obvious that people do not know what they are assuming because no other way of putting things has ever occurred to them. With these assumptions a certain limited number of types of philosophic systems are possible, and this group of systems constitutes the philosophy of the epoch.[1]

These unconscious and fundamental assumptions are presuppositions.

Collingwood pioneered in the theory of presuppositions, and developed an account of the presuppositions of questions, which served as the basis of his "logic of question and answer." On Collingwood's view, every statement is an answer to some question and every question rests on a presupposition, which must be made explicit if the question is to be understood and answered rightly. The following somewhat overemphatic passage conveys some idea of the nature of Collingwood's theory of presuppositions:

> Whenever anybody states a thought in words, there are a great many more thoughts in his mind than are expressed in the statement. Among these there are some which stand in a peculiar relation to the thought he has stated: they are not merely its context, they are its presuppositions.[2]

As Donagan pointed out, Collingwood is unwarrantedly presupposing that presupposing is an act of the mind:

---

[1] Whitehead 1932, 61; cf. ix, x, 108.

[2] Collingwood 1940, 21. Collingwood's theory of presuppositions is developed mainly in chs. 4 and 5; a somewhat different version is presented in Collingwood 1939, ch. 5. Collingwood's limitations—exemplified by his regarding *Principia Mathematica* as "typographical jargon" (1939, 36n)—are amply outweighed by his insights. The best discussion of Collingwood, by far, is Donagan 1962. Another fine discussion is Ritchie 1948.

Collingwood . . . incorporated into the very fabric of his theory a suggestion that presupposing is an act, and implicitly an act of thought. But, by
definition, it cannot possibly be an act of thought . . .. Presupposing something . . . is . . . being logically committed to accept it by the questions you
raise or suffer to be asked . . .. As Collingwood defined it, presupposing is
not an act of consciousness, but the state of being committed by your
questions, at least provisionally, to accepting something.[3]

What you are presupposing by the questions you ask is "a sheer
matter of logic, just as it is a sheer matter of logic that, when you
make a statement, you imply all that it logically entails."[4] So what
you are presupposing is not a matter of what you are thinking, even
unconsciously, any more than what you are implying is a matter of
what you are thinking, even unconsciously. "Since presupposing
something is being committed to accept it by the questions you ask,
it is no more an act of consciousness, and therefore no more an act
of thought, than logically implying something."[5]

Collingwood's theory of presuppositions is a theory of the presuppositions of questions. Strawson later developed a notion of the
presuppositions of statements, contextually defining 'presupposes'
as:

S presupposes S_1 =$_{df.}$ the truth of S_1 is a necessary condition of the truth or
falsity of S.

On the basis of this account, Strawson gave an analysis of the
existential import of universal statements which he took to circum-
vent Russell's theory of descriptions.[6] Black has discussed the
presuppositions of definitions, of words, and of sentences, in the

---

[3] Donagan 1962, 69, 70, 72.

[4] Donagan 1962, 69–70.

[5] Donagan 1962, 270; cf. 269, 271; also 273: "A presupposition of which you are
unaware no more lurks, unseen but powerful, in the recesses of your unconscious
mind than does a conclusion you have failed to draw."

[6] Strawson 1952, esp. 18, 175–76, 213. See also Strawson 1950; Sellars 1954;
and Strawson 1954. On Strawson's account, and how it differs from Collingwood's, Donagan is especially acute; see 1962, 70–72. Strawson's later account of
presuppositions is in his 1959, 184, 190–93, 199–204, 228.

process throwing considerable light on the nature of presuppositions; Black's discussions made it manifest that presuppositions cannot be dispensed with.[7]

The discussion here will concentrate, not on the presuppositions of questions or statements, nor on the presuppositions of definitions, words, or sentences, but on the presuppositions of inference.

Sometimes inferring is like guessing. "I infer that you lost it" can mean "It is my guess that you lost it." It is also like assuming. Assumptions are often inferences, made tentatively. "Since you can't find it anywhere, I assume that you lost it" is only more idiomatic, not more accurate, than "Since you can't find it anywhere, I infer that you lost it." To say "we assume that" or "we have to assume that" is to indicate that the assumption—the inference—referred to, though supported by some evidence, is supported by slender evidence that falls far short of being conclusive but nonetheless will explain the occurrence in question. Inference is a mental process which, when captured in words, becomes an inference, also called an argument, susceptible to logical display and analysis. A purely mental process such as inference, which we think of as taking place in our heads, still involves presuppositions, whether we think of them or not. They are what is involved in the inferences we make, whether we make them silently, in our heads, thinking without utterance, or make them explicitly and overtly.

A *presupposition of an inference* is whatever must hold or be true in order for the inference to be valid. *The principle of an inference* is a general proposition, covering a class of inferences, that brings out the connection between premise and conclusion in virtue of which the inference, if valid, is valid. The principle of an inference is one of its presuppositions, but not all the presuppositions of an inference can serve as its principle.

---

[7] Black 1954, also 53–54, 57; Black 1962, also 165–66. Another discussion worth registering is Rescher 1961.

2 Presuppositions of Formal Logic

In a paper of 1932—"A Set of Postulates for the Foundation of Logic"—Alonzo Church observed that every formal system of logic presupposes a knowledge of the meaning of certain symbols other than the undefined terms of the formal system and assumes "an understanding of a certain body of principles which these symbols are used to express," and that in every such formal system the postulates must use some terms other than the undefined terms of the system.[8] As Church points out, "formulas composed of symbols to which no meaning is attached cannot define a procedure of proof or justify an inference from one formula to another" and "we are . . . obliged to use in some at least of our postulates other symbols than the undefined terms of the formal system, and to presuppose a knowledge of the meaning of those symbols, as well as to assume an understanding of a certain body of principles which these symbols are used to express . . .."[9] Here are some of the "principles of intuitive logic" uncovered by Church.

> We assume an ability to write symbols and to arrange them in a certain order on a page, and the ability to recognize different occurrences of *the same* symbol and to distinguish between such a double occurrence of a symbol and the occurrence of *distinct* symbols. And we assume the possibility of dealing with a formula as a unit, of copying it at any desired point, and of recognizing other formulas as being *the same or distinct* . . ..
>
>   We assume that we know what it is to be a proposition of intuitive logic, and that we are able to assert such propositions, not merely one proposition, but various propositions in succession. And . . . we assume the permanency of a proposition once asserted, so that it may at any later stage be reverted to and used as if just asserted.[10]

These principles of intuitive logic are among the presuppositions of inference. They are presuppositions of formal logic, what must hold if the inferences of formal logic are to be valid, or, indeed, possi-

---

[8] Church 1932, 349–51.

[9] Church 1932, 349.

[10] Church 1932, 350–51.

ble. And Church's ingenious list can be extended almost indefinitely. Here are some other presuppositions of formal logic, that is, of formal inference.

We presuppose that a symbol handwritten on a page is the same as the symbol in a transcribed or typewritten or printed copy of that page, that the symbol printed in different type or a different font is the same symbol carrying the same meaning. We assume, presuppose, also that the location of a symbol on a page—barring special cases—that is to say, whether it occurs in a given rendition of it in my handwriting or yours, or in chalk on a board or in pencil or in ink or in blue or black or green or white, or on the right hand side or middle or left hand side of the page or the board, is indifferent to its interpretation, unless its configuration or color or location is specified as significant by some other specific stipulation of the system. Minding our p's and q's, in this context, consists in being able to distinguish 'p' from 'q' no matter in what form they are set down, and this entails knowing that the microscopic and minute differences in the appearance of 'p' in different locations, no matter what the vehicle of print or writing, are indifferent to the identity of one and the same symbol.

Now all this is a matter of the presuppositions of inference, in this case formal inference. And, although the presuppositions can be altered in particular contexts by specific stipulation or convention, some such presuppositions must hold for the stipulation or convention itself. Nor could such presuppositions be "proved" or "established" without being in turn presupposed. This indeed is the only sort of proof they can have—that they are presupposed in all inference. They cannot be proved by deduction from premises that entail them without such derivations still presupposing them. And this is the best sort of proof there can be. To be presupposed in all inference and all reasoning is conclusive proof of whatever is so presupposed.

3 PRESUPPOSITIONS AND PROOF

In this connection, the following claim has special pertinence:

Proof always presupposes the validity of logical principles. In proving, we must appeal to the capacity of our hearers or readers to distinguish between valid and invalid arguments.[11]

The first statement here is manifestly true. The second statement shifts to thinking of proving as a rhetorical and not a logical act. The first, however, uses 'proof' in a logical manner, in which proving means demonstrating and not convincing. And a proof does presuppose the validity of logical principles, in particular the logical principles used in the "proof." The principles of logic, especially but not solely the principles of "intuitive logic," are what are presupposed in every proof or attempt at proof. ('Proof' is an achievement word, as is 'refutation'; 'invalid proof' is, taken literally, self-contradictory; 'proof' in that expression must be taken as within scare quotes.) They are necessary and omnipresent presuppositions. Proofs are proofs of other things, not of the validity of logical principles, and no one proof can prove the validity of logical principles. To put it another way, the principles of logic cannot be the conclusions of probative arguments, cannot be proved by being deduced from premises. Logical principles are presupposed in, not proved, by specific and particular proofs, are proved by being presupposed in any and every proof. Every refutation, even an attempted refutation of the principles of logic, presupposes them as well; this is the essence of a transcendental proof, and this is the true substance of what Aristotle was maintaining in the famous passage in *Metaphysics* Book Gamma (chs. 3 and 4), in which he argued that the principle of noncontradiction cannot be demonstrated by being deduced from premises more certain than it.

A principle which every one must have who understands anything that is, is not a hypothesis, and that which every one must know who knows anything, he must already have when he comes to a special study. Evidently then such a principle is the most certain of all . . ..[12]

---

[11] Mitchell 1962, 59.
[12] *Metaphysics*, 4:3, 1005b 15–18.

4 IMPLYING AND PRESUPPOSING

What is the difference between implying and presupposing? In an analysis of presupposing that foreshadowed Strawson's, Geach threw considerable light on this matter:

> It is important to distinguish my view that the existence of the present king of France is *presupposed* by the assertion "the King of France is bald" from Russell's view that his existence is *implied* by this assertion. If p implies q, and q is false, p is of course false. But to say p presupposes q is to say that p is an answer to a question that does not arise unless q is true. If q is false, or if q in turn is an answer to a question that does not arise, the assertion of p is not false but simply out of place.[13]

This analysis itself presupposes an account of the logic of question and answer of the sort that Collingwood attempted and that Geach himself takes for granted—that is to say, presupposes—and also of what it is for a question to arise or not to arise and for an answer to be out of place. These are important conceptions indeed. Geach tells us that "When a question does not arise, the only proper way of answering it is to say so and explain the reason; the 'plain' affirmative or negative answer, though grammatically possible, is *out of place*. (I do not call it 'meaningless' because the word is a mere catchword nowadays.)"[14] To be sure, we can learn how to use these ideas by considering the examples to which they are applied, and for many purposes that is enough, but this is really only the beginning of an analysis.

In his account of the fallacy of 'many questions,' Geach provides an illuminating example of the way in which Collingwood's theory of presuppositions—though Geach never mentions Collingwood—ties in with his and Strawson's. *Regardez*:

> . . . let us take a typical example of the fallacy: the demand for "a plain answer—yes or no!" to the question "have you been happier since your wife died?" Three questions are here involved:

---

[13] Geach 1950, 86.
[14] Geach 1950, 85.

1. Have you ever had a wife?
2. Is she dead?
3. Have you been happier since then?

    The act of asking question 2 presupposes an affirmative answer to question 1; if the true answer to 1 is negative, question 2 *does not arise*. The act of asking question 3 presupposes an affirmative answer to question 2; if question 2 does not arise, of if the true answer to it is negative, question 3 *does not arise.*[15]

Note that Geach states that it is the act of asking a question that presupposes, does not say this about the question itself. I am not clear on the implications, or the presuppositions, of this, if any, since I do not see that it is necessary.

What is the difference, in relation to inference, between implying and presupposing? Geach's answer will not avail here, where we are dealing, not with statements construed as answers to questions, but with inferences. Notice how the term 'implies' is used in the following passage: "When one condemns homosexuality or masturbation or the use of contraceptives [or whatever] on the ground that it is unnatural, one implies that whatever is unnatural is bad, wrongful, perverse."[16] 'Implies' is used here to mean the same as 'presupposes.' What one "implies" is that a certain principle holds, and one "implies" it in the sense of presupposing it. The general principle stated is a presupposition of the inference signified by the words 'on the ground that.'

But if an inference presupposes something, does it not at the same time imply it? In a sense, as Bradley would say, but not as such. If *A* presupposes *P*, *P* is more general than *A*, has a wider scope or range. If *A* implies *B*, in the sense of entailing it, then *B* is no more general than *A*. It is the inference that *B* because of *A* that implies *P*, in the sense of presupposing it. If *P* is false, the inference is groundless. And the whole inference is an instance of contextual, not logical, implication. One who says '*B* because of *A*' implies *P* in the sense that, in *saying* '*B* because of *A*,' one implies

---

[15] Geach 1950, 84–85.
[16] Adapted from Leiser 1973, 52.

that one accepts the general principle *P*. But the *speaker* is not thereby presupposing the general principle. The *inference* presupposes it, whether one asserts '*B* because of *A*' or not, and one implies, through stating the inference that *B* on account of *A*, that one accepts it. It is not the proposition, that something is bad because it is unnatural, that implies the generalization that whatever is unnatural is bad. It is the *utterance or assertion* of the proposition that (contextually) implies it.[17] The proposition—or rather, the inference involved in the proposition—presupposes the generalization, in the sense that if the generalization is false, the inference is invalid.

The terms 'implies' and 'presupposes' can be used interchangeably, and often are. However, the relations signified are not identical, and the 'implies' that means the same as 'presupposes' is not the 'implies' either of the ordinary conditional or of strict or necessary implication. If *A* implies *B*, that is, logically implies *B*, *B* is not more general than *A*, unless 'implies' is used in the sense of 'presupposes'.

5 TERMINOLOGY

We now review a number of perfectly familiar logical facts. There is less uniformity on these matters than one might suppose.

An argument is a set of statements or propositions arranged in a definite order, that of premises to conclusion. The premises consist of that proposition or set of propositions—usually two or more, in a limiting case one—*from* which the conclusion follows or is inferred. The conclusion is that statement or proposition implied by or inferred *from* the premises. Clearly 'premise' and 'conclusion,' in

---

[17] Nowell-Smith 1954, 80–84, discusses contextual implication. An excellent discussion is Grant 1958. Whether one speaks of contextual or of pragmatic implication, as Grant recommends, is, to my mind, indifferent. On Grant's view, "genuine pragmatic inferences . . . are neither logical deductions nor ordinary empirical inferences" (1958, 306), but rather inferences of propositions from actions, such as uttering or asserting.

this usage and in this context, are polar terms—whenever there is an instance of the one there is an instance of the other.[18]

In formal logic, an inference is the same as an argument, but outside of formal logic the term 'inference' is often used to refer to the process of inferring or deriving the conclusion—also sometimes called the inference—from the premises. Hence 'inference' can stand for a product, an inference or argument statable in words or symbols, and it can stand for a process, the process that leads to that product. By a common yet still curious transference of meaning 'argument' is often used to stand for the premises of an inference, and as just mentioned 'inference' is often used to stand for the conclusion of the argument, what is inferred. So we could speak of the arguments (premises) for an inference (conclusion), and refer to the whole, indifferently, as an inference or an argument, though there is not much point in it. I do no more here than observe the phenomenon and henceforth use the terms 'inference' and 'argument' interchangeably, counting on the context to make it clear should some other sense be meant. So the presuppositions of inference are the presuppositions of argument.

I regard the distinction between sentences, statements, and propositions as important and useful. There are those who do not, but I am not about to argue the point here. We use or utter sentences to make statements, to express propositions. Sentences are linguistic entities, propositions are logical ones. Except in abstract logical systems, sentences or strings of symbols have no logical relations, have only physical and syntactical properties. When we speak of propositions we are engaging their semantic properties, and when we speak of a statement, or an utterance, we are engaging pragmatic properties. A proposition is whatever can be true or false. Often there is no distinction of consequence between a proposition

---

[18] More precisely, they are existentially, not just conceptually, polar. Terms are conceptually polar if the meaning of one involves the meaning of the other; they are existentially polar if the existence of one entails the existence of the other; and existential polarity entails conceptual polarity. There is interdependence, or multi-polarity, among the concepts of 'argument,' 'premise,' and 'conclusion.' These ideas are explored in Singer 1990–91.

and a statement. When one wants to convey that ambiguity is absent and that what one is saying is as context free as possible—it is impossible to be altogether free from context—one speaks of a proposition. Otherwise one speaks of a statement, and by extension we can speak of a statement being true or false, though it is worth noting that 'statement' is ambiguous as between the act of stating and the thing stated. Nominalists are given to speaking of true or false sentences; in my view what they are doing is unwittingly referring to the interpretations of sentences, either propositions or statements. A sentence is a group of words, and is no more true or false than its constituents. What is true or false is what is said by means of the sentence, that is, the statement or proposition. An ambiguous sentence is one that expresses different propositions; the same sentence, without being ambiguous, can express different propositions in different contexts; and different sentences, in either the same or different contexts, can express the same proposition. The same holds for the relationships between sentences and statements. The distinction important in this context is that, although statements can be ambiguous, propositions, by definition, cannot. But for the most part I speak interchangeably of statements or propositions. The occasions on which the distinction is important are those on which a statement can be understood, owing to the ambiguity of its constituent words or to a shifting of the context, as having different meanings.[19]

---

[19] Barker 1980, has some interesting remarks on this point: "To say that the premises and conclusions of arguments are sentences (as was said earlier in this section) is a serviceable but crude way of speaking . . .. [I]t glosses over the distinction between a declarative sentence and the statement, or assertion, that a speaker makes by uttering the sentence on a particular occasion. Saying that the premises and conclusion of an argument are sentences suggests that sentences as such are true or false and that we can analyze the logic of an argument merely by studying the sentences (the series of words) that occur in it. But we cannot do that . . .." (22). Given what Barker goes on to say on this matter there is some room for wondering whether the usage is even serviceable. For when dealing with concrete arguments or interpreted argument forms one is not dealing merely with sentences—the verdict should precede the sentence. There is also a question whether the terminology used—as between sentence, statement, proposition, judgment, all mentioned by Barker—is merely a matter of taste or choice, as he suggests, or reflects some basic philosophical presuppositions.

An argument or inference is not itself a proposition or statement, but is made up of propositions, so an inference or argument (where by 'inference' one is not referring to the conclusion of the argument) is not appropriately or correctly said to be true or false. Such talk equivocates between saying that the inference, meaning argument, is "logical" and saying that the inference, meaning its conclusion, is true. An argument is valid or invalid, sound or unsound (and may also be appraised as effective or ineffective, persuasive, convincing, plausible, reasonable or unreasonable, significant or trivial, good or bad, conclusive or inconclusive, strong or weak, probable or improbable, and so on, and such appraisals have their points in their proper contexts). In what follows I adhere to the standard logical usage, in which to say that an argument is valid is to say that a certain relationship holds between its premises and its conclusion, the relationship of entailment or logical implication, in virtue of which the conclusion follows from or may validly be inferred from the premises; that is to say, an argument is valid if it is impossible for the premises to be true and the conclusion false; and an argument is sound if it is valid and its premises are true.[20]

Though an argument is not itself a proposition, for every argument there is a corresponding proposition, conditional in form, asserting that the premises imply the conclusion. If we let 'A/B' stand for any argument, with 'A' representing the premises and 'B' the conclusion and '/' ('slash') the connecting term 'therefore' or 'so,' then the statement 'If A then B,' or the proposition that A implies B, is its *corresponding conditional*. On occasion the corresponding or associated conditional is referred to as the principle of

---

[20] Strange as it may seem to those brought up in one tradition, these terms are used differently by those brought up in another, with some writers interchanging the use. We can find a different use in some textbooks of logic, *e.g.* Pollock 1979, 8: "An argument form is sound if, and only if, its corresponding conditional is formally analytic"; and Anderson and Johnstone 1962, 79: "When the deduction of a conclusion from given premises can be found, we shall speak of the inference by which this conclusion is reached as a *sound inference*. (The phrase 'valid argument' is sometimes used in this connection, but we shall want to use the word 'valid' for a different purpose later.) . . . If there is a deduction—*i.e.*, a sound inference—then it is impossible for all its premises to be true when its conclusion is false."

the argument, but this usage is not helpful. The principle of an argument is a general proposition that brings out the connection between premises and conclusion in a nontrivial way, and in this sense, as obscure as it is, the principle of an argument is not identical with its corresponding conditional. If A/B is valid, then 'If A then B' is necessarily (logically) true; conversely, if 'If A then B' is necessarily true, then A/B is valid. Again, just to fix ideas, where it is necessarily true that A implies B, then A necessarily (logically) implies B, and if A necessarily implies B, then A/B is valid; and conversely, if A/B is valid, then A necessarily implies B and it is necessarily true that A implies B.

So much for the familiar facts, some but not all facts of terminology.

6 THE PRINCIPLE OF AN INFERENCE

Peirce referred to the principle of an argument as its guiding or leading principle. In "Some Consequences of Four Incapacities" (1868), Peirce said:

> Every argument implies the truth of a general principle of inferential procedure (whether involving some matter of fact concerning the subject of argument, or merely a maxim relating to a system of signs), according to which it is a valid argument. If this principle is false, the argument is a fallacy . . .[21]

In saying that every argument implies the truth of a general principle, Peirce is in effect saying that every argument presupposes the truth of a general principle, so this principle, in the terminology being used here, is a presupposition of the arguments it governs. Notice that this "general principle of inferential procedure" has the same relation to the argument as presuppositions have—if it is false the argument is invalid. In "The Fixation of Belief" (1877) Peirce spoke of "*guiding* principles of inference":

---

[21] Peirce 1932–34, cited here in the standard way by reference to volume and paragraph number: 5.280, or vol. 5, par. 280, for the passage quoted.

The particular habit of mind which governs this or that inference may be formulated in a proposition whose truth depends on the validity of the inferences which the habit determines; and such a formula is called a *guiding principle* of inference. Suppose . . . that we observe that a rotating disk of copper quickly comes to rest when placed between the poles of a magnet, and we infer that this will happen with every disk of copper. The guiding principle is, that what is true of one piece of copper is true of another. Such a guiding principle with respect to copper would be much safer than with regard to many other substances—brass, for example.[22]

Peirce added that "A book might be written to signalize all the most important of these guiding principles of reasoning,"[23] but he never wrote the book, and it is still not clear how it could be written. For the principle, that "what is true of one piece of copper is true of another," seems to me true only in certain restricted contexts, which Peirce did not signalize. Perhaps he meant, or had in mind, that the magnetic or electrical or chemical properties of copper are invariant, or something akin. Otherwise, what is true of one piece of copper, say the one I have now in my pocket, is not true of another, say the one I have now in my coin collection. The one I have in my coin collection is a rare coin, the one I have in my pocket is a piece of wire. Peirce says that the truth of a guiding principle depends on the validity of the inferences it governs; this may amount only to a difference in emphasis, but it is also true that the validity of the inferences depends on the truth of the principle: if the principle is false, the class of inferences is invalid. (I deliberately bypass the implication that the principle is something thought of or present to the mind.)

In "On the Natural Classification of Arguments" (1867), Peirce wrote:

Every inference involves the judgment that, if *such* propositions as the premisses are are true, then a proposition related to them, as the conclusion is, must be, or is likely to be, true. The principle implied in this judgment,

---

[22] Peirce 1932–34, 5.367.
[23] Peirce 1932–34, 5.368.

respecting a genus of argument, is termed the *leading principle* of the argument . . . .. A *valid* argument is one whose leading principle is true.[24]

Here Peirce speaks of the *leading* principle of an argument and the leading principle is also a general principle covering an indefinite number of concrete arguments—"respecting a *genus* of argument"—and consequently cannot be identified with the associated conditional, though it could be a generalized version of the associated conditional. As to leading and guiding, the only difference I can discern is that the *leading* principle of an argument, as Peirce has implicitly defined it, states that the premisses of an argument necessarily imply its conclusion, whereas no such necessity seems to attach to what he elsewhere called the *guiding* principle of an argument. It is not clear, however, that Peirce meant there to be any distinction between them, and the one suggested seems very implausible.[25] Peirce says about enthymemes that "such an argument is rendered logical by adding as a premiss that which it assumes as a leading principle."[26] On the hypothesis just considered, this would imply that the missing premiss of a valid enthymeme is a necessary truth, which is too implausible to suppose for a moment.[27] Peirce's scattered writings on this matter, so far as I have been able to determine, seem to provide no clear insight into how to define or to formulate the principle of an inference, though it is a suggestive idea.[28]

---

[24] Peirce 1932–34, 2.462–3.

[25] However, see Peirce 1932–34, 2.588–9 and 2.469.

[26] Peirce 1932–34, 2.449 note.

[27] *Cf.* Peirce 1932–34, 2.588–9.

[28] *Cf.* "On the Algebra of Logic" (1880), Pierce 1932–34, 3.164: "A habit of inference may be formulated in a proposition which shall state that every proposition *c*, related in a given general way to any true proposition *p*, is true. Such a proposition is called the *leading principle* of the class of inferences whose validity it implies. When the inference is first drawn, the leading principle is not present to the mind, but the habit it formulates is active in such a way that, upon contemplating the believed premiss, by a sort of perception the conclusion is judged to be true. Afterwards, when the inference is subjected to logical criticism, we make a new inference, of which one premiss is that leading principle of the former inference, according to which propositions related to one another in a certain way are fit to be premiss and conclusion of a valid inference, while another premiss is

7 PRESUPPOSITIONS AND PREMISES

So every argument, in addition to having premises *from* which the conclusion is derived, has a principle *on the basis* of which the conclusion is derived. In addition, every argument has presuppositions, *in accordance with* which the conclusion is derived. A *presupposition of an argument* or inference is any proposition the truth of which—but not the necessary truth of which—is necessary for the argument to be valid. That is to say, an argument *presupposes* any proposition that must be true in order for the argument to be valid. If any of the presuppositions of A/B is false, then A/B is invalid; and if A/B is valid, then all of its presuppositions are true. But if any, as distinct from all, of the presuppositions of A/B are true, it does not follow that A/B is valid. It depends on which ones are true. An argument does not presuppose that its corresponding conditional is merely true, but that it is necessarily true. The *principle* of an argument is what must *necessarily* be true for the argument to be valid. If (N) 'Necessarily, if A then B,' a presupposition of A/B, is true, then A/B is valid. So no argument has just one presupposition. But N is not the principle of A/B. The principle of A/B is the generalization of N stating that, as Peirce would put it, if A_i, all propositions of the class of A, are true then B_i, all propositions of the class of B, must be true. (This, to be sure, leaves undecided the question how to determine the relevant classes of A and B.) Clearly, if the corresponding conditional of an argument is necessarily true, the argument is valid, and there are presuppositions of inference that are as much presuppositions of the corresponding conditional as of the inference itself.

The associated conditional of an argument is also one of its presuppositions, since every argument presupposes that its corresponding conditional is true. Now the presuppositions of an argu-

---

a fact of observation, namely, that the given relation does subsist between the premiss and conclusion of the inference under criticism; whence it is concluded that the inference is valid." *Cf.* Peirce 1932–34, 3.160–61, 165–71; esp. 3.166: "In the form of inference P/C the leading principle is not expressed; and the inference might be justified on several separate principles."

ment are propositions, and some of them, though not all, can be added to the argument as additional premises from which the conclusion can be derived. The argument resulting from this procedure, however, is actually a new one, different from the former, though closely resembling it. This procedure, as others, such as Peirce and Strawson, have pointed out, can clearly be followed with the associated conditional of the argument—though Peirce spoke of adding the principle of the argument as a premiss. Given the argument A/B, its associated conditional is "If A then B." Call this C. If C is added as a premise, the argument resulting is C&A/B, or

(MP)
    If A then B (C)
    A
    _____
    B.

Such a procedure as this will naturally make any argument valid, provided its other presuppositions are true, but it is, as is obvious, perfectly trivial. Yet consider what it involves. It appears that any argument, no matter how blatantly fallacious, can be made valid merely by adding its associated conditional as a premise. However, this is only appearance. For the argument resulting from this bit of legerdemain is, though similar to the original argument, not the same argument.

The new argument resulting from this Lewis Carroll sort of procedure, C&A/B, has a new and different corresponding conditional, namely (C_1) "If A and C, then B." And this conditional can in turn be added to the argument MP as an explicit premise, generating the argument:

(MP_1)
    If (If A then B) and A, then B (C_1)
    If A then B   (C)
    A
    _____
    B.

MP_1 in turn will have an associated conditional, C_2, "If C_1 and C and A, then B." And the process mentioned can of course go on indefinitely. But it is altogether without point. In the case where the principle of the argument, or the associated conditional, is necessarily true (and if one is necessarily true, so is the other), as is C_1, it is not necessary, but otiose, for it to be added to the argument as a premise. The original argument, MP, is valid as it stands, with its original premises alone, and thus is what Peirce called a *complete* argument. This is exemplified by MP, and MP_1 is its *redundant expansion*. However, where the associated conditional of an argument is not necessarily true, the argument is not valid as it stands. In such a case another premise is needed to ensure its validity, and such an argument can, of course, be transformed into a valid one, without the addition of any substantive premise, by adding the associated conditional to the premises, but the argument resulting is really a different one, related to the original by this process of expansion but not identical with or equivalent to it. However, as is evident, this is a trivial way of conferring validity; it simply shifts the question of validity to the questions whether the associated conditional is true and what is its basis.

8 Univocability

What has just been said is for the most part well-established doctrine, logical matter-of-fact, not likely to be questioned except by someone with well-rehearsed philosophical problems with the very notions of validity, entailment, propositions, necessary truth, and the like. But such an eccentric skeptic will have left us long ago and causes no concern. What I shall argue now is that for every argument there is at least one presupposition that not only need not be added to the argument as a premise, but *cannot* be. Doing so would do nothing toward making the argument valid if it is not already; the new argument resulting would involve exactly the same presupposition, with possibly some differences in wording but with no difference in import; and the *requirement* that this necessary presupposition be added to every argument to ensure its validity would lead to a vicious regress and is, in the end—the end that never comes—self-contradictory. This necessary presupposition is that *the terms used essentially in the statement of the argument* (that is, in statements on which its validity hinges) *retain the same meaning throughout the course of the argument.* I shall call this the "presupposition of constancy of meaning," or for short, the "presupposition of meaning" (PCM).

That the presupposition of constancy of meaning is a presupposition of every argument is not at all recondite but really well known, practically self-evident. If a term used essentially in the statement of an argument shifts in meaning in the course of the argument, the argument cannot be valid. This principle is explicit in the theory of the syllogism, where a violation of it gives rise to the fallacy of four terms, and, though the fallacy named may be peculiar to the theory of the syllogism, the general principle—the principle of the constancy of meaning—of which it is a violation is in no way parochial. Thus, the fact that the syllogism is outmoded in logic studies (it is not outmoded in actual use) and hardly ever taught today in institutions of higher learning by those who want to be using the latest techniques, is of no moment. In symbolic logic a similar principle, the principle of univocability, states that each and every symbol used in a given context must be used within that context in exactly the same way, univocally, a condition to be observed in symbolizing statements variables and functions. So in formal logic this condition is built in, as a precondition. But this does not automatically ensure the condition for concrete arguments, involving interpreted argument forms. And it only confirms the point that the principle of constancy of meaning is a presupposition of all arguments.

The "principle of symbolic uniqueness," as it has also been called, has been formulated thus: "Repetition of terms within a verbal argument must be reflected by repetition of the corresponding symbols in any formal schema assigned to the argument . . . . [T]his rule implies that distinct symbols must be replaced by wholly distinct terms . . .," which implies that this principle has implications, which is not surprising.[29] Another formulation is "When in a

---

[29] Neidorf 1967, 17–18, *cf.* 40; Brown and Stuermann 1965, 82; *cf.* 83–84, "principles for symbolization."

given argument a statement is once represented by a specific symbol, that symbol must regularly represent the same statement throughout the argument"—the equivalent principle obviously applies to functions, predicates, *etc*. Such a principle of notation or symbolization, when enunciated explicitly, is a precondition of proceeding correctly. If not enunciated explicitly—usually it is not—it is still taken for granted implicitly. It is, in other words, a presupposition of the procedure, a "principle of intuitive logic" that must be presupposed in any formal treatment or system and in any interpretation of a logical system that aims at consistency. This principle of "intuitive logic," along with others, can be proved to be a requirement, only exactly the same principles would be presupposed in the proof.

That the presupposition of the constancy of meaning is a necessary condition for validity means, not that it is itself necessary—there is no way an application of it to any particular argument can be a necessary truth—but that its truth is necessary for the validity of any argument to which it applies. And it is an omnipresent presupposition. So it is a proposition that must be true in order for an argument to be valid, yet particular applications of it cannot be logically certified as true. And it is not a premise *from which* the conclusion is derived. The presupposition in question can, in another context, be used as a premise from which a conclusion is derived. For example, the argument K,

(K)   One of the terms used essentially in argument H shifts in meaning
between premises and conclusion

_____

H is invalid—

is a valid argument. But it involves, in meaning and import if not in identical wording, exactly the same presupposition of constancy of meaning. And, since the premise of K is not necessarily true, K does not provide an *a priori* proof that H is invalid.

The demand that this presupposition be added to the argument as a premise, suggested by the maxim to "make all the assumptions explicit," would, as just stated, lead to an infinite regress. Consider the familiar argument L—

(L)
(1) All men are mortal
(2) All Greeks are men

___

(3) All Greeks are mortal.

L is of course valid, but only if the terms 'men,' 'mortals,' and 'Greeks,' along with the logical terms 'all' and 'are,' retain the same meaning, whatever it may be, in the course of the argument. Note incidentally that L is not a sound argument unless 'men' is taken to mean 'human beings' and not 'males,' and if in (1) 'men' means 'males' and in (2) it means 'human beings,' the argument is not valid, even though it appears to be an instance of the valid argument form

(AAA_1)
(1F) All M are P
(2F) All S are M

___

(3F) All S are P

Now, let the presupposition of constancy of meaning, in a suitable interpretation, be added to L as an explicit premise, from which, together with the other premises, the conclusion follows. Then we have L_1—

(L_1)
(1) All men are mortal
(2) All Greeks are men
(4) The term 'men' in (1) has the same meaning it has in (2), the term 'mortal' in (1) has the same meaning it has in (3), and the term 'Greeks' has the same meaning in both (2) and (3)

___

(3) All Greeks are mortal.

Although L_1 is valid, it is a very odd argument, since (4) is a second order statement, referring to the others, and L_1 in turn involves the same general presupposition of constancy of meaning.

For L_1 also presupposes that the terms used in the statement of it retain the same meaning throughout. In order for L_1 to be valid, the occurrence of '(1)' in (4) must refer to the statement labeled as (1), the occurrence of '(2)' in (4) must refer to the statement labeled (2), and so on. This is trivial, to be sure, but not something that can be guaranteed by stipulation. It must be presupposed. And this presupposition itself cannot be logically or necessarily true. Now if *this* presupposition, (5), is added to the premises of L_1, to give by expansion the argument L_2, essentially the same presupposition will be involved in—that is, presupposed by—L_2, though the terms used in the particular statement of it will vary somewhat. And so on, indefinitely. It follows that a presupposition of an argument is not a premise of that argument, the demand that it be added as premise is in general unwarranted, and in the case of the presupposition of the constancy of meaning, logically absurd. Although a proposition that is a presupposition of one argument can be a premise of another, every argument, even one employing it as a premise, presupposes the principle of the constancy of meaning, and the conclusion of the argument is not drawn *from* the presupposition, but from the premises of the argument *in accordance with* the presupposition. To paraphrase a remark of Strawson's, there is no possibility of obtaining a valid argument with so many premises that it can dispense with presuppositions.[30]

Let us restate L_1 in a slightly different way, as in L':

---

[30] Strawson 1952, 209 note: "In general, given any valid inference, it is possible to frame a different valid inference incorporating, as an additional premise, a necessary truth corresponding to the principle of the original inference; and in the early stages of the application of this process, the inference obtained may differ in form from its immediate predecessor. (But there is no hope of obtaining a valid inference with so many premises that it can dispense with a principle.)" Strawson is quite right on this point, on which he was anticipated by Peirce. Unfortunately, if Strawson ever provided an explicit account of 'principle of an inference,' I have not found it, and I have no clear idea how he would explicate it.

(L′)
(1) All men are mortal
(2) All Greeks are men
(4′) The terms used in this argument retain the same meaning throughout

---

(3) All Greeks are men.

Here, in L′, the meaning presupposition (4′) certainly looks different from the corresponding proposition (4) in L$_1$. But just as (4′) is a particular specification, with reference to "this argument," of the general presupposition of constancy of meaning, (4) is a particular specification of (4′). So in their contexts (4′) and (4) have exactly the same meaning, and what was true of (4) would be equally true of (4′). Moreover, the second order and self-referential character of (4′) is evident from the occurrence of the indexical expression 'this argument,' which in the context stands for, and can be replaced by, L′. It is therefore a presupposition of L′ that 'this argument' in (4′) refers to the argument L′, and this presupposition of L′ is not a premise of L′. So adding the statement that "The terms used in this argument retain the same meaning throughout" to L as a premise does not mean that the argument resulting, L′, does not presuppose exactly the same thing. It does. And it will not do to rephrase 4′ as "The terms used in L′ retain the same meaning throughout," for L′ in our rephrased 4′ must be taken as referring to the argument labeled L′, and 4′ is only a particular application of PCM, to L′.

Take L″, containing the contradictory of 4′, "The terms used in this argument do not retain the same meaning throughout." If this is true, then the resulting argument L″ is invalid. This shows that 4′ is a pseudopremise, not a premise of L′ but a presupposition of it. For note the peculiar character of this alleged "premise." If it is false, the argument is invalid. But the truth value of genuine premises makes no difference to the validity of the argument. That is why this is a pseudopremise, not a genuine premise at all, a presupposition of the argument, not a premise of it. Otherwise, since every argument presupposes its own validity, the proposition that "This argument is valid" could be added to any and every argument as a premise. This pseudopremise, "This argument is valid," is a presupposition of every argument, not a premise.

Does every argument presuppose its own validity? Given any argument P/Q, this argument presupposes the proposition that P/Q is a valid argument; if the proposition that P/Q is a valid argument is false, then P/Q is not valid (and conversely, in this case, the presupposition is true if and only if the argument is valid). Hence, every argument presupposes its own validity, and this presupposition of validity is not a component in, a premise of, the argument itself. It is another omnipresent presupposition of inference, along with the presupposition of the constancy of meaning, and adding this presupposition of validity to the premises of the original would not validate it if it is not originally valid. For one premise of this expanded argument would be *about* this expanded argument, adds nothing to the validity of the argument and could be dropped without invalidating it, and the expanded argument containing this "premise" would presuppose exactly the same thing, that "this argument is valid." So the presupposition cannot be eliminated by attempts to transform it into a premise.

Hence, a presupposition is not a premise, and neither the meaning presupposition nor the presupposition of validity can be a premise of any argument to which it ostensibly refers. Each can be a premise of an argument about some other argument—though this other argument will still involve exactly the same omnipresent presupposition—but it cannot serve as a premise in any argument referring to the argument in which it is a premise. For the validity of an argument is independent of the truth-value of its components, its premises and conclusion, though its validity is not independent of the truth-value of its presuppositions.

9 EQUIVOCATION

Consider now an example of an argument that is flagrantly invalid, owing to obvious equivocation:

(5) All bishops move only diagonally

(M)   (6) Fulton J. Sheen is a bishop

---

(7) Fulton J. Sheen moves only diagonally.

Here the presupposition of meaning is false, is not satisfied, and the argument is invalid. Now suppose we add the premise (8), "The term 'bishop' in (5) has the same meaning as 'bishop' in (6)," obtaining the expanded argument (M_1). In point of fact, (8) is false. But let us imagine that 'Fulton J. Sheen' is the proper name of a particular chess piece, a bishop, in a specific set of chess pieces; or else that 'moves diagonally' is some esoteric way of describing certain actions of officers of the church. So let us imagine that (8) is true by definition or stipulation. Is the resulting argument then valid? If (8) is taken as a statement of fact, we might be inclined to say that the argument is valid, only obviously unsound, indeed absurd. If (8) is taken as a stipulation, the argument will be valid, and the question of its soundness will remain open, whether anyone is interested in it or not. But if it is valid, it is so only because, if this presupposition holds—if this premise is true—then the argument is an instance of a valid argument form—

All M are P

(AII) S is an M

S is a P—

and of course the argument M_1, which contains (8) as an explicit premise, is not an instance of an argument that is normally dealt with, since (8)—or something like (8)—is a presupposition of the application to M of the schema AII, and not itself a premise. Moreover, there is no *a priori* guarantee that the terms used in (8) have the same meaning in (8) as they have in the rest of the argument, that, for example, the occurrence of '(6)' in (8) refers to the statement labeled (6) in the statement of M_1. This is something that must be presupposed. So the new argument obtained from M by this sort of expansion involves the same presupposition of constancy of meaning, and it should by now be obvious that it is impossible to state an argument so "completely" and "explicitly" that this presupposition is never involved. No matter how many premises of this sort are added, the same presupposition is involved. And, if this presupposition is taken as a premise from which, together with the other premises, the conclusion follows, then, since the argument will not be valid unless this "premise" is true, the validity of the argument will depend on the truth of its premises. But this is self-contradictory. It follows that it is logically impossible for every presupposition of an argument to be a premise of the argument. The validity of an argument depends on the truth of its presuppositions; it does not depend on the truth of its premises. And there is no possibility of formulating a valid inference with so many premises that it can dispense with presuppositions.

10   ENTHYMEMES

An enthymeme is typically defined as a syllogism with a premise that is suppressed or missing or unstated, or a conclusion that is suppressed or unstated. By a natural extension, the term 'enthymeme' can be applied to any argument, whether a syllogism or not, with a missing or suppressed or unstated premise. (For present purposes we can ignore arguments with unstated conclusion.) Now what is meant by 'missing' or 'suppressed'? How is one to tell when a premise is missing or suppressed? In practice there is usually no difficulty; one can usually tell from the context, or from the actual example used. For instance, the words "She must be poor—look at her clothes" clearly express an argument, though there is no explicit statement of a premise, only an indication of what the premises are. In this case there are two plausible choices: (a) "Her clothes are shabby, and All people wearing shabby clothes are poor"; or (b) "Her clothes are shabby, and All poor people wear shabby clothes." The first argument is valid but unsound, the second is invalid. Naturally there is no certainty that either of these is what the user of the form of words mentioned had in mind. But what needs to be noticed here is the language usually employed in discoursing about such cases, and, in general, in talking about enthymemes. It is usually said, to take some phrases from logic books chosen pretty much at random, that the premises missing from an enthymeme are "needed assumptions," "necessary premises," or "assumptions that play an essential part in the argument."[31] And we are frequently told such things as that "The arguments encountered in conversation or writing usually take much for granted. Criticism of such arguments calls for making the unstated premises or *assumptions* explicit."[32] Such language may seem to imply that the missing premises of an enthymeme, which are said to be "assumptions of the argument" or "what the argument takes for granted," are presuppositions of the argument in the sense defined. They are not. If these missing or unstated premises are assumed or presupposed by the argument they are presupposed in some other sense. For they are not required to be *true*, in order for the argument to be valid. They only require to be *made explicit* in order for the argument to be made explicit or complete. And they can be false without the validity of the argument being in any way affected—characteristic of genuine premises and of statements assumed to be needed as premises. What I have defined as the presuppositions of an argument are not missing premises of an argument, for they are not premises at all. Thus, there would appear to be two senses of "assumptions of an argument" or "what is taken for granted in an argument." In one sense these phrases mean what must be *stated* or understood or supplied as premises in order for the argument to be complete; in the other they mean what must be *true* in order for the argument to be valid. The two may be easy to confuse with each other, and in either case there may be difficulty in stating with precision and certainty just what is "presup-

---

[31] *Cf.* Clark and Welsh 1962, 127–28; Copi 1953, 205: "Where a necessary premiss is missing, without that premiss the inference is invalid. But where the unexpressed premiss is easily supplied, in all fairness it ought to be included as part of the argument in evaluating it"; and Black 1952, 27. That I have cited books from some years ago is of no moment; similar books of more recent date say similar things about enthymemes, if they say anything about enthymemes at all.

[32] Black 1952, 28. The example used is adapted from Black.

posed" or assumed or taken for granted in a given inference. None-theless, the difference is genuine and important.

11   FORM AND VALIDITY

It is a standard credo of modern logic that the validity of an argument depends solely on its form, so much so that this credo has become something like an absolute presupposition amongst those who hold it, held on to as beyond question. It has one incidental defect—it is not true. Determining the form of an argument has epistemic value only, not constitutive. It does not *make* the argument valid. It enables us to determine whether the argument is an instance of a valid argument form, on the principle that if an argument is an instance of a valid argument form then it is a valid argument. There is no problem with the principle as just stated. But there are valid arguments that have no abstractable logical form. Sometimes this can be appearance only. Some arguments that appear to have no abstractable logical form can, with sufficient ingenuity, be shown to have one, as with arguments from complex conception or arguments from added determinants. My point here, however, does not depend on such cases as these. An example of a valid inference with no abstractable logical form is "Today is Sunday, so tomorrow is Monday." This inference has analogies, such as "Today is Monday, so tomorrow is Sunday" or "Today is Tuesday, so yesterday was Monday." But there is no way of determining the validity of this inference by reference to its form. The argument—this is true of all arguments—is valid in virtue of the relation that exists between premise and conclusion. The premises entail or necessarily imply the conclusion; the corresponding conditional is necessarily true; therefore, the argument is valid. Form does not generate validity, it only supplies what for a number of purposes, including those of instruction and for working with abstract logic, is a convenient mode of expression. To suppose otherwise is to suppose that if no map exists for a certain place, there is no way to get there or there is no such place, and the slogan that an inference is made valid by its form is actually a form of mysticism. This was brought out some time ago by Cohen and Nagel, in a statement the import of which seems very clear:

> The more general statement or formula is not a constraining force or imperative existing before any special instance of it. An argument is valid in virtue of the implication between premises and conclusion in any particular case, and not in virtue of the general rule, which is rather the form in which we have abstracted or isolated what is essential for the validity of the argument . . ..[33]

When I first read this, a long time ago, at a time when I was first immersed in the study of logic, I failed to note its import, perhaps because it was immediately preceded by the statement that "the correctness of any assertion of implication between propositions depends upon their form or structure," which certainly appears incompatible with the statement that immediately succeeds it. After further study, however, I came back to the successor statement and saw the logic in it, that arguments are valid in virtue of the relation of implication that holds between their premisses and their conclusion, and are not made valid by their form.

There is a general principle relevant to the example just considered: "Take the pattern 'Today is X, so tomorrow is Y,' and substitute for X the name of any day of the week and for Y the name of the following day. Any inference that conforms to this pattern is valid." But knowing that is not a matter of knowing the form of the inference. It is a matter of understanding its presuppositions. In

---

[33] Cohen and Nagel 1934, 12. Smullyan 1962, 75–76, has an account of formalizing an argument from complex conception. For the credo, see 3–4: "Arguments are valid because of their form . . .. There can be no valid argument without a corresponding validating form . . .. Every valid argument is an instance of some validating form or other." Yet, as Smullyan goes on to note, "If 'poet' means a writer of verse, then 'Shakespeare was a poet. Therefore, he was a writer' is a valid argument. This argument is a substitution instance of the argument form, 'a was a poet. Therefore, a was a writer.' And this form is a validating form." This is stretching things a bit in order to hold on to the dogma that "Arguments are valid by virtue of their form." The poets/writers argument is valid not in virtue of its form, but in virtue of its content, the specified meanings of 'poet' and 'writer.' It is not an inference whose validity is determined or guaranteed by the methods of formal logic. Strawson (1952) analyzed, though apparently with not much effect, the problems with the slogan 'validity depends on form alone' (54–56).

the case of examples of this sort, what is presupposed, in addition to the principle of constancy of meaning, is the calendar system, the meanings of the indexical terms 'Today' and 'Tomorrow,' and the names of the days of the week. Another is that we are not in a period in which we are moving from one calendar system to another. If today is Friday and at midnight we are shifting from one calendar system to another by adding eleven days, then on the new calendar tomorrow will not be Saturday, it will be Tuesday; similarly, if we were adding six days, tomorrow would be Friday—— and the people in that circumstance of infrequent occurrence would have two occasions in the same week for saying "TGIF."

An argument that is an instance of a valid argument form is a valid argument. But to know whether an actual argument is an instance of a valid argument form one needs to know certain relevant things about its content, the meaning of the statements composing it. Furthermore, its converse—if an argument is valid, then it is an instance of a valid argument form—does not follow and is not true. Just as there are presuppositions of formal logic, in dealing with and making actual inferences outside of a formal system, inferences of any kind, there are presuppositions one must understand. If any of these presuppositions is false, the inference is invalid. By contrast, if the inference is valid, then its presuppositions are true. If this should lead to the unwelcome further inference that an a priori truth, "this inference is valid," as a consequence implies or presupposes an empirical truth, "the terms used in the statement of the inference retain the same meaning throughout," that is a consequence, and a problem, that remains to be dealt with.[34]

---

[34] This paper, or rather an ancestor of it, has had an unusually long gestation period, has had, and has needed, a number of revisions, and even now may well have miscarried, even though it has now been completely rewritten and more than half of it is new. Over this period I have benefited from the comments, on one or another earlier version, of a number of people, including John Burdick, Michael Byrd, James Duerlinger, Andre Gallois, David Hamlyn, Mark Timmons, Bill Tolhurst, John Watling, Peter Wenz, and Robert Paul Ziff, as well as some others who may not wish to be named.

University of Wisconsin, Madison

References

Anderson, John M. and Henry W. Johnstone, Jr. 1962. *Natural Deduction*. Belmont, Cal.: Wadsworth.

Aristotle. *Metaphysics*. W. D. Ross, tr., Books Gamma (IV) and Kappa (XI).

Barker, Stephen F. 1980. *The Elements of Logic*, 3^d ed. New York: McGraw-Hill.

Black, Max. 1952. *Critical Thinking*, 2nd ed. New York: Prentice-Hall.

Black, Max. 1954. "Definition, Presupposition, and Assertion." In *Problems of Analysis*. Ithaca: Cornell University Press, ch. 2.

Black, Max. 1962. "Presupposition and Implication." In *Models and Metaphors*. Ithaca: Cornell University Press, ch. 4.

Brown, Paul L., and Walter E. Stuermann. 1965. *Elementary Modern Logic*. New York: Ronald.

Carroll, Lewis. 1895. "What the Tortise Said to Achilles." *Mind* N.S. 4: 278–80.

Church, Alonzo. 1932. "A Set of Postulates for the Foundation of Logic." *Annals of Mathematics* 33: 347–55.

Clark, Romane, and Paul Welsh. 1962. *Introduction to Logic*. Princeton, N.J.: Van Nostrand.

Cohen, Morris R., and Ernest Nagel. 1934. *An Introduction to Logic and Scientific Method*. New York: Harcourt, Brace.

Collingwood, R. G. 1939. *An Autobiography*. London: Oxford University Press.

Collingwood, R. G. 1940. *An Essay on Metaphysics*. Oxford: Clarendon Press.

Copi, Irving. 1953. *Introduction to Logic*. New York: Macmillan.

Donagan, Alan. 1962. *The Later Philosophy of R. G. Collingwood*. Oxford: Clarendon Press.

Geach, P. T. 1950. "Russell's Theory of Descriptions." *Analysis* 10: 84–88.

Grant, C. K. 1958. "Pragmatic Implication." *Philosophy* 3: 303–24.

Leiser, Burton. 1973. *Liberty, Justice, and Morals*. New York: Macmillan.

Mitchell, David. 1962. *An Introduction to Logic*. London: Hutchinson University Library.

Neidorf, Robert. 1967. *Deductive Forms*. New York: Harper.

Nowell-Smith, P. H. 1954. *Ethics*. Baltimore: Penguin.

Peirce, Charles Sanders. 1932–34. *Collected Papers*. C. Hartshorne and P. Weiss, eds. Cambridge, Mass.: Harvard University Press.

Pollock, John L. 1979. *An Introduction to Symbolic Logic*. New York: Holt, Rinehart and Winston.

Rescher, Nicholas. 1961. "On the Logic of Presupposition." *Philosophy and Phenomenological Research* 31: 521–27.

Ritchie, A. D. 1943. "The Logic of Question and Answer." In 1948, *Essays in Philosophy*. London: Longmans, Green, 102–18.

Sellars, Wilfrid. 1954. "Presupposing." *The Philosophical Review* 63: 197–215.

Singer, M. G. 1990–91. "Polar Terms and Interdependent Concepts." *Philosophic Exchange* 21 & 22: 55–71.

Smullyan, Arthur. 1962. *Fundamentals of Logic*. Englewood Cliffs, N.J.: Prentice-Hall.

Strawson, P. F. 1950. "On Referring." *Mind* 59: 320–44.

Strawson, P. F. 1952. *Introduction to Logical Theory*. London: Methuen.

Strawson, P. F. 1954. "A Reply to Mr. Sellars." *The Philosophical Review* 63: 216–31.

Strawson, P. F. 1959. *Individuals*. London: Methuen.

Whitehead, Alfred North. 1932. *Science and the Modern World*, 1st ed. 1926, Cambridge: Cambridge University Press.

6

Education as Norm Acquisition

Thomas F. Green

1 CONTEXT

It is the most rudimentary description of education that it consists simply of norm acquisition.[1] I aim to examine that acquisition through a study of moral education, broadly conceived. Moral education may be construed as the formation of conscience, conscience as the exercise of reflexive judgment, and its formation as the acquisition of norms. These three claims may seem, on the surface, to constitute a patently inadequate view of the nature of moral education. In what follows, however, I intend to show how these three claims may be unpacked to form a view remarkably fruitful for grasping the conduct of moral education. I believe that such a perspective represents, furthermore, a useful extension of the work of Frederick L. Will, an extension, moreover, that illustrates in an interesting way how standard formulations of philosophical questions in epistemology and ethics often receive fresh formulations when cast as questions in the philosophy of education. Issues in epistemology, for example, when 'located' in this way, tend to become

---

[1] I am indebted to Dana Radcliffe and to Emily Robertson who read this piece with critical care, and to Ken Westphal whose difficulties with the argument in an earlier form led to useful revisions. The central argument of this paper will appear as a chapter in Green (forthcoming), in which the formation of conscience is explored through its several forms—the conscience of craft, of sacrifice or duty, of membership, of memory and, finally, what might be termed the conscience of imagination.

focused less upon problems of knowledge and truth and more upon learning. Learning, however, is a concept seldom granted a role center stage in the history of philosophy. It was admittedly, a question much favored by Wittgenstein to ask, in analysis, how the use of a certain term or concept could be learned. Answering such a question is nearly always illuminating. To pursue it, however, is merely to employ a useful tool of philosophic method, not to open a central topic of investigation. To this claim of general neglect, it might be countered, 'learning' is a concept of central importance in the Platonic corpus, but, in truth, it figures there primarily as a vehicle to carry the burden of the so-called doctrine of recollection. 'Learning' is a notion that, for some reason philosophers seem to have been content, for the most part, even if only by default, to leave to psychology.[2]

In his efforts to free us from the peculiar limits of Cartesianism and foundationalism, Frederick Will has shed much light upon the ways that norms perform their governing roles in the conduct of many activities and institutions, including those of law, politics, and science. He has written, furthermore, in interesting ways on the philosophical criticism of norms, their mutual interaction and trans-forming configurations. He has written much less, however, on how norms are acquired. Yet, it takes only a little reflection to see that it is not, first of all, in the validation of norms or their criticism, but in their acquisition that we shall find the rudiments of moral education, perhaps the rudiments of any education. Norm acquisition is the central phenomenon of moral education, the matter that most needs understanding.

In what follows I aim to elaborate this view that moral education is the formation of conscience, that conscience is simply reflexive judgment, and the formation of conscience is the acquisition of norms. A deceptively simple rendering of Aquinas's view would

---

[2] In Edwards 1967, for example, there is no entry on 'learning' at all. Yet it is, or ought to be, among the most contested concepts of philosophical interest. By contrast, in Sills 1968, 113–97 there appears an extended article of some twelve sections.

have it that conscience is simply reason commenting upon conduct.[3] Conscience, he said, is to be understood as reflexive judgment exercised in specific cases. Of the two principal elements in this formula, namely, reflexivity and particularity, he emphasized the particularity of judgment, whereas Kant emphasized its reflexivity. The term *conscientia*, wrote Aquinas, "may be resolved into *cum alio scientia* (knowledge applied to an individual case)."[4] But "conscience," as Kant expressed it, "is an instinct to pass judgment upon ourselves" in accordance with moral laws,[5] and he then went on to contrast this judgment of the self measured against moral laws with another kind of reflexive judgment measuring the self against rules of prudence. He says, "Prudence reproaches; conscience accuses."[6] Instead of concentrating upon this difference between the moral and the prudential, however, I wish to focus upon their likeness, which is to say, the reflexivity that Kant finds in both kinds of judgment. It is the reflexive character of judgment that is essential to conscience. Each of us has the capacity to judge our own conduct, the capacity even to stand in judgment on what we discern to be the composition of our own affections. This is a sort of judgment that each of us makes in our own case. Conscience is often described, in fact, as an "interior voice" of the self speaking to the self offering advice, counsel, and judgment, or, as Kant put it, reproachment.

---

[3] The more common—we might even say "instinctive"—view is that conscience is not *reason* commenting, but mother or father, teacher or aunt, preacher or politician etc. The basis for this view, that is, what constitutes its appeal and may make it seem instinctive, will be discussed below together with what may constitute the error implicit in it.

[4] *Summa Theologiae* I.Q.79.Art. 13. Aquinas distinguishes conscience from any innate faculty or power. It is an act of reason, he says, expressed in three ways: ". . . insofar as we recognize that we have done or not done something . . ., insofar as through the conscience we judge that a thing should be done or not done . . ., and insofar as by conscience we judge that something done is well done or ill done." This last kind of judgment, that something is well done or badly done, is what extends the reach of conscience to judgments of excellence in practice, to standards of craft, for example.

[5] Kant 1963, 129.

[6] Kant 1963, 131.

Mill remarks upon yet a third aspect of conscience, namely, its associated feelings, a feature present in this formula, but not explicit. Mill says, of the "internal sanction of duty," that its "binding force . . . consists in the existence of a mass of feeling which must be broken through in order to do what violates our standard of right, and which, if we do nevertheless violate that standard, will probably have to be encountered afterwards in the form of remorse. Whatever theory we have of the nature or origin of conscience, this is what essentially constitutes it."[7]

In these three features—particularity, reflexivity, and the associated moral emotions—we have a characterization of conscience which, if not complete, is nevertheless complete enough to allow for a rather full account of the elements of moral education. I intend to comment, in short, not upon conscience formed, but upon conscience being formed; not upon the rational foundations of what judgments conscience may or may not deliver, but upon how those judgments come to be shaped.[8] To these contextual remarks upon this resolute and fixed attention to the *acquisition* of norms, an additional note of context is needed. It is that by such a perspective, the domain of moral education is considerably enlarged so as to include, for example, what are often described as rules of skill, craft, or 'prudence' in several of its many senses. Expanding the domain of moral education in this way may offend certain philosophical sensibilities since it seems to extend the concerns of moral education beyond the limits of anything usually regarded as moral. However, the judgments of one's performance in the arts, the crafts, and even in the quite mundane tasks of daily life reflect an exercise of reflexive judgment, sufficiently like those more traditionally viewed as moral, so as to make talk of a 'conscience of craft' something more than metaphor. That I have just written a bad paragraph presents no moral crisis to me. But still, I know, and

---

[7] Mill 1895, ch. 3, 41–42.

[8] This distinction between attention to conscience formed and conscience in formation is a central difference, I believe, between a philosophy of moral education and moral philosophy.

everybody else who cares about it knows perfectly well the difference between the unease that accompanies that judgment and the satisfaction, even laughter, that comes with having written a good one. Having the capacity to make such judgments with their accompanying unease or joy is just what I mean by having a "conscience of craft." The feelings associated with such judgments, moreover, are crucial because their presence is the exact sign that judgment has indeed become reflexive, that standards have become one's own and no longer simply mirror the judgments of some external tutor. From this single observation, it should be evident that the expanded domain of 'moral education' is thus made to include the standards of excellence in every department of education. My first and most basic claim is that the formation of conscience can be described as "the acquisition of norms," a process that, for convenience, I shall refer to as "normation."[9]

The second claim is that normation, *i.e.*, the formation of conscience, contrary to what Aquinas seems to hold, is not a special instance of the acquisition of knowledge, although it implies possession of various kinds of knowledge. My meaning is analogous to what Aristotle intends when he suggests that friendship, though not a virtue, nevertheless implies the possession of virtue. It is not a virtue because it is a relation and because virtues are not relations. Friendship, however, implies the possession of virtue because it is a relation among persons that presumes a rough equality of virtue and because the exercise of virtue requires the exercise of practical judgment, which is a kind of knowledge.

There is only this sort of distant connection between the acquisition of norms and knowledge, learning, or coming to know. Yet, if normation is not an instance of "coming to know" or even "coming

---

[9] The term "normation," I am told, is not a part of the standard sociological lexicon. Perhaps it is not a part of any standard vocabulary used in discussing these matters. I introduce it here because the term "socialization" is so loosely used, so vague and ambiguous, so misused in educational discourse, that some fresh approach, hence some fresh, and therefore more malleable, terminology, is needed. Thus do I defend the otherwise foolish step of introducing yet another piece of technical jargon.

to believe," but remains nevertheless the central business of moral education, it follows as a third point that moral education cannot be understood primarily as a matter of inculcating or stimulating "right belief," or even "right reason." Furthermore, because of the intimate conceptual connection between "teaching" and "learning," and between "learning" and "coming to know," it remains problematic in what sense, if any, we can speak of normation as an aim of teaching or even of learning, although there remains no question at all that it is central—perhaps the very core of education. It is admittedly odd that anything so central to education should have so little strong and direct connection to knowing, to learning, to teaching, or to coming to know.

As a fourth claim, I wish to defend Mill's view of "a mass of feeling" as constitutive of conscience. The centrality of feeling in the formation of conscience is implicit in the fact that normation necessarily structures the emotions of self-assessment. That is to say, it is normation that gives specific content to the emotions of guilt, shame, pride, regret, and, as Mill suggests, remorse, among others, and makes it possible for self-deception to have its risks. These emotions stand in a peculiarly strong relation to the formation of conscience because, like the judgments of conscience generally, these are essentially reflexive emotions. They are emotions of self-assessment, emotions in which the self stands in judgment of the self.[10] In that respect they are unlike other emotions, such as fear and hope, which must assume a prominent position in any full exposition of moral education, but are not essentially reflexive and are not essentially structured by normation. All this, however, needs explanation.

2 NORM AND NORMATION: THE ANALYSIS

By "norm" I mean "social norm," not "statistical norm" and I do not refer simply to "the done thing." A social norm is not simply

---

[10] As far as I know, the description of these as the emotions of self-assessment originates with Taylor (1985).

the modal tendency of behavior within some social group. On the contrary, we may take as *a kind of paradigm* that a social norm is a rule of conduct, not the formulation of a modal pattern of behavior. It does not describe how persons behave; rather, it prescribes how they think they ought to or should behave. It is not merely a statement of what people do, but a rule formulating what they think they ought to do. Social norms thus, are rules of "ought" and "should." If persons within some social group conduct themselves in ways that comport with norms significant to them, then there will be observable regularities in their conduct. However, from merely observing such a regularity of behavior within a social group, we cannot infer the presence of any definite social norm, as we might if "social norm" were a statistical concept.

I describe this formulation as presenting "a *kind* of paradigm" because, as will become apparent later, I believe neither that social norms can always be described as rules nor that a moral life consists simply in following rules. Ideals and exemplars also have standing as models and thus provide standards of a sort. However, I do believe that what I say here about the acquisition of norms as rules will apply equally to the acquisition of ideals and to the ways by which exemplars receive their status as models. One connection, for example, between norms as rules on the one hand and as ideals and exemplars on the other is provided by the fact that in both cases some standard is presented for the guidance of reflexive judgment, and it is, after all, this acquisition of reflexive judgment that I aim to describe as normation and as constituting the essence of moral education.

2.1   *Compliance, Obedience, and Observance*

It is easy, for example, to imagine a social group the behavior of whose members is at odds with its norms. Suppose we find that the observable behavior of 20 percent accords with a longstanding situational rule of conduct (say a norm praising cooperation under certain circumstances), but that the behavior of the remaining 80 percent regularly does not accord with the norm. We cannot infer that in such a divided social group, the norm of cooperation has changed or been abandoned. The distribution tells us very little. Beyond merely observing compliance or noncompliance, we need to know whether the miscreant majority feel guilty, ashamed, or remorseful about their noncooperation and whether the seemingly cooperative behavior among the minority is genuine or only apparent. If persons present one face for public inspection and reserve another for their private moments, if they aim to shield their conduct, not alone for the sake of prudence, but to escape from shame, then, in doing so, they advertise the existence of a norm, and testify that it governs even as its demands are ignored. The noncompliant ones, merely by their noncompliance, no more establish the absence of the norm than the compliant ones, merely by their compliance, establish its presence.

If compliant behavior is insufficient to confirm the presence of a social norm, then what would be sufficient? "Observant behavior" comes to mind. But already the vocabulary becomes complex, unwieldy, and possibly confusing. How might observant and compliant behavior differ? We may say that behavior (B) accords with some norm (N) if N describes B. Thus, to say, for example, that the behavior of the planets (their orbits) accords with the laws of motion is to say simply that such laws can be used to describe their orbits. It is not to suggest that such laws are being obeyed. Nothing resembling obedience occurs here. The planets neither obey nor disobey.

Beyond such talk of behavior that accords with a norm, as in the case of planetary orbits, lies a vocabulary of compliance. One might comply with a senseless bureaucratic rule or legal edict, for example. That is to say, one might do whatever the rule directs, but without granting to such a rule or edict any authority. Such compliance may be driven by threat, but it need not be. Complying with a rule might simply be the most convenient thing to do, something done merely because noncompliance, though rationally and perhaps even morally a more reasonable thing than compliance, is nevertheless a greater nuisance. To comply with such edicts is merely to 'take them into account' in the way one takes into account the weather by altering one's dress, or an aching back by altering one's stride. So behavior might either "accord" with a norm or "comply" with a norm. These are distinct phenomena, even though not observably different. Considered as temporal and physical events, the difference will be indiscernable to witnesses, even though experientially they are quite distinct.

To speak of behavior "obedient to" some norm is to invoke yet another vocabulary. A *obeys* N, or A's behavior is obedient to N, only when N is viewed as legitimately commanding. Obedience, in short, is a concept that applies only when a rule or norm is prescriptive rather than descriptive and when the behavior is compliant, but not merely compliant. Obedience requires an important addition to compliance, namely, acceptance of the *authority* of the rule. When 'obedience' to a norm within some social group deconstructs into mere compliance, then, as I shall try to demonstrate, we have what has been called 'alienation.'

Beyond this progression starting with 'accordance' moving to 'compliance,' and thus to 'obedience,' there lies yet a fourth vocabulary. We all know of conduct that is not in accord with some normative rule or standard, and which, therefore, cannot be described as either compliant or obedient to it, but which, at the same time, is undertaken in manifest admission of the norm's authority. Think, for example, of cases in which behavior is 'observant' of a norm, but, nevertheless, disobedient, cases in which the authority of a norm to command is granted, but the agent elects to disobey. By describing behavior as 'observant,' in contrast to 'compliant' or 'obedient,' I mean to pick out just those features of conduct that display the agent's admission of the authority of a norm, leaving aside all questions of obedience or disobedience. Thus, behavior may be disobedient yet at the same time 'observant' of a norm. By this convention, behavior obedient to a norm is necessarily observant, though observant behavior may be either obedient or disobedient.

One might, for example, lie and then feel guilty about doing so, thus disobeying a moral rule while at the same time acknowledging its authority. We cannot describe such behavior as in accord with a norm or compliant with it or obedient to it. But we can describe it as observant of the rule. Behavior observant in this sense, but disobedient, will often be concealed. In fact, the reach for concealment on the part of an actor, as I have noted already, is one thing that counts (though not decisively) in favor of the view that such behavior is undertaken in observance of the norm. In short, concealment suggests that such conduct is undertaken by an agent who acknowledges the authority of the norm to command. Otherwise, concealment would not matter. To establish that conduct is observant in this sense will be sufficient also to establish the presence of a social norm, whereas mere compliance or noncompliance, with whatever frequency it occurs, is insufficient. As an empirical matter, the demeanor of an agent acting in departure from a standard of conduct, and the *response* of others to that deviance, will carry more weight in establishing the operable presence of a social norm or even of an entire moral order than will evidence of compliance. That one's behaior corresponds to what a social norm would prescribe tells us very little. Such conduct might fit any one of these four, drastically different descriptions. But the response of an agent and the response of observers to departures from what the norm would prescribe tells us a great deal about which of these four descriptions is appropriate.

Given this array of distinctions, the interesting cases to study turn out to be not those of obedience or disobedience, but those of defiance. Refusing to sit in the back of the bus in a time and culture of Jim Crow is not so much an act of disobedience as it is an act of defiance, a certain *kind* of noncompliance. The point of such action is not simply to violate the rule, which, it is important to note would be morally nugatory, but to reveal that the rule or norm lacked moral authority to begin with and that what had appeared as obedience to it was not that at all. It was only compliance, the sort of behavior often produced in the face of threat, the only kind, perhaps, that threat can produce. Such defiance, however, can be, and perhaps often is, undertaken in obedience to (and therefore observant of) some other norm to which one is being obedient. "Civil disobedience," is too simple a phrase to describe an action undertaken not simply to disobey, but to repudiate one expression of moral order and its replacement by another. It involves not merely disobedience, but the repudiation of one rule of behavior in affirmation of another. And therein lies its threat. If such behavior were not an act of repudiation, it would have no moral point. It would be merely another case of disobedience, a matter of an entirely different order.

2.2 Norm Acquisition—Criteria

These conceptual points about the acquisition of social norms can be elaborated in another way. Let us ask by what criteria we judge that the behavior of some third person is observant of a social norm. In short, under what conditions would we say of someone that he or she has 'learned' or 'acquired' a social norm? It will be helpful to study this matter through an example as distant as possible from any moral rule and perhaps even from anything that we would typically think of as a social norm. How about a rule of grammar? We might ask what would have to be satisfied in order that we might say of some third person that he or she has 'learned' or 'acquired' a rule of grammar as a norm of speech or writing.

I start at so remote a point partly in search of clarifying simplicity. Even at the risk of triviality, I seek a case that can be examined directly without having to peer through any thick cloud of surrounding moral sentiment. But in addition to this matter of simplicity is also the matter of scope. I hope to show, without need of further comment, that the process of norm acquisition, though central to anything we might call moral education, nevertheless extends far beyond the domain of moral rules and principles, moral dilemmas, or moral problems. It extends, for example, to learning rules of craft and decorum or rules of courtesy and "getting along" at work, in hospitals, or within schools and other institutions. But even beyond this large domain, I want to establish that the criteria we employ in third-person claims of norm acquisition apply also to third-person judgment on the acquisition of ideals and exemplars. The process of norm acquisition, in short, like the business of moral education itself, covers a domain that includes both the moral and the prudential, and even much in addition to that, including the conduct of inquiry and the exercise of craft.

Such a remote and apparently distant case through which to explore these points can be found by considering the simple rule of grammar that subject and verb should agree in person and number. By what criterion could we say confidently that another person had learned to 'observe' this rule of grammar, that is, had come to speak in obedience to it? One test might be that the person can state the rule on demand. But this is plainly inadequate. One's speech might have been guided by this rule long before any encounter with its formulation. Being able to state the rule is neither necessary nor sufficient nor, one might add, is it either necessary or sufficient that one be able to identify a correct formulation of the rule as might be requested in a typical paper and pencil test of many choices. A second possibility would be to record the degree to which a person's speech accords with the rule as revealed in a performance test of some kind. But this too is clearly insufficient for saying that the person is 'observant' of the rule. One's speech might accord with it yet not be governed by it, might accord with the rule without being observant of it.

But suppose we note that A corrects his or her own speech and that of others in the face of departures from the rule. In that case, we will be justified in saying that the rule actually governs A's speech, that A actually applies the rule appropriately first to one's self and then to others. Only under this third condition could we say that A has learned the rule as a norm, that is, has become observant of it.

In short, the criterion that someone has acquired a social norm, even in so simple and remote a case as a rule of grammar, is not that his or her behavior accords with it, or that he or she can state the rule when asked, or even pick it out from a list. Learning to repeat the rule on demand or learning that or knowing that the words "subject and verb should agree in person and number" states a rule of grammar—these kinds of 'learning to . . .' or 'knowing that . . .' are not the kinds of learning and knowing that we have in mind when we think and speak of acquiring or learning norms.

If there is learning or knowing at all in normation, it is certainly not learning or knowing of this kind. If there is learning at all here, but not 'learning to,' or 'learning that,' or 'knowing that,' then what kind of learning is it? The linguistic expression that comes closest to capturing the phenomena being described here as a case of learning would be some form of the expression 'learning to be' as in "Anderson is learning to be more tolerant."

2.3   The Essential Presence of a Critical Attitude

However, if a person corrects his or her own speech and that of others in the face of error or irregularity, then something in addition to mere compliance or obedience is going on. This step requires the adoption of a certain critical attitude toward departures from the rule, the attitude that, in some sense, these departures are wrong, that these errors are indeed errors and not simply artful innovations or merely optional ways of doing things. This critical attitude— apparently a part of our very criterion for saying someone has acquired a norm—is the attitude that such departures call out for correction. With this step, in other words, there is invoked the notion that the rule does more than merely state a social expectation. The rule, in the composition of the person who acquires it, must take on the status of a rule of rectitude, a statement of what is correct. Therefore, in the makeup of the learner, it must become a rule binding not only upon one's own self, but upon others as well. It becomes a kind of public rule, a rule of right. Only with this additional step, only with the adoption of this critical attitude in the face of error, does the rule become the expression of an "ought." Only then does it become a norm or rule that can in any sense be said to 'govern.'

With the appearance of this critical attitude, in other words, there emerge also the ideas of 'correct' and 'incorrect,' 'right' and 'wrong,' 'propriety,' 'impropriety,' 'social gaffe,' and, possibly even, 'moral breach.' Of course, an enormous range of norms and rules and departures from them is covered in that range from 'incorrect' to 'moral breach.' Which it will be, in specific cases, depends upon the setting and the weight attached to the norm in

question. Norms, as we shall see, are always 'situationally specific.'
To get into a cab in Paris on one's way to the railroad station,
especially in a time of civil violence, and to pronounce 'gare' as
'guerre' may produce embarrassment, even momentary damage to
one's self-esteem, but none would count it as a moral breach. At
worst, it will lead the driver to ask nervously, "Where's the battle?"

These notions of 'correct,' 'incorrect,' and so forth are not *produced* by the adoption of this critical attitude in learning. Their
presence is a *part* of that critical attitude, not a consequence.
Between the acquisition of a social norm and the adoption of the
critical attitude that departures from the norm add up to error, we
have not a causal, or even a sequential, but a part-whole relation or
a structural feature of what we mean by norm acquisition. To ask
how we get from the acquisition of a social norm to the adoption
of this critical attitude is like asking how we get from Paris to
France. We have already arrived—not, however, because the travel
is swift or the distance slight.

2.4   . . . And Caring to Be Correct

This "critical attitude" includes also a kind of caring. No matter
that subject and verb should agree in person and number, one
would not allow the rule to be the measure of one's own speech,
let alone use it as a standard by which to judge and correct the
speech of others (even *sotto voce*) unless one cared to speak and
write correctly and unless one supposed that others cared, that is,
unless it has come to matter. The reflexive announcement of the
self must be that rectitude matters, in craft and speech no less than
in matters of morality and propriety. What are we to imagine, if we
attempt to picture a person who, when confronted with departures
from the rule makes corrections but does not care to be correct or
care that others are correct? What could this mean? If this is a
conceivable condition, some actual state of affairs, then what would
be its description?

   This 'correcting, but not caring to be correct,' is one mark (there
are others) of a kind of lethargy, a kind of indolent indifference

toward the rule, perhaps even toward rectitude or propriety in general. Clearly, were such lassitude ever the dominant feature of our relation to social norms generally, then we would no longer have behavior describable as 'obedient' or 'observant.' Such behavior is compliant at best. That's all. When we imagine such caring in the 'critical attitude,' as I have called it, to be missing, then what we imagine is precisely what is meant by 'alienation,' and 'anomie' or 'normlessness.' If this attitude of 'correcting, but not caring to be correct,' were extended to the whole of one's social life, then the surrounding world would have been transformed into an object to be manipulated, but not something to be engaged in. Without the caring aspect of that critical attitude—the view that rectitude matters—we would simply endure a kind of Kafkaesque world where conduct is prescribed, where prescriptions gain compliance, but where social norms lack any semblance of authority, legitimacy, or even sense. The internal speech of the self would be: "It doesn't really matter, but this is the way they like it. I know what they want, so I'll go along with this senseless charade even though nothing vital is at stake." Such a posture of detachment is the perspective of the uninvolved, the apathetic. It is the condition of anomie.

The key to this interior speech lies in that indefinite, obscure, omnipresent, and distant 'they.' How remote 'they' always are! How senseless; yet, at the same time, how pervasive are the norms of everyday life when viewed simply as the edicts that "they" deliver, and how thoroughly, under like circumstances, do those edicts lack even the most minute measure of moral authority! This condition is closely connected with another that the medievals described as *acedia*, *i.e.*, a kind of spiritual torpor or sickness that in our own day is often expressed as *ennui*, or boredom.[11] The ancient idea extended, however, to something more fundamental than mere boredom. It included the notion of a certain rebellion, a

---

[11] "*Acedia*" is the term translated as "sloth" among the traditional so-called seven deadly sins. For an interesting account of how these emotions or states of being are related in a "constructivist" view, see Armon-Jones 1986.

condition of being asleep to life but, at the same time, also resolute in rejecting any possible contentment at being what one is, namely, a human being.

When normation occurs in the sense I have described, that is, when norms are present, then concepts of right, wrong, and the like are also present, and with them the attitude that being right is a good thing, that it matters. Imagine a school in which a youngster is, say, suspended for some breach of conduct. What attitude should the youngster adopt toward the school in order to cope with the discipline? The most immediate, and most decisive reaction would be to withdraw moral authority from the norms of the school and from the institution—to view the institution with disrespect, even contempt. The school will get the apparent compliance it seeks, but only by giving up any semblance of moral authority. It will appear empirically as though all is well, that order is restored, that whatever breach may have occurred in the moral authority of the school has been repaired. But when we grasp the nature of normation, we can easily grasp also that these appearances are remarkably misleading. Compliance is confused with observance. To adopt as a general rule such a 'distant' attitude of compliance with what 'they' desire would be to adopt the posture of the alienated. That this posture of distance is 'anomic,' is all the proof one needs to show that the critical attitude I have been trying to describe is what transforms the rule into a public rule of right. The attitude that rectitude matters is a necessary condition for the existence of the norm *as a norm*. Instead of its acquisition or adoption *as a norm* we get the acknowledgement of a rule as a mere circumstance of life. We get anomie![12] This "critical attitude" has still another aspect. Depending upon the location of the norm in that continuum from 'incorrect' to

---

[12] This "anomic" perspective is not always to be decried (see Mercurio 1972, ch. 5, esp. 5). In this participant-observer study of caning in Boys High School in New Zealand, one cannot help being impressed by the degree to which the practice of caning, though persisting, becomes irrelevant to the lives of the boys subject to it, and the degree to which their withholding of authority from the practice can be seen as a mark of maturity in them, a point at which they begin to "take their lives into their own hands," and withhold authority from the adult community. This is alienation that can also be viewed as a step toward maturity.

'social gaffe' and thence to 'moral breach,' we know that a norm
has been acquired if, and only if, confronting violations of it or
even anticipating one's own violations of it provokes some degree
of shame, guilt, embarrassment, and the like in one's self and, on
the part of others, beyond a mild annoyance, it provokes disap-
proval, censure, moral rejection, or even abhorrence. The central
point is not that there is an emotional or affective side to normation. The point is rather that normation just is this structuring of the
emotions of self-assessment—shame, guilt, embarrassment, pride,
and the like—both in our self-assessment and in our judgments of
others. By saying that normation 'structures' these emotions, I mean
to refer not to the logic of their composition, whether they presuppose some propositional content, for example. I mean to refer rather
to their focus or object. Normation gives content to these emotions
inasmuch as it provides their object. It tells us what things are
going to provoke such emotions. In short, normation makes these
emotions specific. Structuring these emotions in this sense is precisely what merely compliant behavior is powerless to accomplish.
Again, absent these emotions, and the norms themselves will vanish.
Observant behavior will deconstruct into mere compliance.[13]

3 NORMS AND KNOWLEDGE

Clearly, there is something peculiar about speaking of the acquisition of norms, that is, their appearance in the governance of 'observant' behavior, as a kind of knowing or even of learning. If
norm acquisition is viewed as some kind of 'knowing norms,' it is
not propositional knowing. Knowing that Q, where Q is some norm,
would be at best a kind of knowing that produces compliant, not
observant behavior. The expression closer to our educational meaning would be, not that we learn norms, nor even that we come to

---

[13] Hope is not an emotion structured by normation in the way that other emotions
are, even though its formation is essential for the success of any moral education.
Indeed, hope may not be properly viewed as an emotion at all. Hope, although
forward looking in its objects, is always dependent upon memory for its foundations and thus is backward looking in its formation.

know them, but that we acquire them. The point is, not that we come to know the standards of speech (to preserve the example) in some sense of 'know,' but that we come to *have* such standards. We acquire them. Not that we learn them, but that they are impressed upon us. There is point to the suggestion that we do not possess them so much as they possess us.

It is often noted—and as more than a mere etymological aside—that the term "education" is derived from the Latin, *educare* which means "to lead out." But the etymology is weak. The *Oxford Latin Dictionary*[14] suggests that the root is *educo*, the primary meaning of which is the kind of leading out that occurs when a military officer leads the troops out from camp on patrol and not the leading out aimed at drawing out from the child what is already there, something needing only the assistance of an educator to be born. Leading out, in the sense of *educo*, is not midwifery. The *Dictionary* offers a secondary meaning of *educo*, which it describes as "weak" and which means "to tend and support the growth of (offspring)" but primarily of animals and plants, not a meaning that offers much support to the conventional educator's graduation-speech appeal to *educare*.

Actually, when the Romans wished to speak of education, instead of using one or another idea derived from *educo*, they more commonly used *instruere* which, being derived from *struere*, to build or construct, means "to build in" or, literally, to "insert." This is the word from which we get "instruct" and "instrument" in the sense of "tool." The same point is noted in a related Latin term also more commonly used by the Romans than *educo* in discussions of what we would call 'education.' The word is *instituere*, from which we get 'institute.' It is derived from the preposition plus the Latin, *statuo* meaning, "to place in order to remain upright," or to "put up," or "erect." Thus, the root idea of this term also is 'to place in' or 'upon' or, in short, to 'establish.' *Constituere*, from the same stem, together with its descendants, 'constitute,' 'constitution,' 'constitutive,' carries still the same meaning.

---

[14] Glare 1982.

I do not intend by this etymological excursus to prove anything. I aim only to establish that there is an ancient, still viable, and quite literal point in saying that norms are not so much learned as they are inserted or built into us or constituted in us or stamped upon us. Clearly, they are constitutive of our emotional lives. It is easy to say that we 'acquire' norms; harder to say that we 'learn' them; and a yet more remote possibility that we come to know them. This lack of any but a remote association between norm acquisition, on the one hand, and knowing and learning, on the other, is admittedly an odd result. I am concerned that it not be viewed as a mere intellectual contrivance created in order to gloss over some error. To this end, it may be useful to observe that it is quite normal to speak of the developing powers of speech as 'acquisition,' and to speak of 'learning' a language only in the case of a second or third language. In other words, a first language, it seems, is acquired; a second, or third, is learned. We should say, perhaps, not that we learn social norms or come to know them, but simply that we come to be normed. This social process by which we become normed is what I mean by "normation."

4 THE SITUATIONAL LOCATION OF NORMS

As I have already argued in some detail, a social norm does not describe how members of a group behave. Rather *for them*, it prescribes how they ought to or should behave. Moreover, as I have also argued, such norms are always situationally specific and always subject to revision through time. That is to say, the norms or rules expressing a certain value will differ in detail from one institution to another, from one setting to another, and from one time to another. For example, the norms giving shape to relations of co-operation may be more restricted in the school than in the family. Behavior called 'cooperative' in the family, and therefore endorsed, may be called 'collusion,' or more simply 'cheating' in the school. The same behavior endorsed in one setting will be proscribed in another.[15] This undoubted fact that norms are always 'situated' is often interpreted as though to endorse the claim that norms are hopelessly relative to group, to situation, to time, and the like, and for that, an understanding of normation cannot provide any firm basis for understanding the conduct of moral education. In consequence of the proposition that norms are always 'situational,' it is supposed that we must give up any basis for the critical examination of norms and any rational defense for their change and improvement.

This objection—really a family of objections—rests, however, on a number of misconceptions, most of which arise from a tendency to overlook the fact, barely stated here, that *no tradition is without its critical resources, and no rational criticism is without its tradition.*[16] This is a point that will be pursued somewhat later, but, for the moment, it will be better to turn to a different cluster of misunderstandings, *viz.*, those embodying misconceptions of the fact that norms are situationally specific. Just what does "situationally specific" mean?

4.1   *Norms, Judgment, and the Foundationalist Project*

Everyone learns some form of the dictum that situations alter things, but nobody can describe ahead of time all the situations likely to alter things in order that suitable provisions covering all contingencies can be included in the norm. Furthermore, even if such a norm of action could be framed, its complexity would exceed what anyone could learn. Fortunately, however, there is no need to introduce such complication. To have acquired the norms of home and school and their separate, but overlapping, norms of collusion and cooperation is already to have acquired some judgment as to how 'circumstances alter things.' Part of what we mean, in short, when we say that norms are situationally specific is that among those things acquired in the very acquisition of norms is a developed sense of propriety, a grasp of the 'fittingness' of conduct

---

[15] See Dreeben 1968, 66–67.
[16] [See Will 1997, ch. 6.—Ed.]

to setting, the developed judgment, for example, that the school is a place different from the home and in what respects. Indeed, it is difficult to imagine just how any sense of judgment or propriety in such matters could be acquired except *through* some such process of normation. It is partly this 'fittingness of conduct to setting,' the demand for a sense of propriety and judgment, and not the so-called relativity of the norm, that we refer to by saying that norms are situationally specific.

There are really four points here, each crucial to the claim that moral education is education in observing and elaborating the voices of conscience, and that normation is the process by which that aim is accomplished. The first is simply to note that norm acquisition is not habit acquisition, at least not if one views habits as unthinking, fixed responses to situations. As Frederick Will has noted, it is a serious mistake to think of norm acquisition

> as a process in which (persons) are equipped with a repertory of fixed, unthinking modes of response. A person who was so equipped, in whom the norms of his social environment had been absorbed as if they were such modes of response, would not pass for long as a person trained in a certain discipline, occupation, or craft, or as a responsible moral agent.[17]

Indeed! Such is the person whom we recognize as engaged in formula philosophy, and formula writing, the person who plays the score, but not the music, who cooks without imagination, who, only in some Pickwickian sense, as Will suggests, can be said to know and abide by the rules of practice, but who has either forgotten or has never grasped the point, a person who, quite literally, and always dresses rightly as a rule. Doing things always and only by the book, as they say, is all that can be expected when norm acquisition is grasped as something akin to blind conformity to, or habitual compliance with, social norms. Such a person may, for a moment, be regarded as competent in this or that activity, but such a judgment, as Will suggests, will not be sustained. The impression

---

[17] Will 1988, 135.

of competence in such a person will not last simply because it is not competence that such a person displays.

Paramount among things missing in the picture of such a person who plays by the book is precisely any portrayal of that fittingness of action to setting, that exercise of judgment, to which we refer by pointing to the situational character of norms. Still, learning that cooperation is a good thing, yet not always, is not to learn still another rule, a kind of superordinate rule that one needs to apply requiring then still another rule to govern the application of that one, and then still another and another and so on. Anyone who has learned simply that one should tell the truth in all matters and all circumstances, and undertakes to do so by the book, will soon run afoul of the norms of courtesy, for example, when bidding farewell to the host of a dull and uncongenial party. The missing element in such cases is not familiarity with some added rule of conduct needed to referee all conflicts between the norms of honesty and those of courtesy. Candor has its place, but so does decorum. What is missing is not some defect in the norms that govern either candor or courtesy.

The tendency to find some fault in the norm in this and like situations is one thing that leads to the foundationalist project. Having supposedly found a gap deemed to be implicit in the norm, some apparently unstated conditions perhaps, one is tempted to try filling in the gap. If we yield to the temptation, then the resulting project is going to aim at completing the norm either by providing the presumably missing details or by offering some additional norm of a 'higher' order, a norm of rather extraordinary juridical capacities such as are needed to mediate any conflict, remove any uncertainty that might arise. The project presumes that such 'gaps' are deficiencies in the norms. But the thesis here is that there are no such gaps, or that if we acknowledge them to exist—if only as an alternative description of things—they are not to be viewed as deficiencies in the norms of action, but simply as offering further evidence that one aspect of every norm is that its acquisition calls for the acquisition of judgment. To recognize such settings and such boundaries as exist in the difference between school and home is to acquire a kind of judgment that is already a part of norm acquisition, a kind of judgment already implicit in that achievement. Frederick Will, again, has put the matter directly and generally. He writes,

> It is not, of course that a person learns norms as fixed paths of action, and learns also an independent, supervening craft, namely how to judge. Rather, one learns to judge in learning how to act, in being educated in norms of action; and learns to judge only in relation to patterns of action.[18]

4.2 Norms Resident in Practices

In this mention of "patterns of action" there lie a third and yet a fourth important point on the situational nature of norms. It is not merely circumstances that alter things. Norms are specific also to practices and to institutions. Recall the observation stated earlier that part of what we mean by saying norms are situationally specific is that their acquisition entails the exercise of judgment, a sense of the 'fittingness' of conduct to setting. But this fittingness of conduct to setting is often negotiated simply by recognizing what activity it is in which we are engaged. Recognizing the difference between norms of school and home is largely identical with learning what it means to say that this (the place where one is) just *is* the school or the family, or the church. It is pretty much identical with such things as being able to say that we are now not simply tossing the ball, but playing baseball, that we are not now simply stacking stone, but laying a dry-wall. This is the sense of Will's reference to patterns of action. Norm acquisition is always embedded in activities and institutions. Acquisition occurs by engaging in conduct of whatever sort is called for by those activities and institutions and appropriate to them in ways not detached from or abstracted from human action and activities.

The norms of the school or college governing the activity that we call 'grading papers,' for example, are not simply regulations for

---

[18] Will 1988, 136.

sorting, as though this activity were on a par with sorting apples at the orchard or classifying grades of paper in the stock room. The norms of grading papers cannot be grasped and criticized as though there is some purely ideal and airie thing that constitutes the rules of something called 'sorting' or 'ranking,' some rules of action applicable to all situations, waiting only to be brought down and applied in various human settings, in this case for grading papers, in that for grading apples, and in this other for rank ordering these cherry pies. The norms of grading papers are first and foremost the norms of an activity *of the school*. It is *from* that setting and only *in* that setting that a certain activity gains its identity as the thing that we call 'grading papers.' That is where the norms of grading gain their sense. Thus, recognizing that certain modes of behavior endorsed in the home are forbidden by the norms of the school is not a recognition easily distinguished from simply recognizing that one is engaged in the activities *of the school*. Involved here are the norms of membership and participation.

Implicit in this idea that norms are situationally specific is a fourth point, namely, that behavior observant of norms is not 'applicative' in any straightforward sense of 'application.' That is to say, one does not learn the norms of cooperation and then apply them. Such a view of norm observance—that first comes the rule, then its application—virtually never describes what is present wherever normation has been achieved. It may, however, approach a description of some reality in those cases where norm acquisition is incomplete but underway. It is there, amid the struggles of acquisition, after all, that the standards and rules of conduct are most likely to become, not simply guides to conduct or presumptions of rectitude, but the *objects* of discussion. "What does good practice say about *this* situation?" we might ask. In the midst of learning a new craft or practice or settling into a new environment, one may need to discuss the rules and practice something like their application.[19] But this is the description of normation aborning, not

---

[19] It is a matter of considerable interest that such contexts, namely, those in which norm acquisition is taking place by a process of formation, are also the settings in

the character of normation achieved. And even in that situation, this applicative view of norm-observant behavior is, by no means, universal. One need only recall the paradigmatic case of becoming observant of a rule of grammar to recognize that this applicative model of norm governance is almost never an accurate description even in situations of learning.

In a faculty workshop on curriculum reform that I once conducted at a well-known liberal arts college famed for its fine teaching, one of the participants, a teacher of biology, was clear in describing his aim in teaching as leading his students to 'apply' their knowledge of biology when, for example, they looked at the huge maple in the middle of the quad and the richness and interdependence of life in its surroundings. We discussed what, in this context, might be meant by 'applying knowledge' and readily agreed that its meaning was not at all clear. This is not the 'applying' of applying a coat of paint to the barn door, or applying the tape-rule to the floor, or applying oneself to the task at hand. I asked whether it would make any difference to his understanding of teaching were he to describe his aim instead, as simply getting the students to 'see' things biologically, that is, see them as a biologist would. The idea that behavior observant of norms can be understood on the model of norm application is a notion about as obscure as the idea that one is "applying" one's knowledge of biology when one is seeing the ecology of the maple tree in the quad as a biologist would. The 'applicative' understanding of observance is misleading. It should be apparent, however, that what we are stuggling to point at when we speak of 'applying' norms as guides to conduct in some x or y, some task at hand, is simply the exercise of reflexive judgment in doing x or y.

As I have suggested already, one does not learn the norms of cooperation and then apply them. To the question, "What are you doing?" one simply answers "Helping with the dishes" or "Preparing dinner" or "Planting the beans." One does not *apply* the norms of cooperation, one simply comes to *be* cooperative. One comes to

which case studies and casuistry seem to find their natural pedagogical setting.

be normed. The norms operable in any setting with respect to some activity 'native' to that setting are nearly always quite sufficiently identified by simply identifying the activity and its setting. Simply to say "I am grading papers" is already to say what norms govern my current behavior and in what institutional environment they are to be understood. To engage in such an activity is already to be governed by the norms of that activity, by its setting and its residence in whatever is the relevant institution. But this is virtually never a matter of shaping behavior in ways that the 'applicative' image of things would have us suppose.

These points are integrally related to one another. They arise from focusing attention, not upon the nature of norms, but upon the nature of their acquisition. Norm acquisition cannot be understood as the acquisition of 'blind habit'; such acquisition entails the acquisition of judgment and a sense of propriety; it can take place only in the context of human activities and settings; and the 'applicative' model of governance is an inappropriate one to employ in trying to understand the governance of norms. These are all features of norm acquisition that become evident when we seek to explicate what sense we are to attach to the notion that norms are situationally specific.

5 STRONG AND WEAK NORMATION

The model of normation offered so far can be described as strong, that is, the sort that necessarily invokes the moral emotions of self-assessment. Not all normation, however, is of this sort. There can be weak norms or weak normation. When norms, otherwise of considerable weight, come to be construed as mere technical directives—as with rules of craft or rules of thumb in the practice of some craft; or when they are viewed as weak rules of prudence—as when we try to grasp the situational rules of decorum in a society where our relevant social group shifts from time to time—then we may describe the result as weak normation. Still other chances for weak normation have been noted already under a different description, namely, the circumstances producing alienation or anomie.

These also must now be seen, however, in another light, and in order to do that it will be helpful to retreat a few steps in order the better to advance.

5.1   Gemeinschaft and Gesellschaft

In the history of sociological thought is found an extensive exposition of a distinction parallel to the contrast I seek to make between strong and weak normation. The distinction, in one of its forms, appears as a difference between societies in which essential norms are extensively governed by the boundaries of the sacred, in contrast to other systems of social order in which norms are essentially guides to conduct of a purely functional and prudential sort. Ferdinand Tönnies, for example, introduced into sociology the distinction between *Gemeinschaft* (community) and *Gesellschaft* (society).[20] Relations of *Gemeinschaft* tend to be rooted in kinship, blood, a shared memory or tradition, and often a common religion. Those of *Gesellschaft*, however, tend to be rooted more in contractual agreements of utility and transient interest or even in something as simple as a mere coincidence of compatible functions, but not in kinship, memory, or any shared religion. Tönnies's deployment of the distinction was typological. That is to say, the distinction was meant to establish two ends of a continuum, two 'ideal types.' Since actual human associations vary considerably, bearing sometimes a closer resemblance to *Gesellschaft* and sometimes to *Gemeinschaft*, the distinction provides a means of discerning order in the midst of that variation. Given the conceptual distinction, in other words, empirical instances can then be appropriately placed in relation to one another on a scale, depending in each instance on whether it more nearly resembles the conditions of *Gemeinschaft* or those of *Gesellschaft*.

In *Gesellschaft*, persons are separated except when related by agreement, or shared interest, whereas, in *Gemeinschaft* persons remain united, or at least strongly related, despite deep discord or

---

[20] Tönnies 1887.

even enmity. According to the justly famous formulation of Tönnies,

> The theory of the *Gesellschaft* deals with the artificial construction of
> an aggregate of human beings which superficially resembles the
> *Gemeinschaft* insofar as the individuals live and dwell together
> peacefully. However, in *Gemeinschaft* they remain essentially united
> in spite of all separating factors, whereas in *Gesellschaft* they are
> essentially separated in spite of all uniting factors.[21]

We find exemplars of *Gemeinschaft* in relations of friendship and
families. Friendship prototypically is not a relation of utility, of
contract, or agreement. It is useful to have friends, but use them
and they will disappear. Nor can one forge friendships by seeking
to secure whatever utility such ties provide. Cronyism differs from
friendship precisely because it does tend to be based in a kind of
quid pro quo, a utilitarian reciprocity of a sort alien to the relation
of friendship. In this respect, cronyism typifies *Gesellschaft* and
friendship typifies *Gemeinschaft*. Tönnies tended to assign these
types to particular historical epochs, attempting thus to describe the
transformation involved in the emergence of modern European
societies from their earlier origins. I seek no such application of the
distinction. I seek only to exploit its heuristic value. *Gemeinschaft*-
like relations, such as those of family and friends, typically require
strong normation, whereas *Gesellschaft*-like relations of a contractual
and economic sort do not. They are typically relations of weak
normation.

It is a common description of the modern world that in it, strong
social norms have become fewer and weak ones more numerous.
This can be seen as one side of secularization, the expression of the
idea that in modern societies relations among persons are more akin
to the model of *Gesellschaft* than to *Gemeinschaft*. Nevertheless,
even in such a world, there remain certain relations—most obviously those of friendship—to which strong normation seems not merely
propitious, but essential. The norms of friendship, for example,

---

[21] Tönnies 1963, 192.

cannot be construed as mere technical guides to conduct. That one causes pain to one's friend must be viewed, within the institution of friendship itself, as a major normative violation. If such conduct does not evoke strong feelings of shame, guilt, feelings of pain, or the like, then we can doubt that in that instance friendship itself exists.

"All of the cherished elemental states of mind of society—love, honor, friendship, and so on—are emanations of *Gemeinschaft*," thought Tönnies.[22] Yet common experience in the modern world suggests that most relations are "emanations of *Gesellschaft*," relations of craft, convenience, and utility to which we are weakly normed. If it be asked, "Why should we teach history?" the question will be understood to require an answer giving some account of the utility of historical studies—so that we do not repeat the past, so that we may be freed from unthinking submission to the past, and so forth. The answers are familiar and nearly always disingenuous. But if you ask that question of a Jew and specifically about Jewish education, the question will be greeted with incredulity—that is just what education is. How could you not teach history? The difference is the difference in the way that education is conceived within the context of *Gesellschaft* in contrast to the way it is conceived in the context of *Gemeinschaft*.

No doubt the increasing domain of weak normation is central to the expansion of human liberty in contemporary societies. If you are a Jew, then strict adherence to orthodox dietary rules may be difficult to fit into the protocols of lunch within the chambers of commerce, and if you are Japanese, then rituals of greeting are difficult to combine with telephone communication. How does one bow over the phone? Persons become lightly normed to such conventions because observing them, in any strong sense, becomes seriously inconvenient. Fresh rules for conduct in dining and greeting will be introduced and in the process the norms will become situationally excepted. That is to say, people are likely to insist, and for a long time, that the old rules of conduct have not been aban-

---

[22] Nisbet 1966, 76.

doned. They still apply "*except* not so strictly any longer in these circumstances or under those conditions." Cooperation is still a much desired and valued disposition, except not at school or under certain circumstances. Such a transition can be described, in an extended sense, as secularization, a decline in the domain of the sacred and correspondingly in the domain of strong normation.

5.2   *Organic and Mechanical Solidarity*

A related distinction, exploited by Durkheim, provides added perspective on the nature of strong and weak normation. In *The Division of Labor in Society* Durkheim distinguished organic and mechanical solidarity, and related to this distinction, he introduced also the idea of 'collective conscience.' By 'mechanical solidarity' he refers to social cohesion of the sort that has existed throughout most of social history. It is based upon moral and social homogeneity and supported, he thought, by a kind of repression. Following Henry Maine,[23] in his famous account of *Ancient Law*, Durkheim associated mechanical solidarity with penal law. Where there is mechanical solidarity, tradition dominates, justice is predominantly aimed at subordinating the individual to a collective conscience, property is communal, and religion tends to be identified with cult and ritual. Social ties are underwritten by the sacred.

Organic solidarity, in contrast, is based primarily upon the division of labor. Out of the division of labor, and in consequence of it, comes the emergence of individuality from the restraints of collective repression and from submission to a collective conscience. It becomes possible to see society, not under the guise of a kind of mechanical solidarity, but as the organically coordinated efforts of free individuals pursuing different functions, but united, insofar as they are united at all, by the complementarity, perhaps even mutuality, of their different roles. Thus justice, under conditions of organic solidarity becomes less punitive, as in the case of penal law, and becomes more focused upon problems of restitution, a feature more typical of civil law. Individuals thus become disengaged from the

---

[23] Maine 1963.

constraints of kinship, class, localism, and the settled and predetermined roles of an inflexible traditionalism. Or so Durkheim saw it.

This distinction, as Durkheim drew it, will strike nearly everyone as putting things exactly in reverse of their apparent order. The 'mechanical solidarity' of which he speaks will be grasped nowadays precisely as a kind of organic social order, and the 'organic solidarity' of which he speaks will be more easily recognized nowadays as a functional order. But never fear. Both forms of social organization are clearly grasped in the case of Jack Sprat and his wife, that couple liberated from the constraints of a limiting traditionalism into the comparative freedom of strictly functional relations.

It will be recalled that Jack Sprat could eat no fat; his wife could eat no lean; and so, between the two of them they licked the platter clean. This is a wonderful division of labor, but not a very firm basis for marriage. Assuming their different, but complementary disabilities, these two might be brought together and agree thus to accomplish a joint purpose that neither can accomplish alone. But both can be replaced, however, by a disposal or by a dog unlikely to be as discriminating. This couple, of course, do not constitute a society. However, if we imagine a society to be the Sprats writ large, then we imagine a society based exclusively upon the division of labor with no ties of any other sort. Between Jack Sprat and his wife there is only a kind of functional relation, an order of the sort that Durkheim meant by 'organic solidarity' and that we typcially describe as 'mechanical.' By noting how inadequate such relations are as a basis for marriage, I mean to take note of a different kind of relation, typical of what Durkheim meant by a 'mechanical' and what we would mean by an 'organic' association.

Such, according to Nisbet,[24] was the original argument of *The Division of Labor*. Durkheim, however, held that any society based upon human relations of the sort typified by the Sprats, can persist only in the presence of some continuity with the first form of solidarity. "The division of labor," wrote Durkheim,

---

[24] Nisbet 1966, 85–86.

can be produced only in the midst of pre-existing society. There is a social life outside the whole division of labor, but which the latter presupposes. That is, indeed, what we have directly established in showing that there are societies whose cohesion is essentially due to a community of beliefs and sentiments, and it is from these societies that those whose unity is assured by the division of labor have emerged.[25]

In short, in a world where relations of utility, contract, and the ties of interest provide the integuments of a kind of organic solidarity, much depends upon sustaining the shared norms that contracts should be honored promises delivered, and that the conditions of trust should be realized and jealously preserved—*none of which can be understood to emerge out of transient interests, willed agreements and other ties of convenience or social function.* Expressed in Durkheim's terms, "organic solidarity" cannot persist except where some residue of mechanical solidarity remains. In other words, the world of weak normation depends for its persistence on the prior existence of some domain of strong normation.

And so, as Talcott Parsons has written in explicating Durkheim's views,

> Since the collective conscience stresses the commonness of beliefs and sentiments that constitute it, this seems to identify it with mechanical solidarity and suggests that organic solidarity, associated as it is with differentiation in the social structure, must develop at the expense of the conscience collective."[26]

The picture is that with the growth of organic solidarity through the division of labor, the domain of the collective conscience diminishes. It has less and less scope, is less needed, governs smaller and smaller sectors of life. Hence, there is less and less that can be viewed as demanding a shared conscience. This is the picture that allows us to understand in a deeper way the distinction between strong and weak normation.

---

[25] Durkheim 1933, 277.
[26] Parsons 1968.

In the contemporary world, the problem is not so much that there are no shared values or beliefs, no sentiments, no precinct to which it is proper to be strongly normed. The problem is rather to spell out just what the domain of that 'collective conscience' may be, and that is another way of asking just what duties, what rights, and what responsibilities ought to be a part of the collective conscience? What norms must there be, in short, to which, beyond their contractual ties and functional agreements we should expect persons to be strongly normed? As the collective conscience shrinks, shared duties and sentiments are likely to be more abstract, more general, less tied to status and role, and especially more contextual, but for all that, at the same time their formation is more critical to the smooth conduct of a society. It is not an inescapable conclusion that we should be strongly normed to every standard of craft, morality, or civic life. Anyone of whom that can be said is likely to be viewed as rigid, inflexible, doctrinaire, and without judgment. Such are the conditions that describe the fanatic, the morally inflexible, the bigot.

6 MORAL EDUCATION AS SOCIAL CRITICISM

There are relations, however, even in the most secular surroundings, of which strong normation is an essential feature. This fact needs further discussion for at least two reasons. First, because it will help to clarify the role of ideals and exemplars in the conduct of moral education, and second, because it will reveal in what ways norm acquisition is not a path of appeal to some orthodoxy, but is instead a way to place social and moral criticism on solid foundations. These matters can be considered in connection with first, a contrast between the empirical and the normative communities, and second a valuable distinction between what I shall call the internal and the external voices of moral interpretation.

6.1 The Empirical and Normative Communities

The regularity of conduct within a human community, that is, the actual modal behavior that occurs there, the presence of which might be confirmed by an external observer, almost certainly will not be identical with the behavior that would be discoverable there if the community were all that its members think it ought to be. That is to say, among the norms of any community there will be those that proscribe behavior in the strong sense, norms whose violation will, therefore, produce guilt, or shame, or some kind of aversion. It is in their response to violations of such norms that members of the community reveal their acquired sense of what the ideal embodiment of the community would be. What the community is in fact, that is, what is empirically found there, is almost never what members of the community think it would be if it were all that that they think it ought to be.[27] Hence, the normative and the empirical communities need to be distinguished, *and the distinction is itself empirically present in the behavior of the members.*

Being native to the normative community, not to the actual, that is, putting on its standards as one's 'second nature,' is what normation in the strong sense is about,[28] whereas acquiring the norms of the empirical community, without the normative, is what mere compliance is about. As I have pointed out already, this latter form of normation—that producing mere compliance—is the form that converts the norms of any community into something like technical directives, rules of thumb. Instead of describing the conditions under which ideals are realized, such rules then describe only how things work, how the world operates, and thus, what one needs to grasp in order to 'get along.' For illustration one need only consider the fact that any person for whom honesty is merely the best policy, that is, a person who views the standards and rules of honesty merely as an aid in 'getting along,' is a person not to be trusted. If there be a personality type corresponding to this strictly 'instrumental' conversion of norms, it might be the person who is said to know the price of everything and the value of nothing. In some contrast like that between the normative and the empirical communities is to be found the proper parent, perhaps, to a thou-

---

[27] See above, §2.1.

[28] And it is here that we shall discover the parameters of the collective conscience in Durkheim's sense.

sand dualities that lie within the limits of many traditions. One thinks, for example, of the Heavenly City and the Earthly City; the City of God and the City of Man; heaven and earth; value and fact; the Garden and the Fall; being "in the world, but not of it."

Normation to the empirical community is the kind of normation that is often understood both by the lay public and also by educators as 'socialization.' To whatever extent that is so, then by saying that moral education is a process of normation, I do not mean it is socialization. Normation to the empirical community is not what I intend by 'strong normation' nor is that what Durkheim meant. Nothing of any importance depends upon the question whether this distinction, between the empirical and the normative communities, is one that Durkheim devised. It is instructive to observe that, nevertheless, he did deploy it. When, in *The Rules*, Durkheim speaks of social facts, the facts he has in mind are just such norms as I have described in the full sense of the prescriptive rules of a social group expressed in observant behavior. Thus, the social facts of *Suicide* are not the tabulated data, but the norms reflected in those data. The norms are those social facts that he describes in *Rules* as being as objective and implacable as any facts of nature.[29] It is also this view of social facts as norms that allows us to mark the crucial distinction between the empirical community and the normative community, between the way things are and can be discovered to be and the way things would be were they all that the shared norms of a society suggest they ought to be. In this sense, the norms of a society are its ideals, not its empirical mores. Normation thus, for Durkheim, provides the standards against which the actual community is to be assessed *by its members*. To be normed in the strong sense is to be normed to these ideals.

Thus, almost at the height of the Dreyfus Affair, Durkheim, in "*L'Individualisme et les intellectuels*," wrote staunchly against the

---

[29] Durkheim 1965, 13.

anti-Dreyfusards.[30] They had argued that decisions already made by the Army effectively denying Dreyfus's rights could not be reversed. To do so, they argued, would threaten the very survival of a system of national security and authority and thus threaten the very foundations of the French Republic. Durkheim argued, on the contrary, that not to reaffirm and defend Dreyfus's rights would be to commit moral suicide. Like a religion that by successive indifference toward its central practices slowly declines and disappears, to neglect a defense of Dreyfus's rights would be to exercise indifference to the very core of the only set of beliefs that hold the nation together. For the heart of the French Republic, its unity, lay not in preserving the institutions of security, but in securing the rights of individuals, and if the cost of this meant the demise of the existing institutions of security and state, still, it would not mean the end of the Republic, the essentials of which lay not in these realities, but in the normative framework of the nation. In short, he appealed to the normative community, to its constitutive norms, as over against those whose arguments were rooted entirely in the empirical community. He appealed to what he could have called the collective conscience, a set of norms that are nonnegotiable, norms to which strong normation is a necessity.

This distinction between the empirical and normative communities is crucial. It constitutes a vital extension of the idea that moral education is the formation of conscience and the formation of conscience is normation. For in this distinction between the empirical and the normative communities, social criticism and moral critique are assured a lofty position in what might otherwise appear to be a view of education implacable in its defense of the status quo, devoted to the cultivation of mindless habit and conformity. In this distinction between the normative and the empirical community moral education enlists the critical resources of a tradition, in fact, the critical resources of several traditions. Moral education as

---

[30] See Durkheim 1973. A slightly different translation with comment by Steven Lukes is found Durkheim 1993. A valuable discussion of this piece is found in Wallwork 1972, 166–70.

criticism emerges. It begins to appear when the members of a community, normed already, insist upon measuring what the community is against what it claims to be, against, that is, its best portrait.

6.2   *Internal and External Interpretation*

This contrast between the empirical and the normative communities, though framed at a fairly high level of social aggregation, is found also at a much lower level of aggregation. The contrast has its individual expression in a parallel contrast between the internal and external voices of moral interpretation. When I hear a voice addressed to me from some distance saying, in effect, "You are not the generous," or "the honest," or "the sympathetic and sensitive person that you claim to be," then I feel the sting. It hurts. I am charged with being false, of being insincere or inauthentic, of lacking integrity. This voice, has a certain moral bite to it. It gets my attention quickly. I call this the internal voice of criticism because although it always comes, and must, from a point away from me, namely, from another person, it is always from another person like me, not from a God, not from on high, and it is a voice addressed to an internal condition of the self. It is, in short, a critical voice directed against what I am, not against what I believe. And not being addressed to belief, neither will it be quieted by a change of belief. It calls upon me not merely to think something different, but to be something different, namely, to be what I claim to be.

There is another voice, however, addressing me to say there is something wrong with what I claim to be. This is a different voice saying, in effect, that the goods I seek are false, that my opinions about what has worth ought to be revised, that they cannot be justified, that they are groundless. To this latter voice, palms upward, I might shrug my shoulders and respond simply, "So?" "You have your views and I have mine." I call this the external voice of criticism because, though it too comes from a distant point, it is another kind of distance and another kind of point. This is a voice addressed to the need for an external foundation of moral belief, a foundation so distant, so devoid of context that it represents what Thomas Nagel has called "the view from nowhere." This is an Olympian, or if you prefer, a Magisterial voice. It is a voice that demands foundations, not merely in my reason, but in Reason itself or in the very nature of things. It is addressed to me because it is addressed to any reasonable person. Because it is a voice from "nowhere," it purports to be a voice for "any-one." And because it is a voice for any-one, it claims to be a voice for "everyone."

With this external voice from nowhere my quarrel can often seem, not simply academic, but, as we sometimes say, "merely" academic. "What really is the standard of duty?" "Is there any such?" "Is the rule of utility enough?" "Does an acceptable standard of honesty allow for no exceptions?" "What about this one? Can it count as an exception?" Any quarrel I might have with this external voice of criticism is likely to draw heavily on such talk of rules and principles and cases. This is the voice of the philosophic quest in its justificatory practice. It is the Olympian voice of philosophy about to embark upon another evangelical project.

But with the former, the interior voice, the struggle is serious and in no sense merely academic. This voice addresses my personal integrity, not my orthodoxy. With it, I will have to wrestle. I cannot escape it. The external is, as it were, the voice of a public bar of judgment before which my beliefs must gain approval. But the other is the voice of an interior bar of judgment before which I, myself, in all my particularity must stand, all masks aside, and seek approval.

These voices both speak of "true" and "false," but they use these words with different meanings, and the difference is stark. The external voice speaks of "truth" as something like correspondence and thus of falsehood as mistake or error. But the internal voice speaks of "truth" in the logic of "coherence," the coherence of a self, and thus it speaks of truth not as error or as falsehood but as dissembling.

7 CODA

Beginning with the claims that (1) moral education is the formation of conscience, (2) that conscience is the exercise of reflexive judgment, and (3) that conscience is formed in normation, we are led along many paths describing the place of the moral emotions of self-assessment, the intrinsic acquisition of critical judgment, as well as the placement of social criticism as a part of moral education.

Syracuse University

References

Aquinas, Thomas St. 1918f. *Summa Theologiae*. Rome: Leonine.

Armon-Jones, Claire. 1986. "The Thesis of Constructionism." In *The Social Construction of Emotions*. R. Harré, ed. New York: Blackwell, 1986, 32–82.

Dreeben, Robert. 1968. *On what is Learned in School*. Reading, Mass.: Addison-Wesley.

Durkheim, Emile. 1933. *The Division of Labor in Society*. G. Simpson, tr. New York: Macmillan.

Durkheim, Emile. 1965. *The Rules of Sociological Method*. S. A. Solovay and J. H. Mueller, trs. New York: Free Press.

Durkheim, Emile. 1973. "Individualism and the Intellectuals." M. Traugott, tr. In *Emile Durkheim on Morality and Society: Selected Writings*. R. Bellah, ed. Chicago: University of Chicago Press, 43–57.

Durkheim, Emile. 1993. "Individualism and the Intellectuals." S. Lukes, tr. *Political Studies* 17, 1969, pt. I: 14–30. Rpt. in *Emile Durkheim: Critical Assessments*. P. Hamilton, ed. New York: Routledge, IV, 166–83.

Edwards, Paul, ed.-in-chief. 1967. *The Encyclopedia of Philosophy*. New York: Macmillan & The Free Press.

Glare, P. G. W., ed. 1982. *Oxford Latin Dictionary*. Oxford: Clarendon Press.

Green, Thomas F. (Forthcoming). *Voices: The Educational Formation of Conscience*. South Bend, Ind.: Notre Dame University Press.

Kant, Immanuel. 1963. *Lectures on Ethics*. L. Infield, tr. Indianapolis: Hackett.

Maine, Henry J. S. 1963. *Ancient Law*. New York: Beacon Press.

Mercurio, Joseph. 1972. *Caning: Educational Ritual*. New York: Holt, Rinehart and Winston.

Mill, John Stuart. 1895. *Utilitarianism*. London: Longmans, Green and Company.

Nisbet, Robert. 1966. *The Sociological Tradition*. New York: Basic Books.

Parsons, Talcott. 1968. "Emile Durkheim." In Sills, 1968, IV, 311–20.

Sills, David L., ed. 1968. *The International Encyclopedia of the Social Sciences*. New York: Macmillan and The Free Press.

Taylor, Gabriele. 1985. *Pride, Shame and Guilt: Emotions of Self-Assessment*. Oxford: Oxford University Press.

Tönnies, Ferdinand. 1887. *Gemeinschaft und Gesellschaft*, 8th ed. Leipzig: Buske, 1935.

Tönnies, Ferdinand. 1963. *Community and Society*. C. Loomis, tr. New York: Harper.

Wallwork, Ernest. 1972. *Durkheim, Morality and Milieu*. Cambridge, Mass.: Harvard University Press.

Will, Frederick L. 1988. *Beyond Deduction: Ampliative Aspects of Philosophical Reflection*. New York and London: Routledge.

7

Some Comments on the Later Philosophy of Frederick L. Will

Marcus G. Singer

For this work in critical appreciation of Frederick L. Will I had originally contemplated contributing an essay on some of the ideas developed in the later essays and in part embodied in *Beyond Deduction*. I decided, instead, to contribute the essay on presuppositions.[1] However, I may still at some future time return to consider these later Willian views; there is a feature of this later philosophy, as impressive and as impressively worked out as it is, that continues to trouble me.

The problem, briefly stated, is this: if a conflict in a society eventually works itself out, in accordance with features of the practices of the culture, one way or the other, merely on the basis of the norms already embedded in these practices—which in the process are modified, altered, changed, though they still exercise their function of governance—then how can there be any distinction of a right or a wrong way?

Our society is still in the midst of a serious conflict over the morality of abortion, a conflict that has been escalating in scope and intensity since the decision in *Roe* v. *Wade* in 1973 (410 US 113). Instead of that decision settling the conflict, as Supreme Court decisions have on occasion managed to do, by forging a compro-

---

[1] [Essay 5 above.—Ed.]

mise on which the opposing sides can agree and out of which both sides can get some measure of satisfaction, the decision seems to have exacerbated the issue—it is certainly not settled. Now let us suppose that decision reversed, either by an overruling Supreme Court decision, or by certain kinds of legislation, or by Constitutional amendment. There are, at a minimum, two possibilities. One is that the conflict will continue, in possibly a still more intensified way, as those who support the 'Pro-Choice' side take up arms against what they regard as an oppressive measure or decision. The other is that the conflict will be stilled, getting quieter and quieter over time. At the moment, this second alternative does not seem likely, as the present fervor of those on the 'Pro-Life' side can easily be matched by the fervor of those on the other side, who are currently struggling to hold on to a legal right granted them by judicial decision and can be expected to struggle even more vociferously were this right, now actually regarded by some as fundamental, to be taken away from them.

In any case, whether the present situation is overturned or remains as it is, though with a diminution of conflicting rhetoric, neither outcome can reasonably be said to constitute a right or justifiable decision on the matter merely because it comes to prevail. On Professor Will's view, as I understand it, the view that prevails is right, that is, whatever is or comes to be, as a result of such processes of governance and dispute, is right, at least for the time that it prevails. I find this hard to believe, and even harder to accept.

Let us imagine a third outcome, whether technological or theological, that actually settles the controversy—something that *Roe* v. *Wade*, with its division of pregnancy into three trimesters and with its emphasis on the distinction between fetal viability and inviability, conceivably could have achieved but, as is overwhelmingly obvious, did not. If the controversy were to be settled, in the sense of going away, would that outcome, whatever it was that brought it about, thereby be right? As I understand Professor Will, this is the answer his philosophy, operating from an external and neutral standpoint, would yield. In my judgment, any philosophy that has such a consequence must have something wrong with it. The question is whether the later philosophy of Frederick L. Will has this consequence.

It may not, yet I find this view embedded or implied in the later writings.[2] Consider, for example, this passage:

> In a great variety of ways, as in the great controversy over slavery in the last century, partisans of both sides of the abortion-rights issue are envisioning and advancing what are at various places and in some important respects contrary visions of what American life should be. An aspect of the width, depth, and intensity of the issues involved is that not only are the prominent groups of partisans on each side engaged in working for the resolution of them. Together with them in their efforts is a vast array of social agencies, of which the courts and a variety of religious and political agencies are but the most prominent. Likewise engaged at one sector or other of the task are the institutions of higher learning, other research institutions, the press and other media of communication. Those who are appalled by the noise and disorder of the entire process, compared, say, to calculative and computative ones, need perhaps to be reminded that these are characteristics of decision procedures endemic and appropriate to a modern democratic society.[3]

These may be "characteristics of decision procedures *endemic* . . . to a modern democratic society," but the judgment that they are *appropriate* to a modern democratic society is not so easily accepted; it is a value judgment of somewhat doubtful credentials creeping in in the guise of a statement of fact. It should not be forgotten that there are other procedures that are endemic, though hardly appropriate, to "a modern democratic society," such as procedures of intimidation, threats, bribery, corruption, the buying of votes and the drowning out of voices, and the sort of lying and deception characteristic of advertising and propaganda. The fact that they exist

---

[2] In Will 1988 and 1997; *e.g.*, in Will 1997, 118–20; it is especially prominent in ch. 9, esp. §§24, 31–35 (pp. 170, 175–78); abortion and slavery are referred to in §28 (pp. 172–74).

[3] Will 1997, ch. 9 §28 (pp. 172–74).

is no argument for the claim that they ought to; it is rather an argument for the claim that they ought not to. And many of these features "endemic to" a modern democratic society are also features endemic to tyrannies and dictatorships. Furthermore, although this sort of clamor is fairly typical of the way in which political conflicts within the society get dealt with, by brass bands, cheering sections, and muscle, it is not the way in which *moral* questions are to be resolved. In the sort of society referred to with such awe and admiration there are, in addition, questions of science and mathematics, such as the questions of evolution *versus* special creation and of the exact value of pi, that, once they enter the political or social or religious arena, some people try to get settled in the same way, by legislation, decree, propaganda, and broken heads. The not-so-magnificent experiment of the Soviet Union, attempting to settle scientific questions by political means, should demonstrate that with certain sorts of questions such methods are altogether out of place.

In the passage quoted, it is said (1) that "partisans of both sides of the abortion-rights issue are envisioning and advancing . . . contrary visions of what *American life* should be," and (2) that there are "prominent groups of partisans on each side engaged in working for *the resolution* of" the issue. Both these remarks call for comment. As to (1), it should be noted that similar issues about abortion have arisen in other countries, especially in Europe. Surely people in those countries are not "advancing . . . contrary visions of what *American* life should be." Such a characterization might have been true of the Prohibition controversy, but the Prohibition controversy was more clearly a political one, although it was embedded in a moral framework. The questions about slavery and abortion, though in this country embedded in a political framework, are more clearly moral ones, and this is true even if their only means of resolution was, or is, a political-military one.

As to (2), it may be granted that there are members of the opposing sides who are engaged in "working for the resolution" of the issue, who are genuinely seeking what is often referred to as 'dialogue' and looking for common ground, seeking to settle the issue in a peaceful way even more than they are seeking to have their own substantive views on the matter prevail. But there are surely many more on each side, particularly the ardent partisans, who are trying by all means in their power to have their will, and their views, prevail, who are more interested in gaining or holding onto what they want than they are in "working for a resolution" of the issue. On the view espoused by many sincere and militant zealots, there can be no 'resolution' in which the other side prevails or in which their own side does not wholly prevail. Thus, I have some doubts about the adequacy of the way in which Professor Will has characterized the conflict.

It would be possible, not practically but logically, to end the abortion conflict, to make it go away, by exterminating all the advocates of one side or the other. There being no advocates left to contest the matter, the controversy would go away, to become as dead as the issue over Prohibition is now—though that issue in the 1920s was the most agitating and troubling one in the country, something that must sound implausible to those born since and who know little of social history. There is now no issue over Prohibition, at least prohibition of alcoholic beverages, though that now-dead issue has its present-day counterpart in the issue, just beginning to germinate, over the prohibition of presently illegal drugs. However, no one with any vestige of morality could claim that the method of liquidation, practiced with some success in Nazi Germany and the Soviet Union for a long time and in many places in the past and still in the present, is actually a morally legitimate way of resolving, as distinct from eliminating, a moral issue. It would be no justification of such methods to say that they are "endemic and appropriate" to a modern dictatorship. And it would not do to say that the method of liquidation of the opposition is neither endemic nor appropriate to "a modern democratic society." Once the method were used and tolerated in "a modern democratic society," the norms of that society would change and the method would then be endemic to that sort of society. It cannot be put out of court by factual claims to the effect that it isn't done; after all, on the view in question, if I have understood it right, whatever is and prevails is right.[4]

The controversy over slavery in this country was eventually settled, but only by a horrible civil war—which is of course a course still open in the conflict over abortion. The conflict over slavery was settled, and hardly any respectable opinion advocating or justifying slavery is now to be found. But suppose for a moment that the South had won the Civil War and as a result was enabled to hang on to its slave system and that slavery were consequently still an existing institution. On the same logic, one would have to conclude that slavery would then be justified as right and just. I judge that, on logical and emotional grounds, an impossible view, *demonstrably* false; yet it seems to me to be an inevitable consequence of the later philosophy of Professor Will, which leads me to paraphrase a plaintive remark said to have been made long ago by an ardent fan, "Say it ain't so, Fred!"[5]

I add that the processes described, apparently with approval though possibly with a sort of resigned approval, may work to settle moral *issues*, moral controversies, but are irrelevant to solving moral *problems*, as irrelevant to moral problems as they are irrelevant to scientific or philosophical problems.[6] I add further that I may well have misinterpreted Professor Will on this matter, something on which he may be able to set me straight, and I see no

---

[4] [The abortion controversy is addressed further by Martin Perlmutter in "Moral Intuitions and Philosophical Method," Essay 9 below.—Ed.]

[5] [Slavery is discussed further by Wallace and by Kettner, pp. 250–51, 333.–Ed.]

[6] The distinction between *issues*—which are akin to and tend to lead to disputes, controversies, or conflicts—and *problems* is discussed in Singer 1985, esp. 10–16. An acute observation by Dewey (1910, 19) is worth reproducing here: "Intellectual progress usually occurs through sheer abandonment of questions together with both of the alternatives they assume [N.B., presuppose]—an abandonment that results from their decreasing vitality and a change of urgent interest. We do not solve them; we get over them." The trouble is that there are certain problems that cannot be *solved* merely by getting over them, such as questions about the morality of slavery, of torture, and of capital punishment. Whether the abortion issue is of this latter kind, or is rather a problem to be "solved" by "getting over it," is a matter that calls for separate treatment.

need, at this particular time, to detail further the various places and statements in his work that have led me to the position taken here.

This being the situation, I decided to go ahead with the paper printed above, on a matter that had been plaguing me for a very long time and which I needed to get settled, in my own mind at least, in order to proceed with some more comprehensive work of my own, so my procedure has something resembling a pragmatic justification. I hope that the relation the above piece on "presuppositions" bears to the philosophical work of Frederick L. Will is not altogether obscured by my not explicitly detailing it.

University of Wisconsin, Madison

References

Dewey, John. 1910. "The Influence of Darwinism on Philosophy." In *The Influence of Darwin on Philosophy*. New York: Henry Holt and Co., 1–19.

Roe v. *Wade*. 1973. *United States Supreme Court Reports* 410, starting on p. 113 (hence 410 US 113 (1973)).

Singer, M. G. 1985. "Moral Issues and Social Problems." *Philosophy* 60 No. 231: 5–26.

Will, Frederick L. 1988. *Beyond Deduction*. New York and London: Routledge.

Will, Frederick L. 1997. *Pragmatism and Realism*. K. R. Westphal, ed. Lanham, Md.: Rowman & Littlefield.

8

Frederick L. Will on Morality

William H. Hay

In the course of presenting an account of getting knowledge through the use of nondeductive reason, Professor Will has given a framework in which any morality can be described. He also indicates criteria for judging moralities. This part of his work may not have been noticed, because it is tertiary to his main purpose. His earliest work had centered on the so-called problem of induction. Then, in his first book,[1] he explored faults he claimed to find in the posing of the problem and maintained that the source of these faults lay in the acceptance of the foundation theory of knowledge. Two main features of that theory are "(1) the location of secure 'foundations' from which proper claims of knowledge could and must begin, and (2) the 'building' of further claims upon these foundations by strictly deductive methods."[2] He charged that the foundation theory of knowledge leads to "frustrations in the project of understanding how ethical and political judgments can be reasonably formed," and so "to the conclusion that they cannot" be formed by the use of reason.[3]

In his 1988 book, *Beyond Deduction*, Will develops his account of getting knowledge through nondeductive reason. In *Induction and Justification* he had already expressed his dissatisfaction with T. S. Kuhn's characterization of Copernican heliocentric astronomy as a

---

[1] Will 1974.
[2] Will 1988, 18.
[3] Will 1974, 340.

case of revolutionary science that broke with rational processes. Kuhn had claimed that Copernicus had jumped by genius from working within the Ptolemaic paradigm to working out the details within a different paradigm.[4] Will, by contrast, claimed that Kuhn's contrast of what Kuhn called revolutionary science with ordinary science was but a matter of degree. Will believed that Kuhn made this mistake because Kuhn identified the work of rational processes with what is reconstructible in deductive processes. He maintained that Kuhn was wrong in supposing that "fundamental changes in the processes of thought and action are effected basically by nonrational means" (*BD* 38).[5]

Will reminds us that "our quest for truth about the physical world must provide some acceptable account of how knowledge of this truth can be attained."[6] His answer to this quest is stated in terminology of his own devising. 'Norms' he defines as "patterns of procedure that serve as guides to standards of thought and action" (*BD* 1). Norms are "accepted precepts and practices" (*BD* 24). Norms are not templates exemplified in rigidly identical movements. Rather they "are ways of thinking and acting embodied in human life" (*BD* 101). Will refers us to John Dewey's article, "The Reflex Arc Concept in Psychology."[7] Just as a way of walking finds exemplification in a variety of acts, so "action in accordance with norms is not to be considered on the model of pre-established and automatic responses to stimuli" (*BD* 130).

The other term he defines is 'governance.' This Will defines as the ways in which "norms are constantly molded, strengthened and weakened, refined and degraded" (*BD* 95). One cause of "generation, criticism, refinements, reconstruction, maintenance, re-enforcement, and elimination of norms," is "that the norms . . . themselves embody false assumptions about that segment of the world with which they are engaged" (*BD* 43, 96). In governance norms can

---

[4] See Will 1974, 267.

[5] Numbers in parentheses in the text preceded by '*BD*' refer to pages in Will 1988.

[6] Will 1997, 88.

[7] Dewey 1896, 358; *BD* 132.

come to be affected by the world. In this way we can come to know the truth about the physical world (*cf. BD* 96).

How do individuals acquire these norms? Norms "do not subsist in us, fixed and absolute" (*BD* 89). "Rather they are formed in us by . . . the communities of which we are members in family life, in schooling, in vocation, in religious practice, in political affiliation, and in other areas of communal living, . . . creating in us more or less well-composed miniature reflections of themselves" (*BD* 89–90).[8]

From this we can see that Will has provided us with "a theory of governance which emphasizes the social character of the norms of thought and action" (*BD* 227). But we are not restricted to the norms formed in us by "the communities that formed us" (*BD* 90)? "Anyone of us may develop and commit ourselves to standards which diverge from those of the communities that formed us" (*BD* 90). This should not be understood as "evidence that there is in us a capacity to discern standards quite independent of the communities" (*BD* 90).

Professor Will had the longtime aim of showing how processes "not reducible to deductive forms" are none the less entitled to be called 'rational' (*BD* 247). Borrowing a term from C. S. Peirce, Will calls such processes 'ampliative' processes. He warns us that it would be a mistake to expect ampliative processes, however rational, "to yield formulae and techniques comparable to those developed in and for deductive governance" (*BD* 12). Ampliative processes will give "no general blanket philosophical certification of all results generated" (*BD* 12). When ampliative processes succeed, that is known by the fact such processes that would ordinarily be regarded a use of reason as "pondering, wavering, balancing, readjustment, and reassessment" (*BD* 183) have produced a belief that "we do not *at all* doubt we must and do regard as truth."[9] Here

---

[8] [On this topic see Thomas F. Green, "Education as Norm Acquisition," Essay 6 in this volume.—Ed.]

[9] Will 1997, 82.

Will acknowledges his debt to Peirce, who wrote we "must and do regard as infallible and absolute truth."[10]

From the time of his 1969 American Philosophical Association–Western Division Presidential Address, "Thoughts and Things,"[11] Professor Will has been developing an account of the propriety of recognizing as rational processes ones that cannot be reconstructed as deductive processes. It was only in the more recent paper, "Pragmatic Rationality," that he began to treat moral judgment.[12] In *Beyond Deduction*, Will picked out moral judgment in conscientious decisions as an activity in which several norms are combined to arrive at a judgment without the involvement of deductive reason. In the workings of what we call conscience is found the operation of a capacity to weigh many norms and to arrive at a judgment of the form, 'this is what I judge I must do' or 'not do.' The main purpose of that book is, however, to explain ampliative processes and the way in which they are rational.

Will takes note of a pair of articles by D. D. Raphael and J. O. Urmson. Each was convinced that he had made moral judgments and each reached the conclusion that the decision was a matter of 'intuition.' This was not intuition as conceived in the nineteenth century and before, where what was intuited was the truth of certain moral principles. Rather each claimed that what was intuited was what was to be done in a particular situation where moral principles conflicted. And further, each of the authors described the intuitive judgment as involving reasons. Raphael reported that his intuition was a choice of which obligation was the stronger. But the choice was not "irrational or nonrational."[13] For "choice without a reason would not be choice at all, since choice involves deliberation, a process of apparent reasoning."[14] Raphael remembers that that moral

---

[10] Peirce 1905, "What Pragmatism Is," in Pierce 1931–58, 5:298. Quoted in Will 1997, 83.

[11] Will 1997, ch. 1.

[12] Will 1997, ch. 8.

[13] Raphael 1974, 11.

[14] Raphael 1974, 12A–12B.

judgment rested on the conviction that a "rule could be absolute."[15]
He now thinks that that conviction was a mistake, and so that the
"decision is not arbitrary, completely subjective, or completely
nonrational, but it cannot be fitted to a precise formula either."[16]
He had a reason for his decision. Will found that Urmson in his
article maintained that "there is in moral decision-making an unavoidable need for an intuitive weighing and judgment of reasons
for and against competing alternatives" (*BD* 73).

Will recognizes the judgments there described as intuitions as
what we often call decisions of conscience (*cf. BD* 89). There is no
limit as to what kind of act conscience prescribes or proscribes.
Sometimes conscience has demanded total refusal to take part in
military service. At the same time conscience has demanded of
others that they immediately volunteer for service in the army. For
some, conscience has imposed a vegetarian diet, but has allowed
milk, butter, and eggs. For others conscience has prescribed total
abstinence from eating any animal or animal product. Such have
been the variety of deliverances of conscience.

Will has taken care to list the sources of the norms that go into
the deliverances of conscience. "As a child grows to maturity, . . .
he absorbs more and more of the moral standards of his community, or of the various communities of which he is a member. And .
. . the various standards which he absorbs in school, church, or
synagogue, may diverge widely from those derived from older
associates in work or play" (*BD* 137). Will gives as examples, the
Ten Commandments and the Golden Rule. He gives others also,
such as "what matters most is how you played the game, or, by
contrast, that there is no substitute for victory" (*BD* 137). Along
with the rule comes an understanding of "the conditions under
which and the way in which it is applied, its importance in relation
to other ways of proceeding" (*BD* 137). Reflection on the relative
importance of the relevant norms makes possible the decisions of
conscience.

---

[15] Raphael 1974, 12B.
[16] Raphael 1974, 12E.

At this point the expert in traditional ethical theory is likely to ask whether there will not be occasions when two persons come out with opposed moral judgments as the result of conscientious reflection. In such cases the expert will ask how we are to say which judgment is valid. Will, however, has no place in his account of morality for questions about validity out of context. What his account advises is a look at the social fact of morality as found in the community, if any, to which the partners in disagreement belong. They may be involved in rival proposals for change in the community. Will credits Hegel and the intermediary, F. H. Bradley, for calling attention to the role that institutions have in constituting a community and the consequent role that they play in establishing what in that community ought to be done or not done. Will also remarks on Professor Anscombe's article, "On Brute Facts," in which she notes that certain facts of existence establish what ought to be done.[17] As Will puts her point, "in a context of certain institutions, under normal circumstances, the fact that a merchant X supplied a customer Y with certain goods entails the further fact that Y owes X payment for those goods" (*BD* 167).

This answers Hume's challenge to explain how a statement about an 'ought' can be inferred from statements about 'is.' Disagreements between persons who have made conscientious judgments can be resolved only by their coming to agreement on the institutions that constitute their community.

When there are very basic and strongly controverted divisions of opinion over warranted changes or opposition to change—for example, at the present time, concerning abortion, sexual practices, and family life—judgments on the merits of contending alternatives and on a proper resolution of the controversy, before the event, before the slow moving, grinding body of norms of thought and action has come to 'intimate' some disposition, can be rendered by individuals, only with great tentativeness. (*BD* 227–28)

---

[17] Anscombe 1957–58.

Will quotes the summary of Kristin Luker's study of the abortion controversy in the United States today: "The abortion opponent believed in the traditional sex roles and saw motherhood as her highest mission in life, while the abortion supporter saw herself more as her husband's equal and viewed the unavailability of birth control and abortion as limiting her competitive chances in the world."[18] Whether this split will ever be resolved is a matter on which Will is unsure. He is familiar with Hegel's confidence that "the course is upward . . . toward rationality in some absolute form," but Will is "less bold and optimistic." Will holds that "it is not the function of reason . . . to ensure that the human journey of this world will terminate in some Promised Land."[19]

W. H. Walsh has reported a criticism of Hegel's ethics, that it leads to "some form of relativism, or perhaps the dissolution of ethics into sociology."[20] Will recognizes that his framework for ethics leads to relativism, but remarks that "it leads to a displacement of the relativism from a relation between individuals to one between communities."[21] But an ethic that fits the account that Will has given is not condemned to dissolve into sociology. For there is

> instruction available to us in others, and constantly from the course of life in the world, as to what is better and worse for us . . . .. For it is as creatures of this world, formed, clothed, instructed, often firmly corrected, and rarely cosseted by this world that the human species and its civilizations have come to be what they are. (*BD* 173)

There are "limitations and opportunities offered to us by external and internal nature," as adherents of natural law have stressed (*BD* 84). A community may be judged by the good and the harm occurring to individuals in it that can be attributed to the institutions that constitute the community. It is hard to get agreement on what is better for individuals, but it is easy to get agreement on what is

---

[18] Quoted by Will (1997, 173) from *Newsweek*, January 14, 1985, 21.
[19] Will 1997, 81, 82.
[20] Walsh 1969, 11.
[21] Will 1997, 78.

harmful to them. Professor Bernard Gert has developed this theme.[22]

Will's list of the sources of the norms that go into conscientious decisions consists of the many communities to which the person belongs. It does not include anything outside of nature. Will expects an explanation in natural terms of instances such as the answer to President McKinley's prayer for divine guidance as to whether to call on Congress to declare war on Spain. Claims of supernatural sources are sometimes made for moral injunctions, but Will presumes that there is an explanation in terms of natural causes. Will has provided a framework for describing a large variety of moralities and has indicated grounds for judging them in terms of what is better and worse for the individuals who are members of the community in which the morality in question prevails. There is no final enshrinement of any one morality. There is only the question of whether a proposal will be better or worse for the individuals involved than what currently prevails. This judgment requires factual study of what will result, which may well be called sociological study, and a reckoning of whether it is better or worse for the individuals affected.

In terms of Will's framework for every possible morality, persons who appeal to intuitions of right and wrong in arriving at a statement of morality are investigating the morality they live by, not an eternal fact. Will's views are in strong contrast to the pronouncement of Alan Donagan that "'morality' . . . stood for a standard by which systems of mores, actual and possible, were to be judged and by which everybody ought to live, no matter what the mores of his neighbors might be."[23] They are equally in disagreement with Gert's definition of morality. "Morality is a public system applying to all rational persons governing behavior which affects others and which has the minimization of evil as its end, and which includes what are commonly known as the moral rules as its core."[24] What Will

---

[22] Gert 1988.
[23] Donagan 1977, 1.
[24] Gert 1988, 6.

has set forth does not of course rule out such moralities, but his account of morality shows that it is not necessary for morality to be of that sort. They would say that what Will includes as a morality is merely a code of conduct, which in their eyes may well be an immoral code. Medical ethicists and business ethicists devote much of their work to just that, the scrutiny of particular cases in the light of the code of the relevant community. Only part of their work is devoted to proposing changes in that code.

Though some writers on ethics have maintained that the fundamental norms are set for mankind, Will maintains that they are "developed by human beings . . . dealing with the affairs of life" (*BD* 48). Not that they have been devised consciously any more than languages have. As Hayek remarks: "We merely need to consider language, which today nobody believes to have been 'invented by a rational being . . . in order to see that reason and civilization develop in constant mutual interaction."[25]

Will has given a naturalistic account of gaining knowledge and with it a naturalistic account of the sources of morality. He has recognized (1) the vehement, conscientious, but inconsistent judgments made by different individuals, (2) the fact that these individuals are members of communities constituted by institutions that settle that there are certain kinds of acts to be done or not to be done in circumstances of specified kinds, and (3) grounds for judging these communally based obligations in terms of the contrast with proposals for change to others that would better or worse for the individual members.

University of Wisconsin—Madison

References

Anscombe, G. E. M. 1957-58. "On Brute Facts." *Analysis*, 18 No. 3:69-72.

---

[25] *BD* 161, quoting Hayek 1948, 4.

Dewey, John. 1896. "The Reflex Arc Concept in Psychology." *Psychological Review* 3: 357-70. Revised version rpt. as "The Unit of Behavior." In *Philosophy and Civilization*. New York: Minton, Bach.

Donagan, Alan. 1977. *The Theory of Morality*. Chicago: University of Chicago Press.

Gert, Bernard. 1988. *Morality*. New York: Oxford University Press.

Hayek, F. A. 1948. *New Studies in Philosophy, Politics, Economics and the History of Ideas*. Chicago: University of Chicago Press.

Peirce, Charles S. 1931-58. *Collected Papers*. P. Weiss, C. Hartshorne, & A. Burks, eds. Cambridge, Mass.: Harvard University Press.

Raphael, David Daiches. 1974. "The Standard of Morals" and "The Appendix to the Standard of Morals." *Transactions of The Aristotelian Society* 85, 1974-1975: 1-12 and 12A-12E.

Urmson, John O. 1974. "A Defence of Intuitionism." *Transactions of The Aristotelian Society* 85, 1974-1975: 111–19.

Walsh, W. H. 1969. *Hegelian Ethics*. London: Macmillan.

Will, Frederick L. 1974. *Induction and Justification*. Ithaca: Cornell University Press.

Will, Frederick L. 1988. *Beyond Deduction*. New York and London: Routledge.

Will, Frederick L. 1997. *Pragmatism and Realism*. K. R. Westphal, ed. Lanham, Md.: Rowman & Littlefield.

9

Moral Intuitions and Philosophical Method

Martin Perlmutter

1 Frederick L. Will has always been meticulous about philosophical method. His earlier concern with the certainty and incorrigibility of foundational claims was a result of a deep appreciation of the inherent limitations of philosophy, especially when contrasted with the ambitious claims of foundationalists. His focus on induction was a result of his understanding that it exposed in a glaring way the weakness of the foundationalist project, and demonstrated the more proper, albeit more modest, ampliative functioning of philosophical reasoning. Contact with the world was not a product of unmediated sense experience, and the philosophical project was not showing how the structure of knowledge can be built on this bedrock of experience. Rather, philosophy could not transcend the system of knowledge to which it belonged as a member, though it could reflect in a systematic way on the system to which it belonged. Reason itself is rooted in practice, though it can be used to modify the practices in which it is rooted.

Philosophical disciplines, such as philosophy of law and philosophy of science, which had been relegated to second-tier status in the old foundationalist philosophical milieu, were freed to be true exemplars of philosophical method on the model of philosophy as ampliative reasoning. Reason, understood critically and reflectively, was able to have a useful and constructive function within and about well-established intellectual disciplines, such as law and science.

Will's career spans this transition and has contributed to it; his writings express very well the grapplings of an extraordinary thinker with a system undergoing change. From his earlier writings on induction to his most recent papers on the philosophical governance of norms, Will's work demonstrates a self-conscious concern about philosophical method, while at the same time showing the genuine contribution that philosophy can make to systems of knowledge. His attention to detail, especially in his earlier work, and his own cautious nature mask the broad sweep of his writings.

This paper will reflect on the philosophical governance of norms, Will's central concern in many of his later papers. Will views norms as "socio-psychological entities that interlock with each other and are rooted deeply in the practices of individuals and their communities." On his view, norms are not private representations that can be discovered by introspection, nor can reflecting on individual judgments uncover norms from which these judgments are constituted. His view of norms is pragmatic. Norms are deeply rooted in the practices of the community and available to its members as participants in the community. Norms are based on practice, and are not essentially the private mental representations of the practitioners.

My specific focus in this paper will be the philosophical method that uncovers or discovers ethical principles by considering particular examples about which we have strong intuitions. The suggestion implicit in this method is that the intuition needs to be grounded, that there must be some general statement from which this particular judgment follows. This tacit knowledge is what grounds the intuition and this tacit knowledge is available to the agent because it is the basis of the intuition. One aim of moral philosophy is to expose these general principles, thereby rendering coherent our various intuitions, even if some of our intuitions need to be revised by the principles uncovered by such philosophical scrutiny. Examples are central to the method because they provide the opportunity for exposing the appropriate ethical principle; they base the system of ethical knowledge. The tacit knowledge gains support from the example, since the intuition must be grounded by some more general principle. My aim in this paper is to criticize this method.

I will begin with two examples that have been influential in modern moral philosophy—Thomson's violinist example and Singer's example of passing a pond with a child in distress in it. Both Thomson and Singer use these examples as support for general but quite different moral principles. It is difficult to sort through these examples with general principles that handle them in a consistent way. I will suggest that this difficulty shows that our conflicting intuitions might not be based on the application of broad ethical principles to particular cases. Next, I will present some recent research in social psychology that demonstrates how framing identical choices differently results in widely different and inconsistent preferences. That research raises yet more serious problems about the ability to generate ethical principles on the basis of intuitions about particular cases, since our individual judgments are subject to nonrational factors in virtue of which they are internally inconsistent. That is, the only rendition of preferences must make the agent inconsistent, at least prior to reflecting on the preferences. Finally, I will return to some of Will's most recent writings to show how the critical project of this paper is a prelude to his more constructive thoughts about the nature of norms.

2 Perhaps the best known example in the contemporary philosophical literature on ethics is Judith Thomson's example of an ailing violinist whose supporters attach him to your kidney. As the story goes, the violinist needs a kidney to survive, you have the only kidneys that will do the job, you are connected to the violinist without your consent, and at this point unhooking the violinist will result in his death. Thomson concludes that it is ludicrous to think that you are obligated to provide the violinist continued use of your kidneys, even if it is necessary for his continued life, that though the violinist has a right to life, the violinist has no claim on you

for the wherewithal necessary for his continued life, so the violinist has no claim on you for the continued use of your kidneys. She concludes that the right to life is fundamentally different from the right to assistance, that though it would be kind and splendidly decent of you to forego some of your life's pleasures to help the violinist, you are surely under no obligation to do so. This restricted negative conception of the right to life has a liberal result when applied to the abortion controversy. For, on Thomson's view, even if the fetus has a right to life, it does not have any claims on the woman's body in virtue of that right, and abortion is best understood as the pregnant woman appropriately and legitimately declining to assist the fetus. Just as you are entitled to decide to no longer assist the violinist, the woman is entitled to refuse giving the fetus further aid.

Thomson's example is ingenious and her intuition about her case seems correct. It makes us think of the pregnant woman as a person, not merely a receptacle sponsoring another person. We are not obligated to provide strangers with kidneys, especially for long periods of time, even when those kidneys are necessary for life itself. Her analysis of the intuition is more general and less persuasive, since it is hard to generalize from a violinist to a fetus, from a kidnapped kidney provider to a pregnant woman and, most generally and most significantly, from a refusal to provide kidneys to an ailing musician to allowing a fetus with a right to life to be aborted. That is, the intuition about limiting our obligations to the violinist in need of a kidney seems correct, even if the philosophical story that Thomson tells to ground the intuition is unnecessarily complex to support it. Her account is less persuasive than her case. After all, the threat that each of us might be required to donate one of our kidneys to some needy stranger in virtue of being kidnapped is enough to persuade us not to talk of obligations in Thomson's imaginative case. That requirement is too much of an imposition on the sort of life we are accustomed to living in a way that restricting abortions might not be.

Thomson wants to use her case to model moral thought. She wants to restrict our obligations to others and to give women the freedom to have abortions. Her aim is not merely to analyze the violinist example. So, she finds the principle implicit in her case, a restricted view of obligations, assumes it is what governs the violinist case, and applies it to other cases, such as abortion. This tacit knowledge is to extend to other cases as well. But not every case seems to be governed by the same principle. At least our intuitions about abortion do not have the clarity of the violinist example.

Consider the following case, which is similar in structure to the violinist case; at least, it is similar to the structure that Thomson is drawing our attention to, but it has an altogether different outcome. You have been longing for a winter of solitude for some time and have finally arranged your winter escape to a cabin far removed from civilization. Just as the first snow sets in, thereby isolating you for the long winter in your small secluded cabin, and you anxiously lock your provisions in your small, secluded cabin, you discover a small infant wrapped in warm clothes resting on your doorstep. The infant will surely die without your help, but helping the infant would seriously compromise your plans for a winter of solitude. You have done nothing to incur an obligation to the infant; the infant's plight is not a result of anything that you did and you did not consent to help the infant. Moreover, the infant is not responsible for its plight.

This case produces clear intuitions as well. These intuitions require of you that you help the infant, that you not let it die. One can generalize from this case too, but with different results from the Thomson example. One can talk about our obligations to prevent death and the importance of protecting innocent victims' lives, even at some cost to third parties who did not volunteer to protect those innocent victims. One might want to speak impartially about the insignificance of a winter of solitude when compared to the life of an innocent baby and insist that helping the baby is not just an act of charity or of kindness, that one who does not help is more than merely insensitive or unkind. More simply, one can point to the vulnerability of innocent babies and their need for societal protection. This intuition and the story behind it produce an altogether different result when applied to the abortion issue.

Peter Singer draws these conclusions about our obligations to others from his example of passing a shallow pond in which there is a drowning child. Of course, we should wade in and save the child from drowning even if it results in our clothes getting muddy. His principle is that if it is in our power to prevent something bad from happening, without thereby sacrificing anything of comparable moral importance, we ought morally to do it. A life is worth more than soiled clothing; the soiled clothing is not comparable in moral importance to a saved life. Singer's particular interest with his example is famine relief and our obligation to help the destitute, so he insists that distance is not morally relevant, nor is the fact that there are countless others also in a position to help the hungry. Had he been interested in abortion and had he granted Thomson's assumption that the fetus is a child at conception, he could have reached a conservative conclusion on the abortion issue. After all, a life is worth more than the mother's inconvenience.

Singer focuses on consequences to account for our intuition to save the drowning child. He too draws very general conclusions from his example. Like Thomson's analysis of the violinist example, Singer's analysis of our intuition about the drowning child is less persuasive than the case it analyzes. There is no question that we should help the drowning child. But famine relief is a lot less clear. And his analysis would obligate me to stay hooked up to the violinist, an outcome that is ludicrous, as Thomson points out.

These three examples have structural similarities. Each of them describes a situation where a life is at stake, where the life can be saved, and where the person who can save the life has done nothing to incur an obligation to the victim, who is not responsible for his life being at stake. The problem is that they seem to conflict, at least according to plausible analyses of the intuitions. So, on Thomson's analysis, there should be no obligation in the mountain cabin case or even in the drowning baby case, but it seems clear that there is. And a dying violinist's life is morally more significant than my being hooked up to his kidneys, so I should be required to make some sacrifices to help him out, at least according to Singer. But it seems clear that I am not.

3 Our intuitions about the cases are stubborn. They do not change in virtue of the seeming inconsistency between them. Singer's drowning baby example does not make us think differently about the ailing violinist, nor does Thomson's violinist story make us think differently about the drowning baby. Nor do our intuitions change when the apparent inconsistency is pointed out, not even when we are unable to come up with a principle that shows the inconsistency to be only apparent and not real.

Of course, there are important differences between the cases that we can point to in order to account for the apparently conflicting intuitions. There is a reason to help in the one case and not in the other. We have to say something in response to the charge of inconsistency, even if it is not so general as a principle that sorts through the cases in a consistent fashion. So, an infant or a young child is different from a mature adult. A terminal condition is different from temporary distress. Coming upon a situation in which our help is needed is different from being kidnapped. An imposition that is placed in an unusual situation is different from an imposition that would overwhelm everybody's ordinary lives. And so on.

Thomson is wise to use a case that highlights coercion, a terminal condition, a mature adult, and a large imposition placed on everybody's life if generalized. Those features are important for the intuition not to require assistance that Thomson applies with some imagination to abortion. It is imaginative because the fetus did not kidnap the mother, being in a womb is not a terminal condition, and so on. Singer's case too is clever in the features it emphasizes. It emphasizes temporary distress, a young child, and an only occasional and short-lived imposition even if generalized. Singer too is imaginative in extending his drowning baby case to famine relief.

Famine is not temporary distress and famine relief is not an occasional and short-lived imposition. In fact, Singer's principle would have a profound impact on the way in which we are entitled to live our ordinary lives.

Our practices are far more particular than these generalizations suggest. We often have a clear sense of what is required in particular situations. The violinist example and the drowning baby example are such situations. Other situations produce a less clear sense of what is required; abortion and famine relief are such situations.

These generalizations do have a great deal of plausibility. That is, it does seem correct to say that saving a human life is required even if it inconveniences the agent greatly. So, we should contribute to famine relief, and even go without air-conditioning or a car to help the less fortunate. Seen in this way, the worth of a human life is not merely a local norm, restricted to saving a drowning baby. Rather, it reflects a moral principle that ought to govern people's lives, even if people are blinded by their own situation to recognizing the demands of the moral life. That is Singer's argument.

Thomson objects, thinking that the demands that Singer places on us all are excessive, far beyond the morally required. Talking about kidneys is her way of emphasizing the limits on the impositions that the moral life places on us. Thomson thinks that Singer's view of the moral life will overwhelm our entire lives.

We might come up with some principle that papers over the difference between Singer's and Thomson's examples. So, we might say that one ought to save a life if doing so is not a significant inconvenience. Staying hooked up to the violinist is a significant inconvenience, dirtying one's clothing is not. Two points are in order. First, it is not at all clear that this principle captures the important differences between the examples. Losing one's winter of solitude is a much more significant inconvenience than various versions of the kidney example. But one seems obligated in the former in a way that one is not obligated in the latter. Second, this principle is plausible only because of its indeterminacy. As soon as significant inconvenience is specified, the plausibility of the principle evaporates. The principle thus hardly provides the substance necessary for grounding our moral intuitions.

Some more modest generalizations are appropriate, as the following *ceteris paribus* claims indicate. Large impositions are to be avoided more than small ones; younger people in temporary distress have a larger claim on strangers than older people in a terminal condition; the integrity of one's body is more important than the cleanliness of one's apparel. These general claims are far more particular than Singer's principle of maximizing the good or Thomson's negative conception of rights.

These *ceteris paribus* claims indicate that there are differences that we can point to. Different judgments show that there is something different about the cases being judged. But our practices are not informed by generalizations of the wide scope suggested by Thomson and Singer.

Singer and Thomson are providing the sort of account that underlies much of ethical methodology. That is, we have moral intuitions; moral intuitions are grounded on moral principles; we are to be rational; consistency is a minimal condition of rationality; so there should be a consistent account of our moral intuitions, even if we ourselves are unable to come up with it. Thomson and Singer are attempting to provide the principles that they see as underlying our moral intuitions.

It is not surprising that analyses of different cases might produce ethical principles that are inconsistent. Without such seeming inconsistencies, the ethical enterprise would be altogether too easy, requiring only the analysis of easy examples to uncover the appropriate governing ethical principle. What is surprising is the difficulty of coming up with any principle that sorts our intuitions about these cases.

In the next section, I consider some recent psychological research that suggests that the principles according to which consistency might be established about particular cases might well be principles that must be unavailable to the persons with the intuitions. That is, the intuitions themselves are inconsistent with the agent's own view of the situation when the agent reflects on it; the agent will readily concede that irrelevant factors resulted in the judgment. These data raise doubt about the possibility of establishing coherence between our judgments about particular cases, since our judgments are influenced in a predictable way by factors that we ourselves insist are irrelevant.

4 The philosophical model relies on the assumption that there is tacit knowledge that accounts for the judgments about particular cases. This knowledge, while not transparent to the agent, is what supports the particular judgments; it is the general principle on which the judgment is based. This knowledge comprises the more general ethical beliefs of the agent and these general beliefs are necessary for the agent to reach the particular judgment about specific cases.

Recent findings in the psychological literature cast doubt on the possibility of the philosophical enterprise of ordering intuitions according to coherent ethical principles. They suggest that our intuitions are based, not on general principles, but on more local features of cases. In fact, intuitions are often a result of a variety of circumstances of which the agent is unaware. Moreover, the agent is not well positioned to sort through the varying intuitions. I will focus on two examples.

The first finding suggests a fundamental incoherence between an agent's intuitions by focusing on cases that differ only in a small detail, but that generate predictable but conflicting judgments. The detail hardly supports the difference; in fact, individuals will revise their judgments when shown how much the detail mattered to their earlier judgments. The second shows that identical situations occasionally generate different preferences depending on how the situation is presented. Intuitions about the same case vary in predictable ways in virtue of the way in which the case is framed. The first finding confirms the difficulty of coming up with a principle that underlies our own intuitions; the second suggests that the account according to which preferences are to be sorted is not one that an agent could himself accept as a sorting principle.

Miller and McFarland (1986) asked respondents to determine the appropriate compensation for a man shot in the arm during the robbery of a grocery store. Some respondents were told that the robbery happened at the victim's regular store while others were told that it took place at a store that the victim visited for the first time because his regular store happened to be closed that day. The median award given by the respondents was $100,000 larger in the second case, where the victim was visiting a store for the first time. Miller and McFarland hypothesize that this is a result of the second case being more 'poignant.' (People feel more sympathy for a person who is injured in virtue of an irregular, nonroutine occurrence.) The counterfactual undoing of an unusual or irregular event is easier than the undoing of a regular event, and so evokes a sharper response. It is as if the person is less responsible for the injury because it is not something that he regularly does.

Nonetheless, a separate survey of respondents showed that 90 percent thought the difference in poignancy is irrelevant, that there should be no difference in compensation between the two cases. After all, the harm is the same and the agent is not responsible for being shot in either case. This is an instance of the framing effect; a factor that people claim to be irrelevant affects their judgments about cases presented to them. Poignancy matters to people who also believe that it should not. The more poignant case evokes a stronger response, even though it should not according to the agents themselves.

This case provides a difficulty in organizing judgments into a coherent system, since factors that are important in determining individual judgments are ones that the persons themselves deny are important. That is, judgments about particular situations cannot themselves be taken at face value; they might well need to be revised in virtue of the way the situation is presented. Poignancy is a factor that would have to be discounted in virtue of the 'second-order' judgment that it is irrelevant, even though it is relevant to the initial judgment that awarded higher compensation to the more poignant situation.

The difficulty of rendering a person's judgments consistent should be apparent. We can revise the initial judgment about the one case being worth more compensation, but that revision is made only in virtue of the apparent inconsistency between awarding the one case more while at the same time believing that poignancy should not be a factor. The easier way to account for the person's beliefs is to say that the person believes both that the second case is worth more than the first and that poignancy should not be a factor in determining awards. Of course, this would make the agent's beliefs inconsistent. We will return to this issue after we look at a yet more dramatic example of the framing effect.

Tversky and Kahneman (1981) framed the following problem in different ways to groups of respondents. The respondents were asked to give their preferences between two different programs to combat the outbreak of an unusual Asian disease, which is expected to kill 600 people. Program A will save 200 people, whereas Program B will result in a 1/3 probability that 600 people will be saved. Seventy-eight percent of the respondents (150) preferred A; only 28 percent of the respondents preferred B. the majority choice is risk averse; the sure prospect of saving 200 lives is more attractive than a risky prospect of saving everybody, even though the total expected value of the two choices is the same.

Tversky and Kahneman then framed the question about the same program differently to another group of respondents. Program C will result in 400 deaths whereas Program D will result in a 1/3 probability that nobody will die and a 2/3 probability that 600 people will die. 78% of the respondents (155) preferred D; only 22% preferred C. Here the majority choice is risk taking; the certain death of 400 people is less attractive than the two in three chance that 600 people will die.

Program A and Program C are extensionally equivalent; the only difference between them is that one describes the outcomes in terms of lives lost, the other in terms of lives saved. This too is the framing effect. Irrelevant factors are operative in determining particular judgments. The differing preferences violate elementary requirements of consistency and coherence, since the outcomes are extensionally equivalent. That is, rational choice should not depend on the way in which the question is framed. In this case, the issue is not coming up with a principle that would render the two choices coherent, since by their very nature they are inconsistent.

There are principles that make sense of particular judgments. For example, respondents are more sympathetic to more poignant situations and are inclined to award higher damages to individuals harmed in those situations. Also, respondents are not inclined to take poignancy seriously when it is pointed out to them as a factor in judgments. Cognitive psychologists can devise tests to discover principles of this sort. But these principles are sophisticated and not available to the agent on introspection. Moreover, these principles require some particular judgments to be discounted, suggesting both that the representations of the structure of principles cannot be erected on the particular judgments alone and that the agent is not well positioned to come up with a consistent set of principles. In fact, the agent is poorly positioned to come up with an account of the principles on which the individual judgments are based.

The framing effect is striking in the case of the flu epidemic because it calls into question the possibility of rendering coherent the various particular judgments of the agent. An explanation of the inconsistent particular judgments is possible; again, this is a task that cognitive psychologists do well. There is the framing effect—persons are risk averse when the danger is highlighted, but risk takers when the benefits are highlighted. So, the same situation will predictably produce conflicting judgments depending on whether the dangers are highlighted or the benefits are highlighted. But there can be no set of principles that renders the particular judgments consistent, since it is the same situation that is producing the conflicting judgments.

5 This paper has focused on the difficulty of discovering principles that underlie intuitions. It is difficult to order our moral intuitions about specific cases into a coherent system of ethical beliefs, especially if those ethical beliefs are very general. Ethical norms are far more local, appropriate to particular cases but without the generality that would extend to all cases. So, Thomson's attempt to derive a principle from her violinist example that can be applied to the abortion issue is bound to fail.

Her attempt can be viewed differently. She might be urging us to consider abortion in a certain way; she is focusing her attention on certain features of the abortion controversy. So, restricting abortions places a large burden on women; the women did not volunteer; the fetus cannot survive without the help of the woman; people are generally not required to go to great lengths to help others unless they contract to do so. The norms she is recommending for abortion underscore individualistic virtues, the separateness of persons, and the difference between negative rights and positive obligations. Her violinist example does an excellent job of highlighting these particular virtues and the danger of extending obligations too widely.

Singer has different norms that he is advocating in famine relief. His example features a young and innocent victim, helping someone to whom one has made no commitment, and providing a great benefit at a minimum cost. Singer's focus is on the importance of consequences, on communal virtues, and thus on our need to help others in need. Singer's drowning baby example does that very well.

Both individualistic norms and communal norms are part of our rich cultural legacy. Both have clear applications, as Singer's example and Thomson's example show. There are other areas in which the competition between these norms has not yet been worked out. Famine relief and abortion are part of that indeterminate area. Taking a clear case in which one norm is dominant and applying the norm to a case where it is not is hardly decisive.

The focus of this paper has been negative, claiming that the methodology of ethics makes assumptions that the psychological literature might not support. Ethical reasoning might not depend on general principles in the ways that Singer and Thomson urge. We have strong views about particular cases and particular situations. We can provide reasons for our views, but the reasons do not have the generality to provide for a coherent system of intuitions on the part of the agent.

Frederick Will's recent work has been more positive. His reflections on the philosophical governance of norms is a systematic attempt to discuss how norms operate, how they become transformed, and the positive role philosophy can play in that process. His work begins where the negative work of this paper ends. His defense of philosophical reasoning and reflective governance shows how the indeterminacy between conflicting norms is a feature of the landscape in which we live. He says it well toward the end of "Philosophic Governance of Norms":

> The typical occasions of philosophical governance are those in which for one reason or other accepted, ready-to-hand norms are insufficient to guide decision and action. Aspirant governors trained in and committed to deductive procedure will continue to search and fail to discover occult, recondite norms that will enable them to avoid the disagreeable indeterminacy. Here philosophic minds need to learn the merit of the common practice of learning to live with, and then learning to appreciate the absolute indispensability to reflective human life of this indeterminacy. For it is out of occasions of such indeterminacy, out of frustration, indecision and painful travail in them, that new norms, superseding forms of life, are developed.[1]

That is a more positive message. It is also an altogether useful function that philosophers can help execute. There are no discoverable norms that merely need to be applied to indeterminate areas to decide appropriate behavior. The indeterminacy is more fundamental, since norms appropriate to one practice might not be generalizable to another. But the philosophical task is crucial. For the

---

[1] Will, 1997, 190.

role of women and our obligations to the needy will be decided by it, at least in part.

College of Charleston

References

Miller, D. T., and C. McFarland. 1986. "Counterfactual thinking and Victim Compensation: A test of Norm Theory." *Personality and social Psychology Bulletin* 12 No. 4: 513-19.

Singer, Peter. 1979. *Practical Ethics*. Cambridge: Cambridge University Press.

Thomson, Judith Jarvis. 1971. "A Defense of Abortion." *Philosophy and Public Affairs* 1 No. 1: 47-66.

Tversky, A. and D. Kahneman. 1981. "The Framing of Decisions and the Psychology of Choice." *Science* 211: 453-58.

Will, Fredrick L. 1997. *Pragmatism and Realism*. K. R. Westphal, ed. Lanham, Md.: Rowman & Littlefield.

10

Two Problems in Hans Kelsen's Legal Philosophy

Stanley L. Paulson

1 INTRODUCTION

A legal fiction, as Hans Vaihinger writes in his celebrated work, *Die Philosophie des Als Ob*, is "the subsumption of a case under a conceptual construct that does not properly include it."[1] For example, in a number of Western legal systems a man cohabitating with a woman who gives birth to a child is deemed to be the father of that child whether, biologically, he is the father or not. The fiction reflects a laudable policy, that of assuring financial support for the child.

The example stems from the law. Fictions are also familiar from legal philosophy, which is my focus here. In particular, I consider two concepts that spell trouble for Hans Kelsen's legal philosophy. One is the fictitious *legal person*. The second is the fictitious *basic norm*, a doctrine that Kelsen develops in his later (post-1960) work. Where the fictitious legal person is concerned, there is not only a long history of development in German legal theory, both before and after the enactment of the German Civil Code in 1900, but also, as Franz Wieacker has noted,[2] a direct continuum in this

---

[1] Vaihinger 1913, 46 (Part 1: ch. 5).
[2] Wieacker 1973, 340, *cf.* 361–64.

development from Friedrich Carl von Savigny to Kelsen—by way of Georg Friedrich Puchta, Bernhard Windscheid, and Ernst Rudolph Bierling. The second example, that of the fictitious basic norm, represents in one respect a state of affairs diametrically opposed to that of the first example. To my knowledge, no one had anticipated and no one has followed Kelsen's curious doctrine of the basic norm *qua* fiction. Perhaps no one could. For the fictitious basic norm serves in Kelsen's later theory as a kind of rump surrogate for the neo-Kantian philosophy of law that he abandoned late in his career.

My special concern is with Kelsen's understanding of these fictions and with their import for legal philosophy generally. As we shall see, Kelsen takes a dim view of the traditional doctrine of the fictitious legal person, contending that it has been a source of confusion. More important than his analysis of earlier theorists' difficulties with the doctrine, however, is a problem of Kelsen's own making: In the Pure Theory of Law the systemic or theoretical tie between the legal person and the natural person, the human being, is completely severed. It cannot be otherwise, given the unbridgeable gap between "is" and "ought," between radically distinct modes of cognition, one causal or explicative, the other juridico-normative. And Kelsen in fact recognizes that he faces, here, an antinomy.[3]

Kelsen introduces the fictitious basic norm in his late work, following Vaihinger's reading of the fiction, according to which the fiction not only "contradicts reality," but is, indeed, "self-contradictory." Once Kelsen has introduced the fictitious basic norm, however, the normativity of the law also becomes a fiction. For it was the normativity thesis, claiming the irreducibly normative character of the law,[4] that the basic norm was supposed to establish; now, with the fictitious basic norm, one proceeds *as though* the material

---

[3] See the quotations from Kelsen (1925) in the text on p. 230 below.

[4] On Kelsen's normativity thesis see generally Raz 1981; see also Paulson 1992, esp. 313–22. On the distinction between Kelsen's normativity thesis and the counterpart in H. L. A. Hart's theory, see Paulson 1993.

of the law were irreducibly normative. It scarcely need be added that from the standpoint of the classical Pure Theory of Law and its provocative normativity thesis, this is a disastrous result.

I take up, in turn, these two examples of fictions, considering the problems they reflect in Kelsen's legal philosophy. Section 2 is devoted to the doctrine of the fictitious legal person. I look first to Savigny, introducing with reference to his work both the doctrine and the ensuing problem of unity. I then develop Kelsen's position, beginning with his rejection of the natural person or human being as a possible candidate for legal subject, and then moving on to his rejection of the concept of artificial legal person and its replacement with "points of imputation," a part of his thoroughgoing reconstruction of the fundamental concepts of legal theory, already well under way in the *Hauptprobleme der Staatsrechtslehre*, his first major work.[5] In section 3, on the fictitious basic norm, I begin with Kelsen's very early work on the basic norm, turning then briefly to his "transcendental" or neo-Kantian reading of the notion, and, finally, to his introduction of the fictitious basic norm.

2 THE FICTITIOUS LEGAL PERSON: SAVIGNY AND KELSEN

Otto von Gierke underscores the paradigm shift wrought by Savigny.[6] "Departing from the merely collective 'moral person'" of the past, Savigny moves "a self-contained artificial individual, under the rubric of 'legal person,' to stage center" in the private law.[7] In *System des heutigen römischen Rechts*, Savigny, whose civil law system is developed out of the idea of private autonomy and, in that respect, too, marks a new beginning,[8] puts the question: *Who is the legal subject?*[9] His answer stems from a point outside the legal

---

[5] Kelsen 1923; 1st ed. 1911.

[6] Savigny 1840–49, repr. 1981; hereafter cited as "*System I*," "*System II*," with section and page numbers).

[7] Gierke 1895, 464. On the earlier concept, that of "moral person," see Denzer 1977.

[8] See *e.g.* Kiefner 1969, 4. See generally Rückert 1984, and Behrends 1985.

[9] Savigny, *System II*, §60 (p. 1).

system. The legal subject, in a word, is the *human being*. And this point of departure is no accident. Savigny has a Kantian argument,[10] of moral import, that underscores the central significance of the human being in his theory:

> All law is given for the sake of the moral freedom possessed by every individual. Therefore, the original concept of the person or of the legal subject must coincide with the concept of the human being.[11]

Thus, Savigny continues, there is an "original identity" of the concepts 'legal subject' and 'human being.' "Every individual human being, and only the individual human being, has legal capacity."[12]

Savigny does not, however, remain true to the statement that legal subject and human being are identical. His qualifying language respecting an *original* identity suggests exceptions;[13] in particular, he goes on to increase the size of the class of legal subjects by extending it beyond that of natural persons. As he writes:

> Legal capacity has been established above as coinciding with the notion of the individual human being (§60). We have now to consider it as extended to artificial subjects admitted by means of a pure fiction. We designate such a subject a *legal person*, that is to say, a person who is assumed to be so for reasons purely legal in nature. Thus, just as the human being is a bearer of legal relations, so likewise for the legal person.[14]

The artificial legal person is introduced by means of a "pure fiction," and the idea of a fiction—of that which is contrary to fact—

---

[10] An older, influential statement is Binder 1907, 10. See also Wieacker 1967, 353–54, 397 at note 69, and Kiefner 1969.

[11] Savigny, *System* II, §60 (p. 2), see also *System* I, §52 (pp. 331–32).

[12] Savigny, *System* II, §60 (p. 2).

[13] See generally Dießelhorst 1982–83, esp. 322–27.

[14] Savigny, *System* II, §85 (p. 236) (Savigny's emphasis). Savigny's reference back to §60 is a reference to the passage quoted above, p. 222.

is the key to Savigny's doctrine. If legal relations can be attributed only to human beings, then to introduce an additional legal subject, beyond the "original identity" of human being and legal subject, is to introduce a fiction, an invented subject.[15] Fictions being what they are, Savigny's doctrine of the fictitious legal person is not a theory, for it explains nothing. Rather, it amounts to a formula that warrants treating a corporation, a foundation, and the like as a legal subject in spite of the fact that they fail to fit the original mold, that of legal subject *qua* human being.[16]

The next step in tracing the doctrine takes us to anomalies, which Savigny himself develops. Granting that the legal person is fictitious, there can be no question of an attribution of human will or human acts to it. What, then, of property rights, which are acquired by means of acts? "Acts presuppose a thinking and willing being, a human being, precisely what legal persons *qua* fictions are not." The result is an anomaly, the "internal contradiction" of a subject with "the capacity to acquire property rights despite the subject's inability to satisfy the requisite conditions of their acquisition."[17] Savigny purports to resolve the anomaly by appealing to *representation*. A natural person must stand in for the artificial person, performing on behalf of the latter the acts that are required.

Savigny's solution, however, gives rise to another anomaly: The acts performed by the representative are attributed to the artificial legal person *as its own acts*.[18] In Savigny's words: The "real existence" of the legal person "is based on the will of certain human beings"; "in the name of a fiction," their will is attributed to the "artificial legal person as its own will."[19] In this way, the artificial legal person acquires an "artificial will."[20]

---

[15] See Wieacker 1973, 361.
[16] See Wolff 1938, esp. 505–7.
[17] Savigny, *System* II, §90 (p. 282).
[18] Likewise, *mutatis mutandis*, in public law. See below, p. 229.
[19] Savigny, *System* II, §94 (p. 312).
[20] *Ibid.* §94 (p. 316).

Savigny's introduction of the artificial legal person along with the anomalies to which it gave rise sets the stage for a long and protracted debate, in nineteenth-century legal theory, on the status and role of the legal person generally. Following Savigny for the most part, Puchta defines legal personality as "the possibility of legal will." At the same time, Puchta offers what appears to be a second definition of legal personality, namely, as "the capacity to have subjective rights."[21] In so far as the latter definition can be read independently of the former, it marks Puchta's anticipation of things to come. Rather than beginning, as in Savigny's *System*, with a characterization of legal subject from *outside* the legal system, namely, the legal subject *qua* human being, the question of the identity of the legal subject is answered, following Puchta's second definition, *entirely from inside* the legal system:[22] Where "X" is an unspecified reference point, then if subjective rights can be attributed to X, it follows that X is a legal subject.

Others developed altogether different doctrines—with, for example, Alois Brinz arguing that the legal person was not a legal subject at all ("subjectless"), but rather a conceptualization of "property earmarked for a particular purpose,"[23] and with Otto von Gierke arguing that the legal person was a living being, an organism: "The corporation *qua* real collective person not only has legal capacity but is capable of willing and acting, too."[24] Gierke's position, in particular, became notorious. He builds into the collective person precisely those attributes that are conspicuous by their absence in Savigny's fictitious legal person—the capacity to will and to act. Gierke pays an extraordinarily high price for this solu-

---

[21] Puchta 1863, §22 (p. 37).

[22] See John 1977. Wieacker (1973, 363) goes much further, contending that Puchta, far from merely anticipating the later view with its characterization of the legal subject entirely from inside the legal system, gives full expression to it, relegating the legal person to a mere "point of intersection in a logical scheme of normative reference."

[23] Brinz 1873, §§59–61 (pp. 194–205).

[24] Gierke 1887, 603, and see 607 *et passim*. On Gierke, see the critique in Wieacker 1973, 368–70.

tion; he would have us believe that the legal subject is neither a human being nor an invented subject, but nevertheless a living person, albeit a collective person. This, it must be said, is bad metaphysics.

The general debate over the legal person is not, however, my concern here. Rather, I am concerned with a single aspect of it—the problem set by Savigny's doctrine. As we have seen, instead of a *single* concept of the legal person, there are two concepts in Savigny's *System*, radically distinct from each other: the natural person, and the fictitious legal person. The problem here may be understood as the *problem of unity*. Kelsen, to be sure, cannot be read as responding directly to Savigny. He is, however, properly read as representing a further step in a linear development of the concept of the legal person,[25] a development that begins with Savigny.

Kelsen's resolution of the problem of unity is two-fold. First, he rejects—necessarily, given his premises—the natural person as a possible candidate for the legal subject. What remains is the fictitious legal person, *one* concept rather than a duality of concepts. And that counts, *ceteris paribus*, as a solution to the problem of unity.

This statement of Kelsen's solution is couched, however, in the parlance of Savigny, which strictly speaking is not correct. For having rejected the natural person as a possible candidate for the legal subject, Kelsen goes on to replace the artificial legal person with "points of imputation," "conceptually constructed points of normative reference."[26] I take up in turn these two parts of Kelsen's

---

[25] See *e.g.* Kelsen 1920, §4 (pp. 16–21), §31 (pp. 124–30), §38 (esp. pp. 160–161), §59 (pp. 289–194), §62 (pp. 309–314); Kelsen 1925, §§13–15(d) (pp. 62–74); Kelsen 1992, §§20–25(f) (pp. 39–52), §46 (p. 97); Kelsen 1945, 93–109, 181–201; Kelsen 1960, §§29–33 (pp. 130–195), §41(b) (pp. 293–314).

[26] See Kelsen 1923, 71–78, 121–46, 183–87, 517–20, 707–09, *et passim*; Kelsen 1925, §10(c) (pp. 48–51), §13(d) (pp. 65–66), §15(a)(b) (pp. 71–72), §38(c) (pp. 267–68), §43(a) (pp. 310–11); Kelsen 1992, §11(b) (pp. 23–25), §§25(a)(b),(d)(e) (pp. 46–51), §§48(a)(b) (pp. 99–101). I discuss some details of imputation (or *Zurechnung*) in the sixth of the "Supplementary Notes," in *ibid.* at pp. 134–35; for a full statement of the problem of imputation by a younger contemporary of Kelsen's, see Voegelin 1924.

solution to the problem of unity, and close the section with a critique.

Why is it necessary for Kelsen, as stated above, to reject altogether the natural person, the human being, as a candidate for the legal subject? His position is dictated by the general tenets of the Pure Theory, two of which are absolutely fundamental. First, there is the unbridgeable gap between "is" and "ought," between the natural world and an "ideal" or normative sphere, as Kelsen sometimes puts it.[27] Second, Kelsen introduces radically distinct modes of cognition—a causal or explicative mode, and a juridico-normative mode.[28] In a corollary of this tenet, Kelsen shows how the cognitive modes reflect his dualistic ontology: Each mode of cognition has its "proper object"—the causal or explicative mode is directed to the objects and events of reality, while the juridico-normative mode is directed to the objects of an ideal or a normative sphere. Indeed, the connection between mode of cognition and its "proper object" is far stronger than the language here suggests. As Kelsen puts it, the mode of cognition *determines* the object of cognition.[29]

---

[27] See *e.g.* Kelsen 1923, 6–8.

[28] See *e.g.* Kelsen 1923, 4–5. Kelsen adopts the distinction from Wilhelm Windelband. It is reasonable to assume that Kelsen was also influenced by the distinction, familiar in the work of the later nineteenth-century German public law theorists, between two approaches to the law and state, two points of view (*Betrachtungsweisen*). See *e.g.* Gerber 1880, 224 (*Beilage* II): "[T]he so-called organic view of the state and the legal view are related to one another as two approaches to the same object, each from a different standpoint. The aim of the former is to specify the natural life of the state, its physiology, the aim of the latter, to specify the ethico-juridical content of the state."

[29] See *e.g.* Kelsen 1923, "Foreword," xvii. To be sure, the status of this notion, in Kelsen's work, is not at all clear. It antedates his most promising development of a neo-Kantian foundation for his theory—a foundation that, at least on one reading, reflects something of the Marburg School of Hermann Cohen. In the idea that "the mode of cognition determines the object of cognition," there is, however, nothing at all peculiar to the Marburg School. See in this connection Heinrich Rickert, one of the leading figures in the Heidelberg School of neo-Kantianism, who writes (1913, 225) that "we identify the concept of the object on the basis of the concept of the science that investigates it." The neo-Kantian Bruno Bauch comments that the "correlation between cognition and object," stemming, he adds, from a single reference in the work of Rudolf Lotze, is fundamental in Rickert's work. See Bauch 1923–24, 30. See generally Paulson 1994.

The juridico-normative mode of cognition allows no appeal to the natural person, the human being, for the natural person stands altogether *outside* the legal system. Putting a sharp edge on it, the natural person cannot bear a systemic connection to the legal system owing to the unbridgeable gap between "is" and "ought."

If Kelsen rejects the natural person, the human being, as a possible candidate for the legal subject, only the fictitious legal person is left. Or, from a glance at the tradition, so it would appear. Kelsen, however, does not follow the tradition here. In what I am calling the second part of his solution to the problem of unity, he replaces the concept of the fictitious legal person with his own notion, that of "points of imputation." Kelsen's approach, on the one hand, carefully avoids the concept of the legal person. Despite its value in some contexts as a heuristic device, Kelsen sees the anthropomorphizing of legal person, particularly in nineteenth-century German public law theory, as the source of enormous confusion. On the other hand, Kelsen's approach also avoids the suggestion that the concepts of his legal theory are *fictions*. On the contrary, characterized from inside the legal system and accessible by means of the juridico-normative mode of cognition, "points of imputation," like other basic concepts in Kelsen's reconstruction of the fundamental concepts of legal theory, are to be sharply contrasted with the legal fiction. "Points of imputation" *qua* referents of legal relations are "proper objects" of juridico-normative cognition; far from being fictions, they are as "real" as anything inside the legal system can be.

Taking up these aspects of Kelsen's solution in turn, I begin with his antipathy to the "anthropomorphic" dimension of the legal person. He sees the concept of legal person as a heuristic device, a means of conveniently referring to a bundle of legal relations. As he puts it, the "legal person" is a reference to a partial legal system, and a "physical person"—one species of legal person—is a reference to a partial legal system associated with a human being. Talk of the "state *qua* legal person" is still another reference to a legal system—this time around the entire legal system and not just a part of it. Thus, the concept of legal subject or legal person is "simply a personifying expression for the unity of a bundle of legal obligations and legal rights, that is, the unity of a complex of norms."[30]

Kelsen's alternative to "legal person" is "imputation," which is shorthand for the cluster of legal relations turning on the idea of legal power or empowerment: powers, liabilities, disabilities, and immunities. *Points* of imputation are those reference points in the legal system—those "normative referents"—to which liabilities and the like may be ascribed or *imputed*. Kelsen's notion of imputation is simply a device for avoiding the anthropomorphizing tendency that was all too evident in nineteenth-century speculation about the legal person. Here he is thinking less of Gierke than of Carl Friedrich von Gerber and Georg Jellinek. A brief sketch, drawn from Gerber, will help to place Kelsen's concern in perspective.

Gerber, in a most remarkable development of the 1850s and 1860s, transferred the entire "constructivistic" method of the private law Pandectistic to public law. State law, he writes, has to turn to the private law Pandectistic for the idea of the *juridical construction*. Indeed, "state law has need of the entire collection of general legal concepts that have already been dissected and analyzed in private law in their simplicity and pristine purity."[31] In particular, Gerber transfers the private law doctrine of the legal person to the state:

> The legal specification of a commonwealth that manifests itself in a capacity to act unitarily can be provided by legal science in that it invests the commonwealth with *personality*. This is a general means of juridical construction, and just as it is available to private law for other purposes, it is available to public law for shaping the legal form of the powers of the state.[32]

---

[30] Kelsen 1992, §25 (p. 47).
[31] Gerber 1852, 36–37, *cf.* 28. On Gerber see generally Losano 1984, 2:90–113, 130–49; Pauly 1993, 92–167.
[32] Gerber 1880, *Beilage* II, 225 (Gerber's emphasis).

On one reading, it appears as though Gerber, applying the private law concept of the legal person, were following Savigny's *fictitious* legal person to the letter. In particular, Gerber, like Savigny before him, appeals to the notion of *representation*, introducing state organs who, by acting on behalf of the state, serve to represent it. "As with every legal person, the state, too, requires a *representative* through which the abstract power of will ascribed to the state becomes concrete act."[33] Notwithstanding Gerber's explicit reference to the doctrine of representation, the state *qua* legal person is not the "artificial legal person" of Savigny's doctrine. In Gerber's doctrine, the will attributed to the state in virtue of representation is reified as the "general will." In this connection, he explicitly rejects the notion that the "general will" might be understood as an aggregate of the wills of, say, the majority of the state's citizens.[34] And, lest there be lingering doubts about the matter, Gerber rejects, too, the notion that "the personality of the state" might fall within "the category of the legal person of private law." Rather, he contends, "the personality of the state is unique," bearing no relation whatever to other concepts in the law.[35]

It was to these nineteenth-century problems—the state *qua* legal person and in this connection, a reified doctrine of "general will"-—that Kelsen was reacting when he wrote:

> The assumption that the legal person is a reality different from individual human beings, a reality, yet curiously imperceptible to the senses, or a supra-individual social organism made up of individual human beings—this is the naive hypostatization of a thought, of a heuristic legal notion.[36]

Thus, Kelsen's introduction of "points of imputation" serves to guard against the possibility, so familiar from the nineteenth century, of anthropomorphizing the legal person.

---

[33] Gerber 1880, *Beilage* II, 231 (emphasis added).
[34] Gerber 1852, 56 note 1.
[35] Gerber 1865, 9–10, rpt. in Gerber 1872, 448.
[36] Kelsen 1992, §25(b) (p. 49).

Kelsen's second reason for replacing the *fictitious* legal person with "points of imputation" is to avoid the suggestion that concepts of the Pure Theory of Law are artificial or fictitious. The explanation here takes us back to the fundamental tenets of the Pure Theory, in particular to the unbridgeable gap between "is" and "ought," between the order of nature and the normative order, and to the modes of cognition corresponding to each, the causal or explicative mode and the juridico-normative mode, respectively. In Kelsen's theory, the juridico-normative mode of cognition determines what counts as the "proper objects" of juridical cognition, and they in turn establish the standard against which to measure the "fictitious" character of the legal person familiar from the tradition.

Finally, a critique. It can scarcely be overlooked that Kelsen—recalling, *mutatis mutandis*, Gierke's effort—pays a terribly high price for his solution to the problem of unity. Taking his cues from the radically distinct juridico-normative mode of cognition, he grants that "the human being of biology and psychology . . . cannot be comprehended by legal science at all."[37] The result is an "unavoidable antinomy," which, with remarkable candor, Kelsen himself sketches.[38] On the one hand, the theorist "necessarily presupposes the dualism of 'is' and 'ought,' of reality and value," and dualism means a radical separation, an unbridgeable gap between two worlds. On the other hand, the theorist has to recognize "a connection, in content, between the two orders," between the order of reality and that of value. The antinomy means, *inter alia*, that the Pure Theory of Law cannot take account, in systemic terms, of the connection between human being and legal person.

This, as I suggested at the outset, is a disastrous result, and it gives rise to the question: How did Kelsen, well aware of this result, arrive at this point, and why was he willing to condone a conclusion that is so clearly counter-intuitive? The answer is two-fold. The conclusion follows straightaway from Kelsen's normativity

---

[37] Kelsen 1925, §13(b) (p. 62).
[38] Kelsen 1925, §5(c) (p. 19) (emphasis added).

thesis, his general distinction between "is" and "ought"; and the normativity thesis is absolutely indispensable to Kelsen in replying to both naturalism and psychologism in the work of his predecessors.

The normativity thesis and Kelsen's arguments on its behalf take me to the second example of a fiction in Kelsen's theory, the fictitious basic norm.

3 KELSEN'S FICTITIOUS BASIC NORM

To pick up a thread from the previous discussion, Gerber applies the "constructivistic" method of the Pandectistic to public law; Paul Laband and Georg Jellinek follow him—not, to be sure, without important refinements. Neither Gerber's, Laband's, nor Jellinek's juridical constructions were acceptable, however, from Kelsen's standpoint. He takes the argument of constructivism further than his predecessors, seeing naturalism or psychologism in their work, even if they—particularly Laband and Jellinek—had gone to considerable lengths to "purify" their theories, paying homage to the self-evident truth that "methodological syncretism" was to be avoided at all costs.[39] In particular, Kelsen, drawing on the Heidelberg neo-Kantians' doctrine of methodological dualism, introduces in the *Hauptprobleme* a normativity thesis. With its help, he marks a sharp conceptual distinction between "is" and "ought," between an external, physical world, and a normative, ideal sphere. Referring to

---

[39] Although freedom from methodological syncretism was a point on which all of Kelsen's precursors in German public law theory placed great weight, Paul Laband's statement on a "pure" legal method was the one that became best known. Laband claims that one task of legal science is "the construction of legal institutes," which means "tracing particular legal norms (*Rechtssätze*) back to more general concepts and, on the other hand, deriving the consequences of these concepts." He goes on to say that "to attain this end there is no means but logic, no means can replace logic; all historical, political, and philosophical considerations—however valuable they may be in and of themselves—are without significance [for this enquiry], and serve all too often to obscure the lack of 'constructivistic' work" (Laband 1888, xi).

Wilhelm Windelband and Georg Simmel, Kelsen expounds the
normativity thesis as follows:

> The opposition between "is" and "ought" is a logico-formal opposi-
> tion, and in so far as the boundaries of logico-formal enquiry are
> observed, no path leads from the one world to the other, the two are
> separated by an unbridgeable gap. Logically speaking, enquiring into
> the "why" of a concrete "ought" can only lead to another "ought,"
> just as the answer to the "why" of an "is" can only be another "is."[40]

Having set out the normativity thesis, Kelsen now faces the task
of making a case on its behalf. It is in this connection that he
attempts, in the name of a "basic norm," to erect a neo-Kantian
foundation for his theory. To be sure, Kelsen's initial flirtation with
the idea of a basic norm antedates his effort to set out that concept
in neo-Kantian terms. The beginnings, here, come no later than
1914, a mere three years after the publication of the *Hauptprobleme*.

Walter Jellinek, introducing in 1913 what might be seen as an
early and decidedly crude version of the basic norm, served as
Kelsen's stimulus in this direction. In a major treatise,[41] Jellinek
spoke of an "ultimate" norm, a "highest" norm that cannot be
justified by appeal to a still higher norm. This "ultimate" norm, the
"highest" norm of every legal system, runs as follows:

> In a community where there is a highest power (be it the people, a
> monarch, or a particular social class), what this highest power issues
> as a command ought to be obeyed.[42]

In one respect, Jellinek continues, this highest norm can be compared with the laws of nature. It is as unchanging as the laws of
nature, "an unalterable judgment about the coming to be and the

---

[40] Kelsen 1923, 8.
[41] Jellinek, 1913, 26–29.
[42] Jellinek, 1913, 29, cited by Kelsen 1920, §24 (p. 98 note).

passing away of the legal ['ought'] . . .."[43] He adds that this highest norm "owes its validity not to any [human] act but to a conceptual necessity"[44]—a notion that is familiar from the work of his father, Georg Jellinek.[45]

The reasoning that led Walter Jellinek to this "highest" norm is congenial to Kelsen, and in a major paper of 1914, Kelsen alludes to the notion of an "ultimate" or a "final" norm.[46] In all juridical construction, he writes, one must take valid norms as the point of departure. Then, without warning, he fleshes out the notion in a most telling way, contending that whether the question be one of legal facts or of particular legal norms and their relations to one another, the

point of departure must always be some sort of highest, presupposed norm—presupposed, that is, as valid. The question of the validity of this ultimate norm, assumed as a presupposition of all legal cognition, lies outside [the field of] legal cognition itself. This ultimate point, then, as the highest, presupposed norm, is at the same time the Archimedean point from which the world of legal cognition is set into motion.[47]

These lines foreshadow things to come in Kelsen's theory, but he makes no attempt here to provide philosophical underpinnings for this "highest, presupposed norm." On the contrary, he plays right into the hands of critics when he goes on to write:

The choice of this point of departure [namely, the choice of a highest, presupposed norm] is in principle not a legal question, but rather a political question, and must therefore appear arbitrary from the standpoint of legal cognition.[48]

---

[43] Jellinek 1913, 28.
[44] Jellinek 1913, 28.
[45] See Jellinek 1905, 17.
[46] Kelsen 1914, 215–20.
[47] Kelsen 1914, 216–17 (emphasis added).
[48] Kelsen 1914, 217.

Kelsen's talk of a "highest" norm is disingenuous, a transparent surrogate for the will of the state.

In *Das Problem der Souveränität*, the text of which was completed in 1916, Kelsen is no longer prepared to endorse Walter Jellinek's position. On the contrary, Jellinek's limited claim that the highest norm can be compared in one respect with the laws of nature is transformed by Kelsen into a far stronger claim, with Kelsen now contending that Jellinek had treated "the highest norm as akin to the laws of nature." Such a view, Kelsen continues, would be "worthy of discussion" only if the highest norm stood for a *causal* relation. Thus, Jellinek's "conflation" of "highest norm" and law of nature must be emphatically rejected.[49]

This is harsh criticism of Walter Jellinek, who was quite clearly not guilty of confusing the normative with the causal. He is simply making a comparison—the "highest" norm of the legal system is as unchanging, as "unalterable," as the laws of nature. The more important point, however, is that Kelsen shows himself to be increasingly sensitive to the pitfalls of simply "assuming" a highest norm as a defensible alternative to the naturalism and psychologism of the tradition.

This pulling and hauling, characteristic of Kelsen's very early flirtation with the idea of a basic norm, continues into the 1920s, but with a difference. Kelsen shows, from about 1920 on, increasing interest in the promise of a Kantian or neo-Kantian argument as a means of lending support to the normativity thesis. The details, here, would take us too far afield, but a brief general sketch of this Kantian or neo-Kantian dimension in Kelsen's work provides an instructive comparison with Kelsen's later position. For it is no exaggeration to say that the Kantian or neo-Kantian reading of the basic norm is light years away from Kelsen's later fictitious basic norm.

---

[49] Kelsen 1920 §24 (p. 98 note); *cp.* Jellinek 1913, 28.

In Kelsen's middle, classical period,[50] extending from about 1920 up to, and including, the second edition of the *Reine Rechtslehre* in 1960, there is a remarkable preoccupation with Kantian and neo-Kantian doctrines. For example, Kelsen poses his own transcendental question, addressed to the law,[51] he introduces the "ought" as designating a "relative *a priori* category for comprehending empirical legal data,"[52] and he speaks of legal science as being "constitutive" in character.[53] These notions are distinctly Kantian or neo-Kantian. And, most conspicuous of all where Kantian or neo-Kantian interpretations of the normativity thesis are concerned, there is the basic norm, which Kelsen now describes as "reveal[ing] the transcendental logical conditions" of legal cognition.[54]

In an effort to come to terms with the basic norm, described in this way, one might focus on a regressive version of the Kantian transcendental argument, understood as Kelsen's response to a juridical version of the transcendental question. This approach would have Kelsen (1) introducing the notion of normative imputation as his fundamental category, and then (2) adducing a transcendental argument to demonstrate this fundamental category as a presupposition of the data that are given.

The problem with this approach, as has been argued,[55] is that the regressive version of the transcendental argument is not sound—indeed, it *cannot* be sound as long as there is another explanation at hand, another way of rendering the data coherent. And there will always be another way of rendering the data coherent where the transcendental question is addressed to objects of cognition in one or another of the standing disciplines—be it in history, sociology, or legal science. In other words, the Kantian transcendental argu-

---

[50] On the various phases of development in Kelsen's legal theory, see *e.g.* Winkler 1990, 30–69.

[51] Kelsen 1928; tr. in Kelsen 1945, 437; *cf.* Kelsen 1960, §34(d) (p. 205).

[52] Kelsen 1992, §11(b) (pp. 24–25).

[53] Kelsen 1960, §16 (p. 74).

[54] Kelsen 1992, §29 (p. 58). See the quotation below, p. 236 (at note 58).

[55] See Paulson 1992, 324–32.

ment has force only if all other explanations of the data are pre-cluded. And, to repeat, they cannot be precluded in the standing disciplines.

This line of criticism assumes that Kant's analytic or regressive method is being used simply as shorthand for the synthetic or progressive method. There is, however, an alternative. One can "spin off" the analytic or regressive method from Kant's synthetic or progressive method, and employ it independently of the latter.[56] That was pretty clearly Hermann Cohen's tack.[57] Rejecting as "psychology" central parts of Kant's enterprise in the *Kritik der reinen Vernunft*, including the "transcendental deduction of the *a priori* categories of understanding," Cohen introduces in their place his own "analytic" or "transcendental" method. The task, Cohen argues, is take the *Faktum* of a science as something given, and to proceed by setting out the *a priori* conditions on the basis of which knowledge in that science is founded. In the end, the task amounts to an explication of what, exactly, is understood in taking the *Faktum* of a science as given.

Arguably, this is Kelsen's tack, too. Invoking the basic norm, he writes:

> In formulating the basic norm, the Pure Theory of Law is not aiming to inaugurate a new method for jurisprudence. The Pure Theory aims simply to raise to the level of consciousness what all jurists are doing (for the most part unwittingly) when, in conceptualizing their object of enquiry, they . . . understand the positive law as a valid system, that is, as norm, and not merely as factual contingencies of motivation. With the doctrine of the basic norm, the Pure Theory analyses the actual process of the long-standing method of cognizing positive law, in an attempt simply to reveal the transcendental logical conditions of that method.[58]

---

[56] On the various interpretations of the analytic or regressive method, see general-ly Grundmann 1994, 97–103.

[57] See generally Cohen 1871, 1885; Edel 1988, 1991; Stolzenberg 1993.

[58] Kelsen 1992, §29 (p. 58).

Although, as we saw above, Kelsen refers to Kantian and neo-Kantian doctrines alike, his approach here is distinctly neo-Kantian, implying, just as in Cohen's work, a rejection of the Kantian synthetic or progressive method.[59]

In his later (post-1960) work, Kelsen becomes disenchanted with this neo-Kantian approach, abandoning it altogether and invoking in its place the idea of a fiction:

> The cognitive goal of the basic norm is to ground the validity of the norms forming a positive moral or legal order, that is, to interpret the subjective meaning of the norm-positing acts as their objective meaning (*i.e.* as valid norms) and to interpret the relevant acts as norm-positing acts. This goal can be attained only by means of a fiction.[60]

Vaihinger, in his treatise of 1913, contrasts fiction and hypothesis sharply. Whereas *hypotheses* set out assumptions whose truth might well be established by verification, *fictions* are never verifiable, for they are known to be false.[61] Instead, fictions are employed because of their "utility."[62] Wherever one's cognitive material "resists a direct procedure," the fiction makes it possible to reach one's cognitive purpose "indirectly."[63] Kelsen follows Vaihinger to the letter:

> It should be noted that the basic norm is not—as I myself have sometimes characterized it—a hypothesis in the sense of Vaihinger's philosophy of "as if," but is, rather, a fiction. A fiction differs from a hypothesis in that it is accompanied—or ought to be accompanied —by the awareness that reality does not agree with it.[64]

---

[59] Kelsen's neo-Kantian tack emerges clearly in the reconstructive sketch provided by Treves 1933, rpt. 1992, esp. 66–78.

[60] Kelsen 1991, 256.

[61] See Vaihinger 1913, 143–54 (Part One, ch. 21).

[62] Vaihinger 1913, 152.

[63] Vaihinger 1913, 19 (General Introduction, ch. 4); see also Kelsen 1991, 256.

[64] Kelsen 1991, 256.

Taking the first step, with Vaihinger, to say that the concept in question is a fiction for failing to conform to reality is to say that the concept "contradicts" reality. Vaihinger's second step is to claim that constructs are, in the strict sense, fictions "when they are not only in contradiction with reality but self-contradictory in themselves."[65] Kelsen takes this second step, with Vaihinger, too:

> [T]he Basic Norm of a positive moral or legal system is not a positive norm, but a merely thought norm (*i.e.* a fictitious norm), the meaning of a merely fictitious, and not a real, act of will. As such, it is a genuine or "proper" fiction (in the sense of Vaihinger's philosophy of "as if") whose characteristic is that it is not only contrary to reality, but *self-contradictory*.[66]

The basic norm is contradictory, Kelsen says, because it fails to conform to reality. But why *self*-contradictory? Kelsen argues that it is self-contradictory because (1) it "represents the empowering of an ultimate moral or legal authority," and therefore (2) "emanates from an authority . . . even higher" than the ultimate authority. Thus, Kelsen is contending, the basic norm represents the empowerment of an ultimate authority whose empowering source must be still higher. The authority is ultimate and is not ultimate.

The result of Kelsen's use of Vaihinger is unmistakable. By means of the basic norm, now a fictitious construct of Kelsen's, one proceeds *as though* the material of the law were irreducibly normative. This amounts to a concession, based on the fictitious character of the basic norm, that the normativity thesis, claiming the irreducibly normative character of the law, is not defensible.

---

[65] Kelsen 1991, 256, with reference to Vaihinger 1913, 143–54 (Part One, ch. 21).

[66] Kelsen 1991, 256. Kelsen quotes Vaihinger here: "Ideational constructs are in the strict sense of the term real fictions when they are not only in contradiction with reality but self-contradictory in themselves . . . . To be distinguished from them are constructs which not only contradict reality as given, or deviate from it, but are not in themselves self-contradictory . . . . The latter might be called half-fictions or semi-fictions" (Vaihinger 1913, 24; Part One: General Remark on Fictitious Constructs and Forms).

4 CONCLUDING REMARK

These two fictions in Kelsen's legal theory play very different roles. Where the fictitious legal person is concerned, Kelsen is criticizing a traditional doctrine. Although his own "bundle of legal obligations and rights," explicated in the Pure Theory's reconstruction by means of imputation, is a "functional equivalent" of the legal person of the tradition, Kelsen contends that the traditional doctrine has given rise to great confusion and must therefore be replaced. By contrast, it is his own earlier normativistic legal theory that Kelsen is tacitly criticizing with the fictitious basic norm. One could speculate that the fiction may well give rise to confusion here, too, leading the reader to believe that something of Kelsen's normativism survives in the late (post-1960) period. In fact, it disappears at this point without a trace.

Frederick L. Will may be surprised to learn that he has offered, in his fine paper on the "Philosophic Governance of Norms," an apt commentary on Kelsen's fictitious basic norm. Will writes, in the abstract at the outset of his paper, that norms are widely regarded as "templates . . . of performance." As such, Will continues, these templates

> are thought to determine unilaterally what kinds of thought or action accord with them. Under philosophical elaboration this view has led to multiple perplexities: among them the question of how there can be evaluation, justification, and rectification of such unilaterally determining entities. Sometimes one can appeal to other, supervening norms; but the need to terminate the regressive procedure typically leads to appeals to dubious "foundations," to conventions, or to sheer prejudice.[67]

I fear that Kelsen's fictitious basic norm is the most dubious "foundation" of them all.

Washington University, St. Louis

---

[67] Will 1997, 159.

References

Bauch, Bruno. 1923–24. "Das transzendentale Subjekt." *Logos* 12: 29–49.

Behrends, Okko. 1985. "Geschichte, Politik und Jurisprudenz in F. C. v. Savignys System des heutigen römischen Rechts." In *Römisches Recht in der europäischen Tradition. Symposion aus Anlaß des 75. Geburtstages von Franz Wieacker.* O. Behrends, *et al.*, eds. Ebelsbach: Rolf Gremer, 257–321.

Binder, Julius. 1907. *Das Problem der juristischen Persönlichkeit.* Leipzig: A. Deichert. Rpt. Aalen: Scientia, 1970.

Brinz, Alois. 1873. *Lehrbuch der Pandekten*, 2nd ed. Erlangen: Andreas Deichert.

Cohen, Hermann. 1871. *Kants Theorie der Erfahrung*, 1st ed. Berlin: Dümmler.

Cohen, Hermann. 1885. *Kants Theorie der Erfahrung*, 2nd ed. Berlin: Dümmler.

Denzer, Horst. 1977. "Die Ursprünge der Lehre von der juristischen Person (*persona moralis*) in Deutschland und ihre Bedeutung für die Vorstellung von der Staatspersönlichkeit." In *La formazione storica del Diritto moderno in Europa. Atti del terzo Congresso internazionale della Società italiana di storia del Diritto.* Florence: Leo S. Olschki Editore, 1189–1202.

Dießelhorst, Malte. 1982–83. "Zur Theorie der juristischen Person bei Carl Friedrich von Savigny." *Quaderni Fiorentini* 11–12: 319–37.

Edel, Geert. 1988. *Von der Vernunftkritik zur Erkenntnislogik.* Freiburg: Karl Alber.

Edel, Geert. 1991. "Kantianismus oder Platonismus? Hypothesis als Grundbegriff der Philosophie Cohens." *il cannocchiale. revista di studi filosofici* 1: 59–87.

Gerber, Carl Friedrich von. 1852. *Über öffentliche Rechte.* Tübingen: Laupp & Siebeck.

Gerber, Carl Friedrich von. 1865. "Ueber die Theilbarkeit deutscher Staatsgebiete." *Aegidis Zeitschrift für Deutsches Staatsrecht und Deutsche Verfassungsgeschichte* 2: 5–24. Rpt. in Gerber, 1872, vol. 2, 441–69.

Gerber, Carl Friedrich von. 1872. *Gesammelte juristische Abhandlungen.* Jena: Mauke.

Gerber, Carl Friedrich von. 1880. *Grundzüge des Deutschen Staatsrechts*, 3^{d} ed. Leipzig: Bernhard Tauchnitz.

Gierke, Otto von. 1887. *Die Genossenschaftstheorie und die Deutsche Rechtsprechung.* Berlin: Weidmann. Rpt. Hildesheim: Olms, 1983.

Gierke, Otto von. 1895. *Deutsches Privatrecht.* Leipzig: Duncker & Humblot.

Grundmann, Thomas. 1994. *Analytische Transzendentalphilosophie. Eine Kritik.* Paderborn: Schöningh.

Jellinek, Georg. 1905. *System der subjektiven öffentlichen Rechte*, 2nd ed. Tübingen: J.C.B. Mohr. Rpt. Aalen: Scientia, 1979.

Jellinek, Walter. 1913. *Gesetz, Gesetzesanwendung und Zweckmäßigkeitserwägung*. Tübingen: J.C.B. Mohr. Rpt. Aalen: Scientia, 1964.

John, Uwe. 1977. *Die organisierte Rechtsperson*. Berlin: Duncker & Humblot.

Kelsen, Hans. 1914. "Reichsgesetz und Landesgesetz nach österreichischer Verfassung." *Archiv des öffentlichen Rechts* 32: 202–45, 390–438.

Kelsen, Hans. 1923. *Hauptprobleme der Staatsrechtslehre*. 2nd printing with new "Foreword" (1st ed. 1911). Tübingen: J.C.B. Mohr. Rpt. Aalen: Scientia, 1960.

Kelsen, Hans. 1928. *Philosophical Foundations of Natural Law Theory and Legal Positivism*. W. H. Kraus, tr. Appendix to Kelsen, 1945, 389–445.

Kelsen, Hans. 1945. *General Theory of Law and State*. Cambridge, Mass.: Harvard University Press.

Kelsen, Hans. 1960. *Reine Rechtslehre*, 2nd ed. Vienna: Deuticke.

Kelsen, Hans. 1920. *Das Problem der Souveränität*. Tübingen: J.C.B. Mohr. Rpt. Aalen: Scientia, 1960.

Kelsen, Hans. 1925. *Allgemeine Staatslehre*. Berlin, Julius Springer. Rpt. Bad Homburg v.d. Höhe: Max Gehlen, 1966.

Kelsen, Hans. 1991. *General Theory of Norms*. M. Hartney, tr. Oxford: Clarendon Press.

Kelsen, Hans. 1992. *Introduction to the Problems of Legal Theory*. Translation of *Reine Rechtslehre*, 1st ed. 1934. B. L. Paulson & S. L. Paulson, trs. Oxford: Clarendon Press.

Kiefner, Hans. 1969. "Der Einfluß Kants auf Theorie und Praxis des Zivilrechts im 19. Jahrhundert." In *Philosophie und Rechtswissenschaft. Problem ihrer Beziehung im 19. Jahrhundert*. J. Blühdorn & J. Ritter, eds. Frankfurt/Main: Klostermann, 3–25.

Laband, Paul. 1888. *Das Staatsrecht des Deutschen Reiches*, 2nd ed. Freiburg: J.C.B. Mohr.

Losano, Mario G. 1984. *Studien zu Jhering und Gerber*, vol. 2. Ebelsbach: Rolf Gremer.

Paulson, Stanley L. 1992. "The Neo-Kantian Dimension of Kelsen's Pure Theory of Law." *Oxford Journal of Legal Studies* 12: 311–32.

Paulson, Stanley L. 1993. "Continental Normativism and Its British Counterpart: How Different are They?" *Ratio Juris* 6: 227–44.

Paulson, Stanley L. 1994. "Kelsen and the Marburg School: Reconstructive and Historical Perspectives." In *Prescriptive Formality and Normative Rationality in Modern Legal Systems. Festschrift for Robert S. Summers*. W. Krawietz, *et al.*, eds. Berlin: Duncker & Humblot, 481–94.

Pauly, Walter. 1993. *Der Methodenwandel im deutschen Spätkonstitutionalismus*. Tübingen: J.C.B. Mohr.

Puchta, Georg Friedrich. 1863. *Pandekten*, 9th ed. A. A. F. Rudorff, ed. Leipzig: Johann Ambrosius Barth.

Raz, Joseph. 1981. "The Purity of the Pure Theory." *Revue Internationale de Philosophie* 35: 441–59. Rpt. in *Essays on Kelsen*. R. Tur and W. Twining, eds. Oxford: Clarendon Press, 1986, 79–97.

Rickert, Heinrich. 1913. *Die Grenzen der naturwissenschaftlichen Begriffsbildung*, 2nd ed. Tübingen: J.C.B. Mohr.

Rückert, Joachim. 1984. *Idealismus, Jurisprudenz und Politik bei Carl Friedrich v. Savigny*. Ebelsbach: Rolf Gremer.

Savigny, Friedrich Carl von. 1840–49. *System des heutigen römischen Rechts*, 8 vols. Berlin: Veit. Rpt. Aalen: Scientia, 1981.

Stolzenberg, Jürgen. 1993. "Oberster Grundsatz und Ursprung in Hermann Cohens theoretischer Philosophie." *Philosophisches Denken-Politisches Wirken. Hermann-Cohen-Kolloquium Marburg 1992.* R. Brandt and F. Orlik, eds. Hildsheim: Olms, 76–94.

Treves, Renato. 1933. "Il fondamento filosofico della dottrina pure del diritto di Hans Kelsens." *Atti della Reale Accademia delle Scienze di Torino* 69: 52–90. Rpt. in *Hans Kelsen & Renato Treves, Formalismo giuridico e realtà sociale*. S. L. Paulson, ed. Naples: Edizioni Scientifiche Italiane, 1992, 59–87.

Vaihinger, Hans. 1913. *Die Philosophie des Als Ob*, 2nd ed. Berlin: Reuther & Reichard.

Voegelin, Erich. 1924. "Reine Rechtslehre und Staatslehre." *Zeitschrift für öffentliches Recht* 4: 80–131.

Wieacker, Franz. 1967. *Privatrechtsgeschichte der Neuzeit*, 2nd ed. Göttingen, Vandenhoeck & Ruprecht.

Wieacker, Franz. 1973. "Zur Theorie der Juristischen Person des Privatrechts." In *Festschrift für Ernst Rudolf Huber zum 70. Geburtstag.* E. Forsthoff, *et al.*, eds. Göttingen: Otto Schwartz.

Will, Frederick L. 1997. *Pragmatism and Realism*. K. R. Westphal, ed. Lanham, Md.: Rowman & Littlefield.

Winkler, Günther. 1990. *Rechtstheorie und Erkenntnislehre*. Vienna: Springer.

Wolff, Martin. 1938. "On the Nature of Legal Persons." *Law Quarterly Review* 54: 494–521.

11

The Spirit of the Enterprise

James D. Wallace

1 Frederick L. Will's views about the phenomena that he calls the governance of norms of thought and action grew out his work on skepticism, truth, and the problem of induction. The professional activities of scientists, mathematicians, and philosophers—theoreticians—are the focus of his attention as he seeks to provide a basis for a critical understanding of their activities. The account he offers in his later work of how theorists properly proceed in cultivating and expanding an understanding of various phenomena, however, is an application of a more general conception of what it is for any human activity to proceed rightly, intelligently, appropriately. So, Will's description of how norms govern activity embraces—in addition to inquiry and theorizing—politics, law, ethics, art, professions, and the activities of everyday living. One consequence of this way of conceiving matters is that many of the problems that we presently distribute among the subdisciplines of philosophy for separate consideration turn out on Will's view to be amenable to strikingly similar treatment. Issues in law, politics, and ethics are used to shed light on issues in the philosophy of science. Philosophy, practiced as Will does, becomes once again a unified subject. The understanding of one area of life is used to illuminate other areas in a synthesis reminiscent of Plato's *Republic* in its comprehensiveness. The discussion that follows focuses on the very considerable illumination that Will's approach brings to issues in moral, social, and political philosophy.

2 An outstanding feature of Will's account of the governance of norms is connected with his distinction between the manifest and the latent aspects of a norm. A "norm" here can be understood as a learned activity that is taken to be an appropriate way to proceed in a certain domain (*BD* 30–31).[1] In its manifest aspect, the norm is a guide in the sense of an instruction, a "template" for action: As the unit comes down the assembly line, I am supposed to wire a red and green striped resistor across the two terminals that protrude from it. This norm can be taken as defining my rather simple job, although the instruction does suppose that I know how to do such things as identifying resistors, sorting them by color, and connecting a resistor to two terminals. We can think of learned ways of identifying resistors, sorting them by color, wiring a resistor to a terminal, *etc.*, as component norms that, properly related one to another, make up the norm that governs my job. My job is simply one activity which, together with many other such activities, constitute the activity, the enterprise of producing some product. The larger enterprise can be thought of as made up of a structured set of norms. The enterprise of making this product itself is a component of ever larger structures of economic and productive activities, which are in turn components of the life of an entire community.

Even the relatively simple matters involved in my assembly line job exhibit considerable complexity. In its manifest aspect, my job-norm directs me to do the same operation over and over. Its content can be captured in a brief description that can be used as an instruction, an order, a reminder, *etc.* The manifest aspect is sufficient for the routine case—here comes another unit, I turn it so that the terminals are accessible, I pick up a red and green striped resistor, *etc.* One day, though, I look for a red and green coded resistor and there aren't any there—and here comes another unit. My job norm does not cover this contingency. I am paralyzed. Presumably, somebody knows what to do when this happens—more red and green striped resistors need to be obtained, but how is this done, and

---

[1] Numbers in parentheses in the text preceded by '*BD*' refer to pages in Will 1988.

what happens to the assembly line in the meanwhile? Should I let the units go by without the resistor installed? Should the assembly line be stopped? Suppose someone knows about the relationship of volts, amperes, and ohms, and tells me that three yellow and brown striped resistors are the equivalent of one red and green striped one. Should I wire three yellow and brown striped resistors across the two terminals of each unit and send it on down the line? The answer to this question depends on many things. Can the unit with three resistors across the terminals fit with the other components farther down the line when the final product is assembled? Is there room for the unit so configured in the box that houses the final product? Are the yellow and brown striped resistors appreciably more expensive than the red and green ones? Will there be additional expense in adapting other components to the unit with three resistors? Will such expenses matter?

Probably, running out of a part needed on a particular assembly line is sufficiently common so that there will be well worked out procedures to cope with such an occurrence. In Will's terminology, my job norm is then supplemented with an additional norm that explicitly covers this contingency in its manifest aspect. In other words, I have an instruction that tells me what to do if I run out of red and green resistors. Unprecedented occurrences for which I have no instruction are bound to occur, however, even on an assembly line. This is a hard fact about the human predicament that is of the greatest importance. I am imagining that on my job, running out of a certain kind of resistor is unprecedented, so that there exists no norm that indicates explicitly, that is, in its manifest content, what should be done. There are many things one might consider in the absence of an explicit direction covering such a contingency. Here, we encounter what Will calls the latent aspect of norms. Norms are "components of larger complexes of human life and practice" (PGN 165).[2] "They are typically and always at least to some degree, in dynamic relation with other features of life, including other norms, in consequence of which they are liable to alteration both in respect

---

[2] 'PGN' abbreviates "Philosophic Governance of Norms," Will 1997, ch. 9.

to the conditions under which they are properly applied and to the character of the responses that are proper to their application. . . . norms are always in some degree open, rather than closed with respect to their manifest aspects" (PGN 166; *cf. BD* 147–52).

The job norm that constitutes my task at the assembly line indicates an activity that is part of an entire process of creation of a final product. The activity is economic—I and many others are engaged in earning a living. The process is productive; its purpose is to provide something that answers in a particular way to some desire or need of people. These activities, too, will be constituted by a complex of norms. The way to work out what I should do when the manifest direction of my job's norm fails is by reference to "the larger complex of human life and practice." Consider the entire productive and economic activity of which my job is a part. Certain things I might do when I run out of red and green resistors on the line will minimize the disruption of the larger enterprise, and so far these responses will be preferable. If I understand the larger activity of which my job is a part, I will be able to identify the less disruptive responses. I may even be able to find a response that will actually advance the larger enterprise in some respect, and this would be even better. By hypothesis, no existing norm in the complex available to guide the entire economic and productive process explicitly indicates or directs my proper course of action when I run out of red and green resistors. I am not necessarily bereft of any guidance whatsoever. The collection of norms that comprise the larger undertaking can indicate how one in my predicament should proceed. I may be able to modify my job's norm in the light of the body of norms defining the larger activity in which I am taking part—by appealing to the latent aspect of the complex of norms that comprise the larger activity.

The latent aspect of norms that guides one in working out what to do when some unprecedented difficulty arises with one's assembly line job is not something that belongs to the job norm as an isolated thing. It is this norm, together with the enterprise of which it is a part, with all of its normative components, that guides one in working out the reasonable thing to do with an unprecedented difficulty.

Problems analogous to running out of the proper resistor on the assembly line arise for inquirers. In the early seventeenth century, William Harvey measured the quantity of blood that left the human heart with every contraction and estimated that in one hour, a quantity of blood whose weight exceeds the weight of a human being leaves the heart. For us now, this result confirms the firmly established result that the blood circulates in the body, returning continually to the heart that functions as a pump. For an anatomist in Harvey's time, his result was deeply puzzling. Galen taught that blood ebbed and flowed in two independent systems, the veins and the arteries. The system of blood vessels in the human body did not appear to form a loop—there was no apparent way for the blood that left the heart to be channeled back to it. On the assumption that the blood does not circulate, however, there is no way to account for the origin of the enormous quantity of blood that leaves the heart on Harvey's showing and no way to explain what eventually becomes of it. The assumption the blood circulates, on the other hand, requires that there be a circuit of vessels, but no such thing is found in dissections.

What supported Harvey in his conclusion that the blood must circulate was, of course, connected with the entire state of the knowledge of physiology at the moment of his discovery. The "smaller circulation" from the right side of the heart to the lungs and back to the left side of the heart had been described. Harvey's teacher, Fabricius, discovered in veins valves that impede the flow of blood away from the heart. Of very great influence, however, was the importance of mechanical things to the people of his time. Clocks, telescopes, artillery, and other machines, including pumps, were effecting a social and intellectual revolution. The operation of mechanical things was intelligible. Important people were mechanically minded, and the discovery that the human body, too, is a machine had a certain powerful attraction. This puzzle about anatomy was resolved by Harvey partly by appealing to analogies, to phenomena outside anatomy that were better understood. Nothing in the then existing knowledge about these matters said or implied explicitly that the heart is a pump that circulates the blood; it was Harvey who said this, influenced by what was known at the time about the proper way of thinking about a variety of phenomena in anatomy and mechanics. That is, Harvey was guided in formulating his theory by the latent aspects of existing norms of thought in these areas. The microscope was soon invented, and in 1661 capillaries were found in the lungs of a frog. The materials were at hand to answer the question of how blood flowing away from the heart in the arterial system could get into the venous system to return to the heart. Anatomy could turn to the question of what was being carried by the blood in its circuit.[3]

3 A major theme in Will's work is the adverse consequences, for our understanding of our intellectual practices, of the neglect of the importance of the latent aspect of norms of thought and action. Philosophical accounts that countenance only the role of the manifest aspect of norms in our thinking fail notably to account for the growth of knowledge. The philosophical problems of skepticism about the knowledge of the external world and induction are insoluble, Will argues, without an explicit recognition of the role of the latent aspect of norms in their governance of our activity (*BD* 47–63).

Similarly, norms pertaining to activities other than strictly theoretical ones, including moral norms, are not well understood when attention is focused entirely upon norms' manifest contents and their latent content is dismissed. Then, such norms tend to be thought of as simply explicit instructions that tell us what to do—hard and fast rules that provide explicit direction for every contingency. Of course, there are no such moral rules, but if the latent aspect of norms is neglected, then the only guidance that moral rules can provide is through what they explicitly direct. In fact, multiple moral considerations frequently indicate contrary courses of action in the same circumstances, moral norms conflict in particular

---

[3] For a fascinating account of Harvey's discovery see Butterfield 1965, ch. 3.

situations, and unprecedented moral problems are not uncommon. Moral norms, as a consequence, can offer no guidance where we are most in need of help, if we consider only their manifest content. A common response to this problem in moral philosophy is to seek very general and abstract principles that seem to be applicable in every situation—for example, the General Happiness Principle or the Golden Rule. A familiar difficulty with such abstract principles is that their application is problematic. Like the dicta of the Oracle at Delphi, what they have to say about a particular problem can be understood in more than one way.

Generally, Will maintains, norms of any kind cannot perform their guiding function when they are separated from their latent content, that is when they are considered in abstraction from the actual contexts in which people attempt to live in accordance with them. He cites Wittgenstein's account in *Philosophical Investigations* of the necessity of a background of customary practice for a rule to have a clear meaning. Without such a background, Wittgenstein argues, any response can be made out to accord with a given rule, including continuing the series 2, 4, 6, 8, . . . after reaching 1000, by 1004, 1008, 1012, ...[4] (Compare this with the sort of intuitionism in ethics advocated by W. D. Ross and others.)

> Similar glosses may be and have often been made upon other rules or norms that have been for certain philosophical purposes so abstracted from their latent content that they can no longer perform their expected guiding function. Strikingly similar in this aspect are many criticisms advanced against Kant's principle of universality in his Categorical Imperative, and, more recently, in Goodman's effective criticism of an abstract rule of inductive projection. In both these and many other cases a major point of the criticism is that embarrassingly many conflicting courses of action "can be made out to accord with the rule." (PGN 165)

4 Will criticizes the attempts of philosophers to enunciate certain very general and abstract principles that are intended by means of

---

[4] Wittgenstein 1953, Part 1, §§185–202.

their explicit content alone to indicate definitively the solution to complex intellectual and practical problems. For one thing, the procedures proposed do not indicate one particular situation; rather they point in several different directions at once. It appears, though, that a similar criticism can be made of Will's account of the way that the latent contents of norms guide us in the solution of difficult theoretical and practical problems. With respect to a given problem, the latent aspect of norms, that is, the larger social context of accepted practice in which the problem arises, invariably indicates or suggests more than one solution. The vast body of norms here offers many different paradigms that might be brought to bear on the present problem. Norms in their latent aspect too often will not determine a single solution, but rather offer suggestions for many incompatible solutions. This criticism is that the procedure is insufficiently determinate to offer the sort of guidance we seek with difficult problems that arise both in theory and practice.

If the aim in the end is conceived simply as making the entire collection of our many practices as far as possible harmonious and mutually reinforcing in the existing social context, there will seem to be more than one way to attain this result when two or more practical or theoretical considerations conflict in a particular problem. If in a particular circumstance, norm X indicates that we do A, and norm Y indicates that we do B, where we can do either A or B but not both, then a proper solution to our problem would be to modify norm X in such a way that it did not apply to this particular situation. Norms X and Y, then, would be more harmonious in that in circumstances like this, they will not conflict. The proper course of action here is B rather that A. We could just as well, however, modify norm Y instead of norm X, so that Y does not apply in the circumstance. This too would harmonize X and Y, but the result of this is that in the circumstance, we should do A rather than B. The latent content of norms apparently offers no way to choose between these two alternatives. This is not the guidance we seek.

Consider, though, the problem of slavery as it confronted the people of the United States in the first half of the nineteenth century. Slavery existed as an institution in parts of the country; the fortunes of a substantial number of people were invested in slavery. At the same time, this institution existed in a political community that was deeply committed to liberal and egalitarian democratic social ideals. The conflict between the inequalities and cruelties of slavery with the political morality of this community in which slavery was practiced was acute. The conflict was eventually resolved, through the carnage of the Civil War, by abolishing slavery in all of the United States. Of course, the conflict could have been resolved the other way: the political and social morality could have been given up and the institution of slavery preserved. It is important to notice that in fact there were few (if any) proponents of the latter solution. What the pro-slavery faction wanted to do was, in effect, to preserve the situation of slavery in a democracy, with all of its conflicts. There were attempts to establish that slaves were individuals who lacked certain features that entitled others to life, liberty, and the pursuit of happiness, but the differences these arguments alleged were doubtful. As the conflict continued and the political crisis drew near, pro-slavery people generally refused to permit discussion of the issue.

Giving up the norms of political democracy was not seriously considered as an option in response to the slavery issue. The choice, as the participants saw it, was between the continuation of a community (in some form) riven by the inconsistencies of slavery in a political democracy and a political democracy without slavery. In the circumstances, for these people, giving up the political democracy was unthinkable. No one was prepared to abandon the complex of norms that constitute life in a political democracy, and we do not need to postulate some mysterious intuition of the rightness of such a life to explain this. For one thing, political democracy is the best defense against tyranny, and these people knew it. The latent aspect of the social and political norms that defined political life in the United States in 1860 was not neutral on the issue of giving up slavery or giving up the political democracy.

If one reflects abstractly on the thesis that proper problem solving in theorizing and other activities is a matter of being guided by the latent aspect of norms, if one thinks about this proposal apart from concrete problems, it appears that the idea provides insufficient guidance. There will, it seems, be many more than one way of adjusting norms in conflict in a particular situation to the larger social and intellectual context in which the particular problem arises. The latent aspect of the pertinent norms will not indicate a single solution to the problem. It seems here, too, that "every course of action can be made to accord with the rule." When one considers particular concrete problems, however, the latent aspect of norms tends to be considerably more specific than this in its indication.

The mechanical model of the circulatory system, with the heart as a pump, is indicated in the seventeenth century by a number of considerations in anatomy and in the general culture. The Copernican heliocentric theory is indicated over the geocentric theory in the sixteenth century, not by any crucial experiment, but because of the contemporary interest in astronomy as "a realistic representation of the structure of the solar system" rather than as a device for prediction and calculation (*BD* 243–45).

In Europe in the fifteenth century, interest in trade and improvements in transportation created a demand for capital to finance commercial ventures. New nation-states fought wars, and rulers sought money to finance their wars. So eager were such individuals for capital that they were perfectly willing to pay others for the temporary use of their money. Lending at interest, however—usury—was viewed as a form of theft, a form of extorting from others property to which the lender has no just claim. By the end of the sixteenth century, casuists had reached a consensus that it was proper to lend money at interest, provided the interest was not excessive. The prohibition against lending at interest was modified to accommodate the insistent demand for capital, partly because the social and economic circumstances that originally gave moral meaning to the prohibition against lending at interest no longer obtained. In a subsistence economy, where wealth is not itself a commodity, idle goods are just that. When one's neighbor needs a loan, it is typically because the neighbor is in serious trouble. Charity indicates that one lend idle goods to a neighbor in difficulty, and one is entitled to ask for the eventual return of the principal. To make it a condition of the loan that the lender return more than the principal, however, is to extort additional property from the borrower—property to which the lender has no claim. Usury is theft.

When economic circumstances change so that idle capital can be invested to realize a profit, a lender can reasonably claim that the borrower owes compensation for lost profit in addition to the return of the principal. Potential borrowers, moreover, are eager for capital and perfectly willing to pay for its use. Lenders in such circumstances do not coerce the borrower to pay interest, and lenders have a claim to be entitled to more than the return of the principal. This was the situation in Europe in the sixteenth century. The latent aspect of the social and economic norms of the time indicated that the idea that lending money at interest is unjust be given up, and replaced with the notion of reasonable interest.[5]

One may say that the casuists of the sixteenth century might just as well have held to the norm that lending at interest is unjust and demanded that princes and merchants restrain their lust for capital. The principle, however, had ceased to be morally cogent in the way it had once been. It is not reasonable to ask people to forgo exciting new ventures in the name of an ancient prohibition that had substantially lost its point.

In certain historical contexts, very general social and intellectual considerations indicate the proper solution to certain difficult unprecedented problems, even though no explicitly worked out norms for dealing with such problems exist at the time. It is very particular features of the actual context that rule out certain ways of harmonizing the norms directly involved in the problem and that indicate a preferable way of resolving the matter. To appreciate Will's point about the importance of the latent aspect of norms for

---

[5] I am relying here on the account of Jonsen and Toulmin (1988, ch. 9).

providing guidance with unprecedented problems, one must be a particularist. That is, one must think in terms of very concrete actual problems that have a context rich with particular circumstances that rule out some adjustments and indicate others. One must appreciate John Dewey's initially puzzling saying that,

> In quality, the good is never twice alike. It never copies itself. It is new every morning, fresh every evening. It is unique in its every presentation. For it marks the resolution of a distinctive complication of competing habits and impulses which can never repeat itself.[6]

5 As long as one neglects the particular situation, it can seem that, inevitably, too many incompatible solutions to a problem will be consistent with the latent aspect of norms. Selected historical problems and their solutions help to show that vexed problems can be uniquely and satisfactorily resolved with the help of their background complex of norms that constitute the social context in which the problem occurs.

It will seem to some, however, that in these historical examples, what is described as the proper resolution of problems with the guidance of the latent aspect of norms is simply the actual muddling through that follows social and intellectual crises. Occasionally, more or less by chance, people hit on a good solution, a defensible one, in this way. This is not enough to show, the objection continues, that the people who "solved" the problem were guided by reliable problem solving techniques. The concrete examples used above are nothing more than a selection of cases where things worked out well more or less by accident.

This objection is simply the claim that people are guided in their action by intelligence or insight only when they follow norms whose manifest content indicates that they act as they do. One defense consists in arguing, as Will does, that that claim excludes

---

[6] Dewey 1922, 146.

too much that is paradigmatic of human intellectual success in both theoretical and practical domains.

The actual historical examples, however, are complex. Sometimes people are confronted by problems so unprecedented that they have no procedures that apply. The imagined case of the assembly line worker who ran out of resistors of the proper value is an example of such a problem. It sometimes happens in the practical domain that social circumstances change so that a norm that was effective and important loses its point. There is sometimes an interval where the norm retains its adherents, even though it no longer serves its original function. Established norms can retain their hold over people even when the circumstances that gave them their point cease to obtain. When other concerns begin to clash with the outdated norm, it gradually yields, and people at the same time gradually become aware of the need for a modified norm. This process is often intermittent, confused, fumbling, halting, and only incompletely understood by the participants. Frequently, it is only when the process of change is in the later stages that anyone articulates at all clearly what is happening and why. The idea, clearly articulated, cannot be said to have guided the change. It does not seem implausible, by contrast, to suppose that the idea, glimpsed unclearly and intermittently by the participants, played an important role in people's effecting the change.

European peoples once believed that the health, prosperity, and safety of their entire communities depended upon careful and faithful performance of specific religious observances. If the religious ceremonies were not properly observed, famine, plague, and other calamities were expected to result. It fell to the sovereign, whose function it is to serve and protect the general welfare of the community, to use all resources to ensure that the proper religious forms were observed. This was an important part of the job of protecting the public welfare. The notion that it was no part of the business of the state to concern itself with the most vigorous and strict maintenance of proper religious observances could find no acceptance in such circumstances. The details of proper observance of religious forms was a matter of the most urgent public interest.

Europeans gradually ceased to accept the idea that impiety results in public calamity.

> Social changes, both intellectual and in the internal composition and external relations of peoples, took place so that men no longer connected attitudes of reverence or disrespect to the gods with the weal and woe of the community. Faith and unbelief still had serious consequences, but these were now thought to be confined to the temporal and eternal happiness of the persons directly concerned. Given the other belief, and persecution and intolerance are as justifiable as is organized hostility to any crime; impiety is the most dangerous of all threats to public peace and well-being. But social changes gradually effected as one of the new functions of the life of the community the rights of private conscience and creed.[7]

It would be hard to exaggerate the historical importance in the history of the West of the development of the idea that religion is a private rather than a public matter. One of its consequences was the very gradual acceptance of a norm of civil toleration of religious diversity. Even after the Protestant Reformation, wars were fought and people cruelly persecuted in the name of religious orthodoxy. As the history of the Puritans in America shows, even those who had suffered from persecution were capable of practicing civil intolerance of religious diversity.

John Locke set out relatively clearly and concisely a case for civil toleration of religious diversity in his "A Letter Concerning Toleration." Written in Holland in 1685, this letter argues that civil law, backed up with the sanction of coercive force, is an entirely inappropriate way to inculcate religious conviction. Civil power properly defends people's life, liberty, and property by impartial law and the threat of legal punishment; it is incompetent and inappropriate in religious matters.

> True and saving Religion consists in the inward perswasion of the Mind, without which nothing can be acceptable to God. And such is the nature of the Understanding, that it cannot be compell'd to the

---

[7] Dewey 1927, 266–67.

belief of any thing by outward force. Confiscation of Estate, Imprisonment, Torments, nothing of that nature can have any such Efficiency as to make Men change the inward Judgment that they have framed of things.[8]

Critics of Locke note that although there is an absurdity in the notion of attempting to coerce an individual into believing something, the idea of attempting to foster a certain belief in a community by suppressing public dissent and dissenters is not similarly absurd.[9] Locke's argument, though, is not best understood as an *a priori* argument against attempting to maintain religious orthodoxy by coercion. The force of his position emerges most clearly when he argues that religious officials should not attempt to extend their authority over civil matters.

The Church it self is a thing absolutely separate and distinct from the Commonwealth. The Boundaries on both sides are fixed and immovable. He jumbles Heaven and Earth together, the things most remote and opposite, who mixes these two Societies; which are in their Original, End, Business, and in every thing, perfectly distinct, and infinitely different from each other.[10]

The "End" of religion, as Locke conceives it, is the care of one's soul, a matter of "inward conviction." The function of the state, according to Locke, is to protect and foster the public good. These things are "perfectly distinct." The subordination of one to the other is likely to be to the detriment of one or both. This line of argument makes perfectly good sense against the background of the assumption that the public interest is not directly at stake in the matter of individuals' religious beliefs.

In the seventeenth century, many people had ceased to believe departures from religious orthodoxy caused specific calamities such

---

[8] Locke 1983, 27.

[9] See, for example, Waldron 1991, 116–18. Contemporaries of Locke made this criticism too. See the account of Locke's controversy with Jonas Proast in Nicholson 1991.

[10] Locke 1983, 33.

as war, famine, and pestilence. Yet the sense lingered that the public good was somehow at stake in religious matters. Norms that had lost their point through changes in the beliefs and practices of people lingered beyond their term. Religious heterodoxy was a threat to the public order, people felt—vaguely. James I is reported to have said, "No Bishop, no King, no nobility."[11] Locke pointed out that as long as people in their religious practice do not violate civil laws designed to protect the public good, their acts and beliefs are not the business of the state. The matter is private rather than public.

In seventeenth century England, church and state were complexly entangled, for historical reasons. It served the purposes of the ruling classes to appoint the clergy to their offices. For one thing, the pulpit was a crucially important means of communication in a country where many subjects were illiterate. It was advantageous in certain ways for that church that happened to be the state church to wield political power. Of course the feeling lingered that somehow the public good depended crucially upon religious matters.

Increasingly, however, people who were serious about their religion conceived in the modern manner strove to practice and believe in ways that departed from the practice of the Church of England. In the dim past, it might have been possible to oppose such heterodoxy with the argument that specific calamities would befall the entire community if such practices were tolerated. Without this argument, however, the political-religious orthodoxy was unable to stem the fervor of dissenting Protestants and others. A social revolution was going on at the same time; an educated, energetic middle class strove for political power with an entrenched aristocracy. The religious and political revolutions were interconnected.

There were in Locke's time any number of reasons to support or oppose religious toleration and to except certain kinds of individuals from religious toleration: Charles II supported toleration because he desired to protect Catholics and seek alliance with France; certain

---

[11] Hill 1980, 65.

contemporary Whigs favored toleration to protect dissident Protestants, and some merchants favored toleration because they perceived that the reputation for toleration of their Dutch rivals gave the latter an advantage in trade.[12] Locke himself thought that the state should not tolerate atheists or Roman Catholics, because the former could not be trusted to keep oaths, while the latter owed allegiance to a foreign power.[13]

The central point that Locke saw, however, is that religion and politics have very different purposes, and that the particular social practices for achieving those different purposes did not mesh well. The incursion of one practice into the domain of the other was apt to be at the expense of one or both. It may serve certain state ends to control appointments to religious offices so that political orthodoxy is preached from the pulpit, but religious officials appointed on such grounds are not necessarily qualified to serve their flock's religious needs.[14] Priests who use political power to advance religious purposes are not primarily concerned with the public good. Rulers' worldly private interests are not the only thing that might deflect them from the proper execution of their offices. The use of the coercive power of the state in determining matters of religious doctrine, however, is no more appropriate than its use to determine matters of scientific theory. If one views the public good as consisting, at least in part, in the maintenance of circumstances in which important practices such as religion and science can flourish and participants can flourish in these practices, then it is so far not in the public interest for the state to attempt to influence the pursuit of these practices and the convictions of the practitioners by force. The exception, of course, is the circumstance where some aspect of such a practice presents a clear and present danger to the public.

A reader of Locke's *Second Treatise of Government* is struck by Locke's notion that much of the social activity that constitutes

---

[12] See Cranston 1981, 79–80, and Gough 1991, 58.

[13] Locke 1983, 51–52.

[14] See Michael Walzer's explanation of the wrongness of simony in Walzer 1983, 8–10; also see *ibid.*, chs. 5 and 10.

human life is governed by norms that are natural phenomena. So the family and the activities that take place in this domain are regarded as governed by natural law. Work, commerce, and property are likewise natural phenomena, social features of the "state of nature." Religion, too, appears to be possible in the state of nature. Civil government, unlike most of the other important social institutions and practices he discussed, he held to be artificial—a human creation for human purposes. The notion that certain social practices are natural rather than artificial is untenable, for reasons that Hume tried to articulate, but this does not invalidate Locke's account of the functions and interrelationships of these various institutions.[15]

Locke had a very strong sense of the diverse functions of certain social practices and institutions, and he saw clearly that the coercive powers of the state, however important for certain purposes, were very ill-suited for regulating the internal functioning of certain other important practices, particularly religion. He articulated this insight more or less clearly in 1685, after a substantial degree of religious liberty had been realized in England. He saw that religion had become a matter of individuals' spiritual welfare and salvation in accordance with their convictions concerning what God required. This, and not the preservation of the community from calamity, was religion's "End." What Locke articulated, however, was something of which others had been more or less aware for some time. Those who have a sense of what religion conceived in the modern way is about and who care about this are apt to resist the incursion of politics into religion. Those who at the same time keep before themselves a lively sense of the purpose of the exercise of political power in the public interest and who properly appreciate how easily rulers are distracted from their proper concern, will resist the use of such power for religious ends. They may, of course, describe their reasons for such resistance in various ways, or they may be unable

---

[15] Some modern critics will deny that we can ascertain the function of social practices and institutions, but little in the way of argument is offered for the denial. (See Waldron 1991, 100–01.) If we can ascertain the function of such artifacts as carpenters' tools, what is to prevent us from ascertaining the functions of our social artifacts?

to articulate them at all. They see in their existing activities a compelling need for a norm of religious tolerance, and gradually they adopt it and refine it.

6 We are familiar with the distinction between the letter and the spirit of the law. Frederick Will explicitly identifies the latent aspect of norms with what he calls the "spirit" or the "will" of the norms that pertain to some important activity, institution, or enterprise (PGN 183, 187). When the explicit, manifest content of the rules, principles, instructions, or lore that people have articulated in developing and teaching a certain practice do not provide direction for coping with a certain problem, they can still look to the norms of the practice and its social context for direction. They can look to the "spirit" of the undertaking.

This is apt to strike us as mysterious. The idea of appeal to the spirit or will of a collection of principles seems to invite idiosyncratic responses, caprice, and chaos—the very opposite of objective rational determination. We are familiar, however, with the contrast between what we want in a certain situation, on the one hand, and what the situation calls for or demands, on the other. It is the latter that is the objective determination to which our desires must yield if they conflict with it, if we are to respond reasonably and properly. Perhaps situations *demand* only metaphorically (though the metaphor is more dead than alive); it is no more than a natural extension of this familiar way of talking and thinking, however, to attribute spirits and wills to situations. It follows, then, that the will or spirit of a situation that confronts us with a problem has a certain objective force that endows its demands with authority. One may not want to talk about the will or spirit of a certain collection of norms, but there is no doubt that there is such a thing. In complex matters, what the spirit or will of the enterprise indicates may be difficult to discern, especially for those implicated in the problem, but this is to be attributed to complexity, the limited capacities of human beings, and the difficulty of understanding matters as one participates in them. In such circumstances, Will says, "the superiority of any reading of the spirit . . . is something that often can only be guessed at and can be determined with assurance only by the way in which one or other competitor succeeds in effecting a resolution of the conflict that originally gave rise to the governing activity" (PGN 189–90).

John Locke understood that government and religion, as he knew these complex phenomena, had diverse purposes that properly were pursued and fostered by very different means. Assuming that the flourishing of religious activity contributes to the good of the community, Locke argued, in effect, that in order for government to fulfill its purpose of regulating individuals for the common good, government should not intrude into purely religious matters. The force of the position comes from the historical circumstances. Religion, once conceived of as a community's ritual techniques for appeasing the gods and warding off calamities, had increasingly become a matter of individuals' ways of tending their own spiritual needs. It was no longer possible to justify the hardships resulting from civil coercion to maintain religious orthodoxy by the argument that only by such means can community disaster be averted. Once religion has become primarily a matter of individual salvation, such desperate measures are without justification. Coercion in religion seems unnecessary and, given the kind of enterprise religion had become, counterproductive. This change in the understanding of the point and focus of religion, this metamorphosis in the spirit of the religious enterprise, was more the cause than the effect of Protestantism.[16] Locke often wrote about such matters as though he were discovering natural rights that had existed all along. The right of privacy in religious matters was a right that could be discovered, however, only when religion had become a private rather than a public matter.

Despite what he might have thought, Locke was not announcing the discovery of an eternal unchanging natural right in his letter. Neither was he, however, simply proclaiming his own or his class's preferences about the relationship of church and state. Locke was articulating what the social situation indicated with respect to this

---

[16] John Dewey 1927, 266–67.

vexed matter, given that the practice and understanding of religion and of government had changed in a fundamental way. The spirit or will of the enterprise of religion in its altered form indicated that religion be understood as distinct and very different from government. Nothing explicitly said that. Certain existing practices, moreover, together with the persistence of cultural commitment to the idea that religious diversity was tantamount to anarchy, resisted such a new norm. Those individuals who cared about religion as a matter of personal salvation and those who took seriously the notion that government's function is to foster, not to impede, the pursuit of important practices that constitute the life of the community, supported the civil toleration of religious diversity. They spoke and acted objectively as the spirit of the enterprise indicated, as the situation demanded.

7 The assumption in much philosophical thinking in all areas of philosophy that norms of thought and action guide us only by means of the specific direction provided by their manifest contents has the result that they offer no help in novel situations. Efforts to discover or construct norms that explicitly indicate the proper course in every circumstance prove futile. Indeed, how could they succeed? We have no way of knowing of any particular norm that it will explicitly indicate the *right* response in circumstances we cannot now anticipate. The recognition of the importance of the latent aspect of norms for constructive thinking about vexed intellectual and practical problems provides a way out of this impasse. The value of Will's account lies not only in the very considerable intellectual satisfaction of this insight. The way is cleared and the direction is indicated for philosophical work that promises constructive contribution to the discussion of the most important problems we face.

The University of Illinois at Urbana-Champaign

References

Butterfield, Herbert. 1965. *The Origins of Modern Science*, rev. ed. New York: Free Press.

Cranston, Maurice. 1991. "John Locke and the Case for Toleration." In Horton and Mendus, 1991, 78–97.

Dewey, John. 1922. *Human Nature and Conduct*. In Dewey, 1983, vol. 14.

Dewey, John. 1927. *The Public and Its Problems*. In Dewey, 1984, vol. 2.

Dewey, John. 1983. *John Dewey: The Middle Works, 1899–1924*. J. A. Boydston, ed. Carbondale and Edwardsville: Southern Illinois University Press.

Dewey, John. 1984. *John Dewey: The Later Works, 1925–53*. J. A. Boydston, ed. Carbondale and Edwardsville: Southern Illinois University Press.

Gough, J. W. 1991. "The Development of Locke's Belief in Toleration." In Horton and Mendus, 1991, 57–77.

Hill, Christopher. 1980. *The Century of Revolution: 1603–1714*, 2nd ed. New York and London: Norton.

Horton, John and Susan Mendus, eds. 1991. *John Locke: A Letter Concerning Toleration in Focus*. London and New York: Routledge.

Jonsen, Albert and Stephen Toulmin. 1988. *The Abuse of Casuistry: A History of Moral Reasoning*. Berkeley, Los Angeles, and London: University of California Press.

Locke, John. 1983. *A Letter Concerning Toleration*. J. H. Tully, ed. Indianapolis: Hackett.

Nicholson, Peter. 1991. "John Locke's Later Letters on Toleration." In Horton and Mendus, 1991, 163–87.

Waldron, Jeremy. 1991. "Toleration and the Rationality of Persecution." In Horton and Mendus, 1991, 98–124.

Walzer, Michael. 1983. *Spheres of Justice*. New York: Basic Books.

Will, Frederick L. 1988. *Beyond Deduction: Ampliative Aspects of Philosophical Reflection*. New York and London: Routledge.

Will, Frederick L. 1997. *Pragmatism and Realism*. K. R. Westphal, ed. Lanham, Md.: Rowman & Littlefield.

Wittgenstein, Ludwig. 1953. *Philosophical Investigations*. G. E. M. Anscombe, tr. New York: Macmillan.

12

Rationality Beyond Deduction:
A Guide for the Perplexed
and the Disappointed

James E. Tiles

There is no good reason for, and much reason against supposing that for every need in the governance of norms there are extant accessible norms, resort to and application of which will fill the need. At some places, deductive, applicative techniques, however ingenious and elaborate, are insufficient in principle. What is needed to supplement the application of extant, accessible norms is ampliative effects wrought upon the body of norms, not further applications of components of that body, not the development of further applicative techniques, perhaps in some organon of these. Those looking to find in this study of ampliative processes the elaboration of such techniques, or the prospectus of such an organon, will be disappointed. (*BD* ix–x)[1]

1 If one is held fast by (what are in Frederick L. Will's terms) "deductivist norms" of philosophic discourse, one will indeed be disappointed by Will's book, *Beyond Deduction*, for its central claim is that those norms have led us seriously astray. (The hold of deductivism on a philosophically trained mind may well be so pervasive that opening Will's book will not produce disappointment

---

[1] Will 1988. Citations from *Beyond Deduction* will be marked in the text by the letters '*BD*' followed by a page reference.

so much as perplexity and frustration.[2]) This is not to say that being convinced of the inadequacy of 'deductive, applicative techniques' is a promise of finding satisfaction in what Will called 'ampliative effects.' Beyond deductivism there may lie a more profound disappointment: "the ampliative phases of our employment of norms and the functions these phases perform in the governance of norms" (*ibid.*) may—Will's assurances not withstanding—appear insufficiently rational, even to those who are prepared to treat rationality as extending further than deduction can reach.

The aim of this essay is to assess the basis one might have for disappointment in Will's book by reviewing (§§4 and 5) the resources for "ampliative governance" that Will turns up in his investigation and by canvassing (§6) nearby fields (the works of Aristotle, Charles Peirce and John Dewey) for further resources. As a preliminary, an attempt will be made (§§2 and 3) to identify assumptions that stand as obstacles to a sympathetic hearing of what Will has to say and thus serve as sources of perplexity (although obstacles of this nature are frequently not easy to remove). An effort will be made to explain Will's thesis in as nontechnical a vocabulary as possible—for some perplexity is generated in readers who find it difficult to adapt to an author's lexical idiosyncracies.

2 'Norms' are "patterns of procedure which serve as guides or standards of thought and action" (*BD* 1). Although 'norm' is Will's preferred term, he recognizes 'practice' as "roughly equivalent" (17, *cf.* 30f.)—as in the sentence, 'It is the practice in this office to defer without question to one's supervisor.' Will suggests that the corresponding term in Peirce and Dewey would be 'habit' and in Hume, 'custom' (*BD* 1). The former term, which has a long philosophical lineage stretching back to *habitus* in the Scholastics and *hexis* in Aristotle, emphasizes the basis of Will's central concept in

---

[2] Such seems to have been the experience of the reviewer of Will's book in the journal *Philosophy* 64, 1989, 424–25.

the dispositions of individual agents. 'Custom' draws attention to the essential social dimension of this concept: customs are shared dispositions. But stereotypical customs are superficial behavior patterns, easily identified and imitated by outsiders (*e.g.* in such diverse places as Japan and the Czech Republic it is the custom to take off one's shoes before entering someone's house or apartment.) The 'norms' to which Will refers are commonly learned tacitly through participation, like the grammatical principles that govern one's native language, and are often at least as difficult as grammatical principles for practitioners and outside observers alike to articulate.[3]

Far from merely decorating a way of life, as the word 'custom' might suggest, the norms to which Will refers structure all aspects of life, including how situations are perceived. And they are intricately bound up with one another—it is not in general easy to modify one practice without this affecting many others in unanticipated ways (*cf. BD* 2, 94–95). Norms are "approved ways of proceeding in thought and action," they constitute what Wittgenstein referred to as 'forms of life' and Hegel as 'forms of consciousness' (*BD* 24). Norms, in other words, are items which together constitute a culture, but not as the sum of separable or separably identifiable parts. What are spoken of in the singular or plural are aspects selected for attention by participants or outsiders from the flux of social interaction.[4] Norms are all learned in the sense of acquired through experience (especially acculturation), but they are not by

---

[3] The French social philosopher Pierre Bourdieu has revived the Scholastic term *habitus* (singular and plural: *habitus*) to create a technical term that tries to do justice both to the psychological and to the social dimensions of these phenomena. *Habitus* are, "systems of durable, transposable dispositions, structured structures predisposed to function as structuring structures, that is, as principles which generate and organize practices and representations that can be objectively adapted to their outcomes without presupposing a conscious aiming at ends or an express mastery of the operations necessary in order to attain them" (Bourdieu 1990, 53).

[4] Will's attitude to norms emerges in such lines as "a norm cannot be genuinely conceived independently of its relations with other norms . . .. The price of separate identity is some distortion as a norm . . ." (*BD* 94–95). Dewey similarly stressed the 'interpenetration' of habits, (see *Human Nature and Conduct*, *MW* 14:I, ii).

any means all learned or observed in an explicit or consciously controlled fashion.[5] As Dewey observed (*LW* 1:227–28), our behavior is necessarily governed by a vast complex of subconscious habits, "the greater part" of which "is only implicit in any conscious act or state" (*ibid.*, 230). Enough of these habits must be shared, as Bourdieu says, for communication to be possible: "'Communication of consciousnesses' presupposes community of 'unconsciouses' (that is, of linguistic and cultural competences)."[6]

'Governance' is best approached via its etymology. To govern ('*gubernare*') was originally to steer a boat. The rudder has the effect of giving a disposition to the motion of a boat; the steersman is in a position to adjust that disposition. Norms are the dispositions of ongoing human activities; governance of norms is adjustments made to those dispositions. Note that the position of the rudder does not by itself determine the direction of the boat. The direction of the motive force (wind, oar, propeller) also influences the direction; and how the boat responds to adjustments in the position of the rudder also depends on the shape of its hull and nature of its keel. This metaphor from mechanical causation suggests, however imperfectly, the inter-relatedness of norms (what Will refers to as their 'composition' [*BD* 156]) and highlights the error of imagining that any ongoing human activity can be governed entirely by making adjustments in a single norm. One must, however, be cautious about the further use of a metaphor such as this. Conceiving norms on the usual model of natural causation is, according to Will, the source of serious misrepresentations of human action.[7] Will distin-

---

[5] "Norms are learned patterns of conduct rather than unlearned or instinctive ones, [but] not in the extreme sense that *everything* about them can be fully explained as due to some postgametic learning . . ." (*BD* 24; for an explanation of the italics added here, see *BD* 38–39). Will's acceptance of tacit norms is clear from his assertions that the governance of norms is not always conscious, or reflective. See, *e.g.*, the taxonomy of governance *BD* 158–61 and the passage from *BD* 11 quoted below.

[6] Bourdieu 1990, 58.

[7] Bourdieu similarly rejects mechanical explanations, suggesting that the concept of something 'with history' may be used to distinguish *habitus* from mechanisms. "The *habitus* is a spontaneity without consciousness or will, opposed as much to the mechanical necessity of things without history in mechanistic theories as to the

guishes guidance by norms from mechanical causation by denying that the former operate like 'internalized . . . templates of action' whose influence can be isolated and traced through the complexes of normative influences (*BD* 130–31).[8] The claim here, as we shall see, is part of Will's indictment of 'deductivism.'

We have seen, however, that it is not conscious awareness that distinguishes a norm from a mere mechanism. Consciousness is not even essential to governance of norms. Will makes it quite clear that a good deal of governance is nonreflective, "There are ways in which a community unreflectively, largely unknowingly, effects governance of the constitutional commitments under which it lives . . ." (*BD* 11). Here the image of the rudder is clearly prone to mislead. We assume a helmsman adjusts the rudder to make the boat's course conform to some conscious intention. Norms, Will is suggesting, are sometimes adjusted (governed) without there being any 'end-in-view'—at least any 'end-in-view' to which that particular adjustment is seen as a means. Governance, like Bourdieu's *habitus* (see note 3), "can be collectively orchestrated without being the product of the organizing action of a conductor."[9] This is not surprising, however, if one accepts that governance of norms will itself be guided by norms (*BD* 150). How this takes place is, of course, the central question broached in Will's book.

---

reflexive freedom of subjects 'without inertia' in rationalist theories" (Bourdieu 1990, 56). Although it will be suggested in the next note that the basis of the distance between Will's norms and mechanical causation can be expressed in terms of Mill's Law of the Composition of Causes, it is worth pointing out how Will's insistence that norms have to be (have been) governed in order to be norms (*e.g.* "an uncriticized, ungoverned norm is a contradiction in terms" [*BD* 10]) makes them essentially things 'with history.'

[8] The claim here appears to deny what Mill refers to as the "Law of the Composition of Causes," which is that "if we happend to know what would be the effects of each cause when acting separately from the other, we are often [where the Composition of Causes obtains] able to arrive deductively, or *a priori*, at a correct prediction of what will arise from their conjunct agency" (1843, 3:vi). Mill, as a committed methodological individualist, insisted that "In social phenomena the Composition of Causes is the universal law," since, "Human beings in society have no properties but those which are derived from, and may be resolved into, the laws of the nature of individual man." (*ibid.*, 6:vii).

[9] Bourdieu 1990, 53.

Now if one approaches Will's treatement of this question assuming the transparency of consciousness—viz. that what a person believes, the values that govern that individual's conduct and the principles by which changes are brought about in those beliefs or values are all accessible to that individual's attentive mind—one is bound to be perplexed by the way Will conducts his investigation.[10] If, moreover, one insists, as the tradition of analysis has always insisted, on identifying in phenomena entities whose natures (it is supposed) can be investigated in isolation from one another, Will's assumption that norms (practices) are essentially interrelated will appear to be the very negation of sound thought. Both of these common assumptions are characteristic of modern philosophical individualism and help to sustain the further common assumption (known as 'methodological individualism') that all explanations of collective behavior are reducible to the sum of the behaviors of individuals. It is very likely that readers who hold (or are held by) these assumptions will find themselves perplexed (not to say, frustrated) by the stress that Will places on the social formation of knowledge, thought and rationality—"For the natural tendency of a modern philosophical mind and personality is individualistic" (*BD* 35). Readers who are unable or unwilling to think outside of these assumptions will find it difficult to see the point of Will's central thesis.

3 Will criticizes (specifically Anglo-American) philosophy (*BD* 13) for its 'deductivism,' "the extrusion of ampliative processes from the repertory of philosophical reflection" (*BD* 7). The charge is not

---

[10] Those whose previous experience of philosophy has been so thoroughly shaped by the Cartesian problematic that they find it difficult to image what could be wrong with assumptions such as this, may find it instructive to read Will 1974. Note in particular the "summary statement": "The difference between this traditional view and that advanced in these pages is radical. What is being maintained here is, conceding the oversimplification that summary statement requires, that in so elementary an act as meaning red, and hence in discriminating red objects, red patches, or red appearings from orange, green, or blue ones, one is enabled to do what he does because he is acting within and drawing upon the resources of a complex social practice" (*ibid.*, 211).

merely that philosophers have tried to restrict their own contributions to deductive (explicative, 'analytic' [BD 5]) moves, but that they have also tended to misrepresent governance as rational only to the extent that it consists in such moves. This indictment is framed in a vocabulary borrowed from logical theory. There is a danger in this, given that Will is not advancing claims specific to the practices of "argument, reasoning or inference" (BD 5),[11] but about the way norms guide and in their turn are governed—that is about "the actual generation, criticism, refinement, reconstruction, maintenance, re-enforcement, and elimination of norms" (BD 43).

The two main terms that Will borrows are, moreover, not strictly correlative. Peirce divided inferences into those that were 'explicative'—those that spelled out what was already implicit in the premisses—and those that were 'ampliative,' that is where the conclusion went beyond what was contained in the premisses. Peirce recognized only one kind of explicative inference, deduction, and identified two kinds of ampliative inference, induction and a third kind which he labeled variously 'abduction,' 'retroduction,' 'presumption' and 'hypothesis.' Because his indictment is not aimed specifically at the way philosophers have treated argument,[12] Will has little use for Peirce's contributions to the theory of ampliative inference. (These contributions are mentioned briefly at BD 5 note 2.) 'Deductive' serves to mark a conception of norms; 'ampliative' serves to mark what is excluded by that conception.

Will offers four characteristics of 'deductive processes' that serve to distinguish them from 'ampliative processes' (BD 32–33). (1) The former are 'forensic' or 'probative' in the sense that they aim to produce conviction or assent[13] under the presumption that one or

---

[11] "[H]owever valuable the argument model is for illuminating some processes of governance, it is extremely obscuring for others" (BD 6).

[12] One might well, of course, complain about the privileging of deduction in the theory and pedagogy of logic. Induction attracts interest only to the extent that it appears possible to provide rules of inductive inference. Will classifies such attempts as 'deductivist,' as the aim is to do no more than provide applicative rules (see below).

[13] The traditional (but now obsolete) legal use of the term 'deduction' to which Kant refers in The Critique of Pure Reason (A84/B116), is closer to what Will has

more norms already apply and contain definite answers to questions about how to proceed. 'Ampliative processes' by contrast must be used where prevailing norms are perceived to yield no answer or the wrong answer. (2) 'Deductive processes' are "essentially *applicative* or subsumptive, rather than generative or defining." They are (3) engaged in by individuals, whereas it is supposed to be possible (as we have seen) for ampliative governance to be effected on a social level in a way not consciously intended by any individual. Finally, 'deductive processes' are (4) assumed to be conscious and intentional.[14] The second of these four characteristics carries a great deal of the burden of Will's indictment and it will have to be considered carefully.

The false image of norms has behind it, Will maintains, a conception that may well strike the reader as Platonic. Norms have characters that are "display[ed] in their own specific mode or modes" and being guided by them "is replicating them in thought and action" (*BD* 48). The governance of norms follows the same model; "certain master, archetypal norms" are strictly applied to authenticate more common norms (*BD* 49). The 'deductive' use of norms, it appears, is to be characterized by variations on the root '*plicare*' (to fold): it is ex*plica*tion, ap*plica*tion, re*plica*tion. The norm is assumed to fold over the thought or action that is 'subsumed' under it as copy to 'template' (*BD* 131). This conception feeds, among other errors, the view of norms as guiding human beings by a form of mechanical causation.

Will finds material that usefully subverts the replication model in Wittgenstein's reflections on what is involved in following a rule. One of Wittgenstein's examples involves teaching a person to

---

in mind than is the use of the term in logical theory. (On the legal use of 'deduction' prior to the demise of the Holy Roman Empire, see Henrich 1989, 32–39.)

[14] "A not inconsiderable portion of the attraction of this [deductivist] view of governance derived from the fact that the procedure represented seemed to be a kind that, as in its original Cartesian ancestor, could be engaged in by individual minds isolated from the influence of custom and tradition. The cultural roots of this extremely individualistic, asocial and atraditional emphasis are very broad and deep" (*BD* 56).

generate a sequence of natural numbers by successively adding 2. When the subject reaches 1000 by this procedure, he continues the series with 1004, 1008, 1012, *etc.* The aim of this example, as Will sees it, is to call into question the conception "of a rule as a mental or even cerebral construct that serves as a template for action." The challenge is to explain "how did we, in teaching this person the rule by exhibiting applications of it at steps less than 1000, produce such a template in him that faithfulness to it required him to proceed in one way rather than another?" (*BD* 114).

Will, however, is far from embracing the extreme nominalism which holds that correctly following a rule consists solely in what everyone agrees is correct. This nominalism arises from the illusion generated by thinking that a rule or norm guides in isolation. Wittgenstein's example abstracts from the complex linguistic network that supports any attempt to teach someone explicitly.[15]

> Rather than requiring a skeptical solution to the problem of how a rule can determine action in accordance with it, these reflections help us understand how in fact this determination is realized. The rule of adding 2 does not guide a being who, like a newly created Adam, is without tradition, company, practices, and institutions from which our rules of calculation are generated. The rule guides beings like us, with all these developed resources. It is these that perform the function of ballast, providing the kind of responses that we count as steady performance. (*BD* 116–17)

That Wittgenstein's example should be seen as a threatening a new form of skepticism serves only to highlight the effects of the third

---

[15] It is designed, arguably, to serve as a *reductio* of empiricist claims about what can be achieved solely with ostensive procedures. P. M. S. Hacker links the notion that Wittgenstein's attacks, 'mental ostensive definition' with 'unconditional rules which cannot be misapplied' (1972, 135). Deductivism commits the error of thinking that there always need to be (or can be) rules for applying rules, or rules that somehow embody their own interpretation. Wittgenstein was by no means the first to expose this error. Hacker (1972, 135 note) cites Kant's *Critique of Pure Reason* (A133–34/B172–73) on the need for an ability to subsume things under rules, which he calls 'judgment' and which cannot be taught or equipped with rules, but only acquired by practice.

of the four assumed characteristics of 'deductive processes' cited above.

To offset the conception of subsumption based on 'replication,' Will recommends the conclusion to which E. H. Levi came in his treatment of legal reasoning, "the kind of reasoning involved in the legal process is one in which the classification changes as the classification is made. The rules change as the rules are applied" (*BD* 7, *cf.* 67). Stated baldly this sounds like the very negation of what it is to be governed by law, but what Levi is attempting to highlight is the fact that cases brought before the courts may have the effect of clarifying what the law is. Lawyers have been known to say they do not know what a new piece of legislation means and will not know until it has been tested in the courts. At the very least the appeal to precedents in law is a recognition that statutes do not contain within themselves all that is required for their own interpretation. For Will this is a particularly crucial example of the governance of norms that is completely obscured by the 'replication' conception of how norms guide. Laws—explicit legal norms —are clarified and adjusted to new or unfamiliar circumstances through the process of subsuming cases under them.

It perhaps should be stressed that not all subsumption is—either in intention or in effect—governance of norms. Will acknowledges that cases are routinely subsumed under norms without there being any effect on the character of the norm; moreover "Routine subsumption is widespread, and unquestionably an essential part of human life . . . [but that] does not justify the concentration upon it, indeed the almost exclusive preoccupation with it, that has prevailed in modern philosophy" (*BD* 102). For in addition to routine subsumption, there are many cases where it is not obvious that or how a norm is to apply. The outcome of such problematic cases may have the same effect as routine subsumption, that of 'stabilizing, fixing and entrenching' the norm; in other cases, however, subsumption has the effect of adapting, adjusting, redesigning, reconstructing the norm (*BD* 104).

One of the deleterious effects of deductivism and its replication model is that where governance is clearly needed and cannot be effected by the explication of existing norms, it appears that we can only proceed by making arbitrary decisions. For where the conception of governance is based entirely on what takes place in routine application of norms, any alternative must appear completely unconstrained. Thus the governance that Will calls 'ampliative' is viewed as the outcome of processes that are not rationally governed and which in many contexts "appear under the curious banner of 'emotive'" (*BD* 70).

One such context is the doctrine in jurisprudence known as 'legal realism' (*BD* 66–72) according to which a decision is not guided by reason unless it is "logically compelled by prior legal doctrine whose content all reasonable men must recognize on pain of contradiction and which was, in that sense, there for reason to discover." Realists insist as a consequence that "few, if any, important judicial decisions could be said to be entirely guided by reason in this sense."[16] In the history of philosophy this attitude toward what constitutes the use of reason is exemplified best in Hume and the outcome is similar,

> As the effect of deductivism in Hume was to erase the line between science and faith in matters of fact, so the effect in legal realism was to erase the line between legitimate and illegitimate practice in all those cases of juridical judgment in which the definition of law was made on political, moral, economic and other wide social grounds. (*BD* 69)[17]

What is at stake in Will's prosecution of philosophy for 'deductivism' is the question of whether we are to conceive reason in the

---

[16] The words here are those cited by Will from Dworkin 1981.

[17] Will quotes a comment on Dworkin 1981, by Warren Lehman: "It would be hard, I suspect to get through an American law school today without getting the impression that the law is merely an excuse for policy. The law is how policy is mystified. That kind of cynicism is . . . only the latest of the bad consequences of realism" (1981, 52).

narrow manner espoused by Hume or in the broader manner recommended by Hegel.[18]

And what is at stake in the choice between conceptions of reason is what procedures or processes if any will be regarded as legitimating the governance of norms and whether those procedures and processes will be required to adhere to high standards of care and thoroughness.[19] As 'rational' is a "protean and usually honorific term" (*BD* 55) bestowed on thought processes, 'legitimate' is a protean and usually honorific title bestowed on authority and its exercise. To govern a norm, whether consciously or unconsciously, is to exercise authority (power, *auctoritas*). To ask that governance be rational is to insist on an investment of thought capable of producing an explanation of that governance that attempts to justify it.

To anyone who looks to authority simply to be told what to do (in the way the 're*plica*tion' model insists that a norm stamps its template on all that is subsumed under it), explanations serve only to make clear (ex*plica*te) what is required. There is no need for explanations that justify or legitimate. To people whose outlook on their own actions is voluntaristic, that is who regard their own authority over their own thought and conduct on this autocratic model, there is similarly no need to invest thought to justify what they believe or what they pursue.

If they combine this voluntarism with a belief in the transparency of consciousness, they will tend to conceive of themselves (in

---

[18] Will quotes from Sabine 1950, 620–21: "The idealism of Hegel tried to weave reason and tradition into a single unit—the expanding culture of a national spirit or consciousness . . . .. What Hegel's philosophy professed to offer, therefore, was an enlarged conception of reason . . .."

[19] Citing further Dworkin's discussion (1981) of the effects of legal realism on the work of Chief Justice William O. Douglas, Will reports, "Douglas was rendered by the lingering effects of this philosophy incapable of providing a clear and coherent defense of the commitment in his legal opinions. Lacking a clear and coherent philosophical basis for the decisions that he was obliged by his office to make he . . . 'began to write opinions that he knew would be described by the profession as careless, hasty, and contemptuous of the whole process of legal reasoning'" (*BD* 71).

Bourdieu's terms, note 6) as possessing reflexive freedom 'without inertia,' that is, conceive of their beliefs and conduct as unconstrained by habit, unconsciously followed, or by tradition, subconsciously adhered to. There will be no need to explain their own beliefs or projects even to make clear to themselves what they believe or what they are pursuing. They are bound to find Will's enterprise—his indictment of 'deductivism' and his commitment to a kind of rationalism—perplexing; for in challenging the replication model of how norms guide, Will is challenging their conception of authority.

4 So what lies 'beyond deduction'? What kind of rational authority can be exercised in 'ampliative processes of governance'? We will find it useful first to survey 'ampliative processes' in general, bearing in mind that Will does not set out to claim that all such processes are rational or serve properly to legitimate. "It is of course a gross mistake to construe emphasis upon the ampliative character of certain phases of reflection as implying a general blanket philosophical certification of all results generated in these phases" (*BD* 12).

The two main principles of ampliative governance have already been touched upon. (1) The "application of norms to more or less tractable instances" has "direct reactive effects" on them. (2) Because norms are interrelated with one another in a variety of complex ways, tending to reinforce, or conflict with, one another, norms themselves have ampliative effects on one another. (Although some norms can be placed in hierarchical relationships to one another, it would be a—typically 'deductivist'—mistake to assume that all governance of norms by norms is effected through such relationships.) These two kinds of ampliative effects on norms can be combined, that is to say, (3) the effects of subsuming problem cases under norms will be mediated by other related norms and the bearing of related norms on a given norm will be influenced by precedents established in the history of its application to difficult cases.

These three kinds of ampliative process are set out on page 148 of *Beyond Deduction*. It is not claimed that they provide an exhaustive list of ampliative processes, and it is important to note at least one further basic process that would appear capable of ampliative adjustment, *viz.* the effects on norms of changes in the way they are represented. The most striking of such changes would be the formulation as explicit rules of what have hitherto been tacitly followed norms, for example making statutes out of customs such as took place in the formation of English Common Law in the tenth and eleventh centuries and the codification of Prussia's *Allgemine Landrecht* in the late eighteenth century. The tension that can be observed between speakers who think of their language as governed by formal rules of grammar and those who speak the language entirely 'by ear' also illustrates this difference and the effects on norms previously represented only in practice of being represented as explicit rules.[20]

In general when a norm, hitherto followed tacitly, is given any kind of representation, it not only has the effect of stabilizing that norm (the representation may indeed be referred to as a kind of template in order to determine conformity), it also makes the norm a possible subject of discussion. Norms that are open to discussion can be challenged and justifications demanded, affording people, as it were, a tiller where previously there was no option but to go

---

[20] Differences between oral and written representations of norms, differences between norms that are embodied in exemplars (in drama and song) and those in the form of rules, differences between norms conveyed through text and through pictures, also need to be considered. Where, for example, the form in which a norm is represented (say in the character of an epic story) permits a variety of realizations (in the telling of the story), the norm may be governed by the class of people (dramatic poets) responsible for (re)producing those realizations. This is the source of Plato's apprehensions about the power of representational art.

with the flow.[21] (Whether a given person can actually exert influence on the tiller is, of course, a different question.)

We have, so far, three important kinds of ampliative process, *viz.* the reactive effects of subsumption, the interactive effects of norms on each other and modifications effected through changes in a norm's representation. The question we are approaching is, 'under what circumstances and to what extent can these processes be regarded as rational or legitimating?' The way Will addresses this question with respect to the two processes that he identifies will be considered in the next section. As a preliminary the remainder of this section will introduce a taxonomy of governance, which Will provides (*BD* 158–62) and consider a problem raised by the third process, which Will did not identify.

Will's taxonomy of governance is based on three important oppositions, 'ampliative vs. deductive,' 'reflective vs. nonreflective,' 'philosophical vs. nonphilosophical,' which, because each opposition is treated as independent of the others, generates an eight-fold classification by a process familiar to anyone who has dealt with truth tables. The opposition between 'philosophical and nonphilosophical' refers to governance of norms which possess a 'constitutional dimension,' *i.e.* which is broad, deep, and controversial (*BD* 21–22, *cf.* 122). If we are interested in whether ampliative process can qualify for that "protean and usually honorific term" 'rational,' we might hope to see how ampliative *philosophical* governance can be rational. It indeed appears to be Will's strategy to establish the possibility of rationality for (reflective) philosophical governance

---

[21] The effects are similar on norms which, because of taboos, are understood but never discussed, because people are embarrassed or find it distasteful to mention them. 'Understood,' that is, only in the sense that people are aware of what counts as conformity, for a climate of silence may be conducive to a wide variety of understandings of such norms and their rationale. Kristen Luker's survey of the history of abortion in America reveals how large segments of the population could in 1973 believe from the silence about the subject that everyone assumed the unborn were full persons and abortion was therefore morally wrong, while equally large segments of the population held no such belief. Understanding could not be shared because the matter was never discussed as it belonged to the domain of sex and reproduction, which many people avoided in intimate as well as 'polite' conversation. See Luker 1984, ch. 6.

(see *BD* 158), although he insists that "philosophical species of governance cannot be well understood in isolation from other species" (*BD* 21), so we should not concentrate exclusively on the philosophical species.

It might be thought, from the attention Will pays to specifically reflective philosophical governance, that the application of 'rational' to ampliative governance is confined to the category of 'reflective.' A 'rational' adjustment in a norm would appear to be one that at least *post facto* can be provided with an explicit account of why it should be made. It can stand its ground, be defended, in a discursive examination of its claim over alternatives. If correct, this would appear to require that rational governance be reflective, although there is a paradox lurking here.

If rational governance is reflective, then there is a premium on explicit representations of norms and guidance by explicitly represented norms. Is it then possible for a rational examination of norms guiding a practice to discover (have 'good reason' to conclude) that the practice in question is best left governed by implicit norms? The difficulty is that once a norm has been made explicit, it is psychologically impossible to re-enter the practice as before, governed tacitly by that norm. The paradox comes to a head in the realization that if it is best for a norm to remain tacit, the practitioners governed by it cannot possess a rational justification of the judgment that this is the case. (For possessing the justification requires the very kind of representation of the norm that undermines its tacit guidance.)

This paradox does not have to be resolved in order for us to consider the possibility of rational ampliative governance, although in reaching the paradox two threats to that possibility have emerged from the claim that rational governance must be reflective. One appears in the argument that to be 'rational' an adjustment in a norm must be able to 'stand its ground, be defended, in a discursive examination of its claim.' This language is "forensic or *probative*" and (as Will suggested [*BD* 32]) invites deductivist treatment. If, moreover, there is a premium in rational governance (if it is to be reflective) on explicit guidance by explicit representations of norms, there will clearly be a strong pull from the model of guidance that Will stigmatized as 'replication.'

The tendency of the concept of 'rational' governance to be captured so easily by 'deductivist' notions needs to be made clear. There are two possible sources of disappointment in the outcome of Will's investigation. One is that Will is unable to make ampliative processes conform to deductivist expectations. To be disappointed for this reason is tantamount to begging the question against Will's thesis. The other would be that even after deductivist assumptions and expectations have been carefully identified and suspended, there appears to be no sense in which ampliative processes can be said to be rational. Clearly, to assess whether there is any basis of the second kind for disappointment requires constant vigilance against infiltration from the first source.

5 Will could well have helped readers prone to disappointment from either source by squaring up more directly to the question of what it is for a governance to merit that protean and largely honorific term, 'rational.' Clearly, we have to find uses of the term outside forensic contexts and to identify reflective activities that, however explicit, do not rely exclusively on replicating antecedently existing norms. To see what resources Will can offer us here, readers have to comb through his discussion of other philosophers, for example, his criticisms of Stephen Toulmin and Julian Franklin, to find a characterization of what it is to be 'rational' and a glimpse of what ampliative rationality is supposed to be.

According to Will, Toulmin "is seriously hampered in trying to account for the authority that may be claimed" for judgments about how norms apply in problematic cases (*BD* 162).[22] Toulmin wishes to show how such judgments and choices "can be preserved from

---

[22] In Toulmin's terms the problem is the application of 'concepts' to 'cloudy' cases. The matter is best expressed in Will's language as we are considering what resources he has when addressing the question of the rationality of ampliative governance rather than the merits of his criticisms of Toulmin.

subjectivity and idiosyncrasy" (*BD* 163) but because he thinks of norms as functioning in isolation from one another ("Proceeding without benefit of the concept of composition. . ." [*ibid.*]). Toulmin is forced to rely on "the best individual judgement" of certain authoritative individuals (*e.g.*, in constitutional law, that of Supreme Court Justices) about how norms should develop (about "what the law ought to become" [*BD* 165]). We find in this criticism a negative characterization of 'rational'—it is not subjective or idiosyncratic—and a re-emphasis on one of the major claims Will makes about norms, their close interrelatedness. On the basis of this interrelatedness Will goes on to extract from a discussion of Hegel the idea that institutions (such as law) contain within themselves answers to the question how they ought to develop.

This challenge to the is/ought dualism prevailing in contemporary Anglo-American philosophy (not to mention the appeal to that *bête noire*, Hegel) will, no doubt, provoke more perplexity (not to say hostility) on the part of many of Will's readers. Meeting this particular source of perplexity is a task beyond the scope of this essay, but there is a challenge that arises even before entering the toils of objective idealism and one that we need to be able to deal with here. If we recognize that norms are intimately interrelated and that in those interrelations are answers to how a practice or body of norms ought to develop, how do we distinguish judgments about that development that are 'subjective' or 'idiosyncratic' from those that are 'rational' and 'legitimate'? Some of the answer lies in Will's response to Julian Franklin.

Franklin had criticized the views of Michael Oakeshott regarding "the arrangements which constitute a society capable of political activity"—views that Will saw as very similar to his own understanding of the governance of norms in general (*BD* 178). Rejecting what he called "rationalism" in politics (characterized in a way which Will saw as similar to his own understanding of 'deductivism' [*BD* 134–35]) Oakeshott claimed that

> customs or institutions or laws . . . compose a pattern and at the same time they intimate a sympathy for what does not fully appear.

Political activity is the exploration of that sympathy; and consequently, relevant political reasoning will be the convincing exposure of a sympathy, present but not yet followed up, and the convincing demonstration that now is the appropriate moment for recognizing it.[23]

This is an excerpt representing an extended characterization of political reasoning which, Oakeshott hoped to show, could not be reduced to 'acting on hunches' or 'following intuitions.' Franklin's critique of Oakeshott amounted to pressing the charge that Oakeshott could not with his language of 'sympathy' and 'intimation' avoid appeals to intuition.

'Intuitive,' it should be noted, is commonly contrasted to 'discursive' as a basis for arriving at judgments. One way to specify how 'rational' functions as a term of approbation is to say that it is used to mark pieces of discursive reasoning that are thought to be competently carried out. 'Intuitionism' in moral philosophy is the claim that discursive reasoning is, however competently carried out, impotent to evaluate conduct. Will rejects 'intuitionism' in moral philosophy (*BD* 72–74) as another (along with legal realism) deleterious consequence of deductivism. He nevertheless clearly feels that if Franklin's charge against Oakeshott is sustained, his own position is vulnerable to the charge that it comes down in the end to a kind of intuitionism.

Is it the fate of a theory of ampliative processes of governance to devolve into some explicit or implicit form of intuitionism, some view in which governing thought and action under challenge must depend in a substantial way for the validation of their results upon intuition? (*BD* 179).

A 'yes' to this question is grounds for precisely the kind of disappointment—the kind that does not depend on begging the question in favor of deductivism—that we are considering here.

---

[23] This is an extract from a long quotation from Oakeshott 1962, at *BD* 178.

Will's response is to caution once again against bringing such question-begging deductivist expectations to ampliative reasoning, including a caution against the "terminology of 'argument'" (*BD* 180) and against thinking "of response to logical authority as a kind of intellectual submission" (*BD* 182). He goes on to offer this characterization of the attitude and expectations that find no place in deductivism:

> In ampliative processes the individual alone or together with others is led rather than coerced, led to change his position, to see things from a different point of view. One adopts one view in preference to alternatives, not because it, rather than they, is altogether extruded from the realm of the doubtful, but because one develops an appreciation of the superiority, which may be slight, moderate, or extreme, of one over the others. Although in some cases this appreciation may burgeon forth in an instant, in others it may require a protracted period of extended, often on-and-off reflection. (*Ibid.*)

It takes, perhaps, a protracted period of extended reflection on the concept of reasoning itself before a reader will see how some moments of this reflective activity may be competently or incompetently carried out and the term 'rational' applied to the former. Developments of subtle appreciations following extended periods of reflection may well deserve to be distinguished into those that are rational and those that are not, but the process as Will describes it does not appear discursive enough—does not involve enough explicit articulation—to be above the suspicion that it is nothing more than the exercise of that subjectivity and idiosyncrasy that can do little more to claim legitimacy for itself than to appeal to a faculty of 'intuition.'

Readers who reach this far in Will's account of ampliative processes, having tried as honestly as possible to suspend their deductivist presuppositions and expectations, might well be forgiven for being disappointed. They are, apparently, being asked to accept that discriminations of competence and incompetence are possible for a kind of reflective activity, of which they may feel they have little experience, and are being told that it may take a great deal of precisely that activity in order to become fully convinced of this. Is there anything more that might be said to turn disappointment into hope? Do all attempts to articulate justifications—reasons for governance in one direction rather than another—that escape the allegation of intuitionism, collapse into deductivism?

6 One important resource that Will neglects may be found in the area that lies at the boundary of logic and action theory known as 'practical logic' or 'the theory of practical reasoning.' It is understandable that this area might not look promising to Will, given that much of what goes on in it is dominated by struggles over whether deductivism should prevail here as well. This can be illustrated by recent discussions of material from the earliest contribution to the field—what commentators on Aristotle refer to as 'practical syllogisms.' Aristotle offers several examples of what he calls 'syllogisms' that have conclusions presenting something to be done (*i.e.* what ought or needs to be done—imperatives expressed in a variety of grammatical moods). Commentators with deductivist impulses present these uniformly as the application of rules to instances (and hence as closely parallel to the paradigm of a deductively valid syllogism), although several of Aristotle's examples clearly do not fit this pattern.[24]

There is for example a linked pair of syllogisms in *De Motu Animalium* of which only the second is the application of a rule: "I need a covering, a coat is a covering: I need a coat. What I need I ought to make, I need a coat: I [ought to] make a coat" (701a16 –19).[25] The first of these has no claim to anything like deductive validity. 'Coat' identifies a means to, one way to realize, the needed covering. What Aristotle appears to treat indifferently as 'syllo-

---

[24] A relatively early criticism of the deductivist tradition in the interpretation of the practical syllogism can be found in Anscombe 1957, 57ff. Mothersil (1963) contains a reply to Anscombe on behalf of the deductivist interpreters.

[25] The previous two examples (701a14–16) are not connected but are also examples of the two different types: "'No man should walk, one is a man': straightaway one remains at rest . . . Again, 'I ought to create a good, a house is good': straightaway he makes a house."

gisms' include both the straightforward application of general rules and the identification of means to realize ends. There is, however, nothing in the *Prior Analytics* (where Aristotle discusses the validity of syllogisms) that provides an account of the validity of means-ends reasoning.

It is worthwhile to note a parallel between means-ends practical reasoning and the theoretical inference pattern that Peirce identified variously as 'abduction,' 'hypothesis,' *etc.*—one of his two species of ampliative inference (Peirce, 2.710–14). Abduction confronts what it identifies as a result (something needing explanation), identifies a rule, which if a case of the antecedent of that rule obtained would produce that result, and infers (by way of explaining the result) that a case of the antecedent did indeed obtain. Means-ends reasoning confronts a result (something needing realization), identifies a rule, which if a case of the antecedent of that rule were realized, would produce the result and infers (by way of directing action) that the case should be made to obtain. Abductive inference, as Peirce presents it, has the form of a deductive fallacy known as affirming the consequent (*viz.*, the fallacious pattern P $\rightarrow$ Q, Q $\vdash$ P), but that the pattern is not deductively valid in no way diminishes its utility or disqualifies it from being assessed in terms of a different concept of (nondeductive) validity. Its importance in science is part of Peirce's case for recognizing ampliative as well as explicative forms of inference. If means-ends inference is in practical reasoning what abduction is in theoretical reasoning, then its (obvious) importance in everyday life constitutes a case for recognizing ampliative as well as explicative forms of inference in practical logic.

It might not appear that means-ends reasoning qualifies as ampliative. Is it not simply a matter of subsuming a case (means to realization) under the norm that is provided by the specification of an end? To accept this is to miss several important subtleties. Note first why abduction counts as ampliative for Peirce: a conclusion is inescapably true if it follows deductively from premisses that are true. The premisses of an abductive inference may be true and the conclusion false. The inference merely picks out one of several alternative explanations of the result (specified in the minor premise). In practical reasoning if a rule is a valid specification of what is to be done in a range of circumstances and a case falls within that range then the conclusion about what is to be done is inescapable. That is the deductive model in practical reasoning. But it does not follow from the validity of an end (from its being something that ought to be done) that any given means to that end is something to be done. The inference to a means merely picks out one of several alternative ways to realize an end; it does not conform to the deductive model.

Note further that what is required to select from the variety of means available is an awareness of how other norms (rules and specifications of ends) are affected by a given choice of means. What makes one choice better than another is the way it furthers or conflicts with other norms and choices. In other words, the phenomenon of the interrelatedness of norms (which Will refers to as 'composition') affects the judgment of what is to be done (to realize the end). Someone who reasons competently about the choice of means must be sensitive to a whole range of norms and their bearing on one another. To reach a choice of means frequently involves being "led rather than coerced . . . to see things from different points of view." The appreciation of the superiority of one means over another, which comes via this process, "may be slight, moderate, or extreme." The important thing that comes to the fore when one takes this kind of practical reasoning to Will's discussion of ampliative processes is that it obviously involves discursive articulation and has been recognized by long tradition as an exercise of reason, capable of the competence that is praised with the term 'rational' and the incompetence that is condemned with the term 'irrational.'

It is important not to forget that this second point also applies to abduction. To select from the variety of explanations available requires an awareness of how scientific principles (or, if you will, our beliefs about those principles) bear upon a given explanation.

What makes one explanation better than another is the way it furthers or conflicts with other explanations and principles. In other words, the phenomenon that Quine refers to as the corporate way our statements about external reality face the tribunal of experience affects the judgment of what is the best explanation of a given result. (See *BD* 156, where Will links his term 'composition' directly to Quine's doctrine.) Someone who reasons competently about scientific explanations must be sensitive to a whole range of principles and their bearing on one another. To arrive at an explanation frequently involves being "led rather than coerced . . . to see things from different points of view." The appreciation of the superiority of one explanation over another, which comes via this process, "may be slight, moderate, or extreme." If processes of ampliative governance of norms that Will described (especially at *BD* 182) are not sufficiently rational, neither is what goes on in natural science.

7 The point of this comparison of abduction, a star species of ampliative reasoning, and means-ends reasoning has been to show how the description that Will gives of ampliative processes of norm governance can be discursive—and the competent conduct of such processes can be accorded the approbation 'rational'—without being deductive. The argument is intended to buttress Will's position, but there may be a residual uneasiness on his part (or that of his party) to accept this help. Are not ends (the norms to which this argument draws special attention) judged relative to further ends; does the process not presuppose a hierarchy of ends, at the top of which are one or more final ends (*summa bona*) that serve as the foundation of practical reasoning, as ungoverned governors (*BD* 154), whose validity can be established only by appeal to intuition? Does this strategy for displaying the rationality of ampliative governance not offer too many important hostages to deductivism and to those who hold that what is not deductive must be in the end be intuitive?

Defenders of Will's position, who might like to appeal to and develop the strategy outlined here, would do well to take a leaf

from the philosophy of John Dewey. Dewey, as keen as any pragmatist on the importance of finding means to ends-in-view, insisted
there were no final ends (*LW* 1:99), only the network (corporate
whole) of individual means-ends (ends that are means to something
else and means that offer their own intrinsic satisfactions) with
which we confront our environment as we interact with it. To
explain the folly of belief in (that species of what Will called
'ungoverned governors') final ends, Dewey stressed the way that
experience expands our conception of any end we might possess.
To appreciate how this takes place and to understand how this
process might itself be governed by (nondeductive) discursive
activity—and hence be subject to, assessed as, rational or otherwise
—we need to ensure that our conception of means-ends reasoning
is sufficiently comprehensive.

Here a distinction used in recent discussions of Aristotle proves
to be very useful. J. L. Ackrill, for example distinguishes means
into those that are *instrumental to* and those that are *constitutive of*
their ends. Our commercial and technological culture encourages us
to think in terms of instrumental means, for what we use (money)
to exchange for goods (a car or a holiday) does not form part of
those goods and the tools (personal computer and printer) we use to
produce something (a text or graph) does not form part of the
product. But many of the things we use as means to some end do
form parts of the end we seek, whether it be the wood used to
make a box or the notes that are used in the composition of a
sonata. These are constitutive means. The point of making the
distinction is to call attention to the fact that the selection of the
constituents out of which one will realize some end determines in
important ways what that end is; and deliberation about what
constituents to select is a discursive activity that takes the same
general form as selection of instrumental means.

It is not uncommon for people to set for themselves (or at least
acknowledge that their activity should be governed by) objectives
that sound fine but are only vaguely specified. Politicians accept
that they should promote prosperity; doctors hold themselves re-

sponsible for the health of their patients; managers are expected to see that operations run efficiently. It takes a form of deliberation to fill in the description of the objective to the point where it offers some real guidance. What exactly is prosperity? What constitutes health? Relative to what are we to assess whether an operation is efficient? Determining this is formally similar to finding the means to some end: one selects from alternative possible descriptions, in a way that is constrained by the existing understanding of other ends and how they are to be made specific.

It follows that our highest ends are not "ungoverned governors" but among the norms most seriously in need of governance, precisely because their specificity is in constant need of reconsideration. This is not only because their specificity should be constrained by other norms (and thus need to be revised when these other norms undergo governance). Their specificity should also be responsive to what we find out about the world (the conception of health, for example, should grow in specificity with the growth in our knowledge of biology). And their specificity should alter as our material resources advance.

Neither Aristotle nor Dewey distinguished instrumental from constituent means. Commentators make the distinction to call attention to how comprehensive is Aristotle's use of the term 'means' and how comprehensive is Dewey's understanding of 'instrumentality.'[26] Dewey tended to think of all means as constitutive and did not like to think of any means as external to its end. The garment I wear is not one thing and the money handed over for it something else; the garment is not just a coat, but the coat costing $140 (and the $140 in turn constituted of so much paid labor). At the same time Dewey not only pointed to the effect on ends of alterations in the means available to realize them, he saw the respect in which in seeking to specify ends (by engaging in discursive deliber-

---

[26] Dewey indeed is particularly difficult to follow because he in effect treated all means as constitutive while referring to means generally as 'instrumentalities.' I have tried to help readers of Dewey over these difficulties in Tiles 1988, §§VII.b and VIII.c–e.

ation) the role of the unspecific description of the end serves as means to the end(-in-view) of possessing a satisfactorily specific description of that vaguely specified end.

All of these considerations contributed to what Dewey referred to as the 'thoroughly reciprocal character of means and ends' (*MW* 8:37) and to his insistence that there are no exclusively final ends. Partisans of Will's position, who wish to appeal to means-ends reasoning to illustrate how governance can be discursive and susceptible to assessment as rational (or otherwise), need not fear that they will find themselves committed to a species of ungoverned governors, *viz.* final ends.

8 The final two sections of this essay have departed from resources specifically canvassed by Will in *Beyond Deduction* in an attempt to meet what appeared to be reasonable disappointment with the way Will carried out his (implied) promise to show how the governance of norms can be both ampliative and rational. Readers who have gotten past the initial perplexities generated by Will's project and now find themselves disappointed in the outcome should consider whether because their ". . . ambitions in governance were inspired and shaped by deductivist philosophy . . . [they] expect from a study of ampliative processes the development and display of models, decision procedures and paradigm patterns of research for these phases of our philosophical activities." For they were warned at the outset both of *Beyond Deduction* and of this essay that "If the portrayal by [Will's] book of ampliative phases of governance is essentially sound, such an expectation is bound to be disappointed" (*BD* 12).[27]

University of Hawai'i at Mânoa

---

[27] I am grateful to Ken Westphal for his careful and sympathetic reading of an earlier draft of this essay. I attempted to follow his advice in too many places for each to be individually acknowledged. The result, however, has been, I believe, both to clarify and to enrich what I was trying to say.

References

Ackrill, J. L. 1980. "Aristotle on *Eudaimonia.*" In *Essays on Aristotle's Ethics.* A. O. Rorty, ed. Berkeley: University of California Press, 18–33.

Anscombe, Elizabeth. 1957. *Intention.* Oxford: Basil Blackwell.

Aristotle. 1984. *The Complete Works of Aristotle.* Oxford translations revised by Jonathan Barnes (*De Motu Animalium*, A. S. L. Farquharson, tr.). Princeton, N.J.: Princeton University Press.

Bourdieu, Pierre. 1990. *The Logic of Practice.* Cambridge: Polity Press.

Dewey, John. 1969–90. *The Works of John Dewey* in three series, *Early Works, Middle Works, and Later Works* (cited as *EW*, *MW* and *LW* with volume number and page). Jo Ann Boydston, ed. Carbondale, Ill.: Southern Illinois University Press.

Dworkin, Ronald. 1981. "Dissent on Douglas." *New York Review of Books*, 19 February: 3–8.

Hacker, P. M. S. 1972. *Insight and Illusion.* Oxford: Clarendon Press.

Henrich, Dieter. 1989. "Kant's Notion of a Deduction." In *Kant's Transcendental Deductions.* Eckart Förster, ed. Stanford, Cal.: Stanford University Press, 29–46.

Kant, Immanual. 1965. *The Critique of Pure Reason.* N. K. Smith, tr. New York: St. Martin's.

Luker, Kristen. 1984. *Abortion and the Politics of Motherhood.* Berkeley, Cal.: University of California Press.

Mill, John Stuart. 1843. *A System of Logic.* London: George Routledge.

Lehman, Waren. 1981. Comment on Dworkin. *New York Review of Books*, 28 May: 52.

Mothersil, Mary. 1963. "Anscombe's Account of the Practical Syllogism." *Philosophical Review* 70: 448–61.

Oakeshott, Michael. 1962. *Rationalism in Politics and Other Essays.* London: Methuen.

Peirce, Charles S. 1931–35. *Collected Papers of Charles S. Peirce.* C. Hartshore and P. Weiss, eds. Cambridge, Mass.: Harvard University Press. (Cited by Volume and paragraph number.)

Sabine, George. 1950. *A History of Political Theory*, 3^d ed. London: George Harrap.

Tiles, John E. 1988. *Dewey.* London: Routledge.

Will, Frederick L. 1974. *Induction and Justification: An Investigation of Cartesian Procedure in the Philosophy of Knowledge.* Ithaca, N.Y.: Cornell University Press.

Will, Frederick L. 1988. *Beyond Deduction: Ampliative Aspects of Philosophical Reflection.* London: Routledge.

13

Reasons in a World of Practices:
A Reconstruction of Frederick L. Will's
Theory of Normative Governance

Matthias Kettner

1 RATIONAL APPETITES BEYOND DEDUCTIVISM

Frederick L. Will's fascinating restoration of concreteness to philo-sophical thought about normativity contains two central decon-structive lessons. The first is this: According to Will's convincing diagnosis, one of the deepest urges in modern philosophy—whether empiricist or rationalist—is to search for "ungoverned governors" (*BD* 150).[1] This search, he argues, is bound to fail because of the concrete nature of the norms themselves. According to Will's naturalized Hegelian pragmatism, norms are "concrete universals" because they are psycho-sociologically active, open-textured, and agent-guiding; they are composed or organized in constellations, and yet are never fully consistent nor fully determinate. Thus norms are permanently mutating, and—most importantly—they are *ab ovo* governable and governed. Indeed, norms always result from some process of governance, and they always involve some element of learning. Thus, there can be no ungoverned governors. The "hun-ger" (*BD* 154) that fuels the search for ungoverned governors is hard to give up since with it go the hopes of deductivism. "Deduc-

---

[1] Will 1988, is referred to throughout as '*BD*,' followed by a page number. The most profound part of Will's book, the part which most challenges our thinking about norms and normativity, is ch. 2 (*BD* 83–142). A more recent exposition of his view of norms is Will 1997, ch. 9.

tivism" is Will's term for the view that all and only deductive processes can legitimately govern (assess or justify) norms (*cf. BD* 47, 55).[2]

Still harder to discard is the aspiration that a philosophic study of the "omnipresent," "inescapable" (*BD* 152), and continuous processes of ampliative normative governance will reveal universally applicable principles of governance. From the first lesson alone, that there are no ungoverned governors, it does not follow that all ways of governance are equal. Some may well be more important, more influential, more pervasive, and perhaps more rational than others. Some might even reign supreme, though not like absolute sovereign ("ungoverned") monarchs. The demise of deductivism is not the end of the rational appetite for universal principles in philosophical reflection generally; certainly not in philosophical reflection aimed at a comprehensive theory of the most general normative standards of conduct or of rationality.

Will warns against the expectation that a sound nondeductivist theory of governance yields rational principles of governance. His second deconstructive lesson is that there simply are no such principles. Although we can judge whether particular rearrangements or recastings of constellations of norms are more or less successful, the rationale for such a judgment provides no basis for further such judgments. Whereas we expect that principles properly so called can be employed with the same criterial significance in different cases or circumstances, we do not expect the same generalizability of judgments about the relative success of normative governance. In Will's view, we should abandon the lofty universalistic claims enshrined in the principlism and foundationalism extolled by deductivist programs of justification. We should settle for context-dependent assessments of governance.[3]

---

[2] [Also see the preceding essay by Tiles, "Rationality Beyond Deduction: A Guide for the Perplexed and Disappointed."—Ed.]

[3] For example, Will states that there "are no abstract, context-independent criteria as to what constitutes thoroughness in criticism" (*BD* 203).

I contend that Will's first deconstructive lesson holds but his second does not. I shall argue that judgments about the rationality of particular episodes of governance are contextual without being context-bound. The view I present requires rethinking Will's distinction between reflective and nonreflective modes of governance. It requires strengthening the methodological and systematic role of reflective governance against tendencies in Will's approach to underrate the reflective mode. One important resource for this stronger view of the role and importance of reflective governance lies in a pragmatic analysis of the semiotic conditions required to pose and answer questions about the reasons people think they have for doing what they do, and about the merit of their reasons.

The issues Will raises are complex, and my discussion is accordingly somewhat intricate. I proceed as follows. In §2 I show that Will's theory of governance is self-effacing, not owing to philosophical modesty, but owing to his ambivalence about the descriptive or prescriptive nature of his theory (§2.1) and owing to a pair of tensions. One is between Will's prescriptive aim and his meager treatment of rational superiority; another is between Will's discounting of reflective governance and the methodological centrality reflective governance must have in any *theory* of governance (§2.2). In §3 I point out that, on Will's view, normative principles are context bound because, apart from a specific context, they are mere determinables (§3.1). In opposition to Will, I contend that detailed, case-driven comparative and analogical reasoning can generate informative contextual principles that are not context-bound (§3.2). Such principles can be identified and often justified by abductive argument. Such an argument provides a definite sense of rational superiority of some norms and some instances of governance over others (§3.3). This comports with the fact that reasons, not Will's "ways of behaving," must be taken as the basic unit of analysis in a theory of governance (§3.4). In §4 I contend that Will's tendency to discount reflective governance derives in part from his lack of attention to the semiotic basis of criticism and reflective governance. Reflection makes criticism explicit (§4.1). This kind of

reflection is linguistically based and is specific to human beings
(§4.2). Our linguistic abilities enable us to engage in critical discursive practices (§4.3). Will is right to oppose assimilating our practices to formalized reconstructions of them. Unfortunately, he has
not taken into account the rich pragmatic theories of language that
developed out of speech act theory (§4.4). Four basic points about
human language identified by speech act theory show that the
distinction between reflective and nonreflective governance has a
solid semiotic basis, a basis that makes critical assessment and
revision of norms possible (§4.5). Moreover, this basis shows that
mutual acceptability is an important *sine qua non* for good reasons
(§4.6). I then argue that the contemplative character of Will's
theory of governance is betrayed by Will's lack of attention to the
question, 'Who shall use his theory of governance?' (§5.1). Further
evidence of this tendency is found in Will's retrospective, descriptive characterizations of past, purportedly successful cases of normative governance (§5.2). The proper remedy for this problem is to
recognize that proper reflective governance of norms requires
deliberative democratic institutions that foster—and are fostered
by—the critical discursive practices of discussion, debate, and
reasoned argument (§5.3). I conclude by summarizing my discussion
(§6).

2 WILL'S SELF-EFFACING THEORY OF GOVERNANCE

I now argue that Will's theory of governance is self-effacing, not
owing to philosophical modesty, but owing to his ambivalence
about the descriptive or prescriptive nature of his theory (§2.1) and
owing to a pair of tensions between his prescriptive aim and his
meager treatment of rational superiority, and between his discounting of reflective governance and the methodological centrality
reflective governance must have in any *theory* of governance (§2.2).

2.1 Governance and Good Governance

At several points in my discussion it will be helpful to introduce some shorthand designations. Let us call judgments about the rationality of particular episodes of governance "rationality judgments." Rationality judgments are comparative; they judge whether a process of governing norms is more (or less) successful, relative both to the normative governance sought and to what would be achieved through available alternatives of nongovernance or of other kinds of governance.

Showing, as Will does, that the quest for large-scale governance is misguided is one thing. If in general the rational conduct of affairs requires abandoning illusions, the demise of deductivism, with its lofty but vain hopes of hierarchical control over normative structures, is indeed a sobering lesson "for those with an appetite for large-scale governance" (*BD* 227). However, relinquishing the demand for spelling out the justificatory rationale of governance processes and the principles they involve, however localized or specific they may be, is something else altogether. This demand should not be given up easily. Relinquishing it would incapacitate governance theory, whereas relinquishing large-scale governance adds to its realism. How do we, how can we, judge the rational credentials of processes and outcomes of normative governance? Regrettably, Will addresses this question in ambivalent and troubling ways.

The basic issue involved in Will's ambivalence can be seen by drawing an artificially sharp distinction between a descriptive, meta-normative theory (T_1) and a prescriptive, normative theory (T_2) of rational governance. A theory of type T_1 seeks to describe, explain, understand, or otherwise account for processes, effects, and episodes of all kinds of governance of norms. A theory of type T_2 seeks to develop the perspective required for and appropriate to the differential assessment of (actual or possible) governance of norms. The problem, roughly, is that Will's theory of governance says in the voice of T_2 that what is to be said in the voice of T_1 is that T_2 either has no voice or has nothing to say. The following laconic statement contains the full force of Will's ambivalence. Will holds that

> governance in some degree—not, be it noted, *good* governance, but governance—is integral to the character of a norm. (*BD* 201–2)

The informativeness of T_1 is limited to governance and its exercise as a matter of fact in bodies of norms and their normative metabolism as matters of fact. In contrast to this, T_2 would address the merits of governance not only as a matter of fact but primarily for the purpose of distinguishing better from worse. T_2 would help improve our governance of norms, over and above the way governance might be assisted simply by information about the facticity, the vicissitudes, and the variety of its occurrence. Another way of putting this point would be that T_1 treats of governantial effects on norms as processes of change whereas T_2 treats acts of governance as normative learning processes.[4] Now the attempt at 'good governance' might be inherent in any effort at governance; Will often suggests as much. But that does not obviate the distinction between T_1 and T_2. Taking this point into account, the object of T_1 is not merely governance as such but always already attempts at good governance. However, the purpose served by T_1 would still be different from that served by T_2: Whereas T_1 aims to improve our *understanding* of what purports to be good governance, T_2 aims to improve our *governing*.[5]

Some of Will's philosophical reflections on ampliative governance fit the aims of T_1, some fit the aims of T_2. The ambivalence I sense

---

[4] Will makes the important distinction between stasis and change in norms (*cf.* esp. *BD* 207–29). Both can be the effect of governance. However, since stasis is the retention of some part of a normative composition against the tendency to and occurrence of change in some other parts of it, my use of 'change' is meant to cover both stasis and change. To treat of a change in x from x' to x'' not merely as change but as a normative learning process is to have for x, and impute to x, a standard by which alternative possible changes (*e.g.* from x' to x''') can be judged as better or worse.

[5] Compare this with Nietzsche's (1874) analogous distinction between two historical methods which he designates as 'antiquarian' and 'critical' history.

in Will's project lies in the tension between the following two facts: (1) The overall aim of Will's project clearly lies with T_2; after all, his project is to help us get better at governing rational thinking ("philosophizing") about governance. Will did not write a history of philosophical views on norms and normativity; his philosophical project is to improve these views. And this, according to Will himself, is an exercise of nondeductive, ampliative reasoning that provides a critique of rationality.[6] Will's project is properly characterized as reflective, ampliative, and philosophic.[7] (2) However, the upshot of his project is to show that reflective ampliative governance, whether philosophic or not, has only marginal importance in the grand scheme of things (*cf. BD* 223–27). If Will's ambivalence expressed only a consistent realistic modesty with regard to the authority of philosophic inquiry, this would be no problem. There is nothing contradictory in philosophical insight into the impotence of philosophical insight relative to other socio-historic forces.[8] Reason may well be at home in a world of social practices

---

[6] Will, in a passage endorsing Hegel's view of the philosophical understanding of human institutions and their normativity, writes: "There is no gulf between philosophical understanding of the nature of an institution, and criticism of that institution. Criticism grows out of, is itself part of understanding. In philosophical dialect, 'is' and 'ought' are not distinct, nor even complementary. 'Ought,' the 'ought' of reason, is a necessary feature of a fully developed, *i.e.*, philosophical 'is'" (*BD* 166).

[7] See *BD* 158–62 for a combinatory rehearsal of these three characteristics and their negations.

[8] Will criticizes Rorty rather mildly for his deflationary views on the rationality of philosophy (*cf. BD* 251–56). Yet Will does little to dispel the impression that, aside from nominal skirmishes (*e.g.* over the term 'conversation' [*BD* 254, note 19]), his own view in this regard comes very close to Rorty's. There certainly is more than a grain of truth in Will's assertion that where "governance of an ampliative kind is called for, it makes a great difference to the results of it how it is performed" (*BD* 256). But that is the case with virtually any productive activity; how it is performed always makes a great difference to its results. To learn that ampliative processes are no exception is not very helpful unless there is also a good deal to be learned about the conditions under which such governance is needed and about how to perform it. The bottom line against which theoretical enlightenment can be measured is the platitude that governance is needed when it is needed and it gets done however it gets done. See *BD* 192–96 for "diverse examples of the way in which clues to the governance of norms emerge from a broad and concrete understanding of them" (*BD* 176).

without claiming to rule that world. However, Will's project fails to give the kind of governance that he employs as his philosophic method even a *methodological* or *systematic* priority over different kinds of governance. This involves Will's project in two tensions.

2.2   Two Tensions

One tension in Will's project concerns philosophical activity. If Will did not claim that the reflective ampliative philosophical governance he actually employs were better, that is, rationally superior to other ways of considering this matter (*e.g.* by nonreflective deductive philosophical governance), then there would be no point in Will's charge that deductivism is a mistake.[9] Will's 'beyond deductivism' would then properly mean 'beside deductivism.' That is, deductivism would simply be one style, fashion, or *episteme* (to use a familiar nonnormative term from Foucault) different from the one Will favors, but indifferent regarding the relative rational merits of either view. But if Will claims—as surely he does—that his view is rationally superior, then Will must be much more explicit about the rationality of governance (in philosophy and elsewhere) and about how to assess it than he is in his brief remarks on this topic (*cf. BD* 182f.).

A second tension is found in the object domain of the projected theory of governance itself, *i.e.*, with regard to observable processes of governance. In principle all kinds of governance processes must be amenable to the scrutiny of a theory of governance, since such a theory is to be completely general. No matter whether a governance process g is individual or collective, deliberate or unintentional, broad or narrow, rapid or protracted, reflective or unreflective, deductive or ampliative,[10] *etc.*, g must be such as to allow reconstruction by a theory of governance. Any *reconstruction* of g is

---

[9] 'Rationally superior,' that is, relative to the rationality assumptions pertinent to methods of philosophical analysis and thinking.

[10] Will's main contrast is between deductive and ampliative phases (processes, procedures, activities) of governance. For an illuminating introduction of this distinction in terms of four contrastive features, see *BD* 32–34. For a fifth contrastive feature, rational authority, see *BD* 182.

itself a form of *reflective* governance, performed *deliberately* by *consciously thinking* persons engaged in the reconstruction. The theory, whose overall purpose is reconstructive and explicative (rather than metatheoretical and objectifying), provides no external and privileged role for the theoretician regarding that object domain. Governance theory (in its T_2 aspect) must presuppose that the understanding it obtains can be (re-)translated into the perspective of the people involved in or subject to the processes of governance that are the object of the theory (in its T_1 aspect). Any *theory* of governance must give methodological privilege to actual reflective governance. Moreover, the theory's reconstructive aim presupposes that the actual theoretical activity it involves (of reflective reconstruction of *g*) is possible for people in the object domain, *i.e.*, in the original context of *g*. In Will's own theory, the methodological priority of reflective governance about *g* implies at least the possibility of reflective governance in *g* itself. However—here is my criticism—Will's theory downplays the possibility and significance of reflective governance. Although his theory contains the first crucial insight into this possibility, namely the insight that "one learns to judge in learning how to act,"[11] Will's theory doesn't develop this insight adequately. Will's pragmatic aversion to assigning a special role for reflective governance in the rationality of governance simply inverts the equally undue preoccupation with reflective (albeit deductive) governance found in Modern philosophy. Will's rejection of foundationalism leads him to characterize his own view as "critical rather than foundational" (*BD* 139). But his unwillingness or failure to see the cardinal methodological importance of reflective governance leads him to impute to the "norms themselves" (*BD* 139) the process of their "scrutiny and criticism." To speak of the process of their scrutiny and criticism as something occurring through "mutual interaction among norms themselves" (*BD* 139) obscures the crucial fact that scrutiny and criticism are rooted in reflective thinking and in intentional activi-

---

[11] *BD* 136; *cf.* 10, 112, 139, 150, 232, and Will 1997, chs. 4–8.

ties on the part of people involved in the practices themselves
whose governance is sought. Indeed Will's description obscures this
fact with a metaphor that likens the governing of norms to a material mobile's rearranging itself with the changing winds. Identifying
such a *via media* requires identifying precisely why Will thinks
there are no effective generalizable normative principles.

3 DETERMINABLES AND DETERMINATE PRINCIPLES

On Will's view, normative principles are context bound because,
apart from a specific context, they are mere determinables. Thus, he
concludes, there are no effective generalizable universal normative
principles (§3.1). In opposition to Will, I shall argue that detailed,
case-driven comparative and analogical reasoning can generate
informative contextual principles that are not context-bound (§3.2).
Such principles can be identified and often justified by an abductive
argument. Such an argument provides a definite sense of rational
superiority of some norms and some instances of governance over
others (§3.3). This comports with the fact that reasons, rather than
Will's "ways of behaving," must be taken as the basic unit of
analysis in a theory of governance (§3.4).

3.1 *Determinables, Casuistry, and Judging Governance*
Let G(a), G(b), G(c) be accounts of episodes of governance in
normatively diverse practical fields, *e.g.*, (a) playing ping pong, (b)
studying arithmetic, and (c) making health-care policy. These "G-
stories," for short, are illuminating accounts of how certain changes
have occurred in some norms involved in the normative life of their
respective fields of practice. G-stories also indicate what these
changes mean, regarding both the fields of practice in which they
occur and also other practices whose normative compositions are
affected by those changes. When Will denies that informative
general principles of governance are extricable from their specific
contexts he appears committed to the following casuistic position:
Accounts of governance, G-stories, can underwrite judgments about

governantial success, or comparative judgments about relative governantial success, only if they are domain-specific case stories (*cf. BD* 155).

Of course, for any two G-stories $G(x)_1$ and $G(x)_2$, neither the fact that they are domain specific nor the fact that they are case stories implies that they cannot be compared meaningfully. Rather, Will's position appears to imply that none of the aspects in which one can meaningfully compare them provides good reasons for judgments about governantial success of other (*e.g.*, future) episodes of governance $G(x)_3$, $G(x)_4$,—neither in the same respective domains of practice, nor comparative judgments of episodes across altogether different fields of practice, comparing, that is, $G(a)$ to $G(b)$ or $G(b)$ to $G(c)$. Comparisons across different episodes of governance reveal "dimensions, variable determinables" (*BD* 154; *cf.* 216), but no standards or criteria that are determined in principled ways. The determin*ables* or dimensions revealed in G-stories that embody the rationale for respective rationality judgments are, *e.g.*, harmony, coherence, or simplicity of the new normative composition that resulted from the governantial process being judged. Any G-story reveals a rationale of *many dimensions*: a manifold (hence, not simple) of dubious coherence (how does harmony square with simplicity?), which may perhaps even be disharmonious.

Why expect otherwise? The rationale of normative judgments on normative governance (called "rationality judgments" above) embodied in different G-stories is empty of principles, but not because there is an unprincipled manifold of determinables that can provide no supporting categorial matrix for comparative generalizations. Instead, Will's view appears to be that the *abstractness* of the determinables makes them justificatorily pointless when they are extracted from their specific context. Whatever weight the determinables carry in the justification of normative judgments (he suggests) comes with their concrete determin*ation*, a content they acquire only within the specific case under consideration and which they lose when extended across accounts of different cases. This is what it means to hold that the determinables are *merely* abstract.

Notice that Will's contextualist position concerning the rational assessment of outcomes of governance is matched by his contextualism concerning the rational assessment of conditions under which governance is called for in the first place. Harmony, coherence, simplicity, *etc.*, are merely abstract determinables or dimensions of success of governantial effects; likewise, "incoherencies, discrepancies, inconsistencies, and incompleteness" (*BD* 191) are merely abstract determinables or dimensions of the unsatisfactoriness of practice—they are the original stimulus to which governance responds.

Another way to grasp Will's view of the resources available for grounding rationality judgments is to extract from his descriptions of governance-in-context the bases that he identifies as providing the needed grounds or defense of such determinate judgments. Very roughly, all good governance starts from more or less unsatisfactory practice and ends in more or less satisfactory practice. Governance is taken for granted and is inconspicuous as long as the practices concerned work as they are supposed to. (Will calls this "governance in practice."[12]) Governance *of* practice is desirable whenever it is desirable that those practices work better than they actually do. The grounds for rationality judgments provided by satisfactoriness, unsatisfactoriness, and the relative desirability of governance, appear in the following kinds of considerations. Considerations of satisfactoriness relate governable norms to roles these norms play within the practices they help guide, including their (1) purposive role, (2) functional role, (3) role in individual human lives, and (4) role in the life of communities of individuals who share a common socialization (at least in certain respects). Considerations of (5) feasibility relative to accepted practices, and of (6) seriousness of interference with already accepted practices relate governantial effects (actual or possible) to the desirability of such effects and the processes that produce them.[13]

---

[12] Will 1997, 94–97.

[13] These considerations are already exemplified in Will's early writings, *e.g.*, Will 1963 (*cf.* esp. 276, 288). Recently he makes the same points in terms of, *e.g.*,

Here again the impression is unavoidable that these characterizations are "mere abstract determinables" that give little basis for comparative generalizations—principles—based on rationality judgments of governance. I return to this issue in §5, where I discuss two problems for Will's account, one within Will's theory and one revealed from without by a deliberative theory of democracy. In the following two subsections I introduce two structures of reasoning that help governance theory out of the predicament of being either principlist (blind to individual cases) or context-dependent casuistry (empty of comparative generalizations, *i.e.*, principles).

3.2   *Reasoned Genealogies of Good Reasons*

G-stories must not simply describe in normatively neutral ways the ampliative and deductive phases of processes that account for stasis or change in normative compositions of fields of practice. As Will recognizes, they must throw light on the legitimacy of the stasis or change they describe (*cf. BD* 177, 192). In a judgment that normative governance accounted for in $G(x)_1$ is successful (and hence desirable) governance and that $G(x)_2$ is not, $G(x)_1$ must contain, or must give to all reasonable concerned parties with a sense for standard performance in the relevant fields of practice, reasons in light of which governing process g_1 is presented as the source of the legitimacy of the differential effects (change or stasis) attributed to it. $G(x)_2$ must likewise contain or give reasons that present g_2 as producing some specific lack of legitimacy or recognizable illegitimacy. G-stories $G(x)_1$ and $G(x)_2$ must give good enough reasons for endorsing the claim that g_1 is desirable (in a legitimating sense of 'desirable') and that g_2 is not.

The question, How far can the claims of rationality judgments of specific cases transcend the contextual confines of these cases?, then becomes a question of the powers of analogical reasoning, together

---

"how smoothly" governed norms "perform as components of human life" (*BD* 49). The appropriateness of the normative composition emerging from some process of governance is to be judged "by the role which this or that mode of action or response plays in the constitution of individual and communal life" (*BD* 93–94).

with the power of hermeneutic understanding, to "fuse horizons" (in Gadamer's felicitous phrase) between distinct cases of governance. In the judgment that g_1 is rationally desirable, reasons are traced out from $G(x)_1$ that are perceived as making a significant difference to the evaluative aim of such judgments and they are marked off from reasons that are perceived as irrelevant, *i.e.*, as not making a significant difference;[14] likewise for g_2 and $G(x)_2$. In the context $G(x)_1$ those reasons that make a difference are distinguished from those that do not, relative to the aim of judging the rationality of g_1; and *mutatis mutandis* for the context $G(x)_2$. In what appear to be radically different contexts, such as the G-stories about the norms of Ping-Pong, arithmetic, and health-care policy mentioned in §3.1, the distinction between relevant and irrelevant reasons will of course be drawn differently; but however it is drawn, it will not be drawn in a fanciful or arbitrary way. In each domain there will be further reasons that tend to warrant distinguishing significant from insignificant reasons in one way rather than another. Further reasons that are perceived as giving relevance to those warrants (by distinguishing them in turn from other reasons perceived as irrelevant) can be unpacked from the ever expanding horizon of our understanding, if the scope of scrutiny needs to be extended. The constraints on rationality judgments reconstructed in this way may be broader or stricter, more lenient or more determinative, depending on our (more or less) shared understanding of each case and domain.

The important point is that such constraints on relevance in one domain can not be *altogether* different from constraints in some other domain. Consider two kinds of case. In one type of case, within the two case-relative groups of relevant reasons there may be some that overlap. These shared reasons can serve as the basis for appreciating similarities and differences across the two different G-stories. For each shared relevant reason r, the questions are: Is r's contribution within the overall context $G(x)_1$ to the $G(x)_1$-based

---

[14] The generic evaluative aim of rationality judgments is to ascertain the permissibility or unacceptability of something in terms that as many reasonable persons as possible could share.

judgment about g_1 similar to or different from r's contribution within the overall context $G(x)_2$ to the $G(x)_2$-based judgment about g_2? and What reasons are there for the perceived similarities and differences? Note that this second question allows recursive iteration of the analogical reasoning, which provides whatever answer there is to such questions.

In another type of case, the apparently relevant reasons furnished by $G(x)_1$ and by $G(x)_2$ overlap only to an insignificant extent, if at all. This is *prima facie* incommensurability between two apparently radically different governance processes. This type of case is imaginable not only across different domains of governance, as between Ping-Pong and health-care policy, but also within the same practical field at different times, *e.g.* if between $G(b)_1$ and $G(b)_2$ a paradigm shift has occurred. Still there is ample basis for analogical reasoning. *Ex hypothesi* in such a case any reason r relevant in one G-story will be perceived as irrelevant in the other G-story. If the G-stories refer to different practical domains, then pursuing the question, Why is r relevant in one but irrelevant in the other domain?, will again furnish further reasons once we tap and make explicit our background understanding of the two respective domains and their salient differences. The successive deepening of such background understanding is familiar from established hermeneutical and historical procedures in the cultural sciences.[15] Gearing such methods to our question-schema, through successively wider circles we draw more and more content into our answers as we iterate our question-schema 'On what grounds do we make *this* distinction

---

[15] See Schön 1983, esp. Pt. 2, ch. 6 ("Reflective Practice in the Science-Based Professions"); Taylor 1989, 111–390; Clayton 1996, esp. 134–59, 240–71. Closely related points are made in philosophy of science by Gerd Buchdahl. Buchdahl contends that the assessment and revision of any specific scientific theory occurs only within and depends upon a rich complement of methodological considerations, including a probative component (regarding evidential support), a systematic component (regarding rational coherence), and an explicative component (regarding intelligibility or the "possibility" of the theory). Each component is complex and is integrated with the others. See Buchdahl 1980, for a concise discussion.

between reasons that make a difference and reasons that do not make a difference (in *this* rationality judgment)?'[16]

Does this view of comparative generalizability of rationality judgments lead to an unrealistic and hence unreasonable assumption of homogeneity in the object domain of governance theory? I think not. For example, the governance exercised by a specific method for training fast backhand serves in Ping-Pong and the governance exercised in the crafting of a piece of legislation regarding medical requirements for terminally ill patients may really have (not only *prima* but also *ultima facie*) too little in common for us to be able to make specific comparisons of respective case-based and domain-specific rationality judgments that would afford salient generalizations. Yet an understanding even of such specific differences leads to generalizability elsewhere. Consider the following. Assume for the sake of discussion that we are seriously interested in why only uninformative abstract results come from comparative generalizations concerning Ping-Pong and policy. In this case, the pursuit of the kind of recursive elucidation just sketched will at the very least force us to articulate a rich rationale concerning why this is so, far beyond the immediate and poor answer that between the practice of Ping-Pong and the practice of health care there simply lies a world of difference. The richer our understanding of the normative compositions that make Ping-Pong and health-care law the quite distinct practices we know them to be, the better we can compare generalized rationality judgments about cases within each respective body of practices, *e.g.*, the different training methods of the Chinese and the American Olympic Ping-Pong teams, or the recent licensing of euthanasia in the Netherlands and the recent adoption of brain-

---

[16] Phenomena of drastic change in the economy of relevance within a domain, 'paradigm shifts,' do not block this approach. True, a paradigm shift introduces massive discontinuities regarding what is taken to constitute good reasons. However, an adequate understanding of a paradigm shift will not merely reveal that certain reasons go in and out of favor; it will convey reasons for appreciating changes in how certain reasons get evaluated as good or bad reasons. [*Cf.* Will 1997, ch. 4 regarding "paradigm shifts."—Ed.]

death criteria into protocols for organ donation in the German medical system.

3.3 Double Abduction in Normative Governance

Very roughly, all good governance starts from more or less unsatisfactory practice and ends in more or less satisfactory practice. Any resources for grounding rationality judgments reside within the scope of this general relation. Will makes this point at various times in quasi-medical terms, speaking, *e.g.*, of remedies for deficiencies (*cf. BD* 157, 189). Though inconspicuous ampliative processes of governance occur everywhere all the time, ampliative governance becomes salient or "called for" (*BD* 155) when ongoing practices become markedly unsatisfactory and when such loss in their performance is taken to indicate deterioration or derangement of the composition of the norms shaping the life of those practices.[17] The more remedial or salutary some governantial effect, relative to effects that alternative or variant governing processes would produce—as perceived by persons engaged in the field(s) of practice(s) concerned, and measured against the acknowledged deficiencies in the practice(s)—the more desirable it is. This differential desirability of effects supposedly translates into differential legitimacy (or justifiedness) of the governantial processes that serve to bring them about.

Despite Will's reminder that "ampliative conclusions" (or better: results, or effects) "are not conclusions of arguments" (*BD* 6), where 'argument' denotes the derivation of conclusions from premises by logical entailment, one can describe a general form of reasoning or argumentation (though not in the narrow deductive sense) that serves for tracing the constraints that shape would-be ampliative conclusions. Borrowing from Peirce's most favored

---

[17] In the present subsection it is necessary to distinguish expressly between ampliative and deductive phases of governance. What I say elsewhere about governance is naturally more related to ampliative than to applicative ('deductive') governance.

rendition of what he called abductive reasoning, one can formulate these constraints in the following way:[18]

1) There are manifest undesirable results R in the performance of some accepted practice P, where P is oriented by the norms N_i . . . N_j.

2) If some norm N (of those belonging to P) were to be followed routinely, R would be a matter of course.

3) Therefore, it is desirable that P be ampliatively governed with regard to N.

This abduction captures our intuitions about which routine aspects of norms are to blame when normative compositions go wrong.

If we grant four assumptions—assumptions often met in practice—we can further specify the relevant kind of abductive reasoning. The assumptions are these: (1) We have some sense of the range of possible surrogates, successors, or alternatives to N in P; (2) In view of the kind of reasoning outlined in §3.2, we have some idea of the extent to which P allows for change in its normative composition while remaining recognizably (though perhaps unexpectedly) a composition of *that* practice P; (3) Practice P is important enough for us to desire to go on with P; and (4) It is not equally important for us to go on with N. Whenever these assumptions are met, the following supplementary abduction serves to direct and further specify our experiment in reflective normative governance:

1) P is (unexpectedly) recognized as similar when oriented by N_i . . . N_j and when oriented by N_m . . . N_n.

2) If some norm N' (of those belonging to N_m . . . N_n) were to succeed N in P, and were to be followed routinely, R would not occur in P.

3) Therefore, we should change P so that N' succeeds N.

---

[18] See Peirce 1931–58, 5.145, 5.172, 5.189; *cf.* Fann 1970.

Consider $G(P)_1$ and $G(P)_2$, each an account of a 'remedial successor' (*BD* 157) of some norm N whose routine employment contributes to certain deficiencies in the practice P whose normative composition includes those norms. $G(P)_1$ is better governance than $G(P)_2$ whenever the recomposition of P effected by $G(P)_1$ emends more deficiencies in P while creating fewer new deficiencies in P or any other associated practice than does $G(P)_2$. This trade-off clause (". . . while creating fewer . . .") is an important constraint since normative governance of a norm in some domain of practice must always reckon with that norm's, practice's, or domain's direct and indirect interdependence with other norms, practices, or domains. After all, normative compositions are not only composed, typically they are composed of compositions. Metaphorically speaking they are like a (borderless) quilt rather than a grid in space or nuclei in the void (*cf.* esp. *BD* 93–95).

Nothing in Will's discussion of the generic meaning of 'reasonable,' 'rational,' and related terms precludes characterizing $G(P)_1$ at this point as *more rational* in the way of reflective governance than $G(P)_2$. To understand the propriety of characterizing one episode of governance as more rational than another requires recognizing that reasons are the basic unit of analysis in a theory of governance.

3.4 Reasons Are the Proper Unit of Analysis for the Theory of Governance

In his discussion of the reactive effects of subsuming particulars under rules Will states an essential point of his pragmatic view of norms: the basic praxeological units in the analysis of normative compositions must be "not propositions, statements, sentences, not linguistic or quasi-linguistic entities of any sort . . . ." The basic praxeological units are more basic than these; they are "ways of behaving, or proceeding in thought and action" (*BD* 112). Will's reasons for grounding our theoretical understanding of practices and for avoiding the conceptually or semiotically refined *simulacra* of practical activities are clear and convincing.[19] However, I find his recourse to "ways of behaving, or proceeding in thought and action" too behavioristic and too vague to specify adequately the basic unit of analysis in governance theory, especially in the face of the broad spectrum of phenomena Will covers in his use of the terms 'norm' and, nearly synonymous, 'practice' (*BD* 1f., 24, 30f., 124f., 130). According to Will's core meaning of 'norm,' norms are "approved ways of proceeding in thought and action" (*BD* 24), or "guides to what is reasonable procedure" (*BD* 25). Essential "to their capacity to perform as guides in thought and action is an element of generality" (*BD* 125). Compared to these characteristic marks of the normative, Will's characterization of the basic unit of analysis (just cited) seems hopelessly underdetermined.[20] I suggest that taking *reasons* or *grounds* as a basic unit of analysis is more in tune with Will's marks of the normative. Let me explain.

What are reasons? A sound pragmatic concept of reason should begin with the insight that the very idea of a reason is rooted in our practices of asking for reasons and judging those reasons as good, better, or worse than other apparently significant reasons in the light of what we take them to be reasons *for* (*i.e.*, their intelligible point). The concept of a reason is a thoroughly normative concept. To speak of a reason is shorthand for the entire range of our formal and informal practices by which we distinguish better and worse reasons. Of course we do not always have this aim. When things go their normal course, we engage in our business without explicit concern for the reasons that are woven into our activities and practices. Yet switching to explicit concern for reasons is made universally possible by virtue of our language and communicative competence. Explicit concern for reasons is a stance we take rather than a contact we make with a particular range of

---

[19] For Will's critique of what is occluded from theoretical consideration when one chooses to focus on the manifestation of norms in the symbolic order of speech, see *BD* 100f.

[20] In elucidating a concept C, we reveal a "mark" of C when we reveal a property of C that anything has if it falls under C. See Wiggins 1991, 142.

entities called reasons. Whenever we take the proper stance to appreciate reasons we act as *rational evaluators*. Rational evaluators are persons exercising their capacity to discern, appreciate, and assess reasons. Reasons are not particular somethings *besides* beliefs, desires and aims, facts and feelings, thoughts and temptations, promises, sensory promptings, or what have you. Being a reason is pragmatically—not ontologically—specified by fulfilling a suitable role in those discursive practices that we recognize to be our practices of argumentation—'argumentation' broadly construed, so as to include *inter alia* evaluation, assessment, and justification.[21] What makes something *r* a reason is that *r* contributes to making some activity in some generally intelligible sense *worthwhile*.[22] Because the sense in which something is made worthwhile to do if it is done for certain reasons is *generally intelligible*, the social intelligence of the entire community of beings who are able to reciprocate as rational evaluators can (in principle) be brought to bear on the (individual and collective) determination of that sense of worthiness and thereby on the (individual and collective) governance of the activities that *r* helps to guide.

Doing something for some reasons is doing it "in the light of" those reasons rather than because (in a causal sense of 'because') of those reasons (or reason states). What I recognize as my reason(s) for ϕ-ing is what makes my intention to ϕ intelligible. This is shorthand for saying that my reason enables me to give answers that I can anticipate to be acceptable (or unacceptable) should I either want or have to respond to anyone asking why I shall ϕ. One might say that my intention to ϕ is 'governed' (in Will's sense of the term) by what I recognize as the reasons for which I am ϕ-ing.

The diversity of reasons whose incessant circulation and modification comprises the 'life of the individual mind' no less than the communicative life in shared social lifeworlds is truly astonishing.

---

[21] P. Taylor 1961.
[22] See Dewey 1939.

Even more striking is how practices of evaluating reasons can preserve their flexibility as a pervasive medium in which all our efforts of reaching an understanding of our reasons can cross-communicate and be made to bear on each other.

All reasons are norms, in the rich sense that Will's program of "restoring concreteness to norms" reinvests in that term. However, taking reasons as the basic praxeological unit of governance not only increases specificity, it restores methodological priority to reflective governance and thus helps to avoid the tensions (concerning both philosophical and nonphilosophical governance) that were seen to beset Will's approach (§2.1).

4 REFLECTIVE GOVERNANCE AND ITS SEMIOTIC UNDERPINNINGS

The points made in §§3.2 and 3.3 require us to reconsider how Will conceives of reflection in what he calls 'reflective' governance as distinct from nonreflective governance. The aim of §§4.1–4.5 is to amend a semiotic deficit in Will's theory of governance and thereby improve Will's view. I contend that Will's tendency to discount reflective governance derives in part from his lack of attention to the semiotic basis of criticism and reflective governance. Reflection makes criticism explicit (§4.1). This kind of reflection is linguistically based and is specific to human beings (§4.2). Our linguistic abilities enable us to engage in critical discursive practices (§4.3). Will is right to oppose assimilating our practices to formalized reconstructions of them. Unfortunately, he has not taken into account the rich pragmatic theories of language that developed out of speech act theory (§4.4). Four basic points about human language identified by speech act theory show that the distinction between reflective and nonreflective governance has a solid semiotic basis, a basis that makes critical assessment and revision of norms possible (§4.5). Moreover, this basis shows that mutual acceptability is an important *sine qua non* for normative principles (§4.6).

4.1 *Reflection as Making Criticism Explicit*

I do not find Will's remarks about the concept of reflection-in-governance (as distinct from nonreflective ways of governance) especially illuminating. The following passage typifies Will's treatment of this crucial topic:

> [W]hen in our more reflective activities, including our philosophical ones, we engage in the *explicit criticism and reformation* of norms we are not embarking upon activity of an entirely new kind . . .. Rather what *we* are engaging in is a continuation in greatly expanded and *more self-conscious form* of a kind of activity that *we* have engaged in already in some degree in following norms, because it is an aspect of norms themselves, because learning to follow norms always entails in some degree the capacity to expand and modify as well as to exemplify and confirm the routine aspects of them. (*BD* 232; emphasis added.)

The explicitness of criticism, the reformation of norms in the sense of intervening in extant bodies of norms under the guidance of explicit criticism, and a prospective, retrospective, and ongoing awareness of what one is doing and intending to do while engaged in such activities—all these features make it hard to imagine that the reflection required for reflective governance could take place in a world devoid of well entrenched, highly differentiated, hence multipurpose linguistic practices. It remains to be seen how far down the evolutionary ladder it makes sense to employ the concept of "language" for characterizing whatever semiotic structures may be found in communities of nonhuman forms of life. Natural human languages are semiotic vehicles of thought and media for communication. If there is something semiotical distinctive about human language that is also necessary for the possibility of reflective governance of norms, then an appropriate semiotic specification of human language is integral to a sound theory of governance.

4.2   *The Linguistic Return*

Will's delight in continuity-theses notwithstanding,[23] I maintain that a sharp distinction must be recognized between governance *amongst us*, human rational animals, insofar as our governance can be reflective, and nonhuman forms of life, where governance (such as it may be) cannot be reflective. If a theory of governance must proceed by case studies, as Will suggests, informed by a broadly evolutionary view of natural and social history and leading to what he laconically calls a "theory of man and nature" (*BD* 173),[24] then such a theory need not assume that *natura non facit saltu*.

True, what appears as leaps, breaks, qualitatively distinct levels, and other discontinuities may appear as continuities when viewed from suitably different perspectives. As Will aptly observes, "what is radical in one respect, in relation to one domain, may be very much in accordance with norms, practices, arrangements in one or more other domains" (*BD* 215). However, the reverse holds too. Pine trees, pigeons and persons may appear strikingly similar in the light of a highly developed evolutionary perspective on the history of the cosmos. Yet from another perspective, *e.g.* from the point of view of a theory of semiotic structures, drastic differences may be highlighted between kinds of beings who are close kin on the genealogical tree of evolutionary history, as is the case with some species of apes and *homo sapiens*.[25] If the distinction between

---

[23] Will maintains a continuity-thesis regarding reflective and nonreflective forms of ampliative governing (*BD* 161), regarding philosophical and nonphilosophical ones (*BD* 153), and regarding philosophical understanding of an institution and its criticism (*BD* 166).

[24] Peirce's more dramatic term for this kind of endeavour would probably be 'hypothetical metaphysics.'

[25] See Pinker 1994. Pinker notes that there are many species-specific, genetically based adaptations to environmental niches. An innate ability to develop and employ semiotically sophisticated language is, he persuasively argues, a uniquely human adaptation. Pinker also notes, *inter alia*, that a 1 percent chemical difference between the DNA of two organisms equals about 10 megabytes of information content—more than enough for encoding a Universal Grammar and the rest of the differences between humans and chimps. Moreover, in principle that 1 percent difference could be spread across each of the organism's entire complement of genes, which would make for 100 percent different organisms (1994, 351)!

reflective and nonreflective governance makes an important difference to governance itself, and if that distinction has important semiotic implications, then a theory of semiotic structures must be part of any sound theory of governance.

Will laments one consequence of the linguistic turn in philosophy, namely, that "the continuity of the general processes of governance and effecting composition of norms in human thought and action with analogous though much more rudimentary processes in nonhuman forms of life, especially the higher species of vertebrates" has been obscured (*BD* 210). However, Will's reversal of perspective unfortunately tends to obscure the vast and important differences between the practices of sign-mediated communication among nonhuman animal communities and among human communities as we know them. It is not my task here, commenting on Will's views, to develop the whole semiotic component of a general theory of governance. For present purposes it suffices to sketch four core semiotic phenomena pertinent to the philosophical theory of governance.

4.3   The Critical Powers of Human Speech: The Ability to Engage in Discursive Practices

The most important contribution of human linguistic communication to governance appears to consist in the unparalleled potential of human speech to facilitate representing extant norms and normatively composed practices, and to facilitate the criticism of such norms as they are articulated and defined through linguistic representation. Language enables norms to be "brought before us" so that we can identify, recognize, acknowledge or repudiate, affirm or negate, reconsider or modify, in thought what we are or have been doing more or less unthinkingly in our practices. The thrust of the semiotic component of a general theory of governance is set by the discriminatory, reflective and, generally speaking, the critical powers of human speech.

To say of human *speech* that it has discriminatory, reflective, and critical powers is not to indulge in widespread linguistic *proton pseudos* that Will attacks forcefully and relentlessly (*BD* 31f., 52–54, 101f., 123–42). Rather, it is elliptical for saying that human languages (*i.e.* achievements of complex symbolic systems) are linguistically structured in ways that support practices that make the use of language in those practices an intersubjectively meaningful manifestation of discriminatory, reflective, and critical powers that also manifest themselves in human *thinking*. Anyone socialized within the medium of any human natural language has thereby always already acquired, usually to an astonishingly far-ranging extent, the ability to say what one thinks one is doing (being engaged in some practice P) and to ask and answer, in word or thought, questions about why one is doing what one says or thinks one is doing, and to respond in intersubjectively meaningful ways to such questions and answers (*e.g.*, with further questions and answers).

This astonishing ability is common, and thus is intersubjective; it is pervasive, and thus is beyond the control of heteronomous impositions of limits; it is iterative and recursive, and thus is always ongoing; and it is deeply rooted in our linguistic behavior, and thus is translatable among different language-communities. More important, this ability is structurally dialogical. That is to say, it lends itself as much to being exercised by and between different persons as it admits of realization in the first-person. Because this ability is dialogical, not only in its exercise, but already in its constitution, this ability to engage in, to produce and reproduce (what I shall call) *discursive practices*, connects persons, their norms of nonlinguistic activities, and their norms of linguistic activities.

4.4   *The Semiotic Deficit in Will's Theory of Governance*

Will's crusade against substituting the linguistic counterparts, "symbolic replicas" (*BD* 53), or "abstract symbolic surrogates" (*BD* 10) of practice for the philosophical scrutiny of the concrete practices themselves tends to lead him into a global and unhelpfully abstract view of the symbolic reality of linguistic systems of signs (symbolic expressions).[26] According to Will, our practices and doings are "in" the world, as we know it. And so is our thinking, whenever it is "concrete." Why divorce symbolic linguistic expressions from the world of concrete practices? Why should we think that the normative constituents of the linguistic portion of our practices are abstracted from the concreteness of the normative life of our world of nonlinguistic practices?[27] If what persons think and do is inherently world-bound, as Will's naturalism about norms of action *and*

---

[26] Similarly: "The thesis being developed here is that the great success of the symbolic model in illuminating the routine sub-species [of subsumption] led to the mistaken identification of the subsumptive process with this model and with the routine processes of which it is a surrogate" (*BD* 103).

[27] Although Will has devoted considerable effort to identify "replication theory" as the chief antipragmatic obstacle to a sound theory of normative governance beyond deductivism, he has not devoted equal effort to criticizing antipragmatic preconceptions in the philosophy of language. This fact is curious, given that Will's general pragmatic position commits him to a continuity thesis concerning the norms of both linguistic and nonlinguistic practices. (This continuity thesis goes beyond the continuity thesis, reflected in Will's frequent conjunction of the terms 'action' and 'thought' when speaking of norms, concerning the continuity of thinking and doing.) Will's staunch later-Wittgensteinianism on this matter appears in observations like the following, made in an early article. Will observes that even something as seemingly trivial as the adoption of a name for a certain kind of thing is the adoption of a practice: "Furthermore, except in the case of the very young, who must learn the names of things and the practice of using names simultaneously, the new practice adopted represents a kind of variation upon a set of older, already accepted practices, in some harmonious relationship with which the new practice must find a place. What those accepted practices are helps to determine at any given time, and sometimes in a very complex way, what in the way of new practices are desirable or even feasible, just as it determines also when and in what respect the adoption of new practices will entail modifications among the old" (Will 1963, 284). More recently Will aptly observed that "there are a variety of ways in which our thought and action can reflect—clearly, distortedly, or mistakenly—characteristics of the domains in which they are carried on besides pointing out, naming, assigning predicates to, or more generally, speaking falsely or truly about these domains" (*BD* 97), but he does not consider the efforts begun by Austin's theory of speech-acts to explore the great variety of ways in which already our *speech* (*i.e.*, our language-in-use) can reflect characteristics of the domains in which we use it other than stating facts or "representing states of affairs" to ourselves.

thought has it,[28] then so are the linguistic norms and practices insofar as they compose discursive practices.

To be sure, there are influential theories and philosophies of language, old and new, that portray language as an *abstract* semiotic system far removed from the concreteness supposedly enjoyed in practical engagement with the world. Moreover, there is an intrinsic trend in the deductivist bent of philosophy to give pride of place to fact-stating language. On this basis, the view has been promoted that language is a system of representational signs (propositions and their semiotic infrastructures, referential and predicative expressions) that apparently of necessity have to be abstract *vis-à-vis* 'the real world' in order to fulfill the representational role ascribed to them as their prime semiotic function.[29] But why give any credit in the philosophy of language to this kind of representationalism, with its view of language (as an order of abstract symbolic replicas) and linguistic practices (as based on fact stating), when such representationalism is one of the pillars of deductivism, and deductivism harbors a view of norms that is deeply flawed, at least in regard to nonlinguistic practices? Will is highly critical of the consequences of deductivism for a number of fields of philosophical thought.[30] If Will is less cognizant of the consequences of deductivism for philosophical views of language, this would amount to an important omission given the scope of his program of a general theory of philosophical governance. At the very least, Will does not accord language an important role in his program of a

---

[28] *BD* 93–96, 173, 186, 201f.; "What we pick out as norms, what we formulate as norms, are features of the life they compose" (*BD* 95); "Since norms are integrally related to the world, reflective governance is likewise. The achievement of governance is the achievement of a kind of life in the world" (*BD* 96). [Also see Westphal, "Transcendental Reflections on Pragmatic Realism," Essay 2 above.—Ed.]

[29] For penetrating criticism of truth-centered traditions in the philosophy of language, see Apel 1980a and 1986.

[30] See *BD* 64–80 regarding the consequences of deductivism in philosophy of science, legal philosophy, and ethics. [Also see Paulson, "Two Problems in Hans Kelsen's Legal Philosophy," Essay 10 above.—Ed.]

general theory of philosophical governance. This amounts to a semiotic deficit in his program, or so I shall argue.

Following a set of distinctions made familiar by Charles Morris, it can be said that a philosophy of language tends to miss the concreteness of language insofar as it concentrates on 'semantic' and 'syntactic' properties while ignoring the 'pragmatic' properties of language-in-use.[31] A theory of language congenial to the aims of a general theory of normative governance must focus on the much neglected pragmatic properties of language and other semiotic systems. It must treat the 'syntactic' and the 'semantic' as methodologically motivated selective abstractions from the richer and encompassing 'pragmatic' dimensions of language. Pragmatics is linguistically fundamental; these three abstractions are not on equal theoretical footing, and semantics and syntax certainly are not primary. Will focuses almost exclusively on the abstract syntactic and semantic analyses developed, *e.g.*, by Carnap and other logical positivists. He is quite right that such views of language occlude rather than illuminate the phenomena of rational governance.[32] Unfortunately, he overlooks the important developments in pragmatics found, not in Sellars' proposed "pure pragmatics,"[33] but in semiotics and speech act theory, especially as extended by Habermas and Apel.

---

[31] See Morris 1938. Though not developed, the crucial distinction was well captured in terms of language as *langue* (= synchronic sign system) and as *parole* (= actual speech) at the beginning of this century by the swiss linguist Ferdinand Saussure (1916). More recently, Habermas' program of a "universal pragmatics" and Apel's program of a "transcendental pragmatics" seek to criticize and remedy the deficits of abstractivism in the philosophy of language in much the same ways that Will seeks to criticize and remedy the deficits of deductivism in philosophy generally. See Habermas 1979 and 1990, and Apel 1980b and 1995.

[32] [See Westphal, "Transcendental Reflections on Pragmatic Realism," Essay 2 above, §3.—Ed.]

[33] Sellars 1947.

4.5   *The Semiotic Rationale for the Distinction Between Nonreflective and Reflective Governance*

Semiotic studies of nonhuman animal sign systems have identified analogies between the role of propositions in human language when used to convey information about extant features of the world and the role in simpler sign systems, *e.g.* in the 'language' of bees, of significant gestures and other utterances whose causal etiology conveys useful information about states of the environment that are important to the sign-using animals. Bees have developed the ability to exploit features of their environment (*e.g.*, the position of the sun, flight distances, smells, observable regularities in their bodily movements) in order upon returning to the hive to perform dance-like gestures in a way that makes these performances ('utterances') informationally rich and effective guides for fellow bees in their consequent search for food. It is not altogether clear to me whether Will's view of norms as concrete features of the lives of individuals and communities that they compose entails that the regularities in bees' dances are norms proper. For one thing, they seem to have too little composition, too little coherence with other bodies of norms (for lack of other bodies of norms in the life of the hive) to satisfy Will's view of norms as inherently concrete. If Will's remark that norms "guide the actions of persons; it is the action of such beings . . . which are guided by norms" (*BD* 147) is meant to state a necessary constraint on sensible talk of norms then this settles the matter. For all we know, bees are not persons, not even in a very remote way. However, much of Will's characterization of the routine aspect of norms carry over to bee-dance performances.[34]

In order to exclude, *e.g.*, bee-dances from the range of phenomena of concern to a sound theory of governance and to include only practices encountered in human forms of life I recommend a semiotic rationale rather than reference to the malleable and notoriously contested distinction between persons and nonpersons. Will's charac-

---

[34] Perhaps "replication theory," mistaken as a core model for human norms and norm-following behavior, would find a proper place and so would have a grain of truth when referred to bee-dances and similar phenomena of zoosemiotics.

terization of norms as essentially involving governance in virtue of being learned (*BD* 10, 201, *cf.* 147) provides the clue to such a semiotic rationale. To be sure, norms (in Will's sense) always involve governance. And norms always involve to some degree "post-gametic learning," as Will puts it (*BD* 24).[35] But the governance involved in norms specifically in virtue of their being learned is structured by judgment in the sense that learning how or what to do is of a piece with learning how to correct oneself or let oneself be corrected by others with regard to the point of what gets done. (As Will insists, there can be governance *of* practice only because there is already governance *in* practice.[36]) Such correction or governance in practice can affect one's activity regarding either the point of the activity or one's execution, or both. This kind of learning is not reducible to conditioning (whether classical or operant) because it involves an ability to distinguish, contrast, or compare what is done as matter of fact with what is supposed to be done, or what is being done and what is to be done, or what would count as an activity's improving or degenerating, succeeding or failing. Some forms of learning cannot produce, during the learning, a retainable reflection of the practice being learned, a reflection of the practice as change occurs in it, where that reflection is also accessible after and beyond its immediate occurrence.[37] Such forms of learning

---

[35] This clause would preclude reflexes (in the proper neurophysiological sense of the term) and inborn triggering devices (in the proper etiological sense of the term) from being norms. The clause does not exclude the 'language' of bee dances if there is some operant conditioning ('learning') involved, in however small a measure, in the development of their performance over and above the forces shaping the sociobiological evolution of bees.

[36] Will 1997, ch. 5.

[37] I eschew the term 'representation' and use the semiotically less committal 'retainable reflection' partly because I cannot here discuss the issue of whether or how forms of know-how (as distinct from forms of knowing-that) admit of being 'represented.' It seems clear to me that knowing how to play Ping-Pong in humans is, but in pigeons placed inside a "Skinner box" is not, a learning process that generates a retainable reflection of itself. Without the generation of a retainable reflection one might start out hitting a little white ball around and end up being good at playing Ping-Pong while being at a loss to relate what one is doing to anything else one is doing. One would then be in the rather strange position of being unable, *e.g.*, to give up the praxis of Ping-Pong if need be, since one would

cannot distinguish what is done from what ought to be done, nor can they distinguish improving or worsening the practice, or succeeding or erring in it.

Several semiotic structures are crucial to the vast difference between performances of such information-conveying dances among bees and how humans would compose practices that serve to guide finding food in the environment.[38] Three such structures are: (1) negation; (2) distinguishing on the one hand among different particular instances of some activity and on the other between particular instances and the generic type of that activity; and (3) sorting activities in terms of their recognized aims, *i.e.* in terms of established purposes to whose fulfillment they are held to be relevant. These three semiotic structures are found in semiotic systems sufficiently complex to support governing processes that are struc-

---

not know what one is supposed to give up, nor why it should be given up. Operant conditioning as learning mechanism can account for one's getting better at doing something but cannot account for one's knowing what one gets better at doing.

[38] The philosophically most penetrating discussion familiar to me of bee-language in comparison with human language is Bennett 1964. Bennett thinks there is an internal link between the *symbolic* character of a language and the possibility of interpreting an expression as a *reason-giving* utterance: "I think it would be generally conceded that a kind of behavior is not properly described as 'linguistic' unless it is symbolic in character; and to describe behavior as symbolic is to say something about the behavors' reasons for behaving as they do. Specifically, it is to say that most bits of behavior of the kind in question are enacted because such behavior informs other creatures about the location of food, the direction of danger, or whatever the subject-matter of the language may be; and the 'because' here must have something of the force of the giving of a reason" (1964, 44). Hence normal bees can be said neither to have a language proper nor to be rational. If the dances were symbolic it would have to be true of most dances "that the bee performs the dance because it is in the presence of other bees which will be informed by the dance as to the whereabouts of food. That is, for the dance to be symbolic, it is necessary that the dancers should be not merely intelligent about something but intelligent about the relationship between one bee's dancing and another's finding food" (1964, 45). The intelligence must somehow extend to the very governing of the signs and the rules of their usage *i.e.* it must extend to the very linguistic behavior that functions as a mediator between subjects of their relations to states of affairs in a shared world. (Bennett's account of human language is extended in Bennett 1976.)

tured by judgment in the sense Will takes to define the very idea of norms as forms of appropriate response.[39]

In human natural languages, semiotic systems that contain the three structures just mentioned clearly embody another feature of a broad array of utterances, first made explicit philosophically in speech act theory, namely, (4) the complementary structure of an illocutionary component and nonillocutionary component governed by that illocutionary component; e.g., "I warn you (= illocutionary component), a tornado is approaching (= propositional component)." The illocutionary component of a speech-act gives the general point of engaging in a certain kind of practice that is executed by an appropriate performance that follows a linguistic norm. For instance, the general point for anyone engaging in uttering a promise is to commit oneself and to make oneself understood as thereby committing oneself in certain ways for someone else's benefit. The embedded nonillocutionary component assigns a particular content to the illocutionary act. Both components together specify the general point of the illocutionary act into a specific communicative offer (e.g., a specific promise to perform some specific act, or a specific warning about a specific state of affairs) to which all concerned interlocutors (e.g. addressees) can meaningfully respond in ways that are recognized as appropriate within the discursive practices of the linguistic communities of which they are members. When exchanging speech-acts one is expected to be able say what one thinks one is doing, to ask and to answer questions about why one is doing what one says or thinks one is doing, and to respond in intersubjectively meaningful ways to such questions and answers. The semiotic distinction within the speech-act between an illocutionary component and a nonillocutionary component it governs enables us to distinguish the particular point of an activity (e.g., to assert some-

---

[39] "A norm is not just a form of action. It is a form of appropriate action, of appropriate response; and this appropriateness is something that is determined in its relations with, among other things, other norms: by the role which this or that mode of action or response plays in the constitution of individual and communal life" (BD 93–94).

thing, to say of the x that it is F), which is contextually situated within a wider array of practices (*e.g.*, the sorting of different xs into different storage-boxes), from the activity and its full consequential effect and to compare and if need be adjust them to each other,[40] and to do all this within an intersubjective medium, namely within a practice that is multilaterally intelligible and subject to critique through discursive practices.[41]

The intersubjectivity of the medium (human speech) allows for sharing (and comparing, revising, and reproducing) the particular microeffects of individual actors' concrete governance of their particular doings. Such sharing generates norms. The intelligent microeffects that feed them would for the most part, amongst 'mute' creatures, remain enclosed within individual actor-perspec-

---

[40] See *BD* 117f., regarding Will, Wittgenstein, and Stroud on measuring lumber.

[41] In the sixties, some British analytic philosophers (J. Kovesi, J. Kemp, J. G. Brennan)—now unfortunately neglected—argued that even 'empirical' concepts for 'descriptive' employment are formed in such a way that their conceptual structure reflects a distinction between general purposes associated with their employment and a particularizing content governed by that purpose. Most notable is Kovesi (1967), who elaborates the realistically pragmatic position that even those linguistic practices in which we employ so-called 'descriptive terms' (like "table") for stating facts are analogous to practices in which we employ conspicuously evaluative activity-terms (like "murder"), such as in moral judgments, insofar as *any* kind of linguistic practice manifests some point of interest that we invest in those practices. Kovesi states: "Evaluation is not an icing on a cake of hard facts. It is not the case that we have ready-made facts, and that if we want to describe them we state them and say 'yes' about them, and if we want to evaluate them we state them and say 'please' about them. A moral notion does not make a roll-call of facts. There is a point in bringing certain features and aspects of actions and situations together as being relevant, and by removing this point, by removing the 'evaluative element,' we are not left with the same facts minus evaluation.—Standards, needs and wants also enter into the formation of terms that we usually call descriptive terms. What makes a term descriptive is not the lack of these but the point of view from which we organize these and other elements into concepts. While in using descriptive terms we have to follow interpersonal rules in a public language to talk about aspects or relationships of the inanimate world—or if we talk about men and animals we do that in so far as they are part of the rest of the world—in using a moral term we have to follow interpersonal rules in a public language to talk about some aspects or relationships of those very beings whose lives are regulated by interpersonal rules" (Kovesi 1967, 25). Within the 'Frankfurt School' of Critical Theory, the doctrine of 'knowledge interests' that was developed in the mid-sixties by Apel and Habermas served similar purposes. See Apel 1966 and 1980c; Habermas 1971; and Kettner 1996a.

tives, insulated from the experiential intelligence of coactors and therefore lost to the community.

Semiotic systems with the four broad features highlighted by speech-act theory in human natural language (negation, type-token distinguishability of activities, discriminability of activities by standardly associated purposes, discriminability of locutionary and illocutionary components of speech acts) provide the semiotic basis for explicit and self-conscious criticism of normative compositions. Such criticism is essential to reflective ampliative governance. For example, without a means of conveying through communicative acts something that is believed (*e.g.*, that the earth is flat because it appears flat) and distinguishing from it, in a generally intelligible way, a purpose to be achieved in that very act (*e.g.*, claiming truth for one's belief), it would be impossible for members of a community to reciprocate as rational evaluators of reasons (*e.g.*, by doubting that the fact that the earth appears flat provides a better reason for us to believe the earth to be flat than to believe otherwise). To adopt momentarily a computer metaphor, practices of discriminating relevant from irrelevant reasons and appreciating the particular purport of some relevant reason concerning some target matter of deliberation would not "run" on a semiotic system of lesser structural complexity.

4.6   *Reciprocal Criticism and the Mutual Acceptability of Principles*

In this section (§4) I have argued that explicit and self-conscious criticism is essential to reflective ampliative governance; that four semiotic features in a community's linguistic practices are necessary to support self-conscious criticism; and that these features become salient when communication is described pragmatically, as in speech act theory, by distinguishing locutionary and illocutionary acts. This distinction is important for governance theory because it enables speakers to raise validity claims for their speech acts (*e.g.*, for a speaker's act of asserting that the earth is flat) *vis-à-vis* other speakers, and in turn for other speakers to challenge such intersubjective claims by comparing some speaker's illocutionary aim (or intention) with whatever grounds are required to acknowledge that a speaker succeeds with his or her illocutionary aim.

Because our discursive practices enable us linguistically to describe ourselves as doing nonlinguistic things (*e.g.*, frying an egg) and to ascribe such doings to ourselves and to others, *all* kinds of actions are subject to validity claims ("Why did you *fry* my egg when I said I wanted it boiled?").[42] Such challenges are responses within a community of reason-giving communicators that bring into accord or, as the case may be, help to readjust (1) whatever determinate reasons people can have for doing things (within that community) and (2) whatever determinate validity claims they expect their reasons to make on anyone (within that community) in ways that are mutually justifiable in terms that no one with a say in the matter could reject as simply unreasonable—except on the basis of some further reason *r* that in turn must be able to withstand the test of critical consideration, within the group's discursive practice, for everyone with a say in the matter.

Obviously it is not the case that for every reason *r* and for any doing ϕ in some context C, if some person *S* is ϕing-in-C for that reason *r* and there are some persons *S'* (including *S*) who acknowledge *r* as being a good reason for *S* to ϕ-in-C (and who would therefore endorse as valid the corresponding judgment that *S*'s ϕing-in-C is justified since *S* ϕs-in-C for *r*) then *r* is equally good for *everyone*. We have of course a certain stock of very general reasons, which may be called principles, that we think hold good for everyone, *e.g.*, logical principles like *modus ponens* or noncontradiction. Yet the overwhelming majority of the reasons that we acknowledge as good reasons in this or that context are too substantive to admit of unrestricted universalization.[43]

---

[42] See Øfsti 1990 128–72, for a penetrating discussion of act-performance, act-description, and ascriptions of responsibility within communities of users of natural languages.

[43] With regard to moral reasons, see Wiggins 1987. In Kettner 1996b, I argue that universalizability for good reasons can be analyzed in terms of the following principle: If *r* is a good reason for *S* to ϕ in *C* then there is some property *F* of

However, there are some normative pragmatic principles that are undeniably acknowledged whenever we think that we or some other interlocutors are genuinely engaged in discursive practices for the sake of evaluating some reason (no matter how formal or substantive) as good or bad. Such principles are unqualifiedly universal since anyone's act of claiming, for some reason r, not to acknowledge those principles, if meant to be taken as a convincing argument or reason, would be taken to be meant as already expressing their acknowledgment. For example, considering oneself to be an evaluator of reasons (*i.e.*, a participant in argumentative discourse) among other such evaluators does not make sense unless one also thinks that we already share enough ways of evaluating reasons in order for us to make progress identifying whatever differences there may be between our ways of evaluating reasons. This is likely the principle Will has in mind when he observes that "the capacity to disagree implies as a basis some kind of already realized agreement. Divergence of opinion however wide is always rooted in some kind of agreement" (*BD* 199). Moreover, we cannot help thinking that ideally such progress is not arbitrary. One would contradict oneself if one were to claim to do something arbitrarily and to do it for a particular reason. Additionally, we think that ideally evaluators of reasons can determine whether their understanding of the merit of some reason is uncoerced or whether it derives from some fact that allows someone to impose his or her will on others. One would be taken to have lost one's grip on the very possibility of assessing validity claims if one were to claim to take r as good and to claim to do so only because someone else makes or wants one to do so, or only because something other than one's understanding brings one to do so. Having insight into what leads one to take r as a good reason does not suffice to make r a good reason. Rather, purporting to know r to be good presupposes a commitment to respect as an evaluator of reasons just like oneself whoever else

---

S such that r is the same good reason (to ϕ in C) for anyone who is F. Universalizability is thus conditioned by a certain property F that need not hold of everyone.

would purport to know r's merits. Such respect takes the form of reciprocal evaluation. It would be improper to claim to take r to be good and to claim to be prepared to discount without reason anyone's claim that r is not a good reason. Argumentative discourse thus has an *a priori* unlimited potential for expanding the reciprocity of critical evaluation to include in its circle ever new evaluators of reasons. Will's antifoundationalist refusal to countenance some norms as "ungoverned governors" (*BD* 150) is an expression of the fact that the normative composition of argumentative discourse prohibits exempting any particular insight into good reasons from the contest for intersubjective recognition via mutual criticism of possible alternative insights.

5 GOVERNANCE THEORY AND DELIBERATIVE DEMOCRACY

In this final section I return to the issue left pending in §3: Whether governance theory can get beyond abstract determinables such as harmony, simplicity, coherence, discrepancies, inconsistencies, incompleteness, unsatisfactoriness, role in human life, *etc.*, as the roots in reality to which rationality judgments about governance should answer. The contemplative character of Will's theory of governance is betrayed by Will's lack of attention to the question, 'Who shall use his theory of governance?' (§5.1). Further evidence of this tendency is found in Will's retrospective, descriptive characterizations of past, purportedly successful cases of normative governance (§5.2). The proper remedy for this problem is to recognize that proper reflective governance of norms requires deliberative democratic institutions that foster—and are fostered by—the critical discursive practices of discussion, debate, and reasoned argument (§5.3).

5.1   *Who Employs a Theory of Governance?*
Who is to fill the abstract determinables of governance theory with life? In other words, Who does Will's theory designate as its practitioner or would-be agent of application? Whose lives constitute

the reality to which rationality judgments about governance should answer? And how does Will's theory situate the people who are living those lives *vis-à-vis* the people whom the theory supposes to make rationality judgments? These questions throw into relief what is perhaps the most serious deficit in Will's theory, namely, the lack of reflection in his theory on the very conditions that would make for good governance in the application of his theory to some field of practice-to-be-governed. Will's theory of governance does not extend to its own application. Will's theory of governance is silent on the practice, indeed the politics, of implementing governance theory. *Contre coeur* it has the very air of contemplative theorizing that Marx castigated as the hallmark of all idealist philosophy.

5.2 *Whence Rational Social Criticism?*

Will affirms Hume's exhortation "that 'in general, there is a degree of doubt, and caution, and modesty, which, in all kinds of scrutiny and decision, ought for ever to accompany a just reasoner'" (*BD* 228). Accordingly, Will is reluctant to pronounce normatively on changing social arrangements while these are actually still in flux (*BD* 227f.). Of all things, arrangements actually still in flux will not make for clear cases. But they exemplify conditions in which normative change urgently needs reflective governance. However, it appears that on Will's view the more urgently some normative arrangement needs reflective governance, the more modest must such attempts at governance be. If this is a sobering truth, it is also a very disappointing one.

There is little if any consolation in believing (with Will) that *some* governance will invariably take place and that it will take care of itself in *some* way. After all, Will also holds that governantial effects reached in one way may not be as desirable as comparable effects that are reached in some other way. Governance may be inherent in norms, but it is not for that reason necessarily *good* governance (*BD* 201–02). Will recognizes that reflective governance, especially when effected through semiotic means, has a number of advantages lacking in nonreflective (and nonsemiotic) ways of governance (*e.g.*, peaceability, precision, and intelligent novelty; *BD* 212f.). Thus it is bad news to learn that reflective governance, especially when it comes to the appraisal of alternatives routes, is at its worst precisely when its effects, if only such governance were possible, would be most welcome, most desirable, most legitimate, and most urgent.

The quietism of Will's account is reenforced through historic examples that allegedly converge with the results an application of his theory to these examples would have had. However, Will's examples break the avowed rule of Humean modesty. This is particularly obvious in the following passage where the historian Gibbon, a "philosophically judicious citizen of the Roman Empire," and "a similarly alert subject of Louis XVI of France or of Nicholas II of Russia," occupy the place of the theory's practicing subject:

> There are extended periods of history during which one or other of these [attitudes of advocating change, stasis, or conservative resuscitation], or of still other varied attitudes toward the norms and arrangements of life, will have the sanction of balanced philosophical judgment. It was Gibbon's judgment that what he called 'The Golden Age of Antonines,' the period between the death of Comitian and the accession of Commodus, was of all periods of history the one in which the human race was most happy and prosperous. If he was right, the attitude of a philosophically judicious citizen of the Roman Empire alert to his condition would naturally have been one directed to preserving the condition of this felicity. A markedly different attitude was surely recommended to a similarly alert subject of Louis XVI of France or of Nicholas II of Russia. (*BD* 216–17)

The notion that if *we* were *them*, we would side with the cause of the revolutionaries of 1789 and not with its royalist victims, has a disarming obviousness about it. Personally, I endorse Will's judgment. Yet on further thought it is clear that the way in which the political order is perceived as needing governance depends entirely on the practical referent chosen by the theorist and how that subject is in fact situated within that political order, and on how the theorist as practical subject is in fact situated within the political order of his or her actual world. Not every subject of Louis XVI, not even every philosophically alert subject, thought at the time that revolution was the best option. And worse still, not all our contemporaries, not even philosophically alert ones, think in retrospect that it really was the best way to go. Similar remarks apply to Will's view of the Russia of Nicholas II. As to Gibbon's golden age, the time of Antonines surely looked less golden from the perspective of peoples colonized or coerced into the Roman Empire than it did for the average member of the Roman aristocracy. My point in these remarks is not that governance theory underrates the interdisciplinary power it takes to diagnose uncontroversially the signs of the time. Will's theory can accommodate any auxiliary theoretical input from history, political science, sociology, or what have you. My point concerns rather the sense of that telling little phrase, "If he was right . . .." *Was* Gibbon right? This depends crucially on whether the determinate interpretation of harmony (coherence, unsatisfactoriness, desirability, and other relevant determinables) that Gibbon (and, hypothetically, Will) imputes to Antonines' contemporaries, speaks authentically to the self-interpretations of the addressees of the theory's message that their age is really the golden one (or has passed it). If Gibbon *was* right (as Will assumes he was), what would an Antoninian counterpart of Gibbon/Will have had to say to, or perhaps to think about, a contemporaneous militant organizer of slave resistance? Claiming a privilege of theoretical insight would not have made their perspective any more effective in the actual determination of governance of the imperial arrangements concerned.

This thought experiment underscores the political character of rationality judgments about governance of arrangements under which people already are determined or fated to govern their vital affairs. Authors who make the judgments and who claim rational authority for them must be concerned about how they are mandated by their addressees, *i.e.*, by everyone whose concerns would be affected if the policy implied by the rationality judgment were to be practically enacted. Governance theory and a normative political theory of forms of governments, it seems, are close cousins after all.

5.3   *Consensus and Disagreement*

Intended as a theory for us today, Will's theory of governance would, in its socially relevant extensions, have to metamorphose into a theory of democratic political governance. This claim is based on three observations. The first observation (made in §2.2) is that Will's theory of governance, owing to its critical, *i.e.* normative aspirations, must presuppose that the theory's rationality judgments can be (re-)translated into the self-understanding of the very people whose ways of governing their affairs Will (or anyone taking Will's governance theory seriously) would be theorizing *about*. In judging, with regard to certain of your affairs, that a certain governantial arrangement G_1 would be a *better* way of governing them than G_2 I am claiming that G_1 is more acceptable than G_2, and that this relation of G_1 to G_2 is intersubjectively valid in the sense that you and I could appreciate it just like anyone else who is willing and able to put herself hypothetically into your shoes. The second observation is that a minimal but essential trait of *democratic* modes of governance is that democratic governance requires that everyone who must live with the arrangements that are the outcome of such governance have a fair influence on the processes that are responsible for the outcome. The third observation is that, the distinctive requirement of *deliberative* democracy is that everyone who must live with the results of democratic governance have a fair opportunity to engage in reasoning publicly and critically about purportedly good governance, and that actual political decision-making processes be such that their outcomes reflect (at least to a recognizable extent) such public political deliberation. These three observations suggest that discursive practices are both the essential element of reflection in the very general sense in which Will speaks of "reflective governance" (*cf.* §4.1 above) and the core of deliberation in the more specific sense given to that term by political theorists who seek to articulate, under the heading of 'deliberative democracy,' the intuition that the rationale of democracy is not majority rule in order to reach decisions (*e.g.*, by summing preferences) but argumentative debate in order to reach consensus about what ought to be decided for reasons that most citizens can expect one another to accept.[44]

The following passage from one of Will's earlier essays clearly shows his awareness of the methodological priority in democratic arrangements of reflective governance through discursive practices over nonreflective modes of governance and shows that he espouses a notion of deliberative democracy, though without using the term:

> Embedded in our theory of government [*i.e.*, democracy as government by discussion] is a view that there is a way of testing opinion and judgment, of resolving disagreements about both means and ends, that is eminently desirable. Speech and other forms of expression are necessary for this way of proceeding, but they are not by themselves sufficient. Decisions are arrived at, not by yielding to those who can talk the longest or shout the loudest, but by determining who can make the best case, or if no case is clearly best, what elements of conflicting views can be composed into a resolution that competing parties can accept as, if not best, one which they can live with, and in the formulation of which their points of view and interests have had fair consideration.[45]

However, the emphasis in deliberative democracy on reflective governance through discursive practices (discussion, debate, and argument) sits uneasily with Will's tendency to lump argumentation, discourse, and reflection together in order to contrast them with "the argument model" of governance, *i.e.* the extraction of conclusions from premises by deductive operations performed on abstract symbolic replicas of norms (*BD* 6, 180). It is obvious that the operations of discursive practices, *i.e.* argumentation, do not reduce to Will's "argument model." Nor does Will claim they do. But neither do they reduce to (reflective) ampliative governance, as

---

[44] One of the most interesting explorations of this contrast remains Dewey 1927. See also Cohen 1989.

[45] Will 1972, 384.

Will's complementary notions of applicative and ampliative modes of governance would suggest. In argumentative discourse oriented toward reaching a common understanding, "elements of conflicting views" can be reconciled into determined consensus in ways that do not seem to be adequately captured by Will's description of how ampliative processes yield results, namely, as the adoption of a "view in preference to alternatives, not because it, rather than they, is altogether extruded from the realm of the doubtful, but because one develops an appreciation of the superiority, which may be slight, moderate, or extreme, of one over the other" (*BD* 182). Will's characterization of ampliation is ill-suited to characterize argumentative discourse because within critical discursive practices one develops a *grounded* "appreciation of the superiority," an appreciation of good, better, or worse *reasons*. Developing this kind of appreciation is at least subject to the constraints of analogy and abduction discussed earlier (§§3.2, 3.3). To come to appreciate that some reason *r* is better (or worse) than another reason is to gain an understanding of what sorts of disagreements can be overcome or contained by appeal to *r* and where disagreement could resume or continue. Discursively prompted consensus therefore *contains* disagreement. It is not pure agreement but determinate agreement that is mediated by, or supervenes on, determinate disagreement.

I have argued that none of Will's notions of "reasoned argument" (*BD* 180), "the argument model" (*BD* 6), or "ampliative process," sheds sufficient light on the rational potential of argumentative discourse. Will's "argument model" is too close to the deductivist assimilation of justificatory relations between apparently good reasons and what they are claimed to be reasons for, to entailment relations between premises and conclusions. At pains to prevent confounding "reasoned argument" with the applicative "argument model," Will's complementary notion of ampliative processes serves as a counterpoint to that model. However, Will's model appears to be overly contextualist and intuitionist, obscuring the fact that "appreciation" of the superiority of some normative arrangement is appreciation of *reasons*, and is thus always contextual but not altogether context-bound.

Developing more complex, more comprehensive characterizations of argumentative discourse is an urgent priority of the current philosophical agenda.[46] Integrating them into governance theory, or into that self-referential part of the theory that focuses on governing the application of governance theory to politically relevant matters, would greatly enhance the practical resources and appeal of Will's theory.

6 CONCLUSION

I began by pointing out the unduly subdued prescriptive intention of Will's general theory of governance. Governance theory aims at improving our governance. Above and beyond attempting to improve our description of governance, it must therefore be understood as answering questions about how to govern governance well. I also defended the possibility of rationality judgments about governance that are contextual but not context-bound against Will's view that governance theory must settle for context-bound assessments of governance. I then observed the striking and curious contrast between Will's criticism of deductivism—itself a paragon of reflection—and Will's relative silence about reflective modes of governance, as distinct from nonreflective modes. I sought to remedy this lack of balance by appeal to a semiotic conception of reflection. Against Will's tendency to describe the amelioration of normative compositions as objective happenings, I emphasized how reflective governance proceeds through extended mutual criticism that is engendered by our practices of argumentative discourse. The proper object of reflective governance is good reasons, not merely Will's "ways of behaving" or "norms." Finally, I contended that the aspiration of governance theory to engage with socially relevant

---

[46] On Habermas' notion of discourse, see Rehg 1994, and Cook 1994. On his view of deliberative democracy, see Bohman 1996.

issues requires a developed view of deliberative democratic political governance. The methodological priority of reflective modes of governance over nonreflective ones establishes a strong and important affinity between governance theory and deliberative democracy.[47]

Kulturwissenschaftliches Institut Essen

References

Apel, Karl Otto. 1968. "Szientistik, Hermeneutik, Ideologiekritik. Entwurf einer Wissenschaftslehre in erkenntnisanthropologischer Sicht." *Wiener Jahrbuch für Philosophie* 1: 15–45.

Apel, Karl-Otto. 1980a. "Zwei paradigmatische Antworten auf die Frage nach der Logos-Auszeichnung der menschlichen Sprache." In *Kulturwissenschaften*. H. Lützeler, ed. Bonn: Bouvier, 13–68.

Apel, Karl-Otto. 1980b. *Towards a Transformation of Philosophy*. G. Adey and D. Frisby, trs. London: Routledge & Kegan Paul.

Apel, Karl Otto. 1980c. "Scientism, Hermeneutics, and Critique of Ideology. The Project of an Anthropologically Informed Epistemology of Science." In Apel, 1980b, 46–76. (A translation of Apel, 1968.)

Apel, Karl-Otto. 1986. "Die Logos-Auszeichnung der menschlichen Sprache. Die philosophische Relevanz der Sprechakttheorie." In *Perspektiven auf Sprache*. H.-G. Bosshardt, ed. Berlin: de Gruyter, 45–87.

Apel, Karl-Otto. 1995. *Selected Essays I, Towards a Transcendental Semiotics*. E. Mendieta, ed. Atlantic Highlands, N. J.: Humanities Press.

Bennett, Jonathan. 1964. *Rationality. An Essay towards an Analysis*. London: Routledge & Kegan Paul.

Bennett, Jonathan. 1976. *Linguistic Behavior*. Cambridge: Cambridge University Press.

Bohman, James. 1996. *Political Deliberation*. Cambridge, Mass.: MIT Press.

Buchdahl, Gerd. 1980. "Neo-transcendental Approaches Towards Scientific Theory Appraisal." In *Science, Belief and Behaviour*. D. H. Mellor, ed. Cambridge: Cambridge University Press, 1–20.

Clayton, Roberts. 1996. *The Logic of Historical Explanation*. University Park, Penn.: Pennsylvania State University Press.

---

[47] My thanks go to Ken Westphal for detailed comments, discussion, and stylistic advice.

Cohen, Joshua. 1989. "Deliberation and Democratic Legitimacy." In *The Good Polity*. A. Hamlin & P. Pettit, eds. Oxford: Blackwell, 18–34.

Cook, Maeve. 1994. *Language and Reason. A Study of Habermas's Pragmatics*. Cambridge, Mass.: MIT Press.

Dewey, John. 1927. *The Public and Its Problems*. New York: Holt, Rinehart & Winston.

Dewey, John. 1939. *Theory of Valuation*. Foundations of the Unity of Science 2 No. 4. Chicago: University of Chicago Press.

Fann, K. T. 1970. *Perice's Theory of Abduction*. The Hague: Nijhof.

Habermas, Jürgen. 1971. *Knowledge and Human Interests*. J. Shapiro, tr. Boston: Beacon.

Habermas, Jürgen. 1979. "What is Universal Pragmatic?" In *Communication and the Evolution of Society*. London: Heinemann.

Habermas, Jürgen. 1990. *The Theory of Communicative Action*. Cambridge, Mass.: MIT Press.

Kettner, Matthias. 1996a. "Karl-Otto Apel's Contribution to Critical Theory." In *Handbook of Critical Theory*. D. Rasmussen, ed. London: Basil Blackwell, 258–86.

Kettner, Matthias. 1996b. "Gute Gründe. Thesen zur diskursiven Vernunft." In *Die eine Vernunft und die vielen Rationalitäten*. M. Kettner & K.-O. Apel, eds. Frankfurt/Main: Suhrkamp, 424–64.

Kovesi, Julius. 1967. *Moral Notions*. London: Routledge & Kegan Paul.

Morris, Charles. 1938. *Foundations of the Theory of Signs*. Foundations of the Unity of Science 1 No. 2: 1–14. Chicago: University of Chicago Press.

Nietzsche, Friedrich. 1874. "On the uses and disadvantages of history for life." In *Untimely Meditations*. R. J. Hollingdale, tr. Cambridge: Cambridge University Press, 1983, 57–123.

Øfsti, Audun. 1990. "Language Games and 'Complete' Languages: On the Apel/Habermas Reception and Critique of Wittgenstein's Later Philosophy." In *Essays in Pragmatic Philosophy II*. H. v. Hoibraaten, ed. Oslo: Norwegian University Press, 128–72.

Perice, Charles S. 1931–58. *Collected Papers*. C. Hartshorne, P. Weiss, & A. Burks, eds. Cambridge, Mass.: Harvard University Press.

Pinker, Steven. 1994. *The Language Instinct: How the Mind Creates Language*. New York: Morrow.

Rehg, William. 1994. *Insight and Solidarity. The Discourse Ethics of Jürgen Habermas*. Berkeley: University of California Press.

Saussure, Ferdinand. 1916. *Course in General Linguistics*. C. Bally, ed. Rpt. London: Owen, 1974.

Schön, Donald A. 1983. *The Reflective Practitioner. How Professionals Think in Action*. New York: Basic Books.

Sellars, Wilfrid. 1947. "Pure Pragmatics and Epistemology." *Philosophy of Science* 14: 181–202. Rpt. in *Pure Pragmatics and Possible Worlds: The*

Early Essays of Wilfrid Sellars. J. F. Sicha, ed. Atascadero, Cal.: Ridge-view, 1980, 5–26.

Taylor, Charles. 1989. *Sources of the Self.* Cambridge, Mass.: Harvard University Press.

Taylor, Paul. 1961. *Normative Discourse.* Westport, Conn.: Greenwood.

Wiggins, David. 1987. "Universalizability, Impartiality, Truth." In Wiggins, 1991, 85–96.

Wiggins, David. 1991. *Needs, Values, Truth.* 2nd ed. Oxford: Blackwell.

Will, Frederick L. 1963. "Language, Usage, and Judgment." *The Antioch Review* 23: 273–90.

Will, Frederick L. 1972. "Philosophy, Institutions, and Law." *Modern Age* 16: 379–86.

Will, Frederick L. 1988. *Beyond Deduction: Ampliative Aspects of Philosophical Reflection.* London: Routledge.

Will, Frederick L. 1997. *Pragmatism and Realism.* K. R. Westphal, ed. Lanham, Md.: Rowman & Littlefield.

Contributors

WILLIAM P. ALSTON is Professor Emeritus of Philosophy at Syracuse University. He served previously on the faculties of the University of Michigan, Rutgers University, and the University of Illinois at Urbana-Champaign. He is past President of the American Philosophical Association, Central Division (1978–79), and is a fellow of the American Academy of Arts and Sciences. His recent books include *Epistemic Justification* (1989), *Divine Nature and Human Language* (1989), *Perceiving God* (1991), *The Reliability of Sense Perception* (1993), and *A Realist Conception of Truth* (1996).

THOMAS F. GREEN is Professor Emeritus of Education and Philosophy at Syracuse University. He was founding Director or Co-Director of the Educational Policy Research Center at Syracuse (1967–73), President of the Philosophy of Education Society (1975–76). He has been officer or member of the National Academy of Education since 1979. He is a John Simon Guggenheim Fellow, and has been Whitehead Fellow of Harvard University, Fellow of the National Institute of Education and Senior Research Fellow at Princeton Theological Seminary. He has been guest lecturer or visiting Professor at more than a dozen American universities. His publications include *Predicting the Behavior of the Educational System* (1980), *Work and Leisure and the American Schools* (1970), *The Activities of Teaching* (1971), and nearly 100 scholarly articles. He is currently finishing two books, *Voices: The Educational Formation of Conscience*, and *Walls: Education in Communities of Text and Liturgy*.

WILLIAM H. HAY is Professor Emeritus of Philosophy at the University of Wisconsin-Madison. He is past President of the American Philosophical Association, Western (now Central) Division (1974–75). He has published numerous articles and reviews in prominent journals and collections on diverse topics, including philosophy of science, renaissance and modern philosophy, and ethics. He is co-editor (with M. G. Singer) of *Reason and the Common Good: Essays of Arthur E. Murphy* (1963) and (with W. Courteney and K. Yandell) of J. R. Weinberg, *Ockham, Descartes, and Hume* (1977).

MATTHIAS KETTNER is a lecturer in the Deparment of Philosophy and in the Department of Psychology at the Johann-Wolfgang-Goethe University in Frankfurt am Main, and is a research fellow at the Kulturwissenschaftliches Institut in Essen. Since 1987 he has collaborated closely with Karl-Otto Apel and with Jürgen Habermas on the application of discourse-ethics. His publications include *Hegels »Sinnliche Gewißheit«. Diskursanalytischer Kommentar* (1990), "Peirce's Notion of Abduction and Psychoanalytic Interpretation" (1991), "Rational Foundations of Moral Responsibility for Nature" (1992), and "Gute Gründe. Thesen zur diskursiven Vernunft" (1996). He is coeditor (with K.-O. Apel) of *Zur Anwendung der Diskursethik in Politik, Recht und Wissenschaft* (1992), *Mythos Wertfreiheit?* (1994), and *Die Eine Vernunft und die vielen Rationalitäten* (1995). He is coeditor (with A. Dorschel, W. Kuhlmann, and M. Niquet) of *Transzendentalpragmatik* (1993).

STANLEY L. PAULSON is Professor of Philosophy and Professor of Law at Washington University in St. Louis. Over the last decade he has held research fellowships from the National Endowment for the Humanities, the Max Planck Society, the Fulbright Commission, and the Deutsche Forschungsgemeinschaft, with residence at the universities of Münster, Heidelberg, and Göttingen. His translation of Kelsen's *Reine Rechtslehre* (First Edition), together with Bonnie Litschewski Paulson, appeared with the Clarendon Press in 1992 (paperback 1996), and a volume of papers that he has edited,

Normativity and Norms. Critical Perspectives on Kelsenian Themes, is forthcoming with the Clarendon Press.

MARTIN PERMUTTER wrote his dissertation at the University of Illinois with Fred Will as his mentor. He taught at the University of Texas at Austin and the University of Tennessee at Nashville before joining the College of Charleston in 1978, where he served as Chair of the Philosophy Department from 1982–1990. He serves on a variety of ethics committees at the Medical University of South Carolina, he directs the Jewish Studies Program at the College of Charleston, and he works in the areas of applied ethics and philosophy of religion.

NICHOLAS RESCHER is a University Professor of Philosophy at the University of Pittsburgh, where he served for many years as Director at the Center for Philosophy of Science. He is a member of the Institut International de Philosophie and several other learned academies. In 1984 he was awarded the Alexander von Humboldt Prize for Humanistic Scholarship. A visiting scholar at Oxford, Constance, and Salamanca, Professor Rescher has received four honorary degrees from universities of the USA and abroad. He is the author of more than seventy books ranging over many areas of philosophy. He is currently working on a book on the role of prediction in science and in everyday life.

MICHAEL ROOT is Professor of Philosophy at the University of Minnesota. He is the author of *Philosophy of Social Science: The Methods, Ideals, and Politics of Social Inquiry* (1993). His specialties are the nature of language and the methods of the social sciences, and his articles have appeared in *American Philosophical Quarterly*, *Biology and Philosophy*, *Linguistics and Philosophy*, *Notre Dame Journal of Formal Logic*, and *Philosophical Studies* and as chapters in a number of anthologies. He is currently writing a book on systems of classification in the natural and social sciences. MARCUS G. SINGER is Professor Emeritus of Philosophy at the University of Wisconsin. He is the author of *Generalization in Ethics*

(1961), editor of *Morals and Values* (1977) and *American Philosophy* (1986), co-editor of *Legislative Intent and Other Essays on Law, Politics and Morality*, by Gerald C. MacCallum (1993), and editor of *Reason, Reality, and Speculative Philosophy*, by Arthur E. Murphy (1996). He is past President of the American Philosophical Association, Central Division (1985–86).

JAMES E. TILES is Professor of Philosophy at the University of Hawai'i at Mânoa. He is author of *Things that Happen* (1981), *Dewey* (1988), and with Mary Tiles of *An Introduction to Historical Epistemology* (1993). He is editor of *John Dewey: Critical Assessments* (4 vols., 1992).

JAMES D. WALLACE is Professor of Philosophy at the University of Illinois at Urbana-Champaign, where he has taught since 1962. A graduate of Amherst College, he received his Ph.D. degree from Cornell University. He is author of *Virtues and Vices* (1978), *Moral Relevance and Moral Conflict* (1988), and *Ethical Norms, Particular Cases* (1996).

KENNETH R. WESTPHAL is Associate Professor of Philosophy at the University of New Hampshire. He is author of *Hegel's Epistemological Realism* (1989) and *Hegel, Hume und die Identität wahrnehmbarer Dinge* (1997). He is editor of Frederick L. Will, *Pragmatism and Realism* (1997). He has published widely on Kant's and on Hegel's theories of knowledge, moral and social philosophies, and aesthetic theories. He received the 1994 George Armstrong Kelly Prize for "Kant on the State, Law, and Obedience to Authority in the Allegedly 'Anti-Revolutionary' Writings" (1992). He is currently writing a book titled "Kant, Hegel, and the Objective Deduction of Categorial Concepts."

Biographical Notice

FREDERICK L. WILL is Professor of Philosophy Emeritus at the University of Illinois at Urbana-Champaign. He was born on May 8, 1909, in Swissvale, Pa. He received his A.B. from Thiel College (Oxford) in 1929, his M.A. from The Ohio State University in 1931, and his Ph.D. from Cornell University in 1937. He was made D. Litt. by Thiel College in 1965. He was a John Simon Guggenheim Memorial Fellow in 1945–46 and a Senior Research Fulbright Scholar at Oxford in 1961. He held visiting positions as Professor of Philosophy at Cornell University in 1955 and 1964–65, and at the University of California at Irvine in 1978. He was President of the American Philosophical Association, Western (now Central) Division, in 1968–69. He has published three books, *Induction and Justification* (1974), *Beyond Deduction* (1988), and *Pragmatism and Realism* (1997). He also published numerous articles in leading philosophical journals. A complete bibliography of his writings appears in *Pragmatism and Realism*.

Index

abortion controversy: 185–86, 188, 198–99

acedia: 159

Ackrill, John L.: instrumental *vs* constitutive means, 289–91

alienation: 153, 159, 170

Allgemeine Landrecht (Prussia): 278

anomie: 160, 170

Anscombe, Elizabeth: brute facts, 198

Apel, Karl-Otto: 321, 326*n*41

Aquinas, St. Thomas: concepts, 47–48; conscience, 146–47, 150

Aristotle: law of non–contradiction, 118; friendship and virtue, 150; practical syllogism, 285–86; means, 289–91; mentioned, 266

Armstrong, David: externalism, 37; perception, 64, 67–68

Augustine, Saint: 8

Austin, John L.: bizarre fictions, 34–35, 42, 45, 52, 53; speech-acts, 319*n*27

Bayle–Laplace Theorem: 102

Bennett, Jonathan: 324*n*38

Bierling, Ernst Rudolph: 220

Black, Max: on presuppositions, 114–115

Blackburn, Simon: quasi–realism, 49–51; mentioned, 17

Blanchard, Brand: coherentism, 38; perception, 63, 64, 73*n*19, 75

Bourdieu, Pierre: 268, 269, 277

Bradley, Francis: 120, 198

Brennan, J. G.: 326*n*41

Brinz, Alois: 224

Buchdahl, Gerd: 307*n*15

Carnap, Rudolf: anti–realism, 18; realism, 27–34*passim*; subjectivism, 29–34; semantics, 321; mentioned, 38, 49

Cato: 101

Chisholm, Roderick: phenomenal *vs* comparative 'looks', 78–80

Church, Alonzo: 116–117

classification: descriptive and prescriptive aspects of, 326*n*41

Cohen, Hermann: 236, 237

Collingwood, Robin George: presuppositions of questions, 113–114, 119

community: empirical *vs* normative, 6, 177–80

concepts: empirical, open texture of, 34–38

conditioning, psychological: 323

conscience: collective, 174, 180; individual, 181, 197; St.

Thomas Aquinas, 146–47, 150; Kant, 147; John Stuart Mill, 148, 150

consciousness, transparency of: 270

Copernicus, Nicolas: 252

Crane, Tim: perception, 66

criticism: and tradition, 164, 180; and education, 177–82; philosophical, 203–204

deductivism: 265–66, 269–71, 275, 277, 281, 283, 292–293, 320

democracy: deliberative, 330–38

Derrida, Jacques: 36

Descartes, René: evil deceiver, 40; mentioned, 41, 43, 45

Dewey, John: truth, 2–3; naturalism, 37, 54; reflex arc, 194; good, 254; habit, 266, 268; means-ends reasoning, 289–91; mentioned, 10

Donagan, Alan: 200

Dretske, Frederick: information theoretic epistemology, 42n77; non–epistemic seeing, 60n1

Dreyfus affair: 179–80

Durkheim, Émile: organic vs mechanical solidarity, 174–77, 179–80

education: moral, 145–82$passim$; as social criticism, 177–82

empiricism, logical: 36

ends, highest: 290

ennui: 159

enthymeme: 127, 138–40

epistemology: foundationalism vs coherentism, 18, 37–39, 95; foundationalist, 35–36, 95, 193; the given, 49, 69; social,

89–108$passim$, 270; causal explicative vs juridico–normative (Kelsen), 226–27, 230

equivocation: 136–138

externalism: and testimonial evidence, 99; David Armstrong, 37; Frederick L. Will, 17–18, 34–37, 42, 45, 49, 52–53; Michael Williams, 41

Fabricius: 247

fictions: Hans Vaihinger, 219, 220, 237–38. See legal fiction

figure/ground illusion: 77

Foucault, Michel: 300

foundationalism: 166, 193, 294, 301. See epistemology.

Franklin, Juilian: 281–83

Gadamer, Hans-Georg: 306

Galen, Claudius: 247

Geech, Peter: implying vs presupposing, 119; fallacy of many questions, 119–20

Gemeinschaft: vs Gesellschaft, 171–74

Gerber, Carl Friedrich von: 228 –29, 231

Gert, Bernard: 200

Gibbon, Edward: 332–33

Goodman, Nelson: mutual adjustment of rules and inferences, 91, 95; mentioned, 249

governance: in practice vs of practice, 304, 323, $cf.$ 279–80, 315

Grice, Paul: maxims of conversation, 106–108

G[overnance]-stories: defined, 302

Habermas, Jürgen: 321, 326n41

Haldane, John: 47–48
Harvey, William: 247–48, 252
Hayek, F. A.: 201
Hegel, Georg W. F.: forms of consciousness, 267; reason, 276; normative dimensions of social institutions, 299*n*6; mentioned, 198, 199, 282
Heil, John: perception, 63, 64
Hempel, Carl: 38
Hobbes, Thomas: on trust, 105–106
Hume, David: beauty a tertiary quality, 49$_n$104; principles of testimonial evidence, 89–108 *passim*; conventions, 260; custom, 266; deductivism, 275; modesty, 334. *See* is and ought

idealism: absolute, 75; objective 282. *See* Kant
ideals: cognitive and practical, 10–14; pragmatic grounding of, 12–14. *See* norms, ends
implication: contextual, 121. *See* inference
imputation: points of (Kelsen), 221, 225, 227–30
individualism, methodological: 270
inference: presupposition *vs* principle of, 115, 128; principle of, 125–28; form and validity, 140–43
intuitionism, moral: 196–97, 283, 285, 288, 336–38; D. D. Raphael, 196–97; J. O. Urmson, 196–97; William D. Ross, 249

intuitions: moral, 196–97, 203–18*passim*; psychology of, 212–15
is and ought: 198, 220, 226, 227, 230–32, 282

James, William: truth, 1, 2, 10; principles of testimonial evidence, 92–94
Jefferson, Thomas: 101–102
Jellinek, Georg: 228, 231, 233
Jellinek, Walter: 232–34
justification and mutual criticism: 327–30, 334–37. *See* norms

Kahneman, D.: 214–16
Kant, Immanuel: 'I think', 8; anti–realism, 18, 30; formal idealism, 18; affinity of manifold of intuition, 18–26*passim*; transcendental idealism, 22–26; 37; Refutation of Idealism, 23, 26, 53; conscience, 147; transcendental argument, 236; categorical imperative, 249; mentioned, 49, 68, 72
Kelsen, Hans: 219–239*passim*; legal person, 219–30; basic norm, 219–221, 231–39; pure theory of law, 220, 226, 230, 236, 239; normativity thesis, 231–32; points of imputation, 221, 225, 227–30
Kemp, J.: 328*n*41
knowledge by acquaintance: 37, 39
knowledge, perceptual. *See* perception
Kovesi, Julius: 326*n*41
Kuhn, Thomas: incommensurability, 29; scientific revolutions, 193–194

Laband, Paul: 231
Law, pure theory of. *See* Kelsen
legal fiction: 219–239*passim*; basic norm, 219, 231–39. *See* legal person
legal person: Hans Kelsen, 219–30; Otto von Gierke, 224–25, 228, 230
legal realism: 275
Leibniz, Gottfried W.: 34–35
Levi, E. H.: legal reasoning, 274
Lewis, Clarence I.: 2
Locke, John: religion and politics, 256–63
Lovejoy, Arthur: 2
Luker, Kristin: abortion, 199

Maine, Henry: 174
Marx, Karl: 333
McFarland, C.: 213–14
Mill, John Stuart: conscience, 148, 150
Miller, D. T.: 213–14
Morris, Charles: 321

Nagel, Thomas: truth, 39*n*59; view from nowhere, 181
naturalism: John Dewey, 37, 54; Charles S. Peirce, 37, 54; Frederick L. Will, 7, 37, 54, 200, 201, 316–17
Neurath, Otto: 38
nominalism: 273
normation: acquisition of norms, 149, 163, 168–69, 195, 197; strong *vs* weak, 170–78
normativity thesis (Kelsen): 231–32
norms: acquisition, 145–83 *passim*, 195, 266, 325; social, as rules of conduct, 151–63; compliance, obeience, and

observance, 151–61; context of, 164–70; Frederick L. Will, 165, 167, 194–195, 204; governance of, 194–195, 239, 243–63*passim*, 265–91*passim*, 293–338*passim*; basic (Kelsen), 219–220, 231–39; manifest and latent aspects, 244–63*passim*, *cf*. 307–308; composition of, 268, 287–88, 311, 322; semeiotic basis of, 324–27

Oakeshott, Michael: 282–83
open texture. *See* concepts

Pandectistic (German private law): 228
Parsons, Talcot: on Durkheim, 176
particularism: in ethics, 254
Pascal, Blaise: principles of testimonial evidence, 92–93
Peacocke, Christopher: perception, 64–65, 72
Peirce, Charles S.: objectivity, pragmatic standards of, 1, 2, 5, 11; naturalism, 37, 54; truth, 39*n*59; principle of inference, 125–28; complete argument, 130; ampliation, 195–96; kinds of inference, 271; abduction, 286, 311–12; mentioned, 266
Pendlebury, Michael: perception, 63, 73
perception: conceptualism, 59–85*passim*; conceptualism defined, 62; moderate conceptualism, 64; theory of appearing, 59–85*passim*; sense datum theory, 61, 69, 72; adverbial

theory, 61; propositional content theory, 61; hallucinations, 61–62; propositionalism, 63; Frederick Dretske, 60n1; Brand Blanchard, 63, 64, 73n19, 75; David Armstrong, 64, 67–68; John Heil, 63, 64; Christopher Peacocke, 64–65, 72; Michael Pendlebury, 63, 73; George Pitcher, 64, 67–68; John Searle, 64, 65, 71–72; Tim Crane, 66; Joseph Runzo, 67, 69–70, 73–74, 75; Irving Rock, 75; Roderick Chisholm, 78–80

Pinker, Stephen: 317n25

Pitcher, George: perception, 64, 67–68

Plato: 103, 244, 272

polar terms: 122

post–modernism: 4, 5, 13. See Derrida

practical reasoning, theory of: 285–88

Pragmatism: objective vs subjective criteria, 1–14 passim

presuppositions: 111–112; of inference, 115–42 passim; of constancy of meaning, 131–38; Robin George Collingwood, 113–114, 119; presuppositions, Max Black, 114–115; Alfred North Whitehead, 113; Peter Strawson, 114–11, 119; Bertrand Russell, 119

prohibition (of alchoholic beverages): 188–89

Puchta, Georg Friedrich: 220, 224

Putnam, Hilary: brains in vats, 40, 43, 45; internal realism, 47

Quine, Willard V. O.: 288

Ramsey, Frank P.: redundancy theory of truth, 17, 49, 50

Raphael, D. D.: moral intuitionism, 196–97

rationality judgments: defined, 299

realism: metaphysical, 5; quasi-realism, 17; internal realism, 47; legal, 275. See idealism, naturalism

reasons: nature of, 312–13; Richard Rorty, 299n8;

reformation, Protestant: 256

Reid, Thomas: principles of testimonal evidence, 96–101, 103, 104, 106

representations: cognitive intermediaries, 47; representationalism, 320

Rock, Irving: perception, 75

Rorty, Richard: truth, 3; reason, 299n8; mentioned, 2, 38

Ross, William D.: 249

Royce, Josiah: 10

Runzo, Joseph: perception, 67, 69–70, 73–74, 75

Russell, Bertrand: theory of descriptions, 114; presuppositions, 119; mentioned, 38

Saussure, Ferdinand: 321n31

Schiller, F. C. S.: 2

Searle, John: perception, 64, 65, 71–72

Sellars, Wilfrid: pure pragmatics, 321; mentioned, 30, 49

semeiotics: deficit in Will's theory, 314–27; bees, 322

sentences: vs statements or propositions, 122–23

Singer, Peter: child drowning in pond, 205, 208–11, 216–17
slavery: 187, 188, 190, 250–51, 333
socialization: 179
Socrates: 103–104
solidarity: organic *vs* mechanical, 174–77
speech act theory: 325–27
Strawson, Peter: presuppositions of statements, 114–11, 119

testimony: 89–108*passim*; externalism, 99; David Hume, 89–108*passim*; William James, 92–94; Blaise Pascal, 92–93; Thomas Reid, 96–101, 103, 104, 106
Thomson, Judith Jarvis: violinist example, 205–11, 216–17
thought, intimately based in language: 47
Tönnies, Ferdinand: 171–74
Toulmin, Stephen: 281–82
tradition: and criticism, 164, 180
truth: guarantees *vs* regulative guides, 7; correspondence, 39; criteria, 39; redundancy theory, 17, 49, 50; William James, 1, 2, 10; John Dewey, 2–3; Richard Rorty, 3; Frank Ramsey, 17, 49, 50; Thomas Nagel, 39n59; Crispin Wright, 51–53
Tversky, A.: 214–16

Urmson, J. O.: moral intuitionism, 196–97
usury: 252–53

Vaihinger, Hans: fictions, 219, 220, 237–38

voluntarism: 276
von Gierke, Otto: on Kelsen, 220; legal person, 224–25, 228, 230
von Savigny, Friedrich Carl: 220, 229

Waismann, Friedrich: 34, 38
Walsh, W. H.: on Hegel's ethics, 199
Weber, Max: 11
Whitehead, Alfred North: presuppositions in philosophy, 113
Wick, Warner: 30
Will, Frederick L.: truth, 5–14 *passim*, 34–40; naturalism, 7, 37, 54, 200, 201, 318–19; externalism, 17–18, 34–37, 42, 45, 49, 52–53; norm acquisition, 165, 167, 195, 197; right and wrong, 185–91; morality, 193–201; foundationalism in epistemology, 193, 203; norms, 194–95, 204, 217–18, 239; moral judgment, 196; governance of norms, 243–46 *passim*, 293–338*passim*; deductive *vs* ampliative processes, 271–77
Williams, Michael: skepticism, 40; contextualism, 40; intrinsic epistemic status of statements, 41–42; epistemological externalism, 41; appearances, 43–46; experiential knowledge, 44–46; mentioned, 53
Windscheid, Bernhard: 220
Wittgenstein, Ludwig: rule following, 49n104, 249, 252, 272–73; forms of life, 267; mentioned 17, 34

Wright, Crispin: minimalism
about truth, 51–53; cognitive
command, 52–53; best explanation, 52–53